GMAT® STRATEGY GUIDES

- **0** GMAT Roadmap
- **1** Fractions, Decimals, & Percents
- **2** Algebra
- **3** Word Problems
- **4** Geometry
- **5** Number Properties
- **6** Critical Reasoning
- **7** Reading Comprehension
- **8** Sentence Correction
- **9** Integrated Reasoning & Essay

STRATEGY GUIDE SUPPLEMENTS

Math

GMAT Foundations of Math

GMAT Advanced Quant

Verbal

GMAT Foundations of Verbal

October 4, 2016

Dear Student,

Thank you for picking up a copy of *GMAT Foundations of Math*. I hope this book provides the guidance you need to get the most out of your studies.

At Manhattan Prep, we continually aspire to provide the best instructors and study resources possible. We hope that you will find our commitment manifest in this book. If you have any questions or comments, please email us at gmat@manhattanprep.com. Our Student Services and curriculum teams are very interested to hear what you have to say.

Many people were involved in the creation of this book. First and foremost is Zeke Vanderhoek, the founder of Manhattan Prep. Zeke was a lone tutor in New York when he started the company in 2000. Now, more than a decade and a half later, the company serves the needs of thousands of students each year.

Our books are based on the continuing experiences of our instructors and students. Stacey Koprince led the rewriting of *GMAT Foundations of Math*, resulting in this new edition. Numerous other instructors have made contributions to this title over the years. For this edition, I'd like to send particular thanks to Whitney Garner, Andrea Pawliczek, Emily Meredith Sledge, and Ryan Starr.

Our colleagues at Kaplan Publishing managed the production process and made sure all the moving pieces came together at just the right time.

At Manhattan Prep, we are proud of this book and of the people who have worked hard to bring it to you.

Thanks again for trusting us to help you prepare for the GMAT. Best of luck!

Sincerely,

Chris Ryan
Vice President of Academics
Manhattan Prep

HOW TO ACCESS YOUR ONLINE RESOURCES

IF YOU ARE A REGISTERED MANHATTAN PREP STUDENT

and have received this book as part of your course materials, you have *automatic* access to *all* of our online resources. This includes all practice exams, Question Banks, and online updates to this book. To access these resources, follow the instructions in the Welcome Guide provided to you at the start of your program.

IF YOU PURCHASED THIS BOOK FROM MANHATTANPREP.COM OR AT ONE OF OUR CENTERS

1. Go to: **www.manhattanprep.com/gmat/studentcenter**
2. Log in with the username and password you chose when setting up your account.

IF YOU PURCHASED THIS BOOK AT A RETAIL LOCATION

1. Create an account with Manhattan Prep at this website:

www.manhattanprep.com/gmat/register

2. Follow the instructions on the screen.

Your one year of online access begins on the day that you register your book at the above URL.

You only need to register your product *once* at the above URL. To use your online resources any time *after* you have completed the registration process, log in at the following URL:

www.manhattanprep.com/gmat/studentcenter

Please note that online access is nontransferable. This means that only *new* and *unregistered* copies of the book will grant you online access. Previously used books will not provide any online resources.

IF YOU PURCHASED AN EBOOK VERSION OF THIS BOOK

1. Create an account with Manhattan Prep at this website:

www.manhattanprep.com/gmat/register

2. Email a copy of your purchase receipt to **gmat@manhattanprep.com** to activate

your resources. Please be sure to use the same email address to create an account that you used to purchase the eBook.

Email **gmat@manhattanprep.com** or call **800-576-4628** with any questions.

Please refer to the following page for a description of the online resources that come with this book.

YOUR ONLINE RESOURCES

YOUR PURCHASE INCLUDES ONLINE ACCESS TO THE FOLLOWING:

GMAT FOUNDATIONS OF MATH QUESTION BANK

This bank consists of extra practice questions (with detailed explanations) that test the variety of foundational math concepts and skills covered in this book. These questions provide you with extra practice beyond the problem sets contained in this book. You may use our online timer to practice your pacing by setting time limits for each question in the bank.

GMAT MATH READINESS ASSESSMENTS

Know when you're ready to move on to GMAT Math. These four online assessments – designed to be taken during and at the end of your fundamental math prep – test your readiness for higher-level GMAT Math.

5 FREE INTERACT™ LESSONS

Interact™ is a comprehensive self-study program that is fun, intuitive, and directed by you. Each interactive video lesson is taught by an expert Manhattan Prep instructor and includes dozens of individual branching points. The choices you make determine the content you see. This book comes with access to the *first five lessons* of GMAT Interact. Lessons are available on your computer or iPad so you can prep where you are, when you want. For more information on the full version of this program, visit **www.manhattanprep.com/gmat/interact**.

ONLINE UPDATES TO THE CONTENT IN THIS BOOK

The content presented in this book is updated periodically to ensure that it reflects the GMAT's most current trends. You may view all updates, including any known errors or changes, upon registering for online access.

The above resources can be found in your Student Center at manhattanprep.com/gmat/studentcenter.

TABLE OF CONTENTS

Arithmetic

In this chapter...

- Quick-Start Definitions
  - Basic Numbers
  - Greater Than and Less Than
  - Adding and Subtracting Positives and Negatives
  - Multiplying and Dividing
  - Distributing and Factoring
  - Multiplying Positives and Negatives
  - Fractions and Decimals
  - Divisibility and Even and Odd Integers
  - Exponents and Roots (and Pi)
  - Variable Expressions and Equations
- PEMDAS
  - PEMDAS Overview
  - Combining Like Terms
  - Distribution
  - Pulling Out a Common Factor
  - Long Addition and Subtraction
  - Long Multiplication
  - Long Division

Chapter 1

Arithmetic

Your goal in this book is twofold: to review fundamental math skills and to practice applying these skills. To this end, there are a number of "Check Your Skills" questions throughout each chapter. After learning a topic, try these problems (one at a time, if more than one), checking your answers at the back of the chapter as you go.

If you find these questions challenging, reread the section you just finished. Then try the questions again. Whenever needed, use the solution to help you work through the math step-by-step. When you get stuck, don't read the entire solution immediately. Read as much as you need to get yourself unstuck, then continue to try to do the work on your own.

In This Chapter, You Will Learn To:

- Recognize math vocabulary and calculate accordingly
- Apply PEMDAS
- Combine like terms and pull out common factors

Quick-Start Definitions

Whether you work with numbers every day or avoid them diligently, give a good read to this first section, which provides definitions for certain core concepts in order to give your studies a quick start. We'll come back to many of these concepts throughout the book. Moreover, **bolded** terms in this section can be found in the glossary at the back of the book.

Basic Numbers

All the **numbers** that we care about on the GMAT can be shown as a point somewhere on the **number line**:

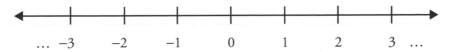

Another word for number is **value**.

1

Counting numbers are 1, 2, 3, and so on. These are the first numbers that you ever learned—the numbers that you use to count individual items.

Digits are 10 symbols (0, 1, 2, 3, 4, 5, 6, 7, 8, and 9) used to represent numbers. If the GMAT asks you specifically for a digit, it wants one of these 10 symbols.

Counting numbers above 9 are represented by two or more digits. The number *four hundred twelve* is represented by three digits in this order: 412.

Place value tells you how much a digit in a specific position is worth. The 4 in 412 is worth 4 hundreds (400), so 4 is the *hundreds digit* of 412. Meanwhile, 1 is the *tens digit* and is worth 1 ten (10). Finally, 2 is the *units digit* and is worth 2 units, or just plain old 2.

412	=	400	+	10	+	2
Four hundred twelve	equals	four hundreds	plus	one ten	plus	two units (or two)

The GMAT always separates the thousands digit from the hundreds digit by a comma. For readability, big numbers are broken up by commas placed three digits apart.

1,298,023 equals one million two hundred ninety-eight thousand twenty-three.

Addition (+, or *plus*) is the most basic operation in arithmetic. If you add one counting number to another, you get a third counting number farther to the right on the number line.

7	+	5	=	12
Seven	plus	five	equals	twelve

Therefore, 12 is the **sum** of 7 and 5.

You can always add in either order and get the same result.

5	+	7	=	12
Five	plus	seven	equals	twelve

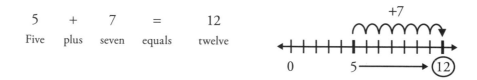

Subtraction (−, or *minus*) is the opposite of addition. Subtraction undoes addition.

7	+	5	−	5	=	7
Seven	plus	five	minus	five	equals	seven

Order matters in subtraction: $6 - 2 = 4$, but $2 - 6 = $ something else (more on this in a minute). By the way, since $6 - 2 = 4$, the **difference** between 6 and 2 is 4.

Any number minus itself equals **zero** (0).

7   –   7   =   0
Seven minus seven equals zero

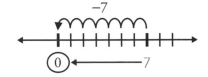

Any number plus zero equals that starting number. The same is true if you subtract zero. In either case, you're moving *zero* units away from the original number on the number line.

$$8 + 0 = 8 \qquad\qquad 9 - 0 = 9$$

Negative counting numbers are $-1, -2, -3$, and so on. These numbers, which are written with a **minus sign** or **negative sign**, show up to the left of zero on a number line.

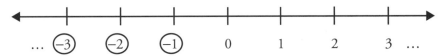

You need negative numbers when you subtract a bigger number from a smaller number. Say you subtract 6 from 2.

2   –   6   =   –4
Two minus six equals negative
                        four

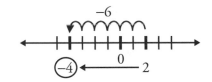

Negative numbers can be used to represent deficits. If you have \$2 but you owe \$6, your net worth is –\$4.

If you're having trouble computing *small minus big,* figure out *big minus small,* then make the result negative.

$35 - 57 = ?$ 57   So $35 - 57 = -22$
                 -35
                  22

Positive numbers are to the right of zero on a number line. **Negative** numbers are to the left of zero. Zero itself is neither positive nor negative—it's the only number right in the middle.

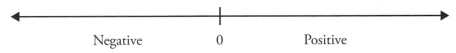

The **sign** of a number indicates whether the number is positive or negative.

1

Integers include all the numbers discussed so far:

- Counting numbers (1, 2, 3, …), also known as **positive integers**
- Negative counting numbers (−1, −2, −3, …), also known as **negative integers**
- Zero (0)

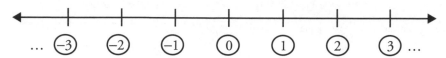

Check Your Skills

Perform addition and subtraction.

1. 37 + 141 =
2. 23 − 136 =

Answers can be found on page 37.

Greater Than and Less Than

Greater than (>) means *to the right of* on a number line. You can also say *bigger* or *larger*, but there is one drawback to using this terminology. Take a look at this example.

Careful! This definition of *greater than* means that, for negative numbers, bigger numbers are *closer* to zero. This may be counterintuitive at first. For example:

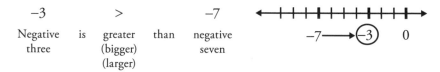

Don't think in terms of "size," even though *bigger* and *larger* seem to refer to size. Bigger numbers are *to the right of* smaller numbers on the number line.

The left-to-right order of the number line is negatives, then zero, then positives. So any positive number is greater than any negative number. For example:

2   >   −3

Two   is greater than negative
                              three

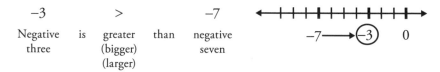

Likewise, zero is greater than every negative number.

0	>		–3
Zero	is greater	than	negative three

Less than (<) means *to the left of* on a number line. You can always re-express a *greater than* relationship as a *less than* relationship—just flip it around.

7	>		3
Seven	is greater	than	three

3	<		7
Three	is less	than	seven

If 7 is greater than 3, then 3 is less than 7.

If you think you are more likely to make mistakes with negatives, test out the following true statements on a number line.

–7 is less than –3	$-7 < -3$
–3 is less than 2	$-3 < 2$
–3 is less than 0	$-3 < 0$

Inequalities are statements that involve greater than (>) or less than (<) relationships.

Check Your Skills

3. What is the sum of the greatest negative integer and the smallest positive integer?

For questions 4 and 5, plug in > and < symbols, and say the resulting statement aloud.

4. 5 __ 16
5. –5 __ –16

Answers can be found on page 37.

Adding and Subtracting Positives and Negatives

Positive *plus* **positive** gives you a third positive. For example:

7	+	5	=	12
Seven	plus	five	equals	twelve

1

Remember that, when adding, you move even farther to the right of zero, so the result is always bigger than either starting number.

Positive *minus* **positive** could give you either a positive or a negative.

> *big positive − small positive = positive*

$$8 \quad - \quad 3 \quad = \quad 5$$

Eight   minus   three   equals   five

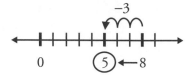

> *small positive − big positive = negative*

$$3 \quad - \quad 8 \quad = \quad -5$$

Three   minus   eight   equals   negative five

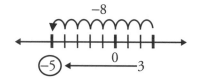

Either way, the result is less than where you started, because you move left.

Adding a negative is the same as subtracting a positive—you move left.

$$8 \quad + \quad -3 \quad = \quad 5$$

Eight   plus   negative three   equals   five

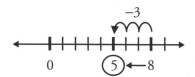

Negative *plus* **negative** always gives you a negative, because you move even farther to the left of zero.

$$-3 \quad + \quad -5 \quad = \quad -8$$

Negative three   plus   negative five   equals   negative eight

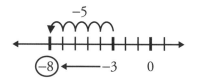

Subtracting a **negative** is the same as adding a positive—you move right. Think "two wrongs (*subtracting* and *negative*) make a right." Add in parentheses so you keep the two minus signs straight.

$$7 \quad - \quad (-5) \quad = \quad 7 \quad + \quad 5$$

Seven   minus   negative five   equals   seven   plus   five,

$$= \quad 12$$

and this equals   twelve

MANHATTAN PREP

In general, any subtraction can be rewritten as an addition. If you're subtracting a positive, that's the same as adding a negative. If you're subtracting a negative, that's the same as adding a positive.

Check Your Skills

6. Which is greater, a positive minus a negative or a negative minus a positive?

Answer can be found on page 37.

Multiplying and Dividing

Multiplication (×, or *times*) is repeated addition.

4	×	3	=	3 + 3 + 3 + 3	=	12
Four	times	three	equals	four threes added up,	and this equals	twelve

Therefore, 12 is the **product** of 4 and 3, which are **factors** of 12.

Parentheses can be used to indicate multiplication. Parentheses are usually written with ( ), but brackets [ ] can also be used, especially if you have parentheses within parentheses.

If a set of parentheses bumps up right against something else, multiply that something by whatever is in the parentheses.

$$4(3) = (4)3 = (4)(3) = 4 \times 3 = 12$$

When writing a multiplication sign, you can use a big dot. Just make the dot big and high so it doesn't look like a decimal point.

$$4 \bullet 3 = 4 \times 3 = 12$$

You can always multiply in either order; you will get the same result.

4	×	3	=	3 + 3 + 3 + 3	=	12
Four	times	three	equals	four threes added up,	and this equals	twelve

3	×	4	=	4 + 4 + 4	=	12
Three	times	four	equals	three fours added up,	and this equals	twelve

Division (÷, or *divided by*) is the opposite of multiplication. Division undoes multiplication.

2	×	3	÷	3	=	2
Two	times	three	divided by	three	equals	two

Order matters in division. 12 ÷ 3 = 4, but 3 ÷ 12 = something else (more on this soon).

1

Multiplying any number by 1 leaves the number the same. One times anything *is* that thing.

1	×	5	=	5	=	5
One	times	five	equals	one five by itself,	and this equals	five

5	×	1	=	1 + 1 + 1 + 1 + 1	=	5
Five	times	one	equals	five ones added up,	and this equals	five

Multiplying any number by zero (0) gives you zero. Anything times zero is zero.

5	×	0	=	0 + 0 + 0 + 0 + 0	=	0
Five	times	zero	equals	five zeros added up,	and this equals	zero

Since order doesn't matter in multiplication, this means that zero times anything is zero, too.

0	×	5	=	5 × 0	=	0
Zero	times	five	equals	five times zero,	and this equals	zero

Multiplying a number by zero destroys it permanently, in a sense. So you're not allowed to undo that destruction by dividing by zero:

Never divide by zero: $13 \div 0 =$ undefined. Stop right there—don't do this!

You *are* allowed to divide zero by any nonzero number. The answer is—surprise!—zero.

0	÷	13	=	0
Zero	divided by	thirteen	equals	zero

Check Your Skills

Complete the operations.

7. $7 \times 6 =$
8. $52 \div 13 =$

Answers can be found on page 37.

Distributing and Factoring

What is $4 \times (3 + 2)$? Here's one way to solve it.

4	×	(3 + 2)	=	4 × 5	=	20
Four	times	the quantity three plus two	equals	four times five,	and this equals	twenty

Turn (3 + 2) into 5, then multiply 4 by that 5.

The other way to solve this problem is to **distribute** the 4 to both the 3 and the 2.

4	×	(3 + 2)	=	4 × 3	+	4 × 2
Four	times	the quantity three plus two	equals	four times three	plus	four times two,

	=	12	+	8
	and this equals	twelve	plus	eight,

	=	20
	and that equals	twenty

Notice that you multiply the 4 into *both* the 3 and the 2.

Distributing is extra work in this case, but the technique will come in handy down the road.

Another way to see how distributing works is to put the sum in front.

	20		=		20	
(3 + 2)	×	4	=	3 × 4	+	2 × 4
5						
Five	times	four	equals	three times four	plus	two times four

Five fours added together			equals	three fours added together	plus	two fours added together
Twenty			equals	twenty		

In a sense, you're splitting up the sum 3 + 2. Just be sure to multiply both the 3 and the 2 by 4.

You distribute when the terms inside the parentheses are connected by addition or subtraction signs. Do *not* distribute if the terms inside the parentheses are connected by multiplication or division; in that case, just drop the parentheses and multiply or divide straight across. For example:

DO distribute:	$3(4 + y) = (3)(4) + (3)(y) = 12 + 3y$
DO NOT distribute:	$3(4 \times y) = 3 \times 4 \times y = 12y$

1

Distributing works similarly for subtraction. Just keep track of the minus sign.

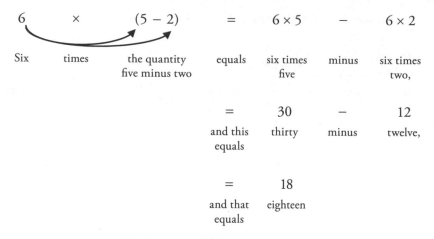

You can also go in reverse. You can **factor** the sum of two products if the products contain the same factor:

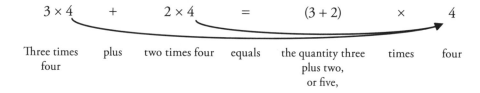

Pull out the **common factor** of 4 from each of the products 4 × 3 and 4 × 2. Next, put the sum of 3 and 2 into parentheses. By the way, *common* here doesn't mean *frequent* or *typical*. Rather, it means *belonging to both products*. A common factor is a factor in common (like a friend in common).

You can also put the common factor at the back of each product, if you like:

$$3 \times 4 \quad + \quad 2 \times 4 \quad = \quad (3 + 2) \quad \times \quad 4$$

Three times   plus   two times four   equals   the quantity three   times   four
four   plus two,
                                                                              or five,

As mentioned before, you can distribute when the math in the parentheses is added or subtracted. Don't distribute if the math in the parentheses is multiplied or divided. For example:

Example	Can I distribute?	
3(4 + 5)	Yes! The math in the parentheses is added.	3(4 + 5) = (3)(4) + (3)(5) = 27
3(4 × 5)	No. When the math in the parentheses is also multiplied (or divided), do the math straight out.	3(4 × 5) = 3 × 4 × 5 = 60

You will use both distributing and factoring in more advanced ways later. Using simple numbers to understand the concepts now will help you to apply these same concepts to more complex problems in future.

Check Your Skills

9. Use distribution to solve: $5 \times (3 + 4) =$
10. Factor a 6 out of the following expression: $36 - 12$

Answers can be found on page 37.

Multiplying Positives and Negatives

Positive × **positive** is always **positive**:

3	×	4	=	4 + 4 + 4	=	12
Three	times	four	equals	three fours added up,	and this equals	twelve

Positive × **negative** is always **negative**:

3	×	−4	=	−4 + (−4) + (−4)	=	−12
Three	times	negative four	equals	three negative fours, all added up,	and this equals	negative twelve

Since order doesn't matter in multiplication, the same outcome happens when you have *negative times positive*. You again get a **negative**:

−4	×	3	=	3 × (−4)	=	−12
Negative four	times	three	equals	three times negative four,	and this equals	negative twelve

What is **negative × negative**? **Positive**. This fact may seem weird, but it's consistent with the rules developed so far. In the same way that something minus a negative turns into something plus a positive ($7 - (-3) = 7 + 3$), a negative times a negative also turns positive. In either case, two negatives make a positive.

All the same rules hold true for division:

Positive Result	Negative Result
Positive ÷ Positive = Positive	Positive ÷ Negative = Negative
Negative ÷ Negative = Positive	Negative ÷ Positive = Negative
Positive × Positive = Positive	Positive × Negative = Negative
Negative × Negative = Positive	Negative × Positive = Negative

Check Your Skills

11. $(3)(-4) =$
12. Use distribution to solve: $-6 \times (-3 + (-5))$

Answers can be found on page 37.

1 Fractions and Decimals

Adding, subtracting, or multiplying integers always results in an integer, whether positive or negative.

$$\text{Int} \quad + \quad \text{Int} \quad = \quad \text{Int}$$
$$\text{Int} \quad - \quad \text{Int} \quad = \quad \text{Int}$$
$$\text{Int} \quad \times \quad \text{Int} \quad = \quad \text{Int}$$

(*Int* is a handy abbreviation for a random integer, by the way, although the GMAT won't demand that you use it.)

However, dividing an integer by another integer does not always give you an integer.

$$\text{Int} \quad \div \quad \text{Int} \quad = \quad \text{sometimes an integer,}$$
$$\text{sometimes not!}$$

When you don't get an integer, you get a **fraction** or a **decimal**—a number between the integers on the number line.

$$7 \div 2 \quad = \quad \frac{7}{2} \quad = \quad 3.5$$

Seven divided by two — equals — seven halves, — and this equals — three point five

Fraction   Decimal

A horizontal **fraction line,** or bar, expresses the division of the **numerator** (above the fraction line) by the **denominator** (below the fraction line).

Numerator

Fraction line $\longrightarrow \dfrac{7}{2} \quad = \quad 7 \div 2$

Denominator

In fact, the division symbol ÷ is just a miniature fraction. People often say things such as "seven *over* two" rather than "seven halves" to express a fraction.

You can express division in three ways: with a fraction line, with the division symbol ÷, or with a slash (/).

$$\frac{7}{2} \quad = \quad 7 \div 2 \quad = \quad 7/2$$

A **decimal point** is used to extend place value to the right for decimals. Each place to the right of the decimal point is worth a tenth $\left(\dfrac{1}{10}\right)$, a hundredth $\left(\dfrac{1}{100}\right)$, and so on.

$$3.5 \quad = \quad 3 \quad + \quad \frac{5}{10}$$

Three point five — equals — three — plus — five-tenths

$$1.25 \quad = \quad 1 \quad + \quad \frac{2}{10} \quad + \quad \frac{5}{100}$$

| One point two five | equals | one | plus | two-tenths | plus | five-hundredths |

A decimal such as 3.5 has an **integer part** (3) and a **fractional part** or **decimal part** (0.5). In fact, an integer is just a number with no fractional or decimal part.

Every fraction can be written as a decimal, although you might need an unending string of digits in the decimal to properly express the fraction.

$$4 \div 3 \quad = \quad \frac{4}{3} \quad = \quad 1.333\ldots \quad = \quad 1.\overline{3}$$

| Four divided by three | equals | four-thirds (or four over three), | and this equals | one point three three three dot dot dot, forever and ever, | and that equals | one point three repeating |

Fractions and decimals obey all the rules you've seen so far about how to add, subtract, multiply, and divide. Everything you've learned for integers applies to fractions and decimals as well: how positives and negatives work, how to distribute, etc.

Check Your Skills

13. Which arithmetic operation involving integers does NOT always result in an integer?
14. $2 \div 7 = 2 \times \underline{\quad}$?

Answers can be found on page 37.

Divisibility and Even and Odd Integers

Sometimes you do get an integer out of integer division.

$$15 \div 3 \quad = \quad \frac{15}{3} \quad = \quad 5 \quad = \quad int$$

| Fifteen divided by three | equals | fifteen-thirds (or fifteen over three), | and this equals | five, | which is | an integer |

In this case, 15 and 3 have a special relationship. You can express this relationship in several equivalent ways.

1

15 is **divisible** by 3.

    15 divided by 3 equals an integer: $15 \div 3 = \text{int}$

15 is a **multiple** of 3.

    15 equals 3 times an integer: $15 = 3 \times \text{int}$

3 is a **factor** of 15.

3 **goes into** 15 evenly.

3 **divides** 15 evenly.

Even integers are divisible by 2.

    14 is even because $14 \div 2 = 7 = $ an integer.

All even integers have 0, 2, 4, 6, or 8 as their units digit (the digit just to the left of the decimal point).

Odd integers are not divisible by 2.

    15 is odd because $15 \div 2 = 7.5 = $ not an integer.

All odd integers have 1, 3, 5, 7, or 9 as their units digit.

Even and odd integers alternate on the number line.

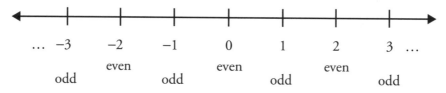

Zero is even because it is divisible by 2.

    $0 \div 2 = 0$, which is an integer

Only integers can be said to be even or odd. Fractions or decimals are not considered even or odd.

Check Your Skills

15. Fill in the blank. If 7 is a factor of 21, then 21 is a _____ of 7.
16. Is 2,284,623 divisible by 2?

Answers can be found on page 37.

Exponents and Roots (and Pi)

Exponents represent repeated multiplication. (Remember, multiplication was repeated addition, so this is just the next step up the food chain.)

In 5^2, the **exponent** is 2, and the **base** is 5. The exponent tells you how many bases you multiply together in the product. When the exponent is 2, you usually say *squared*.

$$5^2 \quad = \quad 5 \times 5 \quad = \quad 25$$

Five squared   equals   two fives multiplied together, or five times itself,   and this equals   twenty-five

When the exponent is 3, you usually say *cubed*.

$$4^3 \quad = \quad 4 \times 4 \times 4 \quad = \quad 64$$

Four cubed   equals   three fours multiplied together, or four times four times four,   and this equals   sixty-four

For other exponents, you say *to the ___ power* or *raised to the ___ power*. You could also say *to the power of ___*. For example:

$$2^5 \quad = \quad 2 \times 2 \times 2 \times 2 \times 2 \quad = \quad 32$$

Two to the fifth power   equals   five twos multiplied together,   and this equals   thirty-two

When you write exponents on your own paper, be sure to make them much tinier than regular numbers, and put them *clearly* up to the right. You don't want to mistake 5^2 for 52, or vice versa.

By the way, a number raised to the first power equals the original number.

$$7^1 \quad = \quad 7 \quad = \quad 7$$

Seven to the first power   equals   just one seven in the product,   and this equals   seven

A **perfect square** is the square of an integer.

     25 is a perfect square because $25 = 5^2 = \text{int}^2$.

A **perfect cube** is the cube of an integer.

     64 is a perfect cube because $64 = 4^3 = \text{int}^3$.

Roots undo exponents. The simplest and most common root is the **square root**, which undoes squaring. The square root is written with the **radical sign** ($\sqrt{}$); if a problem refers to the **radical**, it's talking about that symbol.

$$5^2 \quad = \quad 5 \times 5 \quad = \quad 25, \quad \text{so} \quad \sqrt{25} \quad = \quad 5$$

Five squared   equals   five times five,   and this equals   twenty-five,   so   the square root of twenty-five   equals   five

As a shortcut, *the square root of twenty-five* can just be called *root twenty-five*.

1

Asking for the square root of 49 is the same as asking what number, times itself, gives you 49.

$$\sqrt{49} \qquad = \qquad 7 \qquad \text{because} \qquad 7 \times 7 \qquad = \qquad 7^2 \qquad = \qquad 49$$

Root forty-nine   equals   seven,   because   seven   equals   seven   and this   forty-nine
                                              times   squared, equals
                                              seven

The square root of a perfect square is an integer, because a perfect square is an integer squared.

$$\sqrt{36} \qquad = \qquad \text{int} \qquad \text{because} \qquad 36 \qquad = \qquad \text{int}^2$$

The square root of   is   an integer,   because   thirty-six   equals   an integer
thirty-six   squared

The square root of any *non*-perfect square is an unending decimal that never even repeats, as it turns out.

$$\sqrt{2} \qquad \approx \qquad 1.414213562\ldots \qquad \text{because} \qquad (1.414213562\ldots)^2 \qquad \approx \qquad 2$$

Root two   is   one point four one four   because   that thing squared   is   two
           about   two blah blah,   about

The square root of 2 can't be expressed as a simple fraction, either. So you can leave it as is ($\sqrt{2}$), or you can approximate it ($\sqrt{2} \approx 1.4$).

You'll encounter one other number with an ugly decimal in geometry: **pi** (π).

Pi is the ratio of a circle's circumference to its diameter. It's about 3.14159265… without ever repeating.

Since pi can't be expressed as a simple fraction, it is typically represented by the Greek letter for p (π), or you can approximate it ($\pi \approx 3.14$, or a little more than 3).

Cube roots undo cubing. The cube root has a little 3 tucked into its notch ($\sqrt[3]{}$):

$$\sqrt[3]{8} \qquad = \qquad 2 \qquad \text{because} \qquad 2^3 \qquad = \qquad 8$$

The cube root of eight   equals   two,   because   two cubed   equals   eight

Other roots occasionally show up. For example, the **fourth root** undoes the process of taking a base to the fourth power.

$$\sqrt[4]{81} \qquad = \qquad 3 \qquad \text{because} \qquad 3^4 \qquad = \qquad 81$$

The fourth root of   equals   three,   because   three to the   equals   eighty-one
eighty-one   fourth power

Check Your Skills

17. $2^6 =$

18. $\sqrt[3]{27} =$

Answers can be found on page 38.

Variable Expressions and Equations

Up to now, every number you've dealt with has been an actual, known number. **Algebra** is the art of dealing with *unknown* numbers.

A **variable** is an unknown number, also called an **unknown**. You represent a variable with a single letter, such as x or y.

When you see y, imagine that it represents a number that you don't happen to know. At the start of a problem, the value of y is hidden from you. It could be anywhere on the number line, in theory, unless you're told something about y.

The letter x is the stereotypical letter used for an unknown. Since x looks so much like the multiplication symbol $\times$, you generally stop using $\times$ when writing out algebra to prevent confusion. To represent multiplication, you do other things.

To multiply variables, just put them next to each other.

What you see	*What you say*	*What it means*
xy	"x y"	x times y
abc	"a b c"	The product of a, b, and c

To multiply a known number by a variable, write the known number in front of the variable.

What you see	*What you say*	*What it means*
$3x$	"three x"	3 times x

Here, 3 is called the **coefficient** of x. If you want to multiply x by 3, write $3x$, not $x3$, which could look too much like x^3 ("*x cubed*").

All the operations besides multiplication look the same for variables as they do for known numbers.

What you see	*What you say*	*What it means*
$x + y$	"x plus y"	x plus y, or the sum of x and y
$x - y$	"x minus y"	x minus y
$\dfrac{x}{y}$	"x over y" or "x divided by y"	x divided by y
x^2	"x squared"	x squared, which is just x times x
$\sqrt{x}$	"the square root of x"	the square root of x

1

By the way, be careful when you have variables in exponents.

What you see	What you say	What it means
$3x$	"three x"	3 times x
3^x	"three to the x"	3 raised to the xth power, or 3 multiplied by itself x times

Never call 3^x "three x." It's called "three *to the* x." If you don't call 3^x by its correct name, then you'll never keep it straight.

An **expression** is something that ultimately represents a number; for example, $x + 3$ is an expression. You might not know that number, but you *express* it using variables, numbers you know, and operations such as adding, subtracting, etc.

An expression is like a recipe. If you follow the recipe, you will get the right number, as shown in the examples below:

Expression	What you say	The number represented by the expression
$x + y$	"x plus y"	The sum of x and y. In other words, the recipe is "add x and y." The result is the number.
$3xz - y^2$	"3 x z minus y squared"	First, multiply 3, x, and z, then subtract the square of y. The result is the number.
$\dfrac{\sqrt{2w}}{3}$	"The square root of 2 w, all over 3"	First, multiply 2 and w together. Next, take the square root. Finally, divide by 3. The result is the number.

Within an expression, you have one or more **terms**. A single term involves no addition or subtraction (typically). Often, a term is just a product of variables and known numbers.

It's useful to notice terms so that you can **simplify** expressions, or reduce the number of terms in those expressions. Here are the terms in the previous expressions.

Expression	Terms	Number of terms
$x + y$	x, y	Two
$3xz - y^2$	$3xz, y^2$	Two
$\dfrac{\sqrt{2w}}{3}$	$\dfrac{\sqrt{2w}}{3}$	One

If the last step in the expression recipe is adding or subtracting, then you can split up the expression into more than one term. Many expressions contain just one term, though (just as that last one did).

An **equation** sets one expression equal to another using the **equals sign** (=), which you've seen plenty of times in your life—and in this book already.

What you might not have thought about, though, is that the equals sign is a *verb*. In other words, an equation is a complete, grammatical sentence or statement:

Something   *equals*   something else.

Some expression   *equals*   some other expression.

Here's an example:

$$3 + 2x \qquad = \qquad 11$$

Three plus two x equals   eleven

Each equation has a *left side* (the subject of the sentence) and a *right side* (the object of the verb *equals*). You can say *is equal to* instead of *equals* if you want:

$$3 + 2x \qquad = \qquad 11$$

Three plus two x is equal to   eleven

Solving an equation is solving this mystery:

What is x?

Or, more precisely:

What is the value or values of x that make the equation *true*?

Since an equation is a sentence, it can be true or false, at least in theory. You always want to focus on how to make the equation *true*, or keep it so, by finding the right values of any variables in that equation.

The process of solving an equation usually involves rearranging the equation and performing identical operations on each side until the equation tells you what the variable equals.

$3 + 2x$	=	11	Three plus two x	equals	eleven
-3		-3	Subtract 3		Subtract 3
$2x$	=	8	Two x	equals	eight
$\div 2$		$\div 2$	Divide by 2		Divide by 2
x	=	4	x	equals	four

The solution to the original equation is $x = 4$. If you replace x with 4 in the equation $3 + 2x = 11$, then you get $11 = 11$, which is always true. Any other value of x would make the equation false.

If the GMAT gives you the equation $3 + 2x = 11$, it's telling you something very specific about x. For this particular equation, in fact, just one value of x makes the equation work (namely, 4).

Check Your Skills

19. What is the value of the expression $2x - 3y$ if $x = 4$ and $y = -1$?

Answer can be found on page 38.

1   PEMDAS

Consider the expression $3 + 2 \times 4$.

Should you add 3 and 2 first, then multiply by 4? If so, you get 20.

Or should you multiply 2 and 4 first, then add 3? If so, you get 11.

There's no ambiguity—mathematicians have decided on the second option. **PEMDAS** is an acronym to help you remember the proper **order of operations**.

PEMDAS Overview

When you simplify an expression, don't automatically perform operations from left to right, even though that's how you read English. Instead, follow PEMDAS:

Parentheses	Do P first
Exponents	Then E
Multiplication	Then either M or D
Division	
Addition	Then either A or S
Subtraction	

For $3 + 2 \times 4$, you do the M first (multiply 2 and 4), then the A (add 3 to the result).

$$3 + 2 \times 4 \qquad = 3 + 8 \qquad = 11$$

If you want to force the addition to go first, add parentheses. P always goes first:

$$(3 + 2) \times 4 \qquad = 5 \times 4 \qquad = 20$$

Multiplication and division are at the same level of importance in PEMDAS, because any multiplication can be expressed as division, and vice versa. For example:

$$7 \div 2 = 7 \times \frac{1}{2}$$

In a sense, multiplication and division are two sides of the same coin.

Likewise, addition and subtraction are at the same level of importance. Any addition can be expressed as subtraction, and vice versa.

$$3 - 4 = 3 + (-4)$$

So you can think of PEMDAS this way:

$$\text{PE}^{M}/_{D}\,^{A}/_{S} \longrightarrow$$

MANHATTAN PREP

If you have two operations of equal importance, do them *left to right*.

$$3 - 2 + 3 \qquad = 1 + 3 \qquad = 4$$

However, *override this order* if you have parentheses:

$$3 - (2 + 3) \qquad = 3 - 5 \qquad = -2$$

Consider a more complicated expression:

$$3 + 4(5 - 1) - 3^2 \times 2 = ?$$

Here is the correct order of steps to simplify:

$$3 + 4(5 - 1) - 3^2 \times 2$$

Parentheses $\qquad\qquad\qquad 3 + 4(4) - 3^2 \times 2$

Exponents $\qquad\qquad\qquad\; 3 + 4(4) - 9 \times 2$

Multiplication or **D**ivision $\quad\; 3 + 16 - 18$

Addition or **S**ubtraction $\qquad 3 + 16 - 18 = 19 - 18 = 1$

Try this problem on your own:

$$5 - 3 \times 2^3 \div (7 - 1)$$

P

E

M/D

A/S

Here's the solution:

$$5 - 3 \times 2^3 \div \left(7 - 1 \right)$$
$$5 - 3 \times 2^3 \div 6$$
$$5 - 3 \times 8 \div 6$$
$$5 - 24 \div 6$$
$$5 - 4$$
$$1$$

The answer is 1.

1

Try one more:

$$32 \div 2^4 \times (5 - 3^2)$$

P

E

M/D

A/S

Here's the solution:

$$32 \div 2^4 \times (5 - 3^2)$$

$$32 \div 2^4 \times (5 - 9)$$

$$32 \div 2^4 \times (-4)$$

$$32 \div 16 \times (-4)$$

$$2 \times (-4)$$

$$-8$$

Check Your Skills

Evaluate the following expressions.

20. $-4 + \dfrac{12}{3}$

21. $(5 - 8) \times 10 - 7 =$

22. $-3 \times 12 \div 4 \times 8 + (4 - 6) =$

23. $\dfrac{2^4 \times (8 \div 2 - 1)}{(9 - 3)} =$

Answers can be found on page 38.

Combining Like Terms

How can you simplify this expression?

$$3x^2 + 7x + 2x^2 - x$$

Remember, an expression is a recipe. Here's the recipe in words:

> Square x, then multiply that by 3, then separately multiply x by 7 and add that product in, then square x again, multiply that by 2, and add that product into the whole thing, and then finally subtract x.

That recipe is pretty annoying. Is there a way to simplify it?

There is! First, focus on **like terms**, which contain very similar elements.

Again, a term is an expression that doesn't contain addition or subtraction. Quite often, a term is just a bunch of things multiplied together.

Like terms are very similar to each other. They only differ by a numerical coefficient (the number in front of the variable). Everything else in them is the same.

The expression above contains four terms, separated by $+$ and $-$ operations:

$$3x^2 \quad + \quad 7x \quad + \quad 2x^2 \quad - \quad x$$

Three x squared   plus   seven x plus   two x squared   minus x

There are two pairs of like terms:

Pair one: $3x^2$ and $2x^2$

Pair two: $7x$ and $-x$

Make sure that the variables are identical, including exponents. Otherwise, the terms aren't *like*.

What can you do with two or more like terms? Combine them into one term by adding or subtracting the coefficients. Keep track of $+$ and $-$ signs. For example:

$$3x^2 \quad + \quad 2x^2 \quad = \quad 5x^2$$

Three x squared   plus   two x squared   equals   five x squared

$$7x \quad - \quad x \quad = \quad 6x$$

Seven x minus x equals   six x

Whenever a variable does not have a number in front, the coefficient is 1. In the example above, x can be rewritten as $1x$.

$$7x \quad - \quad 1x \quad = \quad 6x$$

Seven x minus   one x equals   six x

Or you could say that you're adding $-1x$.

$$7x \quad + \quad -1x \quad = \quad 6x$$

Seven x plus   negative one x equals   six x

Either way is fine. A negative sign in front of a term on its own is really a −1 coefficient. For instance, $-xy^2$ has a coefficient of −1.

Combining like terms works because, for like terms, everything *but* the coefficient is a **common factor**. So you can *pull out* that common factor and group the coefficients into a sum (or difference). This is when factoring starts to become really useful.

For a review of factoring, see pages 10–12.

In the first case, the common factor is x^2.

$$3x^2 \qquad + \qquad 2x^2 \qquad = \qquad (3+2)x^2$$

Three *x* squared   plus   two *x* squared   equals   the quantity three plus two, times
x squared

The right side then reduces by PEMDAS to $5x^2$. Of course, once you can go straight from $3x^2 + 2x^2$ to $5x^2$, you'll save a step.

By the way, when you *pronounce* $(3 + 2)x^2$, you should technically say "the quantity three plus two…" The word *quantity* indicates parentheses. If you just say "three plus two *x* squared," someone could (and should) interpret what you said as $3 + 2x^2$, with no parentheses.

In the case of $7x − x$, the common factor is *x*. Remember that *x* should be thought of as $1x$.

$$7x \qquad - \qquad 1x \qquad = \qquad (7-1)x$$

Seven *x*   minus   one *x*   equals   the quantity seven minus one,
times *x*

Again, the right side reduces by PEMDAS to $6x$.

So, if you combine like terms, you can simplify the original expression this way:

$3x^2 + 7x + 2x^2 − x$

$(3x^2 + 2x^2) + (7x − x)$

$5x^2 + 6x$

The common factor in like terms does not have to be a simple variable expression such as x^2 or x. It could involve more than one variable:

$-xy^2 + 4xy^2 = (-1 + 4)xy^2 = 3xy^2$ Common factor: xy^2

Remember that the coefficient on the first term should be treated as −1.

Be careful when you see multiple variables in a single term. For two terms to be like, the exponents have to match for every variable.

MANHATTAN PREP

In $-xy^2 + 4xy^2$, each term contains a plain x (which is technically x raised to the first power) and y^2 (which is y raised to the second power, or y squared). All of the exponents match. So the two terms are like, and you can combine them to $3xy^2$.

Now suppose you had the following series of terms:

$$2xy \quad + \quad xy^2 \quad - \quad 4x^2y \quad + \quad x^2y^2$$

Two x y plus x y squared   minus   four x squared y plus x squared y squared

None of the terms above can combine to a single term. They all have different combinations of variables and exponents. For now, you're stuck. (In the next section, you'll see that there's *something* you can do with that expression, but you can't combine terms.)

The two terms in the following expression *are* like:

$$xy^2 \quad + \quad 3y^2x$$

x y squared   plus   three y squared x

The order of the variables does not matter, since you can multiply in any order. All that matters is that the variables and exponents all match. You can flip around $3y^2x$ to $3xy^2$ to get:

$$xy^2 \quad + \quad 3y^2x \quad = \quad 4xy^2 \quad = \quad 4y^2x$$

x y plus   three y squared x equals   four x y squared,   and that   four y squared x
squared   equals

In general, be ready to flip around products as you deal with numbers times variables. The order of multiplication does not matter. For example

$$x(-3) \quad = \quad -x(3) \quad = \quad -3x$$

x times   equals   negative x times   equals   negative three x
negative three   three

The last form, $-3x$, is the standard form. You can encounter the others as you rearrange terms.

A common factor in like terms could be the square root of a number:

$$\sqrt{2} + 3\sqrt{2} = 1\sqrt{2} + 3\sqrt{2} = (1 + 3)\sqrt{2} = 4\sqrt{2} \quad \text{Common factor: } \sqrt{2}$$

Or the common factor could include pi (π):

$$2\pi r + 9\pi r = (2 + 9)\pi r = 11\pi r \qquad \text{Common factor: } \pi r$$

When terms are *not* like, tread carefully. Don't automatically combine everything; see what you can combine and what you cannot.

As you practice simplifying expressions, keep in mind that your main goal is to reduce the overall number of terms by combining like terms.

1

PEMDAS becomes more complicated when an expression contains terms that are not like and so cannot be combined. Be especially careful when you see terms buried within part of an expression, as in the following cases that you'll come back to later:

Terms inside parentheses

$$-3(x - 2) \qquad x \text{ and } 2 \text{ are not like}$$

Terms in the numerator or denominator of a fraction

$$\frac{1}{1 - x} = 2 \qquad x \text{ and } 1 \text{ are not like}$$

Terms involving exponents

$$\frac{x^{-3} + \left(x^2\right)^4}{x^5} \qquad x^{-3} \text{ and } (x^2)^4 \text{ are not like}$$

Terms under a root sign

$$\sqrt{x^2 + y^2} \qquad x^2 \text{ and } y^2 \text{ are not like}$$

Terms in parentheses, with the parentheses raised to an exponent

$$(x + y)^2 \qquad x \text{ and } y \text{ are not like}$$

Check Your Skills

Combine as many like terms as possible in each of the following expressions.

24. $-3 + 4\sqrt{2} + 6$
25. $4\pi r^2 - 3\pi r + 2\pi r$
26. $8ba + ab^2 - 5ab + ab^2 - 2ba^2$

Answers can be found on page 38.

Distribution

Things become more complicated when multiple terms are found within a set of parentheses.

For a quick review of distribution, go back to pages 10 and 11.

Start by distributing the example from the previous section: $-3(x - 2)$. Remember that you're multiplying -3 by $(x - 2)$. To keep track of minus signs as you distribute, you can think of $(x - 2)$ as $(x + (-2))$. The following example shows the multiplication sign ($\times$) to make it clear that you're multiplying.

MANHATTAN PREP

$$-3 \quad \times \quad (x-2) \quad = \quad -3 \times x \quad + \quad -3 \times -2 \quad = \quad -3x+6$$

| Negative three | times | the quantity x minus two | equals | negative three times x | plus | negative three times negative two, | and that equals | negative three x plus six |

Remember that the negative sign (on -3) distributes across both terms in the parentheses.

When you do all this on your paper, don't use $\times x$ to show multiplication, because you could confuse it with the variable x. Use a big dot or put each term to be multiplied in its own set of parentheses, such as $(-3)(-2)$. You might also put parentheses around the second product to help keep track of sign.

$$-3 \quad \times \quad (x-2) \quad = \quad -3x \quad + \quad (-3 \bullet -2) \quad = \quad -3x+6$$

| Negative three | times | the quantity x minus two | equals | negative three times x | plus | negative three times negative two, | and that equals | negative three x plus six |

How can you simplify this expression?

$$4y^2 - y(5 - 2y)$$

First, distribute negative y, $(-y)$, to both terms in the parentheses:

$$4y^2 - y(5 - 2y) = 4y^2 - 5y + 2y^2$$

Notice that $-y$ times $-2y$ becomes $+2y^2$.

Next, combine $4y^2$ and $2y^2$ because they are like terms:

$$4y^2 - y(5 - 2y) = 4y^2 - 5y + 2y^2 = 6y^2 - 5y$$

Sometimes the term being distributed involves a root or pi. Consider this tougher example:

$$\sqrt{2}\,(1 - x\sqrt{2}\,)$$

The principle is the same. Distribute the first $\sqrt{2}$ to both terms in the parentheses.

$$\sqrt{2} \quad \times \quad (1 - x\sqrt{2}\,) \quad = \quad \sqrt{2} \times 1 \quad + \quad \sqrt{2} \times -x\sqrt{2} \quad = \quad \sqrt{2} - 2x$$

| Root two | times | the quantity one minus x root two | equals | root two times one | plus | root two times negative x root two, | and that equals | root two minus two x |

It turns out that $\sqrt{2}$ times $\sqrt{2}$ is 2.

$$\sqrt{2} \times \sqrt{2} = 2$$

For a more in-depth look at multiplying roots, go to page 111 (or just wait until you get there).

Here's an example with pi:

$$\pi(1 + r)$$

1

Distribute the pi:

π	$\times$	$(1 + r)$	$=$	$\pi \times 1$	$+$	$\pi \times r$	$=$	$\pi + \pi r$
pi	times	the quantity one plus r	equals	pi times one	plus	pi times r,	and that equals	pi plus pi r

Check Your Skills

27. $x(3 + x)$
28. $4 + \sqrt{2}(1 - \sqrt{2})$

Answers can be found on page 39.

Pulling Out a Common Factor

Earlier, you saw the long expression below:

$$3x^2 + 7x + 2x^2 - x$$

This expression has four terms. By combining two pairs of like terms, you can simplify this expression to $5x^2 + 6x$, which has only two terms.

This expression can't go below two terms. The two remaining terms ($5x^2$ and $6x$) aren't *like*, because the variable parts aren't identical. However, these two terms do still have a common factor—namely, x. Each term is x times something, and you can use this fact to rewrite $5x^2 + 6x$.

x is a factor of $6x$, because $6x = 6$ times x.

x is also a factor of $5x^2$, because $x^2 = x$ times x, so $5x^2 = 5x$ times x.

Since x is a factor of both $5x^2$ and $6x$, you can factor it out and group what's left as a sum within parentheses.

$5x^2$	$+$	$6x$	$=$	$x(5x + 6)$
Five x squared	plus	six x	equals	x times the quantity five x plus six

If in doubt, distribute the x back through to verify that you're back where you started.

$x(5x + 6)$	$=$	$5x^2$	$+$	$6x$
The quantity five x plus six, times x	equals	five x squared	plus	six x

In addition, $x(5x + 6)$ can also be written as $(5x + 6)x$. Either way, it may or may not be truly "simpler" than $5x^2 + 6x$. However, pulling out a common factor can be the key move when you solve a GMAT problem.

1

Sometimes, the common factor is hidden among more complicated variable expressions. In the example below, the common factor is *xy*.

$$x^2y \quad - \quad xy^2 \quad = \quad xy(x-y)$$

x squared y   minus   x y squared   equals   x y times the quantity x minus y

Sometimes, the common factor involves a root or pi.

$$\sqrt{2} \quad + \quad \sqrt{2}\,\pi \quad = \quad \sqrt{2}\,(1+\pi)$$

Root two   plus   root two times pi   equals   root two times the quantity one plus pi

Here, the common factor is $\sqrt{2}$. Notice that the first term ($\sqrt{2}$) is the same as the common factor. Whenever the factor you are pulling out is the same as the term, leave a 1 in its place (in the parentheses). For example:

$$\pi r^2 \quad - \quad \pi \quad = \quad \pi(r^2 - 1)$$

pi r squared   minus   pi   equals   pi times the quantity r squared minus one

In the example above, the common factor is π. Again, when you pull π out of the second term (which is π), leave a 1 behind in its place. You can check that this works by distributing π back through.

You might only factor out an integer, or even a negative sign.

$$2 \quad + \quad 4x \quad = \quad 2(1+2x)$$

Two   plus   four x   equals   two times the quantity one plus two x

$$3 \quad - \quad x \quad = \quad -(x-3)$$

Three   minus   x   equals   the negative of quantity x minus three

Remember this monster from a couple of sections ago?

$$2xy \quad + \quad xy^2 \quad - \quad 4x^2y \quad + \quad x^2y^2$$

Two x y   plus   x y squared   minus   four x squared y   plus   x squared y squared

What is the common factor that you can pull out?

Answer: *xy*

$$2xy + xy^2 - 4x^2y + x^2y^2 = xy(2 + y - 4x + xy)$$

Check Your Skills

29. Factor a negative *x*, (–*x*), out of the expression $-2x^3 + 5x^2 + 3x$.
30. Factor the following expression: $4x^2 + 3xy - yx + 6x$

Answers can be found on page 39.

1 ## Long Addition and Subtraction

Sometimes you'll need to add or subtract larger numbers. It has probably been quite some time since you last had to do this on paper, so here's a refresher.

Try this problem.

$$\begin{array}{r} 283 \\ + 654 \\ \hline \end{array}$$

Here are the steps to find the sum of two larger numbers such as these.

$$\begin{array}{r} 283 \\ + 654 \\ \hline \end{array}$$

Begin with the right-most column of numbers and work your way to the left. The right-most column contains the units digits 3 and 4.

$$\begin{array}{r} 283 \\ + 654 \\ \hline 7 \end{array}$$

Sum the units digits: $3 + 4 = 7$.

$$\begin{array}{r} {}^{1}283 \\ + 654 \\ \hline 37 \end{array}$$

Move to the next column, the tens digits 8 and 5, where $8 + 5 = 13$. Place the 3 below and *carry* the 1 (from 13) above the top number in the next column, the hundreds digits.

$$\begin{array}{r} {}^{1}283 \\ + 654 \\ \hline 937 \end{array}$$

Move to the next column, the hundreds digit. Now, there are three numbers: the carried 1, as well as the 2 and 6. Add all of these together to get 9.

When conducting long addition, add the columns of numbers: units digit + units digit, tens digit + tens digit, and so on. If one of those sums is a number greater than 9, you'll need to carry over part of the number to the next column. For example, if the sum is 15, then place the units digit of the sum (the 5) below, but carry the extra part (the tens digit, 1) over to the next column and add it there instead.

Subtraction works similarly, although there is one special circumstance to note.

Try this example:

$$\begin{array}{r} 653 \\ - 472 \\ \hline \end{array}$$

Here's how you subtract when the top number in a column is smaller than the bottom number.

$$\begin{array}{r} 653 \\ -\ 472 \\ \hline \end{array}$$

Begin with the right-most column of numbers and work your way to the left. The right-most column contains the units digits 3 and 2.

$$\begin{array}{r} 653 \\ -\ 472 \\ \hline 1 \end{array}$$

Subtract: $3 - 2 = 1$.

$$\begin{array}{r} ^5\!\!\!\not{6}\,^1\!5\,3 \\ -\ 4\,7\,2 \\ \hline 8\,1 \end{array}$$

$5 - 7 = -2$, but you aren't allowed to put -2 down below. Instead, *borrow* a 10 from the next column. The tens column becomes $15 - 7 = 8$. The 6 in the hundreds column turns into a 5.

$$\begin{array}{r} ^5\!\!\!\not{6}\,^1\!5\,3 \\ -\ 4\,7\,2 \\ \hline 1\,8\,1 \end{array}$$

Finally, subtract the hundreds column: $5 - 4 = 1$.

As long as the top number is greater than the bottom one, you can subtract normally. If the top number is smaller, though, then borrow a 10 from the next number to the left. Once you've done that, proceed normally.

Long Multiplication

In this section, you'll review the basics of long multiplication. It is useful to know this skill for the GMAT, but long multiplication takes time, so think carefully before you use it. Can you simplify the math in any way before you have to multiply? Don't forget to look ahead to the next step or two in the problem: The next step might be to divide. If you do that first, then the multiplication might be easier.

When multiplying two numbers, always put the smaller number in the bottom row. For example, here's how to write 8×57:

$$\begin{array}{r} 57 \\ \times\ 8 \\ \hline \end{array}$$

Multiply the two numbers in the right-most column: $7 \times 8 = 56$.
Put the 6 underneath, then carry the 5.

$$\begin{array}{r} ^5\!57 \\ \times\ 8 \\ \hline 6 \end{array}$$

Multiply the next number over in the top row by the number in the bottom row:
$5 \times 8 = 40$, + the 5 you carried $= 45$.

$$\begin{array}{r} 57 \\ \times\ 8 \\ \hline 456 \end{array}$$

Because you're at the end, put the whole 45 underneath.

1

You may also need to multiply two two-digit numbers, such as 12×85.

$\begin{array}{r} {}^1 85 \\ \times\ 12 \\ \hline 0 \end{array}$

Start with the 2 in the bottom row: $5 \times 2 = 10$.

Put the 0 underneath, then carry the 1.

$\begin{array}{r} {}^1 85 \\ \times\ 12 \\ \hline 170 \end{array}$

$8 \times 2 = 16$, + the 1 you carried = 17. Because you are done multiplying by 2, place the 17 underneath.

$\begin{array}{r} {}^{\not1} 85 \\ \times\ 12 \\ \hline 170 \\ 0 \end{array}$

Now deal with the 1 in the second row. Remember that the 1 actually represents 10.

Place a 0 underneath the right-most column. Don't forget to cross out the 1 you carried last time!

$\begin{array}{r} {}^{\not1} 85 \\ \times\ 12 \\ \hline 170 \\ 50 \end{array}$

$5 \times 1 = 5$. Place the 5 underneath.

$\begin{array}{r} {}^{\not1} 85 \\ \times\ 12 \\ \hline 170 \\ 850 \end{array}$

$8 \times 1 = 8$. Place the 8 underneath.

$\begin{array}{r} {}^1 170 \\ +\ 850 \\ \hline 1020 \end{array}$

Now add the rows underneath, starting from the right: $0 + 0 = 0$; $7 + 5 = 12$, so place the 2 underneath and carry the 1; $1 + 8 +$ the carried $1 = 10$. Because you are done with the addition, place the 10 underneath.

$12 \times 85 = 1{,}020$

Don't let multiplication slow you down on the GMAT. Do multiplication drills to become quick and accurate; 5 minutes a day will make a big difference after a few weeks!

Long Division

As with long multiplication, think carefully before you dive into long division. For instance, what would you do with this problem?

What is 468 divided by 26?

(A) 12

(B) 18

(C) 22

You could do long division…but you don't need to! You can estimate.

$26 \times 10 = 260$

$26 \times ?? = 486$

$26 \times 20 = 520$

Answer (C) is definitely too large. Answer (A) is between 260 and 520, but since 486 is closer to 520 than 260, the answer should be closer to 20 than 10; answer (A) is too small. Therefore, the answer must be (B), 18. Done without having to resort to long division!

On other problems, you may be able to simplify before you do long division. For example:

What is the result when 440 is divided by 11 and then divided by 2?

Don't be fooled by the language! When multiplying or dividing, you can do the work in any order; that's why M and D go together in the PEMDAS order of operations. You don't have to do the work in the order presented. In this case, it's easier to divide by 2 first:

$440 \div 2 = 220$

Now, if you can't simplify any further or estimate your way to an answer, you can try long division.

$$11 \overline{)220}$$ 11 goes into 22 two times.

$$\begin{array}{r} 2 \\ 11{\overline{)220}} \\ -22 \\ \hline 0 \end{array}$$ Place a 2 on top of the unit's digit of the portion of the number you used. In this case, place the 2 above the second 2 in 22.

$$\begin{array}{r} 20 \\ 11{\overline{)220}} \\ -22 \\ \hline 00 \end{array}$$ Bring down the next digit in 220 (in this case 0). 11 goes into 0 zero times, so add a 0 to the top row and you're done. The answer is 20.

1

In the previous example, the answer was an integer ($220 \div 11 = 20$). However, the answer will not always be an integer.

Try dividing 123 by 6.

$6\overline{)123}$ 6 doesn't go into 1, but it does go into 12 two times.

$$\begin{array}{r} 2 \\ 6\overline{)123} \\ -12 \\ \hline 03 \end{array}$$

Place a 2 on top of the digit farthest to the right in 12.

$2 \times 6 = 12$, so subtract 12 from 12, then bring down the next digit (3).

$$\begin{array}{r} 20 \\ 6\overline{)123.0} \\ -12 \\ \hline 030 \end{array}$$

6 doesn't go into 3, so place a 0 on top of the 3.

You're not done! 123 is equal to 123.0. Add the decimal point and a 0 in the tenths column. Bring down the 0.

$$\begin{array}{r} 20.5 \\ 6\overline{)123.0} \\ -12 \\ \hline 030 \\ -30 \\ \hline 0 \end{array}$$

6 goes into 30 five times. Place a 5 on top of the 0. Don't forget to put a decimal between the 0 and the 5.

Also, check your answers. Only carry the calculation as far as you need to in order to find the answer.

Check Your Skills Answer Key

1

1. **178:**

$$
\begin{array}{r}
141 \\
+37 \\
\hline
178
\end{array}
$$

2. **−113:** Do the subtraction in reverse to find the positive difference, then add a negative sign (so the answer is −113, not +113).

$$
\begin{array}{r}
136 \\
-23 \\
\hline
113
\end{array}
$$

3. **0:** The greatest negative integer is −1 and the smallest positive integer is 1: −1 + 1 = 0.

4. **5 < 16:** 5 is less than 16.

5. **−5 > −16:** Negative 5 is greater than negative 16.

6. **A positive minus a negative:** (+) − (−) will always be positive, whereas (−) − (+) will always be negative. Any positive number is greater than any negative number.

7. **42:** $7 \times 6 = 42$

8. **4:** $52 \div 13 = 4$

9. **35:** $5 \times (3 + 4) = (5 \times 3) + (5 \times 4) = 15 + 20 = 35$

10. **6(6 − 2):** $36 − 12 = (6 \times 6) − (6 \times 2) = 6(6 − 2)$

11. **−12:** $(3)(−4) = −12$

12. **48:** $−6 \times (−3 + (−5)) = (−6 \times −3) + (−6 \times −5) = 18 + 30 = 48$

13. **Division:** Sometimes an integer divided by an integer equals an integer (e.g., 6 ÷ 2 = 3), and sometimes it does not (e.g., 8 ÷ 5 = 1.6).

14. $2 \times \dfrac{1}{7}$ **:** $2 \div 7 = 2 \times$ the reciprocal of 7, or $\dfrac{1}{7}$.

15. **Multiple:** If 7 is a factor of 21, then 21 is a multiple of 7.

16. **No:** 2,284,623 ends in 3, which means that it is an odd number. It is not divisible by 2.

1

17. **64:** $2^6 = (2 \times 2) \times (2 \times 2) \times (2 \times 2) = 4 \times 4 \times 4 = 64$

18. **3:** $\sqrt[3]{27} = 3$ because $3^3 = 27$.

19. **11:** Plug the values of the variables back into the expression to find the value of the expression.
    $2x - 3y = 2(4) - 3(-1) = 8 + 3 = 11$

20. **0:**

$$-4 + \frac{12}{3} =$$ Divide first.

$$-4 + 4 = 0$$ Next, add the two numbers.

21. **−37:**

$$(5 - 8) \times 10 - 7 =$$

$$(-3) \times 10 - 7 =$$ First, combine what is inside the parentheses.

$$-30 - 7 =$$ Next, multiply −3 and 10.

$$-30 - 7 = -37$$ Subtract the two numbers.

22. **−74:**

$$-3 \times 12 \div 4 \times 8 + (4 - 6) =$$

$$-3 \times 12 \div 4 \times 8 + (-2) =$$ First, combine what is inside the parentheses.

$$-36 \div 4 \times 8 + (-2) =$$ Multiply −3 and 12.

$$-9 \times 8 + (-2) =$$ Divide −36 by 4.

$$-72 + (-2) = -74$$ Multiply −9 by 8 and subtract 2.

23. **8:**

$$\frac{2^4 \times (8 \div 2 - 1)}{(9 - 3)} =$$ $8 \div 2 = 4$ and $9 - 3 = 6$.

$$\frac{2^4 \times (4 - 1)}{(6)} =$$ $4 - 1 = 3$ and $2^4 = 16$.

$$\frac{16 \times (3)}{6} =$$

$$\frac{16 \times \cancel{3}^{1}}{\cancel{6}_{2}} =$$ When you have larger numbers, simplify (divide) before you multiply.

$$\frac{\overset{8}{\cancel{16}} \times 1}{\cancel{2}_{1}} =$$

$$= 8$$

24. $\mathbf{3 + 4\sqrt{2}:}$ $(-3 + 6) + 4\sqrt{2} = 3 + 4\sqrt{2}$

25. $\mathbf{4\pi r^2 - \pi r:}$ $4\pi r^2 + (-3\pi r + 2\pi r) = 4\pi r^2 - \pi r$

26. $\mathbf{3ab + 2ab^2 - 2a^2b:}$ $(8ab - 5ab) + (ab^2 + ab^2) + (-2a^2b) = 3ab + 2ab^2 - 2a^2b$

MANHATTAN PREP

27. **$3x + x^2$:** $x(3 + x) = (3)(x) + (x)(x) = 3x + x^2$

28. **$2 + \sqrt{2}$:** $4 + \sqrt{2}\left(1 - \sqrt{2}\right) = 4 + \left(\sqrt{2} \times 1\right) + \left(\sqrt{2} \times -\sqrt{2}\right) = 4 + \sqrt{2} - 2 = 2 + \sqrt{2}$

29. **$-x(2x^2 - 5x - 3)$:** Pull an x out of each term. Switch the sign on each term in the parentheses in order to pull out a negative sign.

30. **$2x(2x + y + 3)$:** First, combine the two middle terms, which are like terms: $3xy - yx = 2xy$. In the expression $4x^2 + 2xy + 6x$, the terms all contain $2x$. Pull $2x$ out of each term.

Chapter Review: Drill Sets

Drill 1

Evaluate the following expressions.

1. $39 - (25 - 17)$
2. $3(4 - 2) \div 2$
3. $15 \times 3 \div 9$
4. $(7 - 5) - (3 - 6)$
5. $14 - 3(4 - 6)$
6. $-5 \times 1 \div 5$
7. $(5)(-3)(-4)(2)$
8. $5 - (4 - (3 - (2 - 1)))$
9. $-4(5) - \dfrac{12}{2 + 4}$
10. $17(6) + 3(6)$

Drill 2

Evaluate the following expressions.

11. $-12 \times -2 + 5$
12. $\dfrac{24}{2 + 6 \div 3}$
13. $-10 - (-3)^2$
14. -5^2
15. $\dfrac{-2^3}{2}$
16. $5^3 - 5^2$
17. $5^{(2+1)} + 25$
18. $(-2)^3 - 5^2 + (-4)^3$
19. $7(4) + 7(3) + 7(2) + 7(1)$
20. $3 \times 99 - 2 \times 99 - 1 \times 99$

Drill 3

Combine as many like terms as possible.

21. $\pi r^2 - (2\pi r + \pi r^2)$
22. $5\sqrt{3} + 5\sqrt{2} - 2\sqrt{3}$
23. $12xy^2 - 6x^2y^2 + (2)^2 x^2 y^2$
24. $3\pi + x\pi - 2\pi$

25. $\sqrt{2} + x\sqrt{2} - 2\sqrt{2}$
26. $12xy - (6x + 2y)$
27. $5x - (4x + 2 - (5x - 3))$
28. $\pi^2 r^2 - \pi r + 2\pi r^2 + \pi r^2 + \pi^2 r^2 + 2\pi r$
29. $2x^2 - (2x)^2 - 2^2 - x^2$
30. $4x^2 + 2x - (2\sqrt{x})^2$

Drill 4

Distribute the following expressions. Simplify as necessary.

31. $3(5 - y)$
32. $-(a - b)$
33. $(m + 2n)4m$
34. $2b(3a + b)$
35. $52r(2t - 10s)$
36. $(-37x + 63)10^2$
37. $6kl(k - 2l)$
38. $-\sqrt{2}(18 - 8x)$
39. $d(d^2 - 2d + 1)$
40. $xy^2z(x^2z + yz^2 - xy^2)$

Drill Sets Solutions

Drill 1

1. **31:**

$$39 - (25 - 17) =$$
$$39 - 8 = 31$$

Tip: You could also distribute the minus sign
if you prefer: $(39 - 25 + 17) = 14 + 17 = 31$.

2. **3:**

$$3 \times (4 - 2) \div 2 =$$
$$3 \times (2) \div 2 =$$
$$6 \div 2 = 3$$

3. **5:**

$$15 \times 3 \div 9 =$$
$$45 \div 9 = 5$$

4. **5:**

$$(7 - 5) - (3 - 6) =$$
$$(2) - (-3) =$$
$$2 + 3 = 5$$

5. **20:**

$$14 - 3 (4 - 6) =$$
$$14 - 3(-2) =$$
$$14 + 6 = 20$$

6. **−1:**

$$-5 \times 1 \div 5 =$$
$$-5 \div 5 = -1$$

7. **120:**

$$(5)(-3)(-4)(2) =$$

$$(10)(12) = 120$$

Tip #1: When multiplying several numbers together, look for 5s and 2s in the product. Combine these first to create 10; it is easier to multiply 10 into other numbers.

Tip #2: To determine whether a product will be positive or negative, count the number of negative terms you are multiplying. An even number of negative terms will give you a positive product; an odd number of negative terms will give you a negative product.

8. **3:**

$$5 - (4 - (3 - (2 - 1))) =$$
$$5 - (4 - (3 - 1)) =$$
$$5 - (4 - 2) =$$
$$5 - (2) = 3$$

Tip: Start with the innermost parentheses. Write everything down, and don't try to do multiple steps at once; you'll just open yourself up to careless mistakes.

9. **−22:**

$$-4(5) - \frac{12}{2+4} =$$
$$-20 - \frac{12}{6} =$$
$$-20 - 2 = -22$$

Tip: In order to avoid making a careless mistake with negatives, you may want to write the last line as −20 + (−2) = −22.

10. **120:** Most people would think of this path first:

$$17(6) + 3(6) =$$
$$102 + 18 = 120$$

However, if you find that math annoying (most people would), then don't just start doing it. Take a moment: Is there an easier way to do this math? Yes! Factor a 6 out of both terms:

$$17(6) + 3(6) =$$
$$6(17 + 3) =$$
$$6(20) = 120$$

Drill 2

11. **29:** Do the multiplication first, then the addition.

$$(-12 \times -2) + 5 =$$
$$24 + 5 = 29$$

12. **6:**

$$\frac{24}{2 + (6 \div 3)} =$$

$$\frac{24}{2 + 2} =$$

$$\frac{24}{4} = 6$$

13. **−19:**

$$-10 - (-3)^2 =$$
$$-10 - (-3)(-3) =$$
$$-10 - (9) = -19$$

You could also write the last line as $-10 + (-9) = -19$.

14. **−25:**

$$-5^2 =$$
$$-(5^2) = -25$$

15. **−4:**

$$\frac{-2^3}{2} =$$

$$\frac{-8}{2} = -4$$

16. **100:**

$$5^3 - 5^2 =$$
$$125 - 25 = 100$$

17. **150:**

$$5^{(2+1)} + 25 =$$
$$5^3 + 25 =$$
$$125 + 25 = 150$$

18. **−97:**

$$(-2)^3 - 5^2 + (-4)^3 =$$
$$(-2)(-2)(-2) - (5^2) + (-4)(-4)(-4) =$$
$$(-8) - 25 + (-64) =$$
$$-33 - 64 = -97$$

19. **70:** To make the math faster, factor a 7 out of each term:

$$7(4) + 7(3) + 7(2) + 7(1) =$$
$$7(4 + 3 + 2 + 1) =$$
$$7(10) = 70$$

You can also multiply out each term and then add, as shown below, but that will generally take longer when the numbers are at all large or annoying:

$$7(4) + 7(3) + 7(2) + 7(1) =$$
$$28 + 21 + 14 + 7 = 70$$

20. **0:** Think a moment before you work. Because the number 99 is large, the math is made easier if you factor 99 out of each term:

$$3 \times 99 - 2 \times 99 - 1 \times 99 =$$
$$99(3 - 2 - 1) =$$
$$99(0) = 0$$

Here is the longer way to do the math:

$$3 \times 99 - 2 \times 99 - 1 \times 99 =$$
$$297 - 198 - 99 =$$
$$99 - 99 = 0$$

Drill 3

21. **$-2\pi r$:** The two terms in the parentheses cannot be combined, so start by distributing the negative sign before combining like terms:

$$\pi r^2 - (2\pi r + \pi r^2) =$$
$$\pi r^2 - 2\pi r - \pi r^2 =$$
$$(1\pi r^2 - 1\pi r^2) - 2\pi r =$$
$$0 - 2\pi r = -2\pi r$$

Tip: You don't have to write out a coefficient of 1, but consider doing so if this helps you to minimize careless mistakes.

22. **$3\sqrt{3} + 5\sqrt{2}$:** Group and combine like terms.

$$5\sqrt{3} + 5\sqrt{2} - 2\sqrt{3}$$
$$\left(5\sqrt{3} - 2\sqrt{3}\right) + 5\sqrt{2}$$
$$3\sqrt{3} + 5\sqrt{2}$$

23. **$12xy^2 - 2x^2y^2$:** Simplify before grouping and combining like terms.

$$12xy^2 - 6x^2y^2 + (2)^2x^2y^2 =$$
$$12xy^2 - 6x^2y^2 + 4x^2y^2 =$$
$$12xy^2 + (-6 + 4)x^2y^2 =$$
$$12xy^2 + (-2)x^2y^2 =$$
$$12xy^2 - 2x^2y^2$$

24. **$(x + 1)\pi$:** Group like terms and then combine.

$$3\pi + x\pi - 2\pi =$$
$$3\pi - 2\pi + x\pi =$$
$$(3 - 2)\pi + x\pi =$$
$$1\pi + x\pi =$$
$$(1 + x)\pi = (x + 1)\pi$$

25. **$(x - 1)\sqrt{2}$:**

$$\sqrt{2} + x\sqrt{2} - 2\sqrt{2} =$$
$$1\sqrt{2} + x\sqrt{2} - 2\sqrt{2} =$$
$$(1 + x - 2)\sqrt{2} =$$
$$(-1 + x)\sqrt{2} = (x - 1)\sqrt{2}$$

26. **$12xy - 6x - 2y$:** The terms in the parentheses are not like terms, so distribute the negative sign before grouping and combining like terms.

$$12xy - (6x + 2y) =$$
$$12xy - 6x - 2y$$

Note that you cannot actually combine any of the terms in this problem; none are like terms!

27. **$6x - 5$:** Work from the innermost parentheses out.

$$5x - (4x + 2 - (5x - 3)) =$$
$$5x - (4x + 2 - 5x + 3) =$$
$$5x - (4x - 5x + 2 + 3) =$$
$$5x - (-x + 5) =$$
$$5x + x - 5 = 6x - 5$$

28. **$2\pi^2 r^2 + \pi r + 3\pi r^2$:**

$$\pi^2 r^2 - \pi r + 2\pi r^2 + \pi r^2 + \pi^2 r^2 + 2\pi r =$$
$$(1\pi^2 r^2 + 1\pi^2 r^2) + (-1\pi r + 2\pi r) + (2\pi r^2 + 1\pi r^2) =$$
$$2\pi^2 r^2 + 1\pi r + 3\pi r^2$$

29. **$-3x^2 - 4$:**

$$2x^2 - (2x)^2 - 2^2 - x^2 =$$
$$2x^2 - 2^2 x^2 - 4 - 1x^2 =$$
$$2x^2 - 4x^2 - 1x^2 - 4 =$$
$$(2 - 4 - 1)x^2 - 4 =$$
$$(-3)x^2 - 4 =$$
$$-3x^2 - 4$$

1

30. **$4x^2 - 2x$:**
$$4x^2 + 2x - (2\sqrt{x})^2 =$$
$$4x^2 + 2x - 2^2(\sqrt{x})^2 =$$
$$4x^2 + 2x - 4x =$$
$$4x^2 + (2 - 4)x =$$
$$4x^2 + (-2)x =$$
$$4x^2 - 2x$$

Drill 4

31. **$15 - 3y$:**
$$3(5 - y) =$$
$$3 \times 5 + 3 \times (-y) =$$
$$15 - 3y$$

32. **$-a + b$ OR $b - a$:** The minus sign in front of the left parenthesis should be interpreted as: -1 times the expression $(a - b)$. Because $(-1) \times a = -a$ and $(-1) \times (-b) = b$, the solution is: $-(a - b) = (-1) \times (a - b) = -a + b$.

33. **$4m^2 + 8mn$:** Ordinarily, you see the Distributive Property in this form:

$$a(b + c) = ab + ac$$

If you place a to the right of the parentheses, you can still distribute in the same way.

$$(b + c)a = ba + ca$$

This works because the order in which numbers are multiplied does not matter. The GMAT sometimes disguises a possible distribution by presenting it in this alternative form:

$$(m + 2n)4m = 4m^2 + 8mn$$

34. **$6ab + 2b^2$:**
$$2b(3a + b) = (2b)(3a) + (2b)(b) = 6ab + 2b^2$$

35. **$104rt - 520rs$:** When distributing more complicated expressions, remember to multiply out numbers and combine any copies of the same variable.

$$52r(2t - 10s) =$$
$$(52r)(2t) - (52r)(10s) =$$
$$104rt - 520rs$$

36. **$-3,700x + 6,300$:**
$$(-37x + 63)10^2 =$$
$$(-37x)(100) + (63)(100) =$$
$$-3,700x + 6,300$$

37. **$6k^2l - 12kl^2$:** First, distribute normally. Next, combine like terms. (Note: This solution shows what it looks like to use a big dot to mean multiplication. You can also use parentheses, as other explanations do.)

$$6kl(k - 2l) =$$
$$6kl \cdot k - 6kl \cdot 2l =$$
$$6k^2l - 12kl^2$$

38. **$-18\sqrt{2} + 8x\sqrt{2}$** : Distribute carefully to keep track of those negative signs!

$$-\sqrt{2}(18 - 8x) =$$
$$\left(-\sqrt{2}\right)(18) + \left(-\sqrt{2}\right)(-8x) =$$
$$-18\sqrt{2} + 8x\sqrt{2}$$

39. **$d^3 - 2d^2 + d$:** Even though there are three terms inside the parentheses, distribution works exactly the same. Multiply d by every term in the parentheses.

$$d(d^2 - 2d + 1) =$$
$$(d \times d^2) - (d \times 2d) + (d \times 1) =$$
$$d^3 - 2d^2 + d$$

40. **$x^3y^2z^2 + xy^3z^3 - x^2y^4z$:** The term xy^2z on the outside of the parentheses must be multiplied by each of the three terms inside the parentheses. You can then simplify the expression as much as possible.

$$xy^2z(x^2z + yz^2 - xy^2) =$$
$$(xy^2z)(x^2z) + (xy^2z)(yz^2) - (xy^2z)(xy^2) =$$
$$x^3y^2z^2 + xy^3z^3 - x^2y^4z$$

Divisibility

In this chapter...

- Divisibility
  - Memorize Divisibility Rules for Small Integers
  - Factors Are Divisors
  - Prime Number: Only Divisible by 1 and Itself
  - Prime Factorization: All the Primes on the Tree
  - Every Number Is Divisible by the Factors of Its Factors
  - Factors: Built Out of Primes
  - Factor Tree of a Variable: Contains Unknowns
  - Factors of x with No Common Primes: Combine
  - Factors of x with Primes in Common: Combine to LCM

Chapter 2
Divisibility

In This Chapter, You Will Learn To:

- Apply divisibility rules
- Find the factors of a number
- Answer GMAT questions related to divisibility

Divisibility

Divisibility has to do with **integers**. Recall that integers are the counting numbers (1, 2, 3, etc.), their opposites (−1, −2, −3, etc.), and 0. Integers have no decimals or fractions attached.

Also recall that most integer arithmetic is boring:

integer + integer = always an integer	$4 + 11 = 15$
integer − integer = always an integer	$-5 - 32 = -37$
integer × integer = always an integer	$14 \times 3 = 42$

However, when you divide an integer by another integer, sometimes you get an integer ($18 \div 3 = 6$), and sometimes you don't ($12 \div 8 = 1.5$).

If you get an integer out of the division, then the first number is **divisible by** the second. For example, 18 is divisible by 3 because $18 \div 3 =$ an integer. On the other hand, 12 is *not* divisible by 8 because $12 \div 8$ is not an integer.

Memorize Divisibility Rules for Small Integers

These rules come in very handy. An integer is divisible by:

2 if the integer is even.

Even numbers, such as the number 12, are integers that end in 0, 2, 4, 6, or 8. The number 12 is divisible by 2 because $12 \div 2 = 6$, an integer. Any even number is always divisible by 2.

3 if the sum of the integer's digits is a multiple of 3.

Take the number 147. Its digits are 1, 4, and 7. Add those digits to get the sum: $1 + 4 + 7 = 12$. The sum, 12, is a multiple of 3, so 147 is divisible by 3.

5 if the integer ends in 0 or 5.

The numbers 75 and 80 are divisible by 5, but 77 and 84 are not. Any integer that ends in 0 or 5 is divisible by 5. Any integer that ends in something other than 0 or 5 is *not* divisible by 5.

9 if the sum of the integer's digits is a multiple of 9.

This rule is very similar to the divisibility rule for 3. Take the number 288. Add the digits: $2 + 8 + 8 = 18$. The sum, 18, is a multiple of 9, so 288 is divisible by 9.

10 if the integer ends in 0.

The number 8,730 is divisible by 10, but 8,753 is not. Any integer that ends in 0 is divisible by 10. Any integer that ends in something other than 0 is *not* divisible by 10.

Check Your Skills

1. Is 123,456,789 divisible by 2?
2. Is 732 divisible by 3?
3. Is 989 divisible by 9?

Answers can be found on page 73.

Factors Are Divisors

The integer 6 is divisible by what positive integers?

Test the positive integers less than or equal to 6: 1, 2, 3, 4, 5, and 6.

$6 \div 1 = 6$ Any number divided by 1 equals itself, so an integer divided by 1 will always be an integer.

$6 \div 2 = 3$
$6 \div 3 = 2$ 6 is divisible by 2, and 6 is divisible by 3. Note that these form a pair: $3 \times 2 = 6$.

$6 \div 4 = 1.5$

$6 \div 5 = 1.2$ 〉 Not integers, so 6 is *not* divisible by 4 or by 5.

$6 \div 6 = 1$ Any number divided by itself equals 1, so an integer is always divisible by itself.

Therefore, 6 is divisible by 1, 2, 3, and 6. That means that 1, 2, 3, and 6 are **factors** of 6. Learn all the ways you might see this relationship expressed on the GMAT.

2 is a factor of 6	6 is a multiple of 2
2 is a divisor of 6	6 is divisible by 2
2 divides 6	6 goes into 6 (evenly, without a remainder)

To find all the factors of a small number, use **factor pairs**. A factor pair of 60 is a pair of integers that multiplies together to 60. For instance, 15 and 4 are a factor pair of 60 because $15 \times 4 = 60$.

Here's an organized way to make a table of factor pairs of 60:

1. Label two columns Small and Large.

2. Start with 1 in the small column and 60 in the large column. (The first set of factor pairs will always be 1 and the number itself.)

3. After 1, try the next smallest integer: 2. Since 2 is a factor of 60, write 2 underneath the 1 in your table. Divide 60 by 2 to find 2's "sibling" in the pair: $60 \div 2 = 30$. Write 30 in the large column.

4. Repeat this process until the numbers in the small and the large columns run into each other. In this case, 6 and 10 are a factor pair, but 7, 8, and 9 are not factors of 60. The next number after 9 is 10, which appears in the large column, so you can stop.

If you…	Then you…	Like this:	
		Small	Large
		1	60
	Make a table of factor pairs, starting with 1 and 60	2	30
		3	20
Want all the factors of 60		4	15
		5	12
		6	10

Check Your Skills

4. Find all the factors of 90.
5. Find all the factors of 72.
6. Find all the factors of 105.
7. Find all the factors of 120.

Answers can be found on pages 73–74.

Prime Number: Only Divisible by 1 and Itself

The integer 7 is divisible by what positive integers?

Test out the positive integers less than or equal to 7: 1, 2, 3, 4, 5, 6, and 7.

$7 \div 1 = 7$ Every number is divisible by 1—no surprise there!

$7 \div 2 = 3.5$
$7 \div 3 = 2.33...$
$7 \div 4 = 1.75$ 7 is not divisible by *any* integer besides 1 and itself. (You don't need to do these calculations. It's enough to know that the answer is not an integer.)
$7 \div 5 = 1.4$
$7 \div 6 = 1.16...$

$7 \div 7 = 1$ Every number is divisible by itself—boring!

So 7 has only two factors—1 and itself. Numbers that have exactly two factors are called **prime numbers**. Primes are extremely important in any question about divisibility.

There are a few key details to note. First, the concept of prime applies only to positive integers. Second, note that 1 is *not* prime; it has exactly one factor (itself!). Finally, 2 is the only even prime number. Every even number greater than 2 has at least one more factor besides 1 and itself, namely the number 2.

Every positive integer can be placed into one of two categories—prime or not prime. Memorize the smaller primes: 2, 3, 5, 7, 11, 13, 17, and 19.

Check Your Skills

8. List all the prime numbers between 20 and 50.

Answer can be found on page 74.

Prime Factorization: All the Primes on the Tree

Take another look at the factor pairs of 60. It had 12 factors and 6 factor pairs.

$60 = 1 \times 60$ Always the first factor pair—boring!
and 2×30
and 3×20
and 4×15 5 other factor pairs—interesting!
and 5×12 Let's look at these in a little more detail.
and 6×10

Consider 4×15. One way to think about this pair is that 60 breaks down into 4 and 15. Use a **factor tree** to show this relationship.

Keep going. Neither 4 nor 15 is prime, so they both have factor pairs that you might find interesting: 4 breaks down into 2 × 2, and 15 breaks down into 3 × 5.

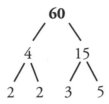

Can you break it down any further? Not with interesting factor pairs. For instance, 2 = 2 × 1, but that's nothing new. The numbers you have reached (2, 2, 3, and 5) are all primes.

When you find a prime factor, that branch on the factor tree has reached the end. Circle prime numbers as you go, as if they were fruit on the tree. The factor tree for 60 looks like this:

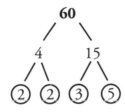

After you break down 60 into 4 and 15, and then break 4 and 15 down further, you end up with 60 = 2 × 2 × 3 × 5.

What if you start with a different factor pair of 60? Create a factor tree for 60 in which the first breakdown you make is 6 × 10.

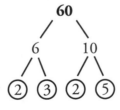

According to this factor tree 60 = 2 × 3 × 2 × 5. These are the same primes as before (though in a different order). Any way you break down 60, you end up with the same prime factors: two 2's, one 3, and one 5. The **prime factorization** of 60 is 2 × 2 × 3 × 5.

Note: The factor tree doesn't list *all* factors of 60; for that, make a table of factor pairs. The factor tree represents the *prime* factors of 60.

Prime factors are like the DNA or the fingerprint of a number. Every number has a unique prime factorization. Sixty is the only number that can be written as 2 × 2 × 3 × 5.

Your first instinct on divisibility problems should be to *break numbers down to their prime factors*. A factor tree is the best way to find a prime factorization.

2

Find the prime factorization of 630.

One way to start is by finding the smallest prime factor of 630. Check 2 first: 630 is even, so it is divisible by 2. On your factor tree, break down 630 into 2 and 315.

Now you still need to factor 315. It's not even, so it's not divisible by 2. Check 3 by adding up the digits of 315. That's 3 + 1 + 5 = 9, which is a multiple of 3, so 315 is divisible by 3. Add this next level of information, 315 = 3 × 105, to your factor tree.

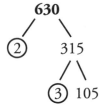

The number 105 might still be divisible by another integer. Check it out: 1 + 0 + 5 = 6, so 105 is divisible by 3. Since 105 ÷ 3 = 35, the tree now looks like this:

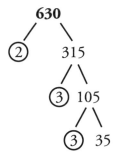

The number 35 is not divisible by 3 (3 + 5 = 8, which is not a multiple of 3), so the next number to try is 5. The number 35 ends in a 5, so it is divisible by 5. Since 35 ÷ 5 = 7, the tree now looks like this:

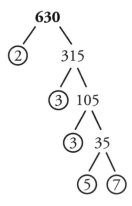

Every number on the tree has now been broken down as far as it can go. The prime factorization of 630 is 2 × 3 × 3 × 5 × 7.

Alternatively, you could have split 630 into 63 and 10, since it's easy to see that 630 is divisible by 10. Then you would proceed from there, breaking 10 into 2 and 5 and breaking 63 into 7 and 9 (which then breaks down into 3 and 3). As you practice, you'll spot shortcuts.

Either way will get you to the same set of prime factors.

If you...	Then you...	Like this:
Want the prime factorization of 96	Break 96 down to primes using a tree	96 → 2, 48; 48 → 12, 4; 12 → 3, 4; 4 → 2, 2; 4 → 2, 2

Check Your Skills

9. Find the prime factorization of 90.
10. Find the prime factorization of 72.
11. Find the prime factorization of 105.
12. Find the prime factorization of 120.

Answers can be found on page 74.

Every Number Is Divisible by the Factors of Its Factors

If a is divisible by b, and b is divisible by c, then a is divisible by c as well. For instance, 12 is divisible by 6, and 6 is divisible by 3. Therefore, 12 is divisible by 3 as well.

This **factor foundation rule** also works in reverse to a certain extent. If d is divisible by two different *primes*, e and f, then d is also divisible by $e \times f$. In other words, if 20 is divisible by 2 and 5, then 20 is also divisible by 2×5 (or 10).

Divisibility travels up and down the factor tree. Consider the factor tree of 150:

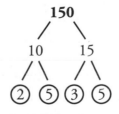

2

Prime factors are *building blocks*. In the case of 150, you have one 2, one 3, and two 5's at your disposal to build other factors of 150. In the example above, you're moving down the tree—from 150 down to 10 and 15, and then down again to 2, 5, 3, and 5. But you can also build upward, starting with the four building blocks. For instance, 2 × 3 = 6, and 5 × 5 = 25, so your tree could also look like this:

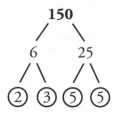

(Even though 5 and 5 are not different primes, 5 appears twice on 150's tree. So you are allowed to multiply those two 5's together to produce another factor of 150, namely 25.)

The tree above isn't even the only other possibility. Here are more:

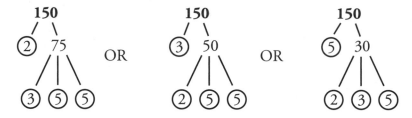

Beginning with four prime factors of 150 (2, 3, 5, and 5), you build different factors by multiplying any two, any three, or even all four of those primes together in different combinations. All of the factors of a number (except for 1) can be built with different combinations of that number's prime factors.

Factors: Built Out of Primes

Take one more look at the number 60 and its factors. Consider the prime factorization of each factor.

Building blocks	Small	Large	Building blocks
1	1	60	2 × 2 × 3 × 5
2	2	30	2 × 3 × 5
3	3	20	2 × 2 × 5
2 × 2	4	15	3 × 5
5	5	12	2 × 2 × 3
2 × 3	6	10	2 × 5

All of the factors of 60 (except 1) are different combinations of some or all of the four prime factors of 60. To say this another way, every factor of a number (again, except 1) can be expressed as the product of a subset of its prime factors. This relationship between factors and prime factors is true of every number.

2

To recap what you've learned so far:

1. If *a* is divisible by *b*, and *b* is divisible by *c*, then *a* is divisible by *c* as well. For instance, 100 is divisible by 20, and 20 is divisible by 4, so 100 is divisible by 4 as well.

2. If *d* has *e* and *f* as prime factors, *d* is also divisible by *e* × *f*. For instance, 90 is divisible by 5 and by 3, so 90 is also divisible by 5 × 3 = 15. You can let *e* and *f* be the same prime, as long as there are at least two copies of that prime in *d*'s factor tree.

3. Every factor of a number (except 1) is the product of a different combination of that number's prime factors. For example, 30 = 2 × 3 × 5. The factors of 30 are 1, 2, 3, 5, 6 (2 × 3), 10 (2 × 5), 15 (3 × 5), and 30 (2 × 3 × 5).

4. To find all of the factors of a number in a methodical way, set up a factor pairs table. For example, 30 has the factor pairs (1, 30), (2, 15), (3, 10), and (5, 6).

5. To find all of the *prime* factors of a number, use a factor tree.

Check Your Skills

13. The prime factorization of a number is 3 × 5. What is the number and what are all of its factors?
14. The prime factorization of a number is 2 × 5 × 7. What is the number, and what are all of its factors?
15. The prime factorization of a number is 2 × 3 × 13. What is the number and what are all of its factors?

Answers can be found on page 75.

Factor Tree of a Variable: Contains Unknowns

Say that you are told that some unknown positive number *x* is divisible by 6. You can represent this fact on paper in several different ways. For instance, you could write "*x* = multiple of 6" or "*x* = 6 × integer." You could also write the information as the result of division: $\frac{x}{6}$ = integer.

You could also represent the information with a factor tree. Since the top of the tree is a variable, add in a branch to represent what you *don't* know about the variable. Label this branch with a question mark (?), three dots (…), or something to remind yourself that you have *incomplete* information about *x*:

What *else* do we know about *x*? What can you definitely say about *x* right now?

Take a look at these three statements. For each statement, decide whether it *must* be true, whether it *could* be true, or whether it *cannot* be true.

> I.   *x* is divisible by 3.
>
> II.   *x* is even.
>
> III.   *x* is divisible by 12.

Begin with statement I: *x* is divisible by 3. Think about the multiples of 6. If *x* is divisible by 6, then *x* is a multiple of 6. List out the first several multiples of 6 to see whether they're divisible by 3.

$$
\begin{array}{ccl}
 & 6 & 6 \div 3 = 2 \\
\text{\textit{x} is a number} & 12 & 12 \div 3 = 4 \\
\text{on this list.} & 18 & 18 \div 3 = 6 \\
 & 24 & 24 \div 3 = 8 \\
 & \dots & \dots
\end{array}
\qquad
\begin{array}{l}
\text{All of these numbers are}\\
\text{also divisible by 3.}
\end{array}
$$

At this point, you can be fairly certain that *x* is divisible by 3. In divisibility problems (and elsewhere), listing out possible values of a variable can help you wrap your head around a question or a pattern.

But you can also *prove* that *x* is divisible by 3. Just make one modification to the tree.

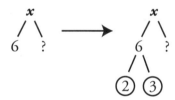

The purpose of the tree is to break integers down into primes, which are the building blocks of greater integers. Now that the factor tree is broken down as far as it will go, apply the factor foundation rule. Since *x* is divisible by 6, and 6 is divisible by 3, you can definitively say that *x* is divisible by 3. Statement I *must* be true.

Statement II says *x* is even. Must that be true? Return to your factor tree.

Again, make use of the factor foundation rule: 6 is divisible by 2, so you know that *x* is divisible by 2 as well. Since *x* is divisible by 2, *x* is even. Statement II *must* be true.

Statement III says *x* is divisible by 12. Compare the factor tree of *x* with the factor tree of 12.

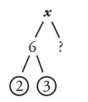 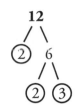

What would you have to know about *x* to guarantee that it is divisible by 12?

The number 12 is 2 × 2 × 3, so 12's building blocks are two 2's and a 3. To guarantee that *x* is divisible by 12, you need to know for sure that *x* has two 2's and one 3 among its prime factors. That is, *x* would have to be divisible by everything that 12 is divisible by.

Look at the factor tree for *x*. There is a 3 but only *one* 2. So you can't claim that *x must be* divisible by 12. But *could x* be divisible by 12?

Consider the question mark on *x*'s factor tree. That question mark is there to remind you that you *don't* know everything about *x*. After all, *x could* have other prime factors. If one of those unknown factors were another 2, your tree would look like this:

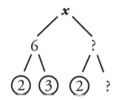

If an unknown factor were a 2, then *x* would indeed be divisible by 12. So *x could* be divisible by 12.

To confirm this thinking, list out a few multiples of 6 and check whether they are divisible by 12.

Some of the possible values of *x* are divisible by 12, and some aren't. *x could* be divisible by 12. Statement III *could* be true but doesn't have to be true.

$$
x \text{ is a number on this list.} \left\{
\begin{array}{ll}
6 & 6 \div 12 = 0.5 \\
12 & 12 \div 12 = 1 \\
18 & 18 \div 12 = 1.5 \\
24 & 24 \div 12 = 2 \\
\ldots & \ldots
\end{array}
\right\}
\begin{array}{l}
\text{Some, but not all, of these} \\
\text{numbers are also divisible} \\
\text{by 12.}
\end{array}
$$

If you...	Then you...	Like this:
Use a factor tree with a variable on top	Put in a question mark (or something similar) to remind yourself what you *don't* know	x / \ 6 ?

Check Your Skills

For each question, the following is true: *x* is divisible by 24. Determine whether each statement below *must* be true, *could* be true, or *cannot* be true.

16. *x* is divisible by 6.
17. *x* is divisible by 9.
18. *x* is divisible by 8.

Answers can be found on pages 75–76.

Factors of *x* With No Common Primes: Combine

Try this problem.

> *x* is divisible by 3 and by 10. Decide whether each statement below *must* be true, *could* be true, or *cannot* be true.
>
> I.   *x* is divisible by 2.
> II.   *x* is divisible by 15.
> III. *x* is divisible by 45.

First, create two factor trees to represent the given information.

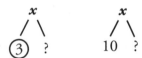

Why not write them together at once? "*x* is divisible by 3" is a different fact from "*x* is divisible by 10." *Initially, always write two given facts about a variable separately.* That way, you can think carefully about how to combine those facts.

Continue to break down the factors until you have only primes:

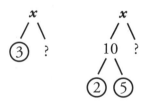

Now you can examine statement I. *x* is divisible by 10, and 10 is divisible by 2, so *x* is definitely divisible by 2. Statement I *must* be true.

Statement II is more difficult. Study the trees. Neither one provides complete information about *x*, but you know for certain that *x* is divisible by 3 and that *x* is divisible by 2 and by 5. These primes are all different. *When the primes from two trees are all different, you can put all the primes on one tree.*

MANHATTAN PREP

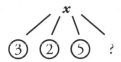

Return to the statement: x is divisible by 15. Can you guarantee this? If x definitely has all the prime factors that 15 has, then you can guarantee that x is divisible by 15.

The prime factors of 15 are 3 and 5. Being divisible by 15 is the same as being divisible by 3 and by 5.

Look at the combined factor tree. x has both a 3 and a 5, so x is definitely divisible by 15. Statement II *must* be true.

In order to understand better how prime factors work, you may want to sketch out some other possible factor trees for this information. If you know that x is divisible by 3, 2, and 5, you can combine these primes to form other definite factors of x.

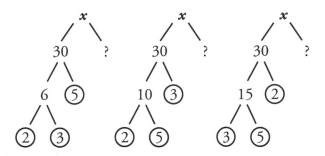

You get 15 on the third tree (don't write all this out on the test, of course). Notice what all three trees have in common. No matter how you combine the prime factors, each tree ultimately leads to 30, which is $2 \times 3 \times 5$.

Therefore, you know that x is divisible by $2 \times 3 \times 5 = 30$. And if x is divisible by 30, it is also divisible by everything 30 is divisible by. Since 15 is a factor of 30, x must be divisible by 15. Statement II *must* be true.

Statement III says that x is divisible by 45. What do you need to know in order to claim that x is divisible by 45? Build a factor tree of 45:

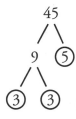

Your tree shows that 45 is divisible by 3, 3, and 5. For x to be divisible by 45, you need to know that x has all the same prime factors. Does it?

2

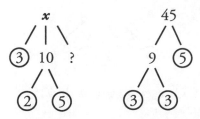

x has a 5, but only *one* 3 for sure. Since you don't know whether x has the second 3 that the 45 needs, you can't say for certain whether x is divisible by 45. x *could* be divisible by 45, but you don't know what the question mark contains. If it contains a 3, then x is divisible by 45. If not, then x is not divisible by 45. Statement III *could* be true but does not have to be.

If you...	Then you...	Like this:
Know two factors of x that have no primes in common	Combine the two trees into one	 becomes

Check Your Skills

For each question, the following is true: x is divisible by 28 and by 15. Determine whether each statement below *must* be true, *could* be true, or *cannot* be true.

19. x is divisible by 14.
20. x is divisible by 20.
21. x is divisible by 24.

Answers can be found on pages 76–77.

Factors of *x* with Primes in Common: Combine to LCM

In the last section, you were told that x was divisible by 3 and by 10, and you figured out the consequences. For instance, you could conclude that x was divisible by 30, the product of 3 and 10.

Now consider a slightly different situation. Let's say that x is divisible by 6 and by 9. Is x divisible by 54, the product of 6 and 9?

Here is the question in tree form:

Given: Question: Do we necessarily get this tree?

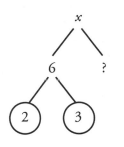
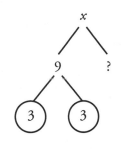
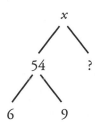

The earlier situation, in which x was divisible by 3 and by 10, was simpler, because 3 and 10 do not share any prime factors. You were able to keep all of the prime factors because no factors were shared. If you multiply those factors together, you'll find find the **least common multiple**, or **LCM**. The least common multiple of two numbers, say A and B, is the smallest number that is a multiple of both A and B. For the 3 and 10 example, the LCM is $3 \times 10 = 30$.

In the new question, though, 6 and 9 do share a prime factor, namely a 3.

Try listing out the multiples of each number, 6 and 9, to find the first number that appears on both lists:

Multiples of 6	Multiples of 9
6	9
12	**18**
18	27
24	

The LCM of 6 and 9 is 18. This is *not* the same number as 6×9, which equals 54. You can't just multiply the two numbers together this time. Why is that?

Take a look at how this works when you are using factor trees:

Given: Conclusion:

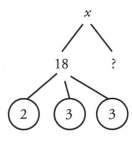

The conclusion contains only two of the three 3's that were part of the given information. The third 3 was dropped.

Imagine this scenario. On a table in front of you sits a box. Sally looks in that box and tells you, "I see an apple and an orange in the box." Linus looks in the box and tells you, "I see two oranges in the box." (Assume Sally and Linus are both telling the truth; they just may not be telling you *everything* they see in the box.)

Does that mean that the box contains three oranges?

No, it doesn't. Linus did see two oranges. But Sally's orange could have been one of those same two that Linus saw. Therefore, at a *minimum*, the box contains two oranges and one apple. You have to strip out one orange, because it represents overlap between the two pieces of information. (Note: The box *could* contain more oranges or apples; it could even contain bananas! You just don't know for sure that it does.)

In the same way, you need to strip out the 3 from the factor tree of 6, because that 3 could just be an overlap with the two 3's from the factor tree of 9. At a minimum, you have a 2 and two 3's. The LCM of 6 and 9 is $2 \times 3 \times 3 = 18$, so x must be divisible by 18, but it does not have to be divisible by 54.

Here's why the LCM is important: *If x is divisible by A and by B, then x is divisible by the LCM of A and B, no matter what.*

For instance, if you are told that x is divisible by 3 and by 10, then you can conclude that x is definitely divisible by the LCM of 3 and 10, which equals 30 (since 3 and 10 don't overlap at all).

The same principle holds true for 6 and 9, though you have to *strip out any common factors*. If x is divisible by 6 and 9, then x is definitely divisible by 18, the LCM of 6 and 9.

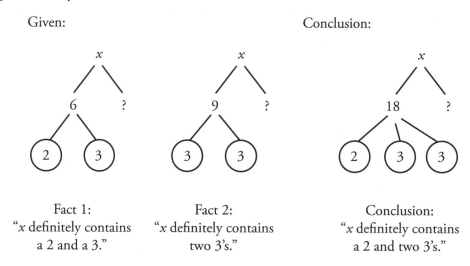

Given:		Conclusion:

Fact 1:
"x definitely contains a 2 and a 3."

Fact 2:
"x definitely contains two 3's."

Conclusion:
"x definitely contains a 2 and two 3's."

The two given facts are like statements given by two witnesses. The witnesses aren't lying, but they could have seen the same things. *Don't double-count the evidence.* All you can prove about x is that it contains a 2 and *two* 3's. The two witnesses could have seen the *same* 3, as Sally and Linus could have seen the same orange.

When two numbers don't share prime factors, their LCM is their product. For example:

3 and 10 don't share any prime factors, so their LCM = $3 \times 10 = 30$.

However, when two numbers share prime factors, their LCM will be *smaller* than their product, because you have to strip out overlap.

6 and 9 share prime factors, so their LCM is not 6 × 9 = 54. In fact, their LCM (18) is smaller than 54.

Listing the two sets of multiples to find the smallest number on both lists works well for small numbers, but it can be messy when the numbers are greater. In that case, break the numbers into their primes and then take only the *greater number of instances of* any particular prime.

For instance:

6 = 2 × 3 and 9 = 3 × 3
How many 2's should you take? The number 6 has one 2 and 9 has no 2's, so take one 2.
How many 3's should you take? The number 6 has one 3 and 9 has two 3's, so take two 3's.

The LCM = 2 × 3 × 3 = 18. That's a lot of steps to find the LCM when the numbers are small, but for more complicated situations, it's definitely faster.

Try another question.

If x is divisible by 8, 12, and 45, what is the greatest number that x must be divisible by?

The "greatest number that x must be divisible by" is code for: *What is the LCM of 8, 12, and 45?*

First, draw three separate trees for the given information:

Given:

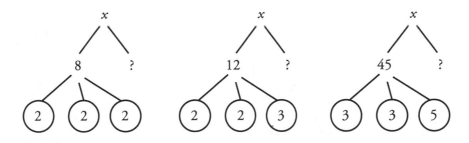

You could find this number by listing all the multiples of 8, 12, and 45 and looking for the first number on all three lists. That would be annoying. Instead, find the LCM by counting up prime factors that you *know* are in x, while stripping out the overlap.

Start with 2. How many 2's are guaranteed to be in x? There are three 2's in 8, two 2's in 12, and none in 45. To cover all the bases, there must be at least *three* 2's in x.

Take 3 next. Since 45 has two 3's, the most in any tree above, x must contain at least *two* 3's. Finally, x must have at least *one* 5 because of the 45. So here's the picture:

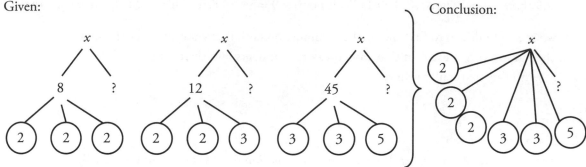

Now calculate the LCM:

$$2 \times 2 \times 2 \times 3 \times 3 \times 5 = (2 \times 2) \times (3 \times 3) \times (2 \times 5) = 4 \times 9 \times 10 = 360$$

Tip: Whenever you have to multiply a lot of numbers, try to pair 2's and 5's to create 10's, because 10 is an easy number to multiply into the greater number.

The LCM of 8, 12, and 45 is 360. It is the greatest number that x *must* be divisible by.

One final note: If the facts are about different variables (e.g., x and y), then the facts don't overlap when multiplying x and y.

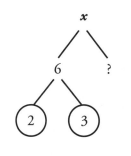

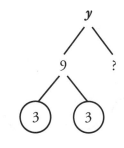

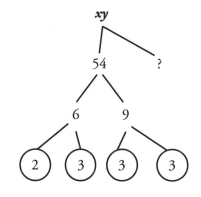

MANHATTAN PREP

The two witnesses are looking at different crime scenes (x and y), so the product counts up everything you see across all the trees. Therefore:

If you...	Then you...	Like this:
Know two factors of x that have primes in common	Combine the two trees into one, eliminating the overlap = Know that x is divisible by the LCM of the factors	x is divisible by 6 x is divisible by 9 becomes x is divisible by 18, the LCM of 6 and 9

Check Your Skills

For each question, the following is true: x is divisible by 6 and by 14. Determine whether each statement below *must* be true, *could* be true, or *cannot* be true.

22. x is divisible by 42.
23. x is divisible by 84.

Answers can be found on page 77.

Check Your Skills Answer Key

1. **No:** 123,456,789 is an odd number, because it ends in 9. Therefore, 123,456,789 is *not* divisible by 2.

2. **Yes:** The digits of 732 sum to a multiple of 3 (7 + 3 + 2 = 12), so 732 is divisible by 3.

3. **No:** The digits of 989 do not sum to a multiple of 9 (9 + 8 + 9 = 26), so 989 is *not* divisible by 9.

4. The factors of 90 are:

Small	Large
1	90
2	45
3	30
5	18
6	15
9	10

5. The factors of 72 are:

Small	Large
1	72
2	36
3	24
4	18
6	12
8	9

6. The factors of 105 are:

Small	Large
1	105
3	35
5	21
7	15

7. The factors of 120 are:

Small	Large
1	120
2	60
3	40
4	30
5	24
6	20
8	15
10	12

8. **23, 29, 31, 37, 41, 43, and 47** are the prime numbers between 20 and 50.

9.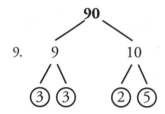

10.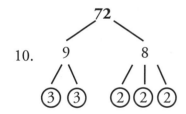

11.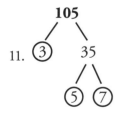

12.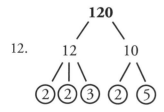

MANHATTAN PREP

2

13. **15**:

$3 \times 5 = 15$

Small	Large
1	15
3	5

14. **70**:

$2 \times 5 \times 7 = 70$

Building blocks	Small	Large	Building blocks
1	1	70	$2 \times 5 \times 7$
2	2	35	5×7
5	5	14	2×7
7	7	10	2×5

15. **78**:

$2 \times 3 \times 13 = 78$

Building blocks	Small	Large	Building blocks
1	1	78	$2 \times 3 \times 13$
2	2	39	3×13
3	3	26	2×13
2×3	6	13	13

For questions 16–18, x is divisible by 24.

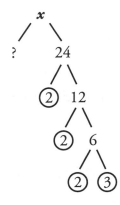

16.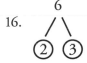

Must be true: For x to be divisible by 6, it must contain the same prime factors as 6, which contains a 2 and a 3. x also contains a 2 and a 3, so x must be divisible by 6.

2

17.

> **Could be true:** For x to be divisible by 9, it must contain the same prime factors as 9, which contains two 3's. x only contains one known 3. But the question mark means x may have other prime factors and may contain another 3. For this reason, x could be divisible by 9 but does not have to be.

18.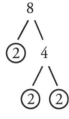

> **Must be true:** For x to be divisible by 8, it must contain the same prime factors as 8, which contains three 2's. x also contains three 2's, so x must be divisible by 8.

For questions 19–21, x is divisible by 28 and by 15.

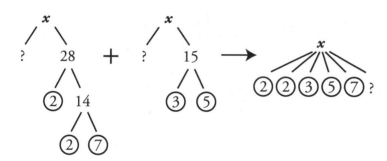

19.

> **Must be true:** For x to be divisible by 14, it must contain the same prime factors as 14, which contains a 2 and a 7. x also contains a 2 and a 7, so x must be divisible by 14.

20.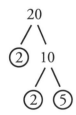

> **Must be true:** For x to be divisible by 20, it must contain the same prime factors as 20, which contains two 2's and a 5. x also contains two 2's and a 5, so x must be divisible by 20.

MANHATTAN PREP

21.

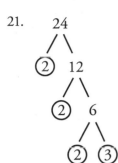

   Could be true: For x to be divisible by 24, it must contain the same prime factors as 24, which contains three 2's and a 3. x contains a 3, but only two 2's for sure. But the question mark indicates that x may have other prime factors, so it may contain another 2. For this reason, x could be divisible by 24 but does not have to be.

For questions 22–23, x is divisible by 6 and by 14.

22. $6 = 2 \times 3$ and $14 = 2 \times 7$. Therefore, the LCM of 6 and 14 is $2 \times 3 \times 7 = 42$. (Remember to strip out the overlapping 2.)

   Must be true: Since the LCM of 6 and 14 is 42, x must be divisible by 42.

23. **Could be true:** The LCM is 42. x could be divisible by 84, but it does not have to be.

Chapter Review: Drill Sets

Drill 1

1. Is 4,005 divisible by 5?
2. Does 51 have any factors besides 1 and itself?
3. $x = 20$
The prime factors of x are:
The factors of x are:
4. If 33 is a factor of 594, is 11 a factor of 594?
5. Is 6,750 divisible by 18?

Drill 2

6. Is 123 divisible by 3?
7. Does 23 have any factors other than 1 and itself?
8. $x = 100$
The prime factors of x are:
The factors of x are:
9. If 2,499 is divisible by 147, is 2,499 divisible by 49?
10. What are all of the positive multiples of 18 that are less than 60?

Drill 3

11. Is 285,284,901 divisible by 10?
12. Is 539,105 prime?
13. If $x = 36$, what are all of the factors of x?
    (A) 2, 2, 3, 3
    (B) 2, 3, 4, 6, 9, 12, 18
    (C) 1, 2, 3, 4, 6, 9, 12, 18, 36
14. Find at least four even divisors of 84.
15. What are the prime factors of 30×49?

Drill 4

16. Is 9,108 divisible by 9 and/or by 2?
17. Is 937,184 prime?
18. $x = 39$
The prime factors of x are:
The factors of x are:
19. How many more prime factors does the product of 42×120 have than the product of 21×24?

Drill 5

20. Is 43,360 divisible by 5 and/or by 3?
21. Is 513,501 prime?
22. $x = 37$
The prime factors of x are:
The factors of x are:
23. What are the two greatest odd factors of 90?

Drill 6

24. Determine which of the following numbers are prime numbers. A prime number has exactly two factors: 1 and itself.

2	3	5	6
7	9	10	15
17	21	27	29
31	33	258	303
655	786	1,023	1,325

2

Drill 7

25. If x is divisible by 33, what other numbers is x divisible by?

26. The prime factorization of a number is $3 \times 3 \times 7$. What is the number, and what are all of its factors?

27. If 6 and 14 are factors of y, must y be divisible by 21?

28. If $7y$ is a multiple of 210, must y be a multiple of 12?

29. If integer a is *not* a multiple of 30, but ab is, what is the smallest possible value of integer b?

Drill 8

30. If 40 is a factor of x, what other numbers must be factors of x?

31. The only prime factors of a number are 5 and 17. What is the number, and what are all of its factors?

32. 5 and 6 are factors of x. Is x divisible by 15?

33. If q is divisible by 2, 6, 9, 12, 15, and 30, is q divisible by 8?

34. If p is a prime number, and q is a non-prime integer, what are the minimum and maximum numbers of factors p and q can have in common?

Drill 9

35. If 64 divides evenly into n, what are all of the known divisors of n?

36. The prime factorization of a number is $2 \times 3 \times 11$. What is the number, and what are all of its factors?

37. 14 and 3 divide evenly into n. Is 12 a factor of n?

38. The sum of the positive integers x and y is 17. If x has only two factors and y is a multiple of 5, which of the following is a possible value of x?

    (A) 3

    (B) 7

    (C) 12

39. If n is the product of 2, 3, and a two-digit prime number, how many of its factors are greater than 6?

Drill 10

40. If n is a multiple of both 35 and 44, is 14 a divisor of n?

41. 4, 21, and 55 are factors of n. Is n divisible by 154?

42. If n is divisible by both 196 and 15, is 270 a factor of n?

Drill Sets Solutions

Drill 1

1. **Yes:** 4,005 ends in 5, so it is divisible by 5.

2. **Yes:** The digits of 51 sum to a multiple of 3 (5 + 1 = 6), so 3 is a factor of 51. (In fact, both 3 and 17 are factors of 51, since 3 × 17 = 51.)

3. **Prime factors: 2, 2, 5**
   Factors: 1, 2, 4, 5, 10, 20
   The prime factors of x are:

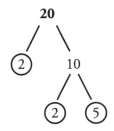

   The factors of x are:

Small	Large
1	20
2	10
4	5

4. **Yes:** You could divide 594 by 11 to determine divisibility, but it is faster to use the Factor Foundation rule. If 594 is divisible by 33, 594 is also divisible by all of the factors of 33. The number 11 is a factor of 33 (33 = 11 × 3). Therefore, 594 is also divisible by 11.

5. **Yes:** In order to be divisible by 18, a number must be divisible by both 2 and 9, factors that make up 18. Because 6,750 ends in a 0, it is even, so it is divisible by 2. The digits of 6,750 sum to 18 (6 + 7 + 5 = 18), and 18 is divisible by 9, so 6,750 is also divisible by 9. Because 6,750 is divisible by both 2 and 9, it is also divisible by 18.

Drill 2

6. **Yes:** The digits of 123 sum to a multiple of 3 (1 + 2 + 3 = 6), so 123 is divisible by 3.

7. **No:** 23 is a prime number. It has no factors other than 1 and itself.

8. **Prime factors: 2, 2, 5, 5**
   Factors: 1, 2, 4, 5, 10, 20, 25, 50, 100
   The prime factors of x are:

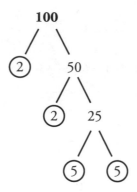

   The factors of x are:

Small	Large
1	100
2	50
4	25
5	20
10	10

9. **Yes:** The Factor Foundation rule is helpful in this question. The problem states that 2,499 is divisible by 147. The Factor Foundation rule states that if 2,499 is divisible by 147, then 2,499 is also divisible by all of the factors of 147. And 147 is divisible by 49 ($147 \div 49 = 3$). Since 2,499 is divisible by 147, it is also divisible by 49.

10. **18, 36, and 54:** In order to generate multiples of 18 that are less than 50, multiply 18 by small integers.

    $18 \times 1 = 18$
    $18 \times 2 = 36$
    $18 \times 3 = 54$

    All other positive multiples of 18 are greater than 60.

Drill 3

11. **No:** 285,284,901 ends in a 1, not a 0. It is not divisible by 10.

12. **No:** 539,105 ends in a 5, so 5 is a factor of 539,105. So are 1 and 539,105. There are other factors, such as 107,821, since $539,105 = 5 \times 107,821$. Prime numbers have only two factors, so 539,105 is not prime.

13. **(C):** The question asks for *all* of the factors of *x*, not just the prime factors. Use a table to find the factor pairs of 36. (Note: 1 and the number itself are always your first factor pair; don't forget them! Also, trap answer (A) represents only the prime factors, not all factors.)

Small	Large
1	36
2	18
3	12
4	9
6	6

14. **2, 4, 6, 12, 14, 28, 42, and 84:** Make a factor pair table to see which factors are even:

Small	Large
1	**84**
2	**42**
3	**28**
4	21
6	**14**
7	**12**

15. **2, 3, 5, 7, and 7:** While you could multiply the numbers together to find the prime factors (annoying because the numbers are large!), there is a faster way. The prime factors of the product of 30 and 49 will consist of the prime factors of 30 and the prime factors of 49. The prime factors of 30 are 2, 3, and 5. The prime factors of 49 are 7 and 7. Therefore, the prime factors of 30 × 49 are 2, 3, 5, 7, and 7.

Drill 4

16. **9,108 is divisible by 9 AND by 2:** The digits of 9,108 sum to a multiple of 9 (9 + 1 + 0 + 8 = 18), so it is a multiple of 9. Because 9,108 ends in 8, it is even, which means it is divisible by 2.

17. **No:** 937,184 ends in 4, which means it's even. Therefore, it's divisible by 2. It's also divisible by 1 and itself. Prime numbers have only two factors, so 937,184 is not prime.

18. **Prime factors: 3, 13**
    Factors: 1, 3, 13, 39 The prime factors of *x* are:

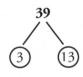

The factors of x are:

Small	Large
1	39
3	13

19. **Two:** You could multiply these products out or identify all of the prime factors of each number, but there is a more efficient way. Because the question asks you to make a comparison, focus only on the *differences* between the two products.

$$42 \times 120$$
$$21 \times 24$$

Compare 42 and 21: $42 = 21 \times 2$. That is, 42 contains 21 (and all of its factors), but 42 also has one additional factor of 2.

Compare 120 and 24: $120 = 24 \times 5$. That is, 120 contains 24 (and all of its factors), but 120 also has one additional factor of 5.

Therefore, the only *additional* prime factors in 42×120 are the 2 in 42 and the 5 in 120. The product of 42×120 has two more prime factors than the product of 21×24.

Drill 5

20. **43,360 is divisible by 5 but is NOT divisible by 3:** 43,360 ends in 0, so it is divisible by 5. The digits of 43,360 do not sum to a multiple of 3 ($4 + 3 + 3 + 6 + 0 = 16$), so it is not divisible by 3.

21. **No:** The sum of the digits is $5 + 1 + 3 + 5 + 0 + 1 = 15$. The number 15 is divisible by 3, so the number 513,501 is also divisible by 3. Prime numbers have only themselves and 1 as factors, so 513,501 is not prime.

22. **Prime factors: 37**
    Factors: 1, 37

Small	Large
1	37

23. **15, 45:** Break 90 down into its factor pairs.

Small	Large
1	90
2	**45**
3	30
5	18
6	**15**
9	10

The two greatest odd factors of 90 are 45 and 15.

Drill 6

24. **Prime numbers: 2, 3, 5, 7, 17, 29, 31:** The numbers in bold below are prime numbers.

2	**3**	**5**	6
7	9	10	15
17	21	27	**29**
31	33	258	303
655	786	1,023	1,325

All of the even numbers other than 2 (6, 10, 258, 786) are not prime, since they are divisible by 2.

All of the multiples of 5 other than 5 itself (10, 15, 655, 1,325) are not prime, because they are divisible by 5.

Next, check whether any remaining numbers have digits that sum to a multiple of 3: 9, 21 (digits sum to 3), 27 (digits sum to 9), 33 (digits sum to 6), 303 (digits sum to 6), and 1,023 (digits sum to 6). All of these numbers are divisible by 3.

For the remaining numbers, you may already know that certain ones are prime. For the rest, check to see whether they are divisible by any prime numbers smaller than the number you are checking. For instance, to check 17, determine that it is not divisible by 2 (it's not even), by 3 (the digits don't sum to a multiple of 3), by 5 (it does not end in 0 or 5), or by 7 (actually check the division here: you don't get an integer).

Drill 7

25. **1, 3, 11:** If x is divisible by 33, then x is also divisible by everything 33 is divisible by. The factors of 33 are:

Small	Large
1	33
3	11

26. **The number is 63, and the factors are 1, 3, 7, 9, 21, and 63:**

$3 \times 3 \times 7 = 63$.

Small	Large
1	63
3	21
7	9

27. **Yes:**

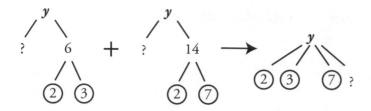

The factors of 6 are 2 and 3. The factors of 14 are 2 and 7. The 2's do overlap, so strip out one instance of that double-counted factor. The combined factors are 2, 3, and 7. The 3 and 7 can be used to create 21 ($3 \times 7 = 21$), so y must be a multiple of 21.

28. **No:** For y to be a multiple of 12, it would need to contain all of the prime factors of 12: 2, 2, and 3. $7y$ is a multiple of 210, so $7y$ contains the prime factors 2, 3, 5, and 7 (because $2 \times 3 \times 5 \times y = 210$). However, the question asks about y, not $7y$, so divide out the 7. Therefore, y must contain the remaining primes: 2, 3, and 5. Compare this to the prime factorization of 12: y does have a 2 and a 3, but it does not necessarily have *two* 2's. Therefore, y could be a multiple of 12, but it doesn't have to be.

Alternatively, you could start by dividing out the 7. If $7y$ is divisible by 210, y is divisible by 30. Therefore, y contains the prime factors 2, 3, and 5, and you can follow the remaining reasoning from above. Alternatively, since y is divisible by 30, y could be 30, which is *not* divisible by 12, or y could be 60, which *is* divisible by 12.

29. **2:** For integer a to be a multiple of 30, it would need to contain all of the prime factors of 30: 2, 3, and 5. Since a is not a multiple of 30, it must be missing at least one of these prime factors. So if ab is a multiple of 30, b must supply any missing prime factors. The smallest possible missing prime is 2. If $b = 2$ and $a = 15$ (or any odd multiple of 15), then the initial constraints will be met: ab will be a multiple of 30, but a by itself will not be.

Drill 8

30. **1, 2, 4, 5, 8, 10, and 20:** If 40 is a factor of x, then any factor of 40 is also a factor of x. List out the factors of 40.

Small	Large
1	40
2	20
4	10
5	8

31. **The number is 85, and the factors are 1, 5, 17, and 85:** If 5 and 17 are the only prime factors of the number, then the number equals 5×17, which means the number is 85.

Small	Large
1	85
5	17

32. Yes:

None of the factors overlap, so you can combine them all: *x* is divisible by 2 × 3 × 5. For *x* to be divisible by 15, it must contain all of the prime factors of 15 (3 × 5). Since *x* does contain a 3 and a 5, *x* is divisible by 15.

33. Maybe: To be divisible by 8, *q* needs three 2's in its prime factorization. Don't find the full list of (non-overlapping) factors. Concentrate only on the 2's, since that's all you need to answer the question.

Because there might be some overlapping factors of 2, you cannot simply count all of the numbers that contain 2. For instance, 6 is a multiple of 2 and 3, so the fact that *q* is divisible by both 2 and 6 indicates only that there is at least one 2 (and at least one 3); there aren't necessarily two factors of 2 just because *q* has the factors 2 and 6.

Instead, look for the greatest number of 2's *in one factor*. The number 12 contains two known 2's, so *q* must be a multiple of 4, but it's unclear whether *q* contains three 2's. It might or it might not.

If you ever do need to check all of the factors, not just the 2's, then do this:

2: *q* must be divisible by 2.

6: The 3 is new. Ignore the overlapping 2 and add a 3 to your list of factors: *q* must be divisible by 2 and 3.

9: The second 3 is new. Add it to your list: *q* must be divisible by 2, 3, and 3.

12: The second 2 is new. Add it to your list: *q* must be divisible by 2, 2, 3, and 3.

15: The 5 is new. Add it to your list: *q* must be divisible by 2, 2, 3, 3, and 5.

30: Nothing new. *q* must be divisible by 2, 2, 3, 3, and 5.

There are only two 2's for certain. Therefore, *q* must be a multiple of 180 (i.e., 2 × 2 × 3 × 3 × 5), but it does not necessarily have to be a multiple of 8.

34. Minimum = one; maximum = two: Start with the more constrained variable: *p*. Because it is prime, it has exactly two factors—itself and 1. Therefore, the maximum number of "factors in common" cannot be more than two. Can *p* and *q* have exactly two factors in common? Certainly; *q* can be a multiple of *p*. (For instance, if *p* = 3 and *q* = 12, the common factors are 1 and 3.)

2

What about the minimum? Can p and q have absolutely no factors in common? Try some numbers. If $p = 3$ and $q = 10$, then the two numbers don't have any prime factors in common, but notice that they are both divisible by 1. Any integer has 1 as a factor. Therefore, the minimum possible number of shared factors is one (the number 1 itself), and the maximum is two (the two factors of prime number p).

Drill 9

35. **1, 2, 4, 8, 16, 32, 64:** If 64 divides evenly into n, then any divisors of 64 will also be divisors of n.

Small	Large
1	64
2	32
4	16
8	8

36. **The number is 66, and the factors are 1, 2, 3, 6, 11, 22, 33, and 66:** $2 \times 3 \times 11 = 66$.

Small	Large
1	66
2	33
3	22
6	11

37. **Maybe:**

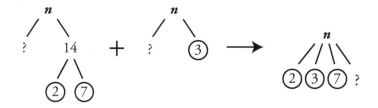

The two sets of factors don't overlap, so you can keep them all. For 12 to be a factor of n, n must contain all of the prime factors of 12 ($2 \times 2 \times 3$). n contains a 3, but only contains one 2 for sure, so 12 *could* be a factor of n but does not have to be.

38. **(B):** Since x has only two factors, it must be a prime number (with factors itself and 1). Since y is a positive multiple of 5, it must be 5, 10, or 15. List out the possible scenarios; start with y since you know there are only three possible values.

$y + x = 17$

$5 + 12 = 17$ No good: 12 isn't a prime number.

$10 + 7 = 17$ Bingo! 10 is a multiple of 5, and 7 is a prime number.

 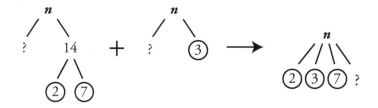

You could write out the third scenario, but wait! Check the answers whenever you have a possible solution. There is a 7 in the answers, so you're done. (It turns out that 15 + 2 = 17 also fits the criteria given in the problem, but 2 is not among the answer choices.)

39. **Four:** Because you have been asked for a concrete answer, you can infer that the answer will be the same regardless of which two-digit prime you pick. So, to make your job easier, pick the smallest one: 11.

If n is the product of 2, 3, and 11, then $n = 66$, and its factors are:

Small	Large
1	**66**
2	**33**
3	**22**
6	**11**

There are four factors greater than 6: 11, 22, 33, and 66.

Why is the answer always four factors, even if you try a different two-digit prime number? Notice that because the other given prime factors of n (2 and 3) multiply to get exactly 6, you have to multiply by the third factor, the two-digit prime number, in order to get a number greater than 6. The right-hand column represents that third factor multiplied by all of the other factors: 11×6, 11×3, 11×2, and 11×1. If you replace 11 with another two-digit prime, you will get the same result. (If you're not sure, test it out! That's a great way to prove a principle to yourself.)

Drill 10

40. **Yes:**

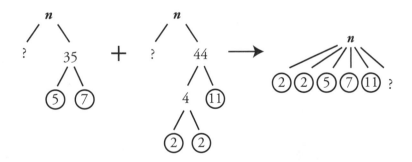

There is no overlap among the factors, so you can keep them all. In order for 14 to be a divisor of n, n has to contain all of the prime factors of 14 (2×7). Since n does contain 2 and 7, 14 is a divisor of n.

2

41. **Yes:**

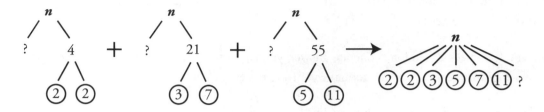

None of the factors overlap, so you can keep all of them. For 154 to divide evenly into *n*, *n* has to contain all the same prime factors as 154 (2 × 7 × 11). *n* also contains 2, 7, and 11, so *n* is divisible by 154.

42. **Maybe:**

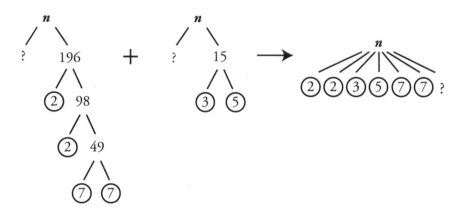

None of the factors overlap, so you can keep all of them. For 270 to be a factor of *n*, *n* must contain all the same prime factors as 270 (2 × 3 × 3 × 3 × 5). *n* contains a 2 and a 5, but only one known 3. Therefore, 270 *could* be a factor of *n*, but it does not have to be.

Exponents & Roots

In this chapter...

- Basics of Exponents
- Multiply Terms with Same Base: Add the Exponents
- Divide Terms with Same Base: Subtract the Exponents
- Pretty Much Anything to the Power of Zero: One
- Negative Power: One Over a Positive Power
- Apply Two Exponents: Multiply the Exponents
- Apply an Exponent to a Product: Apply the Exponent to Each Factor
- Add or Subtract Terms with the Same Base: Pull Out a Common Factor
- Roots: Opposite of Exponents
- Square Root: Power of One-Half
- Cube Roots Undo Cubing
- Multiply Square Roots: Put Everything Under the Root
- Simplify Square Roots: Factor Out Squares
- Add or Subtract Under the Root: Pull Out Common Square Factors

Chapter 3
Exponents & Roots

In This Chapter, You Will Learn To:

- Apply exponent rules to solve problems
- Manipulate square and cube roots

Basics of Exponents

Exponents represent repeated multiplication. The **exponent**, or power, tells you how many **bases** to multiply together. In the example below, 5 is the base and 3 is the exponent.

5^3	=	$5 \times 5 \times 5$	=	125
Five cubed	equals	three fives multiplied together, or five times five times five,	which equals	one hundred twenty-five

An **exponential expression** or term is one that contains an exponent. Exponential expressions can contain variables as well. The variable can be the base, the exponent, or even both. For example:

a^4	=	$a \times a \times a \times a$
a to the fourth	equals	four a's multiplied together, or a times a times a times a

3^x	=	$3 \times 3 \times \ldots \times 3$
Three to the x	equals	three times three times ... times three (there are x three's in the product, whatever x is)

Any base to the first power equals that base.

7^1	=	7
Seven to the first	equals	seven

Memorize the following powers of positive integers. Create flash cards for any that you don't already know.

Squares
$1^2 = 1$
$2^2 = 4$
$3^2 = 9$
$4^2 = 16$
$5^2 = 25$
$6^2 = 36$
$7^2 = 49$
$8^2 = 64$
$9^2 = 81$

More Squares
$10^2 = 100$
$11^2 = 121$
$12^2 = 144$
$13^2 = 169$
$14^2 = 196$
$15^2 = 225$
$20^2 = 400$
$30^2 = 900$

Cubes
$1^3 = 1$
$2^3 = 8$
$3^3 = 27$
$4^3 = 64$
$5^3 = 125$
$10^3 = 1{,}000$

Powers of 2
$2^1 = 2$
$2^2 = 4$
$2^3 = 8$
$2^4 = 16$
$2^5 = 32$
$2^6 = 64$
$2^7 = 128$
$2^8 = 256$
$2^9 = 512$
$2^{10} = 1{,}024$

Powers of 3
$3^1 = 3$
$3^2 = 9$
$3^3 = 27$
$3^4 = 81$

Powers of 4
$4^1 = 2^2 = 4$
$4^2 = 2^4 = 16$
$4^3 = 2^6 = 64$
$4^4 = 2^8 = 256$
$4^5 = 2^{10} = 1{,}024$

Powers of 5
$5^1 = 5$
$5^2 = 25$
$5^3 = 125$

Powers of 10
$10^1 = 10$
$10^2 = 100$
$10^3 = 1{,}000$

Remember PEMDAS? Exponents come before everything else, except parentheses. That includes negative signs. For example:

$$-3^2 \quad = \quad -(3^2) \quad = \quad -9$$

The negative of three squared   equals   the negative of the quantity three squared,   and this equals   negative nine

To calculate -3^2, square the 3 *before* you multiply by negative one (-1). If you want to square the negative sign, throw parentheses around -3.

$$(-3)^2 \quad = \quad 9$$

The square of negative three   equals   nine

In $(-3)^2$, the negative sign and the 3 are both inside the parentheses, so they both get squared. If you say *negative three squared*, you probably mean $(-3)^2$, but someone listening might write down -3^2, so say *the square of negative three* instead.

Negative numbers raised to an even power are always positive. Negative numbers raised to an odd number are always negative.

$$(\text{Negative})^{\text{even}} = \text{Positive} \qquad (\text{Negative})^{\text{odd}} = \text{Negative}$$

The powers of −1 alternate between 1 and −1. Even powers of −1 are always 1 (e.g., $(-1)^2 = 1$), while odd powers of −1 are always −1 (e.g., $(-1)^3 = -1$).

A positive base raised to any power is always positive, because positive times positive is positive—no matter how many times you multiply. For example 2^{45} is positive because it represents 2 multiplied by itself 45 times.

Since an even exponent always gives a positive result, *an even exponent can hide the sign of the base*. Consider this equation:

$$x^2 = 16$$

In Chapter 6, Equations, you will cover in greater depth how to solve an equation such as this one. For now, notice that *two* different numbers for *x* would make the equation true:

$$4^2 = 16 \qquad\qquad (-4)^2 = 16$$

The value of *x* could be either 4 or −4. *Always be careful when dealing with even exponents in equations.* Look for more than one possible solution.

Check Your Skills

1. Which is greater, -5^8 or $(-5)^8$?

Answer can be found on page 117.

Multiply Terms with Same Base: Add the Exponents

Imagine that you multiply together a string of five *a*'s. Now multiply a second string of three *a*'s together. Finally, because you love multiplication, go ahead and multiply the two strings together. How many *a*'s do you end up with?

Write it all out longhand:

$$(a \times a \times a \times a \times a) \times (a \times a \times a) = a \times a \times a \times a \times a \times a \times a \times a$$

Now use exponential notation:

$$a^5 \qquad \times \qquad a^3 \qquad = \qquad a^8$$

a to the fifth   times   a to the third   equals   a to the eighth

What happens to the exponents 5 and 3? They add up: $5 + 3 = 8$. This works because there are only *a*'s in the equation. The two terms on the left (a^5 and a^3) have the same base (*a*), so there are eight *a*'s on each side of the equation.

When you multiply exponential terms that have the same base, add the exponents.

Treat any term without an exponent as if it had an exponent of 1.

$$y(y^6) = y \times y^6 = y^1 \times y^6 = y^{(1 + 6)} = y^7$$

Adding exponents works with numbers in the base, even weird numbers such as π. You just have to make sure that the bases are the same.

$$5^3 \times 5^6 = 5^9 \qquad \pi \times \pi^2 = \pi^3$$

The rule also works with variables in the exponent.

$$2^3 \times 2^z = 2^{(3+z)} \qquad 6(6^x) = 6^1 \times 6^x = 6^{1+x} \text{ or } 6^{x+1}$$

You can choose whether to use parentheses around the exponent, as in the first example—this can help to minimize careless mistakes. If you don't think you're likely to make a careless mistake here, then feel free to skip the parentheses, as in the second example.

Check Your Skills

Simplify the following expressions.

2. $b^5 \times b^7$
3. $(x^3)(x^4)$

Answers can be found on page 117.

Divide Terms with Same Base: Subtract the Exponents

Now divide a string of five a's by a string of three a's. Again, these are strings of *multiplied* a's. What is the result?

$$\frac{a \times a \times a \times a \times a}{a \times a \times a} = \frac{a \times \cancel{a} \times \cancel{a} \times \cancel{a} \times a}{\cancel{a} \times \cancel{a} \times \cancel{a}} = a \times a$$

In exponential notation, you have this: $\dfrac{a^5}{a^3} = a^2$

What happens to the exponents? You subtract the bottom exponent from the top exponent: $5 - 3 = 2$.

When you divide exponential terms that have the same base, subtract the exponents.

This rule works the same for numbers as for variables.

$$\frac{2^{16}}{2^{13}} = 2^{16-13} = 2^3 = 8 \qquad\qquad \frac{x^y}{x^2} = x^{y-2}$$

As before, treat any term without an exponent as if it had an exponent of 1.

$$\frac{f^9}{f} = \frac{f^9}{f^1} = f^8$$

Just make sure that the bases are the same. If the bases are not the same, then you can't combine the two terms into one.

MANHATTAN PREP

Here's the rule book so far.

If you...	Then you...	Like this:
Multiply exponential terms that have the same base	Add the exponents	$a^2 \times a^3 = a^5$
Divide exponential terms that have the same base	Subtract the exponents	$\dfrac{a^5}{a^3} = a^2$

Check Your Skills

Simplify the following expressions.

4. $\dfrac{y^5}{y^2}$

5. $\dfrac{d^8}{d^7}$

Answers can be found on page 117.

Pretty Much Anything to the Power of Zero: One

Divide a string of five *a*'s by a string of five *a*'s. As before, each string is internally multiplied. What do you get?

Using longhand, you get 1.

$$\frac{a \times a \times a \times a \times a}{a \times a \times a \times a \times a} = \frac{\not{a} \times \not{a} \times \not{a} \times \not{a} \times \not{a}}{\not{a} \times \not{a} \times \not{a} \times \not{a} \times \not{a}} = 1$$

Using the exponent subtraction rule, you get a^0.

$$\frac{a^5}{a^5} = a^{5-5} = a^0$$

So a^0 must equal 1. That's true for practically any value of *a*. For example:

$$1^0 = 1 \qquad 6.2^0 = 1 \qquad (-4)^0 = 1 \qquad \left(\frac{3}{4}\right)^0 = 1 \qquad \left(\sqrt{2}\right)^0 = 1$$

The *only* base value for which this doesn't work is 0 itself. The expression 0^0 is called *undefined*. Notice that the exponent subtraction rule above required you to divide by *a*. Since you can't divide by 0, you can't raise 0 to the 0 power either. The GMAT will never ask you to do so.

For any nonzero value of *a*, $a^0 = 1$.

3

Now you can extend the powers of 2 to include 2^0.

<u>Powers of 2</u>

$$2^0 = 1$$
$$2^1 = 2$$
$$2^2 = 4$$
$$2^3 = 8$$
$$2^4 = 16$$

Notice the pattern: Each power of 2 is 2 times the previous power of 2.

Negative Power: One Over a Positive Power

What happens if you divide a string of three a's by a string of five a's?

Using longhand, you get a leftover a^2 in the denominator of the fraction.

$$\frac{a \times a \times a}{a \times a \times a \times a \times a} = \frac{\cancel{a} \times \cancel{a} \times \cancel{a}}{a \times a \times \cancel{a} \times \cancel{a} \times \cancel{a}} = \frac{1}{a \times a} = \frac{1}{a^2}$$

Using the exponent subtraction rule, you get a^{-2}.

$$\frac{a^3}{a^5} = a^{3-5} = a^{-2}$$

So those two results must be equal. *Something with a negative exponent is "1 over" that same thing with a positive exponent.*

$$a^{-2} \qquad\qquad = \qquad\qquad \frac{1}{a^2}$$

a to the negative two   equals   one over a squared

In other words, a^{-2} is equal to the **reciprocal** of a^2. The reciprocal of 5 is 1 *over* 5, or $\frac{1}{5}$. You can also think of reciprocals this way: Something times its reciprocal always equals 1. For example:

$$5 \times \frac{1}{5} = 1 \qquad\qquad a^2 \times \frac{1}{a^2} = 1 \qquad\qquad a^2 \times a^{-2} = a^{2-2} = a^0 = 1$$

Now you can extend the powers of 2 to include negative exponents.

<u>Powers of 2</u>

$$2^{-3} = \frac{1}{2^3} = \frac{1}{8} = 0.125$$

$$2^{-2} = \frac{1}{2^2} = \frac{1}{4} = 0.25$$

$$2^{-1} = \frac{1}{2} = 0.5$$

$$2^0 = 1$$
$$2^1 = 2$$
$$2^2 = 4$$
$$2^3 = 8$$
$$2^4 = 16$$

The pattern still holds! Each power of 2 is 2 times the previous power of 2.

The rules you've seen so far work the same for negative exponents.

$$5^{-3} \times 5^{-6} = 5^{-3+(-6)} = 5^{-9}$$

$$\frac{x^3}{x^{-5}} = x^{3-(-5)} = x^8$$

Negative exponents are tricky, so it can be useful to *rewrite negative exponents using positive exponents*. A negative exponent in a term on top of a fraction becomes positive when you move the term to the bottom.

$$\frac{5x^{-2}}{y^3} = \frac{5}{x^2 y^3}$$

Here, x^{-2} moved from the numerator to the denominator and the sign of the exponent switched from -2 to 2. Everything else stayed the same.

Likewise, a negative exponent in the bottom of a fraction becomes positive when the term moves to the top.

$$\frac{3}{z^{-4} w^2} = \frac{3z^4}{w^2}$$

Here, z^{-4} moved from the denominator to the numerator and the sign of the exponent switched from -4 to 4.

If you move the entire denominator, leave a 1 behind.

$$\frac{1}{z^{-4}} = \frac{1 \times z^4}{1} = z^4$$

The same is true for a numerator.

$$\frac{w^{-5}}{2} = \frac{1}{2w^5}$$

Don't confuse the sign of the base with the sign of the exponent. The sign of the base does not change.

A positive base raised to a negative exponent stays positive. For example:

$$3^{-3} = \frac{1}{3^3} = \frac{1}{27}$$

A negative base stays negative. Odd powers of a negative base still produce negative numbers.

$$(-4)^{-3} = \frac{1}{(-4)^3} = \frac{1}{-64} = -\frac{1}{64}$$

Even powers of a negative base still produce positive numbers.

$$\frac{1}{(-6)^{-2}} = (-6)^2 = 36$$

Here are additional rules for the rule book.

If you...	Then you...	Like this:
Raise anything to the power of zero (besides zero itself)	Get 1	$a^0 = 1$
Raise anything to a negative power	Get 1 over that same thing to the corresponding positive power	$a^{-2} = \dfrac{1}{a^2}$
Move a term from top to bottom of a fraction (or vice versa)	Switch the sign of the exponent	$\dfrac{2a^{-2}}{3} = \dfrac{2}{3a^2}$

Check Your Skills

Simplify the following expressions.

6. 2^{-3}

7. $\dfrac{1}{3^{-3}}$

Answers can be found on page 117.

Apply Two Exponents: Multiply the Exponents

How do you simplify this expression?

$(a^2)^4$

Use the definition of exponents. First you square a. Next, you multiply four separate a^2 terms together. In longhand:

$$(a^2)^4 = a^2 \times a^2 \times a^2 \times a^2 = a^{2+2+2+2} = a^8$$

What happens to the exponents 2 and 4? You multiply them: $2 \times 4 = 8$. On each side, you have eight a's multiplied together.

When you raise something that already has an exponent to another power, multiply the two exponents together.

Always keep these two cases straight:

If you multiply the bases, *add* the exponents. $a^2 \times a^4 = a^{2+4} = a^6$

If you raise a power to a power, *multiply* the exponents. $(a^2)^4 = a^{2 \times 4} = a^8$

If you see see *two* bases multiplied together, as in $a^2 \times a^4$, then you'll add the exponents. If you see just *one* base with two exponents, as in $(a^2)^4$, then you'll multiply the exponents.

The "apply two exponents" rule works perfectly with negative exponents as well.

$$(x^{-3})^5 = x^{-3 \times 5} = x^{-15}$$

$$(4^{-2})^{-3} = 4^{-2 \times -3} = 4^6$$

If you...	Then you...	Like this:
Raise something to two successive powers	Multiply the powers	$(a^2)^4 = a^8$

Put it all together. Now you can handle this expression:

$$\frac{x^{-3}\left(x^2\right)^4}{x^5}$$

First, simplify the parentheses $(x^2)^4$.

$$(x^2)^4 = x^{2 \times 4} = x^8$$

The fraction now reads:

$$\frac{x^{-3}x^8}{x^5}$$

Now follow the rules for multiplying and dividing terms that have the same base. That is, add and subtract the exponents.

$$\frac{x^{-3}x^8}{x^5} = x^{-3+8-5} = x^0 = 1$$

If you have *different* bases that are numbers, try breaking the bases down to prime factors. You might discover that you can express everything in terms of one base. For example:

$$2^2 \times 4^3 \times 16 =$$

(A) 2^6

(B) 2^{12}

(C) 2^{18}

The bases are all different, but they have something in common: Both 4 and 16 are powers of 2. Try rewriting those terms with 2 as the base.

$$4 = 2^2 \text{ and } 16 = 2^4$$

Everything can now be expressed with 2 as the base.

$$\begin{aligned} 2^2 \times 4^3 \times 16 \quad &= 2^2 \times (2^2)^3 \times 2^4 \\ &= 2^2 \times 2^6 \times 2^4 \\ &= 2^{2+6+4} \\ &= 2^{12} \end{aligned}$$

The correct answer is (B).

Check Your Skills

Simplify the following expressions.

8. $(x^3)^4$

9. $\dfrac{a^{15}}{a^0(a^3)^3}$

Answers can be found on page 117.

Apply an Exponent to a Product: Apply the Exponent to Each Factor

Consider this expression:

$(xy)^3$

How can you rewrite this? Use the definition of exponents. You multiply three xy terms together.

$(xy)^3 = xy \times xy \times xy$

So you have three x's multiplied together and three y's multiplied together. You can group these separately, because everything's multiplied.

$(xy)^3 = xy \times xy \times xy = (x \times x \times x)(y \times y \times y) = x^3y^3$

When you apply an exponent to a product, apply the exponent to each factor in the product.

This rule works with every kind of base and exponent you've seen so far. For example:

$(3x)^4 = 3^4x^4 = 81x^4$

$(wz^3)^x = w^xz^{3x}$

$\left(2^{-2}y^2\right)^{-3} = 2^{-2\times-3}\,y^{2\times-3} = 2^6\,y^{-6} = 64y^{-6} = \dfrac{64}{y^6}$

Do the same thing with division. In particular, if you raise an entire fraction to a power, separately apply the exponent to the numerator and to the denominator.

$\left(\dfrac{3}{4}\right)^{-2} = \dfrac{3^{-2}}{4^{-2}} = \dfrac{4^2}{3^2} = \dfrac{16}{9}$

In this example, the top and the bottom of the fraction each have a negative exponent. In this case, you can flip the whole fraction and get rid of the negative exponents in both pieces.

Notice that the following case is different.

$\dfrac{3^{-2}}{4} = \dfrac{1}{4\times3^2} = \dfrac{1}{36}$

In $\dfrac{3^{-2}}{4}$, the exponent applies only to the numerator (3). Respect PEMDAS, as always. Here's more for the rule book.

If you...	Then you...	Like this:
Apply an exponent to a product	Apply the exponent to each factor in the product	$(ab)^3 = a^3 b^3$
Apply an exponent to an entire fraction	Apply the exponent separately to the top and bottom	$\left(\dfrac{a}{b}\right)^4 = \dfrac{a^4}{b^4}$

You can use this principle to write the prime factorization of big numbers without computing those numbers directly. For example:

What is the prime factorization of 18^3?

Don't multiply out $18 \times 18 \times 18$. Instead, figure out the prime factorization of 18 itself, then apply the rule above.

$$18 = 2 \times 9 = 2 \times 3^2$$

$$18^3 = (2 \times 3^2)^3 = 2^3 \times 3^6 = 2^3 3^6$$

The prime factorization of 18^3 is 2, 2, 2, 3, 3, 3, 3, 3, 3.

Simplify this harder example.

$$\frac{12^2 \times 8}{18} =$$

First, break each base into its prime factors.

$$12 = 2^2 \times 3 \qquad\qquad 8 = 2^3 \qquad\qquad 18 = 2 \times 3^2$$

$$\frac{12^2 \times 8}{18} = \frac{\left(2^2 \times 3\right)^2 \times 2^3}{2 \times 3^2}$$

Next, apply the exponent to the parentheses.

$$\frac{\left(2^2 \times 3\right)^2 \times 2^3}{2 \times 3^2} = \frac{2^4 \times 3^2 \times 2^3}{2 \times 3^2}$$

Finally, combine the terms with 2 as their base. Remember that a 2 without a written exponent really has an exponent of 1. Separately, combine the terms with 3 as their base.

$$\frac{2^4 \times 3^2 \times 2^3}{2 \times 3^2} = 2^{4+3-1} \times 3^{2-2} = 2^6 \times 3^0 = 2^6 \times 1 = 2^6 = 64$$

Occasionally, it's faster *not* to break down all the way to primes. If you spot a greater common base, feel free to use it. Try this example:

$$\frac{36^3}{6^4} =$$

You can simplify this expression by breaking 36 and 6 down to primes. But if you recognize that $36 = 6^2$, then you can go much faster.

$$\frac{36^3}{6^4} = \frac{\left(6^2\right)^3}{6^4} = \frac{6^6}{6^4} = 6^2 = 36$$

One last point: Be ready to rewrite a^3b^3 as $(ab)^3$.

Consider $2^4 \times 3^4$. Here's a way to see that $2^4 \times 3^4$ equals $(2 \times 3)^4$, or 6^4:

$$2^4 \times 3^4 = (2 \times 2 \times 2 \times 2) \times (3 \times 3 \times 3 \times 3)$$

$$= (2 \times 3) \times (2 \times 3) \times (2 \times 3) \times (2 \times 3) \qquad \text{by regrouping}$$

$$= (2 \times 3)^4 = 6^4$$

More often you'll need to change $(ab)^3$ into a^3b^3, but occasionally it's handy to go in reverse.

If you...	Then you...	Like this:
See two factors with the same exponent	Might regroup the factors as a product	$a^3b^3 = (ab)^3$

Check Your Skills

Simplify the following expressions.

10. $\left(\dfrac{x^2 y}{z^{-3}}\right)^2$

11. $\dfrac{75^3 \times 45^3}{15^8}$

Answers can be found on pages 117–118.

Add or Subtract Terms with the Same Base: Pull Out a Common Factor

Every case so far in this chapter has involved *only* multiplication and division. What if you are adding or subtracting exponential terms?

Consider this example:

$$13^5 + 13^3 =$$

*Do **not** add the exponents* to get 13^8. That is the answer to a similar but different question (namely, $13^5 \times 13^3$), so it can't also be the correct answer when the multiplication symbol has changed to an addition symbol.

Instead, *look for a common factor and pull it out*. Both 13^5 and 13^3 are divisible by 13^3, so that's the common factor. If necessary, rewrite 13^5 as $13^3 13^2$ first.

$$13^5 + 13^3 = 13^3 13^2 + 13^3 = 13^3(13^2 + 1)$$

You could go farther and rewrite 13^2 as 169. The right answer choice would possibly look like this: $13^3(170)$.

Remember that whenever you pull a term out of itself (e.g., pull 13^3 out of 13^3), you'll always be left with 1.

If you were given x's instead of 13's as bases, the factoring would work the same way.

$$x^5 + x^3 = x^3x^2 + x^3 = x^3(x^2 + 1)$$

Now try this example:

$$3^8 - 3^7 - 3^6$$

(A) $3^6(5)$
(B) 3^6
(C) 3^{-5}

All three terms (3^8, 3^7, and 3^6) are divisible by 3^6, so pull 3^6 out of the expression.

$$3^8 - 3^7 - 3^6 = 3^6(3^2 - 3^1 - 1) = 3^6(9 - 3 - 1) = 3^6(5)$$

The correct answer is (A).

This time, note that when you're pulling from a term whose exponent is just one number higher, you're always left with that term to the first power: Pulling 3^6 from 3^7 returns 3^1, which is the same as 3. Once you get used to that, feel free to skip the step of writing out 3^1 and just write 3 (or whatever number is in the base) directly.

Now try to simplify this fraction:

$$\frac{3^4 + 3^5 + 3^6}{13}$$

Ignore the 13 on the bottom of the fraction for the moment. On the top, each term is divisible by 3^4.

$$\frac{3^4 + 3^5 + 3^6}{13} = \frac{3^4\left(1 + 3^1 + 3^2\right)}{13}$$

Continue to simplify the small powers of 3 in the parentheses.

$$\frac{3^4 + 3^5 + 3^6}{13} = \frac{3^4\left(1 + 3^1 + 3^2\right)}{13} = \frac{3^4\left(1 + 3 + 9\right)}{13} = \frac{3^4\left(13\right)}{13}$$

The 13's on the top and bottom of the fraction can cancel.

$$\frac{3^4 + 3^5 + 3^6}{13} = \frac{3^4\left(1 + 3^1 + 3^2\right)}{13} = \frac{3^4\left(1 + 3 + 9\right)}{13} = \frac{3^4\left(\cancel{13}\right)}{\cancel{13}} = 3^4$$

If you *don't* have the same bases in what you're adding or subtracting, you can't immediately factor. If the bases are numbers, break them down to smaller factors to see whether you now have anything in common. Try this example:

$$4^6 + 20^6 =$$

Again, don't answer the wrong question. $4^6 \times 20^6 = (4 \times 20)^6 = 80^6$, but that doesn't answer this question. This problem asks you to *add* 4^6 and 20^6, *not* multiply them.

3

Since 4 is a factor of 20, rewrite 20 as 4×5 and apply the exponent to that product.

$$4^6 + 20^6 = 4^6 + (4 \times 5)^6 = 4^6 + (4^6 \times 5^6)$$

Now pull out the common factor of 4^6.

$$4^6 + 20^6 = 4^6 + (4 \times 5)^6 = 4^6 + (4^6 5^6) = 4^6(1 + 5^6)$$

That's as far as you'd reasonably go, given the size of 4^6 and 5^6. Finally, try simplifying this one:

$$4^5 + 20^3 =$$

Start it the same way as before. Rewrite 20 as 4×5 and apply the exponent.

$$4^5 + 20^3 = 4^5 + (4 \times 5)^3 = 4^5 + (4^3 \times 5^3)$$

Now the common factor is 4^3, so pull it out:

$$4^5 + 20^3 = 4^5 + (4 \times 5)^3 = 4^5 + (4^3 \times 5^3) = (4^3 4^2) + (4^3 5^3) = 4^3(4^2 + 5^3)$$

The result isn't especially pretty, but it's legitimate. Here's more to add to the rule book:

If you...	Then you...	Like this:
Add or subtract terms with the same base	Pull out the common factor	$2^3 + 2^5$ $= 2^3(1 + 2^2)$
Add or subtract terms with different bases	Break down the bases and pull out the common factor	$2^3 + 6^3$ $= 2^3 + (2^3 3^3)$ $= 2^3(1 + 3^3)$

Check Your Skills

Simplify the following expression by factoring out a common term.

12. $5^5 + 5^4 - 5^3$

Answer can be found on page 118.

Roots: Opposite of Exponents

Squaring a number means raising it to the second power (or multiplying it by itself). Square-rooting a number undoes that process. For example:

3^2	=	9	and	$\sqrt{9}$	=	3
Three squared	is	nine,	and	the square root of nine	is	three

If you square-root first, then square, you get back to the original number.

$$\left(\sqrt{16}\right)^2 \qquad = \qquad \sqrt{16}\times\sqrt{16} \qquad = \qquad 16$$

| The square of the square root of sixteen | equals | the square root of sixteen times the square root of sixteen, | and that equals | sixteen |

If you square first, then square-root, you get back to the original number if the original number is positive.

$$\sqrt{5^2} \qquad = \qquad \sqrt{5\times5} \qquad = \qquad 5$$

| The square root of five squared | equals | the square root of five times five, | and that equals | five |

If the original number is negative, you just flip the sign, so you end up with a positive.

$$\sqrt{(-5)^2} \qquad = \qquad \sqrt{25} \qquad = \qquad 5$$

| The square root of the square of negative five | equals | the square root of twenty-five, | and that equals | five |

If you...	Then you...	Like this:
Square a square root	Get the original number	$\left(\sqrt{10}\right)^2 = 10$
Square-root a square	Get the positive value of the original number	$\sqrt{10^2} = 10$ $\sqrt{(-10)^2} = 10$

Because 9 is the square of an integer ($9 = 3^2$), 9 is called a **perfect square**: its square root is an integer. In contrast, 2 is not the square of an integer, so its square root is an ugly decimal, as you saw in Chapter 1.

Memorize the perfect squares on page 94 so you can take their square roots easily. Also memorize these approximations:

$$\sqrt{2} \approx 1.4 \qquad\qquad \sqrt{3} \approx 1.7$$

Here's a neat way to remember them: February 14th, or the date 2/14, is Valentine's Day, and March 17th, or the date 3/17, is St. Patrick's Day.

You can approximate the square root of a non-perfect square by looking at nearby perfect squares. Try this example:

$\sqrt{70}$ is between which two consecutive integers?

Two nearby perfect squares are 64 and 81. $\sqrt{64} = 8$ and $\sqrt{81} = 9$, so $\sqrt{70}$ must be between 8 and 9. It's almost halfway in between, so you could say that $\sqrt{70} \approx 8.5$.

When you take the square root of any number greater than 1, your answer will be smaller than the original number.

$$\sqrt{2} < 2 \qquad \sqrt{21} < 21 \qquad \sqrt{1.3} < 1.3$$

However, the square root of a number between 0 and 1 is *greater* than the original number.

$$\sqrt{0.5} > 0.5 \qquad\qquad \sqrt{\frac{2}{3}} > \frac{2}{3}$$

$$\sqrt{0.5} \approx 0.7 \qquad\qquad \left(\sqrt{\frac{2}{3}} \approx 0.8\right)$$

Whether a number is greater than 1 or between 0 and 1, the square root of the number is **always closer to 1** than is the original number.

The square root of 1 is 1, since $1^2 = 1$. Likewise, the square root of 0 is 0, since $0^2 = 0$.

$$\sqrt{1} = 1 \qquad \sqrt{0} = 0$$

You cannot take the square root of a negative number in GMAT world. What is inside the radical sign must never be negative.

Likewise, the square root symbol never gives a negative result. This may seem strange. After all, both 5^2 and $(-5)^2$ equal 25, so shouldn't the square root of 25 be either 5 or −5? No. Mathematicians like to have symbols mean one thing.

$\sqrt{25} = 5$, and that's that.

When you see the square root symbol on the GMAT, *only consider the positive root*.

In contrast, when *you* take the square root of both sides of an equation, you have to consider both positive and negative roots.

$$x = \sqrt{25} \qquad \text{Solution: } x = 5$$
$$x^2 = 25 \qquad \text{Solutions: } x = 5 \text{ OR } x = -5$$

Be careful with square roots of variable expressions. The expression must not be negative, or the square root is illegal.

If you...	Then you...	Like this:
Take the square root of a number greater than 1	Get a smaller number (a number that is closer to 1)	$\sqrt{25} = 5$
Take the square root of a number between 0 and 1	Get a greater number (a number that is closer to 1)	$\sqrt{0.5} \approx 0.7$
Take the square root of 1 or 0	Get the number you started with	$\sqrt{1} = 1$ $\sqrt{0} = 0$

Check Your Skills

13. $\sqrt{27} \times \sqrt{27} =$

Answer can be found on page 118.

Square Root: Power of One-Half

Consider this equation:

$$\left(9^x\right)^2 = 9$$

Rewrite the expression using the tools you already have.

$$\left(9^x\right)^2 = 9$$
$$9^{2x} = 9^1$$

Since the bases are equal, the exponents must also be equal. Therefore, $2x = 1$, or $x = \dfrac{1}{2}$.

Consider this equation:

$$\left(9^{\frac{1}{2}}\right)^2 = 9$$

The equation above is true because the exponents are multiplied together: $\left(\dfrac{1}{2}\right)(2) = 1$. You also learned earlier that $\left(\sqrt{9}\right)^2 = 9$.

Put these two equations together:

$$\text{If } \left(9^{\frac{1}{2}}\right)^2 = 9 \text{ and } \left(\sqrt{9}\right)^2 = 9,$$

$$\text{then } 9^{\frac{1}{2}} = \sqrt{9}.$$

For expressions with positive bases, *a square root is equivalent to an exponent of* $\dfrac{1}{2}$.

Try to simplify this example:

$$\sqrt{7^{22}} =$$

You can approach the problem in either of two ways.

1. Rewrite the square root as an exponent of $\dfrac{1}{2}$, then apply the two-exponent rule (multiply exponents).

$$\sqrt{7^{22}} = \left(7^{22}\right)^{\frac{1}{2}} = 7^{\frac{22}{2}} = 7^{11}$$

2. Rewrite what's inside the square root as a product of two identical numbers. The square root is therefore one of those numbers.

$$7^{22} = 7^{11} \times 7^{11}$$

$$\sqrt{7^{22}} = \sqrt{7^{11} \times 7^{11}} = 7^{11}$$

Notice that you get an exponent that is an integer. This tells you that the number 7^{22} is a perfect square, or the square of another integer: $7^{22} = \left(7^{11}\right)^2$. An integer raised to a positive, even power is always a perfect square.

Here's the rule book:

If you…	Then you…	Like this:
Take a square root of a positive number raised to a power	Rewrite the square root as an exponent of $\frac{1}{2}$, then multiply exponents	$\sqrt{5^{12}} = \left(5^{12}\right)^{\frac{1}{2}}$ $= 5^6$
	OR Rewrite what's inside the root as a product of two identical numbers	$\sqrt{5^{12}} = \sqrt{5^6 \times 5^6}$ $= 5^6$

Avoid changing the square root to an exponent of $\frac{1}{2}$ when you have variable expressions underneath the square root (or radical) sign, since the output depends on the sign of the variables.

Check Your Skills

14. If x is positive, $\sqrt{x^6} =$

Answer can be found on page 118.

Cube Roots Undo Cubing

Cubing a number means raising it to the third power. Cube-rooting a number undoes that process. For example:

4^3	$=$	64	and	$\sqrt[3]{64}$	$=$	4
Four cubed	is	sixty-four,	and	the cube root of sixty-four	is	four

Many of the properties of square roots carry over to cube roots. You can approximate cube roots the same way.

$\sqrt[3]{66}$ is a little more than 4, but less than 5, because $\sqrt[3]{64} = 4$ and $\sqrt[3]{125} = 5$

Like square-rooting, cube-rooting a positive number pushes it toward 1.

$\sqrt[3]{17} < 17$ but $\sqrt[3]{0.17} > 0.17$

The main difference in behavior between square roots and cube roots is that you *can* take the cube root of a negative number. You wind up with a negative number.

$\sqrt[3]{-64} = -4$ because $(-4)^3 = -64$

As a fractional exponent, cube roots are equivalent to exponents of $\frac{1}{3}$, just as square roots are equivalent to exponents of $\frac{1}{2}$. Going further, fourth roots are equivalent to exponents of $\frac{1}{4}$, and so on.

Now you can deal with **fractional exponents**. Consider this example:

$$8^{\frac{2}{3}} =$$

Rewrite $\frac{2}{3}$ as $2 \times \frac{1}{3}$, making two successive exponents. This is the same as squaring first, then cube-rooting.

$$8^{\frac{2}{3}} = 8^{2 \times \frac{1}{3}} = \left(8^2\right)^{\frac{1}{3}} = \sqrt[3]{8^2} = \sqrt[3]{64} = 4$$

You could also rewrite $\frac{2}{3}$ as $\frac{1}{3} \times 2$ instead, allowing you to take the cube root first and then square the result. Look at the numbers; which way is easier for this math?

$$8^{\frac{2}{3}} = 8^{\frac{1}{3} \times 2} = \left(8^{\frac{1}{3}}\right)^2 = \left(\sqrt[3]{8}\right)^2 = 2^2 = 4$$

Whichever path you choose, you don't have to write out every step of the math above. Talk yourself through the steps:

$\sqrt[3]{8^2}$	First, I square the 8 to get 64, and then I take the cube root of the 64 to get 4.
$\left(\sqrt[3]{8}\right)^2$	First, I take the cube root of 8 to get 2, and then I square the 2 to get 4.

If you…	Then you…	Like this:
Raise a number to a fractional power	Apply two exponents—the numerator as a power and the denominator as a fractional root, in whatever order seems easiest to you	$125^{\frac{2}{3}} = \left(\sqrt[3]{125}\right)^2$ $= 5^2 = 25$

Check Your Skills

15. $64^{2/3} =$

Answer can be found on page 118.

Multiply Square Roots: Put Everything Under the Root

Consider this example:

$$\sqrt{8} \times \sqrt{2} =$$

Earlier, you learned that $8^a 2^a = (8 \times 2)^a$. This principle holds true for fractional exponents as well.

$$\sqrt{8} \times \sqrt{2} = 8^{\frac{1}{2}} \times 2^{\frac{1}{2}} = (8 \times 2)^{\frac{1}{2}} = \sqrt{8 \times 2}$$

3

In practice, you can usually skip the fractional exponents. *When you multiply separate square roots, you can put everything under the same radical sign.*

$$\sqrt{8} \times \sqrt{2} = \sqrt{8 \times 2} = \sqrt{16} = 4$$

This shortcut works for division, too. *When you divide square roots, you can put everything under the same radical sign.*

$$\frac{\sqrt{27}}{\sqrt{3}} = \sqrt{\frac{27}{3}} = \sqrt{9} = 3$$

As long as you're only multiplying and dividing, you can deal with more complicated expressions.

$$\frac{\sqrt{15} \times \sqrt{12}}{\sqrt{5}} = \sqrt{\frac{\cancel{15}^{3} \times 12}{\cancel{5}_{1}}} = \sqrt{36} = 6$$

Don't forget to simplify before you multiply!

If you…	Then you…	Like this:
Multiply or divide square roots	Combine everything under one radical sign, then simplify	$\sqrt{a} \times \sqrt{b} = \sqrt{ab}$ $\dfrac{\sqrt{a}}{\sqrt{b}} = \sqrt{\dfrac{a}{b}}$

Check Your Skills

Simplify the following expressions.

16. $\sqrt{20} \times \sqrt{5}$

17. $\dfrac{\sqrt{216}}{\sqrt{2} \times \sqrt{3}}$

Answers can be found on page 118.

Simplify Square Roots: Factor Out Squares

What does this product equal?

$$\sqrt{6} \times \sqrt{2} =$$

First, put everything under one radical.

$$\sqrt{6} \times \sqrt{2} = \sqrt{12}$$

You might think that you're done—after all, 12 is not a perfect square, so you won't get an integer out of $\sqrt{12}$. But what if you glance at the answers and $\sqrt{12}$ isn't there? It turns out that $\sqrt{12}$ is mathematically correct, but it can be simplified further.

Here's how: $12 = 4 \times 3$ and 4 is a perfect square, so it can be pulled out from under a square root sign.

$$\sqrt{12} = \sqrt{4 \times 3} = \sqrt{4} \times \sqrt{3}$$

Nicely, $\sqrt{4} = 2$, so finish up:

$$\sqrt{12} = \sqrt{4 \times 3} = \sqrt{4} \times \sqrt{3} = 2\sqrt{3}$$

If the answer you get isn't a perfect square itself but does have a perfect square as a factor, then the GMAT will typically expect you to simplify that answer as far as it can go. Glance at the answers before you actually do that simplification, just to make sure—but expect that you will probably have to do so.

To simplify square roots, factor out squares.

If you...	Then you...	Like this:
Have the square root of a large number (or a root that doesn't match any answer choices)	Pull perfect-square factors out of the number under the radical sign	$\sqrt{50} = \sqrt{25 \times 2}$ $= \sqrt{25} \times \sqrt{2}$ $= 5\sqrt{2}$

Sometimes you can spot the square factor, if you know your perfect squares. Consider this example:

$$\sqrt{360} =$$

If you have your perfect squares memorized, then 360 will likely make you think of the perfect square 36.

$$\sqrt{360} = \sqrt{36 \times 10} = \sqrt{36} \times \sqrt{10} = 6\sqrt{10}$$

What if you don't spot a perfect square? You can always **break the number down to primes**. This method will take longer, but it will work when you need it.

Consider $\sqrt{12}$ again. The prime factorization of 12 is $2 \times 2 \times 3$, or $2^2 \times 3$. Therefore, you can break it down:

$$\sqrt{12} = \sqrt{2^2 \times 3} = \sqrt{2^2} \times \sqrt{3} = 2\sqrt{3}$$

Each pair of prime factors under the radical (2×2, or 2^2) turns into a single copy as it emerges (becoming the 2 in $2\sqrt{3}$). In this exercise, it can be useful to write out the prime factorization without exponents so that you can spot the prime pairs quickly.

Take $\sqrt{360}$ again. Say you don't spot the perfect square factor (36). Write out the prime factorization of 360.

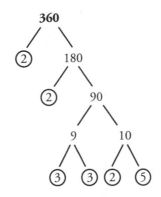

$$360 = 2 \times 2 \times 2 \times 3 \times 3 \times 5$$

Now pair off two 2's and two 3's, leaving an extra 2 and 5. Any pair of primes under a radical sign becomes a single copy of that prime outside the radical.

$$\sqrt{360} = \sqrt{2 \times 2} \times \sqrt{3 \times 3} \times \sqrt{2 \times 5} = 2 \times 3 \times \sqrt{2 \times 5} = 6\sqrt{10}$$

Check Your Skills

Simplify the following roots.

18. $\sqrt{96}$

19. $\sqrt{225}$

Answers can be found on page 118.

Add or Subtract Under the Root: Pull Out Common Square Factors

Consider this example:

$$\sqrt{3^2 + 4^2} =$$

Don't fall into the trap. You *cannot* break this root into $\sqrt{3^2} + \sqrt{4^2}$. You can only break up *products*, not sums, under the square root. For instance, this is correct:

$$\sqrt{3^2 \times 4^2} = \sqrt{3^2} \times \sqrt{4^2} = 3 \times 4 = 12$$

But you can't do that when you're adding under the root. To evaluate $\sqrt{3^2 + 4^2}$, follow PEMDAS under the radical, *then* take the square root.

$$\sqrt{3^2 + 4^2} = \sqrt{9 + 16} = \sqrt{25} = 5$$

The same goes for subtraction.

$$\sqrt{13^2 - 5^2} = \sqrt{169 - 25} = \sqrt{144} = 12$$

Often, you have to crunch the numbers if they're small. However, when the numbers get large, the GMAT will give you a necessary shortcut: factoring out squares.

You'll need to find a square factor that is common to both terms under the radical. Consider this example:

$$\sqrt{3^{10} + 3^{11}} =$$

First, consider $3^{10} + 3^{11}$ by itself. What is the greatest factor that the two terms in the sum have in common? 3^{10}. Note that $3^{11} = 3^{10} \times 3$. Therefore, you can put that in the equation:

$$3^{10} + 3^{11} = 3^{10}(1 + 3) = 3^{10}(4)$$

MANHATTAN PREP

Now plug that back into the square root.

$$\sqrt{3^{10}+3^{11}}=\sqrt{3^{10}(1+3)}=\sqrt{3^{10}(4)}=\sqrt{3^{10}}\times\sqrt{4}$$

Since $3^{10}=\left(3^{5}\right)^{2}$, $\sqrt{3^{10}}=3^{5}$.

Alternatively, apply the square root as an exponent of $\frac{1}{2}$.

$$\sqrt{3^{10}}=\left(3^{10}\right)^{\frac{1}{2}}=3^{\frac{10}{2}}=3^{5}$$

And, of course, $\sqrt{4}=2$. Plug everything back in.

$$\sqrt{3^{10}+3^{11}}=\sqrt{3^{10}(1+3)}=\sqrt{3^{10}(4)}=\sqrt{3^{10}}\times\sqrt{4}=3^{5}\times2$$

The answer also might be in the form $3^{5}(2)$.

If you...	Then you...	Like this:
Add or subtract underneath the square root symbol	Factor out a square factor from the sum or difference OR Go ahead and crunch the numbers as written, *if they're small*	$\sqrt{4^{14}+4^{16}}=\sqrt{4^{14}\left(1+4^{2}\right)}$ $=\sqrt{4^{14}}\times\sqrt{1+16}$ $=4^{7}\sqrt{17}$ $\sqrt{6^{2}+8^{2}}=\sqrt{36+64}$ $=\sqrt{100}=10$

Check Your Skills

20. $\sqrt{10^{5}-10^{4}}=$

Answer can be found on page 118.

Check Your Skills Answer Key

1. **$(-5)^8$**: $-5^8 = -1 \times 5^8$, and is thus negative. $(-5)^8$ will be positive, since the exponent is even. A positive is always greater than a negative.

2. **b^{12}**: The bases are the same, so add the exponents.

    $b^5 \times b^7 = b^{5+7} = b^{12}$

3. **x^7**: The bases are the same, so add the exponents.

    $x^3 \times x^4 = x^{3+4} = x^7$

4. **y^3**: The bases are the same, so subtract the bottom exponent from the top exponent.

    $$\frac{y^5}{y^2} = y^{5-2} = y^3$$

5. **d or d^1**: The bases are the same, so subtract the bottom exponent from the top exponent. d^1 is more commonly written d.

    $$\frac{d^8}{d^7} = d^{8-7} = d^1 = d$$

6. **$\frac{1}{8}$**:

    $$2^{-3} = \frac{1}{2^3} = \frac{1}{8}$$

7. **27**:

    $$\frac{1}{3^{-3}} = 3^3 = 27$$

8. **x^{12}**:

    $$(x^3)^4 = x^{3 \times 4} = x^{12}$$

9. **a^6**:

    $$\frac{a^{15}}{a^0 \left(a^3\right)^3} = \frac{a^{15}}{a^0 a^9} = a^{15-0-9} = a^6$$

10. **$x^4y^2z^6$**:

    $$\left(\frac{x^2 y}{z^{-3}}\right)^2 = \frac{x^{2 \times 2} y^{1 \times 2}}{z^{-3 \times 2}} = \frac{x^4 y^2}{z^{-6}} = x^4 y^2 z^6$$

3

11. **15:**

$$\frac{75^3 \times 45^3}{15^8} = \frac{\left(3 \times 5^2\right)^3 \times \left(3^2 \times 5\right)^3}{\left(3 \times 5\right)^8} = \frac{3^3 \times 5^6 \times 3^6 \times 5^3}{3^8 \times 5^8} = \frac{3^9 5^9}{3^8 5^8} = 3^1 5^1 = 15$$

12. **$5^3(5^2 + 5 - 1)$ or $5^3(29)$:**

$$5^5 + 5^4 - 5^3 = 5^3(5^2 + 5^1 - 1) = 5^3(25 + 5 - 1) = 5^3(29)$$

13. **27:** Any square root times itself equals the number underneath the square root symbol.

14. **x^3:** Since x is positive, x^3 is positive, too.

$$\sqrt{x^6} = \sqrt{x^3 \times x^3} = x^3$$

15. **16:**

$$64^{\frac{2}{3}} = \left(\sqrt[3]{64}\right)^2 = 4^2 = 16$$

You could also square the 64 first, but that would be very annoying math to do without a calculator.

16. **10:**

$$\sqrt{20} \times \sqrt{5} = \sqrt{20 \times 5} = \sqrt{100} = 10$$

17. **6:**

$$\frac{\sqrt{216}}{\sqrt{2} \times \sqrt{3}} = \sqrt{\frac{\overset{108}{\cancel{216}}}{\cancel{2} \times 3}} = \sqrt{\frac{108}{3}} = \sqrt{36} = 6$$

Simplify before you multiply!

18. **$4\sqrt{6}$:**

$$\sqrt{96} = \sqrt{3 \times (2 \times 2) \times (2 \times 2) \times 2} = (2 \times 2)\sqrt{3 \times 2} = 4\sqrt{6}$$

19. **15:** Did you recognize this root? This is one of the common ones; if you have it memorized, you don't have to do any work at all! The square root of 225 is 15. Here's the math:

$$\sqrt{225} = \sqrt{(3 \times 3) \times (5 \times 5)} = 3 \times 5 = 15$$

20. **300:**

$$\sqrt{10^5 - 10^4} = \sqrt{10^4(10 - 1)} = \sqrt{10^4 9} = 10^2 \times 3 = 300$$

Chapter Review: Drill Sets

Drill 1

Simplify the following expressions by combining like terms. If the base is a number, leave the answer in exponential form (e.g., use 2^3, not 8).

1. $x^5 \times x^3$

2. $7^6 \times 7^9$

3. $\dfrac{5^5}{5^3}$

4. $(a^3)^2$

5. $7^{-4} \times 7^3$

6. $\dfrac{(-3)^a}{(-3)^2}$

7. $(3^2)^{-3}$

8. $\dfrac{11^4}{11^x}$

9. $x^2 \times x^3 \times x^5$

10. $(5^2)^x$

Drill 2

Simplify the following expressions by combining like terms. If the base is a number, leave the answer in exponential form (e.g., use 2^3, not 8).

11. $3^4 \times 3^2 \times 3$

12. $\dfrac{x^5 \times x^6}{x^2}$

13. $\dfrac{5^6 \times 5^{4x}}{5^4}$

14. $y^7 \times y^8 \times y^{-6}$

15. $\dfrac{x^4}{x^{-3}}$

16. $\dfrac{z^5 \times z^{-3}}{z^{-8}}$

17. $\dfrac{3^{2x} \times 3^{6x}}{3^{-3y}}$

18. $(x^2)^6 \times x^3$

19. $(m^y)^5 \times m^{y+5}$

20. $\dfrac{\left(2^x\right)^{-2} \times 2^3}{2^{2x}}$

Drill 3

Follow the directions for each question.

21. Compute the sum of $27^{\frac{1}{3}} + 9^{\frac{1}{2}} + \dfrac{3}{9^0}$.

22. Which of the following has the greatest value?
    (A) -5^6
    (B) 6^{-5}
    (C) $(-6)^5$
    (D) $(-5)^6$
    (E) 5^{-6}

23. Compute the sum of $6^{-3} - \left(\dfrac{1}{6}\right)^3 + 8^{\frac{2}{3}}$.

24. Which of the following is equal to $\left(\dfrac{4}{7}\right)^{-4}$?

    (A) $-\left(\dfrac{4}{7}\right)^4$

    (B) $\left(\dfrac{7}{4}\right)^4$

    (C) $\left(\dfrac{4}{7}\right)^{\frac{1}{4}}$

    (D) $\left(-\dfrac{4}{7}\right)^{\frac{1}{4}}$

    (E) $-\left(\dfrac{7}{4}\right)^4$

25. Which of the following has a value less than 1? (Select all that apply.)

    (A) $\dfrac{2^{-2}}{3^0}$

    (B) $\dfrac{3^{-2}}{4^{-2}}$

    (C) $\dfrac{(-3)^3}{(-5)^2}$

    (D) $\left(\dfrac{2}{3}\right)^{-2}$

    (E) $(-4)^3$

Drill 4

Simplify the following expressions by finding common bases. If the base is a number, leave the answer in exponential form (e.g., use 2^3, not 8).

26. $8^3 \times 2^6$

27. $\dfrac{36^3}{6^4}$

28. $25^4 \times 125^3$

29. $9^{-2} \times 27^2$

30. $2^{-7} \times 8^2$

Drill 5

Simplify the following expressions by pulling out as many common factors as possible.

31. $6^3 + 3^3$
    - (A) 3^5
    - (B) 3^9
    - (C) $2(3^3)$

32. $81^3 + 27^4$
    - (A) $3^7(2)$
    - (B) $3^{12}(2)$
    - (C) 3^{14}

33. $15^2 - 5^2$
    - (A) $5^2(2)$
    - (B) $5^2 2^3$
    - (C) $5^2 3^2$

34. $4^3 + 4^3 + 4^3 + 4^3 + 3^2 + 3^2 + 3^2$
    - (A) $4^4 + 3^3$
    - (B) $4^{12} + 3^6$
    - (C) $4^3(3^2)$

35. $\dfrac{3^{12} - 9^4}{27^2 + 9^4}$
    - (A) $3^2(8)$
    - (B) $\dfrac{5}{3^3}$
    - (C) $3^3(20)$

Drill 6

Simplify the following expressions. All final answers should be integers.

36. $\sqrt{3} \times \sqrt{27}$

37. $\sqrt{2} \times \sqrt{18}$

38. $\dfrac{\sqrt{48}}{\sqrt{3}}$

39. $\sqrt{5} \times \sqrt{45}$

40. $\dfrac{\sqrt{5,000}}{\sqrt{50}}$

41. $\sqrt{36} \times \sqrt{4}$

42. $\dfrac{\sqrt{128}}{\sqrt{2}}$

43. $\dfrac{\sqrt{54} \times \sqrt{3}}{\sqrt{2}}$

44. $\dfrac{\sqrt{640}}{\sqrt{2} \times \sqrt{5}}$

45. $\dfrac{\sqrt{48} \times \sqrt{7}}{\sqrt{21}}$

Drill 7

Simplify the following roots. Not every answer will be an integer.

46. $\sqrt{32}$

47. $\sqrt{24}$

48. $\sqrt{180}$

49. $\sqrt{490}$

50. $\sqrt{216}$

51. $\sqrt{135}$

52. $\sqrt{224}$

53. $\sqrt{343}$

54. $\sqrt{208}$

55. $\sqrt{432}$

Drill 8

Simplify the following roots. You will be able to eliminate the root completely in every question. Express answers as integers.

56. $\sqrt{36^2 + 15^2}$
57. $\sqrt{35^2 - 21^2}$
58. $\sqrt{10(11^5 - 11^4)}$
59. $\sqrt{8^4 + 8^5}$
60. $\sqrt{2^9 + 2^7 - 2^6}$
61. $\sqrt{50^3 - 50^2}$
62. $\sqrt{\dfrac{10(13^4 + 13^2)}{17}}$
63. $\sqrt{5^7 - 5^5 + 5^4}$

Drill Sets Solutions

Drill 1

1. x^8:

$$x^5 \times x^3 = x^{(5+3)} = x^8$$

2. 7^{15}:

$$7^6 \times 7^9 = 7^{(6+9)} = 7^{15}$$

3. 5^2:

$$\frac{5^5}{5^3} = 5^{(5-3)} = 5^2$$

4. a^6:

$$(a^3)^2 = a^{(3 \times 2)} = a^6$$

5. 7^{-1} or $\dfrac{1}{7}$:

$$7^{-4} \times 7^3 = 7^{(-4+3)} = 7^{-1} = \frac{1}{7}$$

6. $(-3)^{a-2}$:

$$\frac{(-3)^a}{(-3)^2} = (-3)^{(a-2)}$$

7. 3^{-6}:

$$(3^2)^{-3} = 3^{(2 \times -3)} = 3^{-6}$$

8. 11^{4-x}:

$$\frac{11^4}{11^x} = 11^{(4-x)}$$

9. x^{10}:

$$x^2 \times x^3 \times x^5 = x^{(2+3+5)} = x^{10}$$

10. 5^{2x}:

$$(5^2)^x = 5^{(2 \times x)} = 5^{2x}$$

Drill 2

11. **3^7:**
$$3^4 \times 3^2 \times 3 = 3^{(4+2+1)} = 3^7$$

12. **x^9:**
$$\frac{x^5 \times x^6}{x^2} = x^{(5+6-2)} = x^9$$

13. **5^{4x+2}:**
$$\frac{5^6 \times 5^{4x}}{5^4} = 5^{(6+4x-4)} = 5^{4x+2}$$

14. **y^9:**
$$y^7 \times y^8 \times y^{-6} = y^{(7+8+(-6))} = y^9$$

15. **x^7:**
$$\frac{x^4}{x^{-3}} = x^{(4-(-3))} = x^7$$

16. **z^{10}:**
$$= \frac{z^5 \times z^{-3}}{z^{-8}} = z^{(5+(-3)-(-8))} = z^{10}$$

17. **3^{8x+3y}:**
$$\frac{3^{2x} \times 3^{6x}}{3^{-3y}} = 3^{(2x+6x-(-3y))} = 3^{8x+3y}$$

18. **x^{15}:**
$$\left(x^2\right)^6 \times x^3 = x^{(2 \times 6 + 3)} = x^{(12+3)} = x^{15}$$

19. **m^{6y+5}:**
$$\left(m^y\right)^5 \times m^{y+5} = m^{(5 \times y + y + 5)} = m^{(5y+y+5)} = m^{6y+5}$$

20. **2^{-4x+3}:**
$$\frac{\left(2^x\right)^{-2} \times 2^3}{2^{2x}} = 2^{-2 \times x + 3 - 2x} = 2^{(-2x+3-2x)} = 2^{-4x+3}$$

Drill 3

21. **9**: If you are comfortable handling fractional exponents, you do not need to rewrite those forms using radical signs, as shown below.

$$27^{\frac{1}{3}} + 9^{\frac{1}{2}} + \frac{3}{9^0} = \sqrt[3]{27} + \sqrt{9} + \frac{3}{1} = 3 + 3 + 3 = 9$$

22. **(D):** The question asks for the answer with the greatest value. How can you compare efficiently? In general, don't calculate actual values unless you have to; without a calculator, this math would be messy.

(A) -5^6: Since there are no parentheses around -5, apply the exponent first, then apply the negative. This value will be negative, so if any answer is positive, that answer will automatically be greater than this answer.

(B) 6^{-5}. A positive value raised to a negative power always stays positive. Cross off answer (A). To get rid of the negative exponent, take the reciprocal: $\dfrac{1}{6^5}$.

(C) $(-6)^5$. A negative number raised to an odd exponent will stay negative. Answer (B) is positive, so eliminate this choice.

(D) $(-5)^6$. A negative number raised to an even exponent will turn positive. This value is equivalent to 5^6, which is greater than answer (B). Eliminate (B).

(E) 5^{-6}. This choice is similar to choice (B): to get rid of the negative, take the reciprocal: $\dfrac{1}{5^6}$. This is also smaller than answer (D), so eliminate (E).

23. **4:**

$$6^{-3} - \left(\frac{1}{6}\right)^3 + 8^{\frac{2}{3}} = \frac{1}{6^3} - \frac{1^3}{6^3} + \left(\sqrt[3]{8}\right)^2 = \frac{1}{6^3} - \frac{1}{6^3} + 2^2 = 4$$

The first two terms in the expression are in fact the same. Because these terms are equal, when the second is subtracted from the first, they cancel out leaving only the third term.

24. **(B):** Make the answer choices work for you. Glance at them before you start manipulating the given statement. Two of them flip the fraction and the question prompt has a negative exponent, which involves taking a reciprocal or flipping a fraction. Try that:

$$\left(\frac{4}{7}\right)^{-4} = \left(\frac{7}{4}\right)^4$$

25. **(A), (C), and (E):** The problem asks for values less than 1, so any expressions with negative values, zero itself, or values between 0 and 1 will work:

(A) $\dfrac{2^{-2}}{3^0} = \dfrac{1}{3^0 \times 2^2} = \dfrac{1}{1 \times 4} = \dfrac{1}{4}$

Answer (A) is less than 1. Note: Dividing a smaller positive number by a greater positive number will result in a number less than 1. If you know this, you can stop at the second step.

(B) $\dfrac{3^{-2}}{4^{-2}} = \dfrac{4^2}{3^2} = \dfrac{16}{9}$

3

Answer (B) is greater than 1. Note: Dividing a greater positive number by a smaller positive number will result in a number greater than 1. If you know this, you can stop at the second step.

(C) $\dfrac{(-3)^3}{(-5)^2} = \dfrac{-27}{25} =$ negative

Answer (C) is negative; therefore, it is less than 1. As soon as you realize this one is negative, you can stop.

(D) $\left(\dfrac{2}{3}\right)^{-2} = \left(\dfrac{3}{2}\right)^2 = \dfrac{3^2}{2^2} = \dfrac{9}{4}$

Answer (D) is greater than 1. As with (B), dividing a greater positive number by a smaller positive number will result in a number greater than 1.

(E) $(-4)^3 =$ negative

Answer (E) is negative; therefore, it is less than 1.

Drill 4

26. $\mathbf{2^{15}}$:

$$8^3 \times 2^6 = (2^3)^3 \times 2^6 = 2^9 \times 2^6 = 2^{9+6} = 2^{15}$$

27. $\mathbf{6^2}$:

$$\frac{36^3}{6^4} = \frac{\left(6^2\right)^3}{6^4} = \frac{6^6}{6^4} = 6^{6-4} = 6^2$$

28. $\mathbf{5^{17}}$:

$$25^4 \times 125^3 = (5^2)^4 \times (5^3)^3 = 5^8 \times 5^9 = 5^{17}$$

29. $\mathbf{3^2}$:

$$9^{-2} \times 27^2 = (3^2)^{-2} \times (3^3)^2 = 3^{-4} \times 3^6 = 3^2$$

30. $\mathbf{2^{-1}}$:

$$2^{-7} \times 8^2 = 2^{-7} \times (2^3)^2 = 2^{-7} \times 2^6 = 2^{-1}$$

Drill 5

31. **(A):** Begin by breaking 6 down into its prime factors:

$$6^3 + 3^3 =$$
$$(2 \times 3)^3 + 3^3 =$$
$$(2^3)(3^3) + 3^3$$

Now each term contains 3^3. Factor it out.

$$(2^3)(3^3) + 3^3 =$$
$$3^3(2^3 + 1) =$$
$$3^3(9) =$$
$$3^3(3^2) = 3^5$$

32. **(B):** Both bases are powers of 3. Rewrite the bases and combine.

$$81^3 + 27^4 =$$
$$(3^4)^3 + (3^3)^4 =$$
$$3^{12} + 3^{12} =$$
$$3^{12}(1 + 1) =$$
$$3^{12}(2)$$

33. **(B):** Begin by breaking 15 down into its prime factors.
$$15^2 - 5^2 =$$
$$(3 \times 5)^2 - 5^2 =$$
$$(3^2)(5^2) - 5^2$$

Now both terms contain 5^2. Factor it out.

$$(3^2)(5^2) - 5^2 =$$
$$5^2(3^2 - 1) =$$
$$5^2(9 - 1) =$$
$$5^2(8)$$

Compare that to the answers. What else can you manipulate?

$$5^2(8) =$$
$$5^2(2^3)$$

34. **(A):** Factor 4^3 out of the first four terms and factor 3^2 out of the last three terms.

$$4^3 + 4^3 + 4^3 + 4^3 + 3^2 + 3^2 + 3^2 =$$
$$4^3(1 + 1 + 1 + 1) + 3^2(1 + 1 + 1) =$$
$$4^3(4) + 3^2(3) =$$
$$4^{3+1} + 3^{2+1} =$$
$$4^4 + 3^3$$

35. **(A):** Every base in the fraction is a power of 3. Begin by rewriting every base.

$$\frac{3^{12} - 9^4}{27^2 + 9^4} = \frac{3^{12} - \left(3^2\right)^4}{\left(3^3\right)^2 + \left(3^2\right)^4} = \frac{3^{12} - 3^8}{3^6 + 3^8}$$

The terms in the numerator both contain 3^8, and the terms in the denominator both contain 3^6. Factor the numerator and denominator.

$$\frac{3^{12} - 3^8}{3^6 + 3^8} = \frac{3^8\left(3^4 - 1\right)}{3^6\left(1 + 3^2\right)} = \frac{3^8(80)}{3^6(10)}$$

Simplify the numerator and denominator.

$$\frac{3^8(80)}{3^6(10)} = 3^{8-6}(8) = 3^2(8)$$

Drill 6

36. **9**: Before you multiply larger numbers together, think about whether you can make the math easier by breaking down into primes and pairing integers to pull out of the square root.

$$\sqrt{3} \times \sqrt{27} = \sqrt{3 \times 27} = \sqrt{3 \times 3 \times 3 \times 3} = 3 \times 3 = 9$$

In this case, you can break 27 down into three 3's. Then, each pair of 3's can be pulled out of the square root to give one 3.

37. **6**:
$$\sqrt{2} \times \sqrt{18} = \sqrt{2 \times 18} = \sqrt{36} = 6$$

38. **4**:
$$\frac{\sqrt{48}}{\sqrt{3}} = \sqrt{\frac{48}{3}} = \sqrt{16} = 4$$

39. **15**: You can break 45 down to get a second 5 to match the first one.

$$\sqrt{5} \times \sqrt{45} = \sqrt{5 \times 5 \times 9} = 5 \times 3 = 15$$

Alternatively, you can multiply first and then simplify, as shown below. Which way is easier for you?

$$\sqrt{5} \times \sqrt{45} = \sqrt{5 \times 45} = \sqrt{225} = 15$$

40. **10**:
$$\frac{\sqrt{5,000}}{\sqrt{50}} = \sqrt{\frac{5,000}{50}} = \sqrt{100} = 10$$

41. **12**: Careful! You might get so used to combining automatically that you fail to notice that these two are already perfect squares. They can be simplified first and then multiplied.

$$\sqrt{36} \times \sqrt{4} = 6 \times 2 = 12$$

42. **8**:

$$\frac{\sqrt{128}}{\sqrt{2}} - \sqrt{\frac{128}{2}} = \sqrt{64} = 8$$

43. **9**: Simplify the numerator and denominator before you multiply, then break 27 down into 3's.

$$\frac{\sqrt{54} \times \sqrt{3}}{\sqrt{2}} = \sqrt{\frac{^{27}\cancel{54} \times 3}{\cancel{2}_1}} = \sqrt{3 \times 3 \times 3 \times 3} = 3 \times 3 = 9$$

44. **8**:

$$\frac{\sqrt{640}}{\sqrt{2} \times \sqrt{5}} = \sqrt{\frac{640}{2 \times 5}} = \sqrt{\frac{640}{10}} = \sqrt{64} = 8$$

45. **4**: Simplify before you multiply.

$$\frac{\sqrt{48} \times \sqrt{7}}{\sqrt{21}} = \sqrt{\frac{48 \times {}^1\cancel{7}}{\cancel{21}_3}} = \sqrt{\frac{^{16}\cancel{48} \times 1}{\cancel{3}_1}} = \sqrt{16} = 4$$

Drill 7

46. **$4\sqrt{2}$** : Keep track of all those 2's carefully!

$$\sqrt{32} = \sqrt{2 \times 2 \times 2 \times 2 \times 2} = \sqrt{2 \times 2} \times \sqrt{2 \times 2} \times \sqrt{2} = 2 \times 2 \times \sqrt{2} = 4\sqrt{2}$$

47. **$2\sqrt{6}$** :

$$\sqrt{24} = \sqrt{2 \times 2 \times 2 \times 3} = \sqrt{2 \times 2} \times \sqrt{2 \times 3} = 2\sqrt{6}$$

48. **$6\sqrt{5}$** : If needed, use a factor tree to break down large numbers.

$$\sqrt{180} = \sqrt{2 \times 2 \times 3 \times 3 \times 5} = \sqrt{2 \times 2} \times \sqrt{3 \times 3} \times \sqrt{5} = 2 \times 3 \times \sqrt{5} = 6\sqrt{5}$$

49. **$7\sqrt{10}$** :

$$\sqrt{490} = \sqrt{2 \times 5 \times 7 \times 7} = \sqrt{7 \times 7} \times \sqrt{2 \times 5} = 7\sqrt{10}$$

50. **$6\sqrt{6}$** : Break 216 down into its primes.

$$\sqrt{216} = \sqrt{2 \times 2 \times 2 \times 3 \times 3 \times 3} = \sqrt{2 \times 2} \times \sqrt{3 \times 3} \times \sqrt{2 \times 3} = 2 \times 3 \times \sqrt{2 \times 3} = 6\sqrt{6}$$

51. **$3\sqrt{15}$** :

$$\sqrt{135} = \sqrt{3 \times 3 \times 3 \times 5} = \sqrt{3 \times 3} \times \sqrt{3 \times 5} = 3\sqrt{15}$$

52. $4\sqrt{14}$: Count out those 2's carefully.

$$\sqrt{224} = \sqrt{2\times2\times2\times2\times2\times7} = \sqrt{2\times2}\times\sqrt{2\times2}\times\sqrt{2\times7} = 2\times2\times\sqrt{14} = 4\sqrt{14}$$

53. $7\sqrt{7}$:

$$\sqrt{343} = \sqrt{7\times7\times7} = \sqrt{7\times7}\times\sqrt{7} = 7\sqrt{7}$$

54. $4\sqrt{13}$:

$$\sqrt{208} = \sqrt{2\times2\times2\times2\times13} = \sqrt{2\times2}\times\sqrt{2\times2}\times\sqrt{13} = 2\times2\times\sqrt{13} = 4\sqrt{13}$$

55. $12\sqrt{3}$:

$$\sqrt{432} = \sqrt{2\times2\times2\times2\times3\times3\times3} = \sqrt{2\times2}\times\sqrt{2\times2}\times\sqrt{3\times3}\times\sqrt{3} = 2\times2\times3\times\sqrt{3} = 12\sqrt{3}$$

Drill 8

56. **39:** It is tempting to use the square root to eliminate the exponents on 36 and 15 immediately, but you cannot break up a root over addition. You could multiply out both terms and add them, but you should always try to simplify before doing large calculations. Pull out the greatest common factor of 36^2 and 15^2, namely 3^2. (Tip: Find the greatest number that 36 and 15 have in common. Then square that number. $15 = 3 \times 5$. 36 contains a 3 but not a 5.)

$$\sqrt{3^2\left(12^2+5^2\right)} = \sqrt{3^2(144+25)} = \sqrt{3^2(169)}$$

Both 3^2 and 169 are perfect squares ($169 = 13^2$). Therefore:

$$\sqrt{3^2(169)} = \sqrt{3^2\left(13^2\right)} = 3\times13 = 39$$

57. **28:** Pull out the greatest common factor of 35^2 and 21^2, namely 7^2.

$$\sqrt{7^2\left(5^2-3^2\right)} = \sqrt{7^2(25-9)} = \sqrt{7^2(16)}$$

Both 7^2 and 16 are perfect squares ($16 = 4^2$). Therefore:

$$\sqrt{7^2(16)} = \sqrt{7^2\left(4^2\right)} = 7\times4 = 28$$

58. **1,210:** Pull out the greatest common factor of 11^4 and 11^5, namely 11^4.

$$\sqrt{10(11^5-11^4)} = \sqrt{10\left(11^4(11-1)\right)} = \sqrt{10\left(11^4(10)\right)}$$

$(10)(10)$ is the same as 10^2. The other term, 11^4, is also a perfect square ($11^4 = 11^2 \times 11^2$). Pull the squares out of the square root.

$$\sqrt{10\left(11^4(10)\right)} = (10)\left(11^2\right) = (10)(121) = 1,210$$

59. **192**: Pull out the greatest common factor of 8^4 and 8^5, namely 8^4.

$$\sqrt{8^4(1+8)} = \sqrt{8^4(9)} = \sqrt{8^4(3^2)}$$

Both 8^4 and 3^2 are perfect squares ($8^4 = 8^2 \times 8^2$). Therefore:

$$\sqrt{8^4(3^2)} = 8^2 \times 3 = 64 \times 3 = 192$$

60. **24**: Pull out the greatest common factor of 2^9, 2^7, and 2^6, namely 2^6.

$$\sqrt{2^6(2^3 + 2 - 1)} = \sqrt{2^6(8 + 2 - 1)} = \sqrt{2^6(9)} = \sqrt{2^6(3^2)}$$

Both 2^6 and 3^2 are perfect squares ($2^6 = 2^3 \times 2^3$). Therefore:

$$\sqrt{2^6(3^2)} = 2^3 \times 3 = 8 \times 3 = 24$$

61. **350**: Pull out the greatest common factor of 50^3 and 50^2, namely 50^2.

$$\sqrt{50^2(50-1)} = \sqrt{50^2(49)} = \sqrt{50^2(7^2)} = 50 \times 7 = 350$$

62. **130**: First focus on the numerator of the fraction under the radical. Pull out the greatest common factor of 13^4 and 13^2, namely 13^2.

$$\sqrt{\frac{10\left(13^2\left(13^2+1\right)\right)}{17}} = \sqrt{\frac{10\left(13^2\left(169+1\right)\right)}{17}} = \sqrt{\frac{10\left(13^2\left(170\right)\right)}{17}}$$

The denominator (17) divides evenly into 170, and the remaining terms are perfect squares:

$$\sqrt{\frac{10\left(13^2\left(170\right)\right)}{17}} = \sqrt{10\left(13^2\left(10\right)\right)} = \sqrt{\left(10^2\right)\left(13^2\right)} = (10)(13) = 130$$

63. **275**: Pull out the greatest common factor of 5^7, 5^5, and 5^4, namely 5^4.

$$\sqrt{5^4(5^3 - 5 + 1)} = \sqrt{5^4(125 - 5 + 1)} = \sqrt{5^4(121)} = \sqrt{5^4(11^2)}$$

Both 5^4 and 11^2 are perfect squares ($5^4 = 5^2 \times 5^2$). Therefore:

$$\sqrt{5^4(11^2)} = 5^2 \times 11 = 25 \times 11 = 275$$

Fractions

In this chapter...

- Basics of Fractions
- Add Fractions with the Same Denominator: Add the Numerators
- Add Fractions with Different Denominators: Find a Common Denominator
- Compare Fractions: Use the Double-Cross
- Change an Improper Fraction to a Mixed Number: Divide
- Change a Mixed Number to an Improper Fraction: Add
- Simplify a Fraction: Cancel Common Factors on the Top and Bottom
- Multiply Fractions: Simplify First, Then Multiply
- Square a Proper Fraction: It Gets Smaller
- Take a Reciprocal: Flip the Fraction
- Divide by a Fraction: Multiply by the Reciprocal
- Addition in the Numerator: Pull Out a Common Factor
- Addition in the Numerator: Split into Two Fractions (Maybe)
- Addition in the Denominator: Pull Out a Common Factor, but Never Split
- Add, Subtract, Multiply, Divide Nasty Fractions: Add Parentheses
- Fractions within Fractions: Work Your Way Out

Chapter 4

Fractions

In This Chapter, You Will Learn To:

- Add, subtract, multiply, and divide fractions
- Manipulate fractions in complex scenarios

Basics of Fractions

A fraction expresses division.

The **numerator** on top is divided by the **denominator** on bottom.

Numerator

Fraction line $\longrightarrow$ $\dfrac{3}{4}$ $=$ $3 \div 4$

Denominator

Three-fourths is three divided by four.

The result of the division is a number. If you punch "$3 \div 4 =$" into a calculator, you get the decimal 0.75. But you can also think of 0.75 as $\dfrac{3}{4}$, because $\dfrac{3}{4}$ and 0.75 are two different ways to write the same number. (You'll learn about decimals in the next chapter.)

Fractions express a part-to-whole relationship.

$$\frac{3}{4} = \frac{\text{part}}{\text{whole}}$$

3 pieces = part

4 pieces = whole

In the above figure, a circle represents a whole unit—a full pizza. The pizza has been divided into four equal parts, or fourths, because the denominator of the fraction is 4. In any fraction, the denominator tells you how many equal slices something has been broken into, in this case a pizza. In other words, the denominator indicates the size of a slice: Each slice is one-quarter of the pizza.

The numerator of the fraction is 3. This means that the fraction is talking about three slices of the pizza.

In any fraction, the numerator tells you how many of the slices you are talking about. Together, you are talking about three slices out of four total, or three parts to the total four. You can also say that you are talking about three-quarters of the pizza.

Since fractions express division, all the arithmetic rules of division apply. For instance, a negative divided by a positive gives you a negative, and so on.

$$\frac{-3}{4} = -3 \div 4 = -0.75 \qquad\qquad \frac{3}{-4} = 3 \div (-4) = -0.75$$

So $\frac{-3}{4}$ and $\frac{3}{-4}$ represent the same number. You can also write that number as $-\frac{3}{4}$. Just don't mix up the negative sign with the fraction bar.

PEMDAS also applies. The fraction bar means that you always *divide the entire numerator by the entire denominator*.

$$\frac{3x^2 + y}{2y^2 - z} = \left(3x^2 + y\right) \div \left(2y^2 - z\right)$$

The entire quantity $3x^2 + y$ is being divided by the entire quantity $2y^2 - z$.

If you rewrite a fraction, be ready to put parentheses around the numerator or denominator to preserve the correct order of operations.

Finally, remember that you can't divide by zero. So *a denominator can never equal zero*. If you have a variable expression in the denominator, that expression cannot equal zero. If a problem contains the fraction $\frac{x}{y}$, then y cannot equal zero. The problem will tell you that $y \neq 0$ (that's a "does not equal" sign).

If the problem tells you that $\frac{3x^2 + y}{2y^2 - z}$, then what cannot equal zero?

The entire denominator cannot equal zero. In other words:

$$2y^2 - z \neq 0 \qquad \text{or} \qquad 2y^2 \neq z$$

If the GMAT tells you that something does *not* equal something else (using the $\neq$ sign), the purpose is often to rule out dividing by zero somewhere in the problem.

To compare positive fractions with the same *denominator*, compare the numerators. The numerator tells you how many pieces you have. *The greater the numerator, the greater the fraction* (assuming positive numbers and the same denominators). You have more same-sized slices of pie.

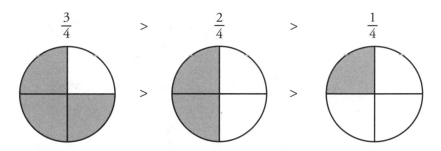

To compare positive fractions with the same *numerator*, compare the denominators. *The greater the denominator, the smaller the fraction.* Each slice of pie is smaller. So the same number of smaller slices represents a smaller amount of the pie.

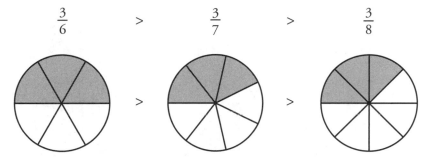

If the numerator and denominator are the same, then the fraction equals 1.

$$\frac{4}{4} \qquad = \qquad 4 \div 4 \qquad = \qquad 1$$

Four-fourths   equals   four divided by   and that equals   one
four,

If the numerator is greater than the denominator (again, assume positive numbers), then you have more than one pizza.

$$\frac{5}{4} \qquad = \qquad 5 \div 4 \qquad = \qquad 1 \qquad + \qquad \frac{1}{4}$$

Five-fourths   equals   five divided   and that   one   plus   one-fourth
by four,   equals

Another way to write $1 + \frac{1}{4}$ is $1\frac{1}{4}$ (read *one and one-fourth*). This is the only time in GMAT math when you put two things next to each other (1 and $\frac{1}{4}$) in order to *add* them. In all other circumstances, two things right next to each other means *multiplication*.

A **mixed number** such as $1\frac{1}{4}$ contains both an integer part, 1, and a fractional part, $\frac{1}{4}$. You can always rewrite a mixed number as a sum of the integer part and the fractional part: just split the integer and the fraction.

$$3\frac{3}{8} = 3 + \frac{3}{8}$$

In an **improper fraction** such as $\dfrac{5}{4}$, the numerator is greater than the denominator. Improper fractions and mixed numbers are two different ways to express the same thing. Later, you'll learn how to convert between them.

A **proper fraction** such as $\dfrac{3}{4}$ has a value between 0 and 1. In a proper fraction, the numerator is smaller than the denominator.

Add Fractions with the Same Denominator: Add the Numerators

The numerator of a fraction tells you how many slices of the pizza you have. So when you add fractions, you add the numerators. You just have to make sure that the slices are the same size—in other words, that the denominators are equal.

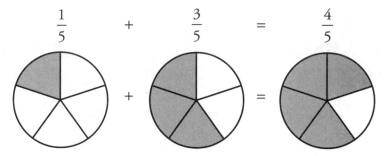

In words, one-fifth plus three-fifths equals four-fifths. The *fifth* is the size of the slice, so the denominator (5) doesn't change.

Since 4 = 1 + 3, you can write the fraction with 1 + 3 in the numerator.

$$\frac{1}{5} + \frac{3}{5} = \frac{1+3}{5} = \frac{4}{5}$$

The same process applies with subtraction. Subtract the numerators and leave the denominator the same.

$$\frac{9}{14} - \frac{4}{14} = \frac{9-4}{14} = \frac{5}{14}$$

If variables are involved, add or subtract the same way. Just make sure that the denominators in the original fractions are equal. It doesn't matter how complicated they are.

$$\frac{3a}{b} + \frac{4a}{b} = \frac{3a+4a}{b} = \frac{7a}{b} \qquad \frac{5x^2}{z+w} - \frac{2x^2}{z+w} = \frac{5x^2 - 2x^2}{z+w} = \frac{3x^2}{z+w}$$

If you can't simplify the numerator, leave it as a sum or a difference. Remember that the denominator stays the same, because it just tells you the *size* of the slices you're adding or subtracting.

$$\frac{x}{y} + \frac{z}{y} = \frac{x+z}{y} \qquad \frac{3n}{2w^3} - \frac{5m}{2w^3} = \frac{3n-5m}{2w^3}$$

Here's another rule for your book:

If you…	Then you…	Like this:
Add or subtract fractions that have the same denominator	Add or subtract the numerators, leaving the denominator alone	$\dfrac{2}{7}+\dfrac{3}{7}=\dfrac{2+3}{7}$ $=\dfrac{5}{7}$

Check Your Skills

1. $\dfrac{3x}{yz^2}+\dfrac{7x}{yz^2}=$

Answer can be found on page 163.

Add Fractions with Different Denominators: Find a Common Denominator

Consider this example:

$$\frac{1}{4}+\frac{3}{8}=$$

The denominators (the sizes of the slices) aren't the same, so you can't just add the numerators this time.

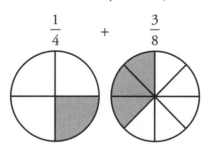

To add these fractions correctly, you will need to manipulate the fractions so that the slices are the same size. In other words, the fractions need to have a **common denominator**—that is, the *same* denominator. Once they have the same denominator, you can add the numerators.

Since a fourth of a pizza is twice as big as an eighth, take the fourth in the first circle and cut it in two.

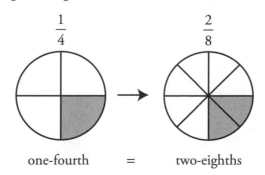

one-fourth   =   two-eighths

You have the same amount of pizza—the shaded area hasn't changed in size. So one-fourth $\left(\dfrac{1}{4}\right)$ equals two-eighths $\left(\dfrac{2}{8}\right)$.

When you cut the fourth in two, you end up with twice as many slices. So the numerator is doubled. But you're breaking the whole circle into twice as many pieces, so the denominator is doubled as well. If you double both the numerator and the denominator, the fraction's value stays exactly the same (this is why you are allowed to make this move!).

$$\frac{1}{4} = \frac{1 \times 2}{4 \times 2} = \frac{2}{8}$$

Without changing the value of $\dfrac{1}{4}$, you have renamed it $\dfrac{2}{8}$. Now you can add it to $\dfrac{3}{8}$.

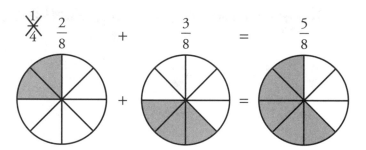

All in one line:

$$\frac{1}{4} + \frac{3}{8} = \frac{1 \times 2}{4 \times 2} + \frac{3}{8} = \frac{2}{8} + \frac{3}{8} = \frac{5}{8}$$

To add fractions with different denominators, find a common denominator. That is, rename the fractions so that they have the same denominator. Then add the new numerators. The same holds true for subtraction.

How do you rename a fraction without changing its value? Multiply the top and bottom by the same number. For example:

$$\frac{1}{4} = \frac{1 \times 2}{4 \times 2} = \frac{2}{8} \qquad \frac{3}{4} = \frac{3 \times 25}{4 \times 25} = \frac{75}{100} \qquad \frac{5}{9} = \frac{5 \times 7}{9 \times 7} = \frac{35}{63}$$

Here's why this works. Doubling the top and doubling the bottom of a fraction is the same as multiplying the fraction by $\dfrac{2}{2}$. (More on fraction multiplication later.)

Notice that $\dfrac{2}{2}$ is equal to 1. And multiplying a number by 1 doesn't change the number. So when you multiply by $\dfrac{2}{2}$, you aren't really changing the number, you're just changing its appearance.

$$\frac{1}{4} = \frac{1}{4} \times \frac{2}{2} = \frac{1 \times 2}{4 \times 2} = \frac{2}{8}$$

You can rename fractions that have variables in them, too. You can even multiply the top and bottom by the same variable.

$$\frac{x}{y} = \frac{x}{y} \times \frac{2}{2} = \frac{x \times 2}{y \times 2} = \frac{2x}{2y} \qquad\qquad \frac{a}{2} = \frac{a}{2} \times \frac{b}{b} = \frac{a \times b}{2 \times b} = \frac{ab}{2b}$$

Just make sure the expression on the bottom can never equal zero, of course. Here's another rule for your book:

If you...	Then you...	Like this:
Want to give a fraction a different denominator but keep the value the same	Multiply the top and bottom of the fraction by the same number	$\frac{1}{4} = \frac{1 \times 2}{4 \times 2} = \frac{2}{8}$

Say you have this problem:

$$\frac{1}{4} + \frac{1}{3} =$$

What should the common denominator of these fractions be? It needs to be both a multiple of 4 *and* a multiple of 3. That is, it should be a multiple that 3 and 4 have in common. The easiest multiple to pick is usually the **least common multiple** (LCM) of 3 and 4. If you need a refresher on that concept, return to Chapter 2.

The least common multiple of 4 and 3 is 12. Rename the two fractions so that they each have a denominator of 12.

$$\frac{1}{4} = \frac{1 \times 3}{4 \times 3} = \frac{3}{12} \qquad\qquad \frac{1}{3} = \frac{1 \times 4}{3 \times 4} = \frac{4}{12}$$

Once you have a common denominator, add the numerators.

$$\frac{1}{4} + \frac{1}{3} = \frac{1 \times 3}{4 \times 3} + \frac{1 \times 4}{3 \times 4} = \frac{3}{12} + \frac{4}{12} = \frac{7}{12}$$

The process works the same if you subtract fractions or even have more than two fractions. Try this example:

$$\frac{5}{6} + \frac{2}{9} - \frac{3}{4} =$$

First, find the common denominator by finding the least common multiple. All three denominators (6, 9, and 4) are composed of 2's and 3's.

$$6 = 2 \times 3 \qquad\qquad 9 = 3 \times 3 \qquad\qquad 4 = 2 \times 2$$

The LCM will contain two 2's (because there are two 2's in 4) and two 3's (because there are two 3's in 9).

$$2 \times 2 \times 3 \times 3 = 36$$

To make each of the denominators equal 36, multiply the fractions by $\frac{6}{6}$, $\frac{4}{4}$, and $\frac{9}{9}$, respectively.

$$\frac{5}{6} = \frac{5 \times 6}{6 \times 6} = \frac{30}{36} \qquad\qquad \frac{2}{9} = \frac{2 \times 4}{9 \times 4} = \frac{8}{36} \qquad\qquad \frac{3}{4} = \frac{3 \times 9}{4 \times 9} = \frac{27}{36}$$

Now that the denominators are all the same, add and subtract normally.

$$\frac{5}{6}+\frac{2}{9}-\frac{3}{4}=\frac{30}{36}+\frac{8}{36}-\frac{27}{36}=\frac{30+8-27}{36}=\frac{11}{36}$$

The process works even if you have variables. Try adding these two fractions:

$$\frac{2}{x}+\frac{3}{2x}=$$

First, find the common denominator by finding the least common multiple of x and $2x$. The LCM is $2x$. So give the first fraction a denominator of $2x$, then add:

$$\frac{2}{x}+\frac{3}{2x}=\frac{2\times2}{x\times2}+\frac{3}{2x}=\frac{4}{2x}+\frac{3}{2x}=\frac{4+3}{2x}=\frac{7}{2x}$$

Now that you know how to do the math in the traditional way, it's time to learn a useful shortcut: the double-cross. (In general, you'll be better able to remember how to implement a shortcut when you first understand the textbook approach.)

Here's an example that you solved earlier.

$$\frac{1}{4}+\frac{1}{3}=\frac{1\times3}{4\times3}+\frac{1\times4}{3\times4}=\frac{3}{12}+\frac{4}{12}=\frac{7}{12}$$

This time, you're going to take some different steps. First, draw three arrows on the problem and rewrite the addition sign just above the top arrows.

The arrows mean multiplication. Multiply along each arrow, and place the product where the arrow points.

The new denominator, 12, is the result of multiplying along the bottom, as shown above.

To get the new numerator, add the two new numbers on top.

The result is the same whether you use the shortcut or do the math in the traditional way; the shortcut just compresses several steps.

The double-cross will always work, and it is usually faster, but there is one circumstance in which the traditional approach is faster.

Take a look at this example:

$$\frac{1}{3} + \frac{1}{6}$$

In this case, 3 and 6 share a common denominator of 6, so you only need to change one fraction: $\frac{1}{3}$. Since this is the case, it's faster to find common denominators.

$$\frac{1}{3} + \frac{1}{6} = \frac{2}{6} + \frac{1}{6} = \frac{3}{6} = \frac{1}{2}$$

Try one more.

$$\frac{5}{6} + \frac{3}{8}$$

Traditional	The Double-Cross
Find a common denominator. The smallest one is 24: $$\frac{5 \times 4}{6 \times 4} + \frac{3 \times 3}{8 \times 3}$$ Add the two fractions: $$\frac{20}{24} + \frac{9}{24} = \frac{29}{24}$$	Draw your arrows and multiply. Add the numerators. Note that 58 and 48 are both divisible by 2, so simplify as a last step: $$\frac{58}{48} = \frac{29 \times \cancel{2}}{24 \times \cancel{2}} = \frac{29}{24}$$

As usual, the traditional method has more work up front (finding a common denominator), but this time the shortcut had an extra step at the end: You have to simplify. Why?

This will happen when the two denominators share factors, as 6 and 8 do. The smallest common denominator, 24, is smaller than multiplying those two numbers together: $6 \times 8 = 48$. If you choose the double-cross in this circumstance, be aware that you will need to simplify at the end (you'll learn various methods for doing this later in this chapter). If the numbers are large enough to be annoying, then you may want to use the traditional method, even though you do have to find common denominators.

If you...	Then you...	Like this:
Add or subtract fractions with different denominators	Put the fractions in terms of a common denominator, then add or subtract OR Use the double-cross shortcut	$$\frac{1}{3} - \frac{1}{6} = \frac{1 \times 2}{3 \times 2} - \frac{1}{6}$$ $$= \frac{2}{6} - \frac{1}{6} = \frac{1}{6}$$ OR

Check Your Skills

2. $\dfrac{1}{2} + \dfrac{3}{4} =$

3. $\dfrac{2}{3} - \dfrac{3}{8} =$

Answers can be found on page 163.

Compare Fractions: Use the Double-Cross

The double-cross is very versatile; it can also be used to compare two fractions.

Which is greater, $\dfrac{3}{5}$ or $\dfrac{4}{7}$?

Use a modified version of the double-cross. Multiply along the top two crossed arrows, but ignore the denominator:

1. Set the two fractions up near each other.

$$\dfrac{3}{5} \qquad \dfrac{4}{7}$$

2. Multiply "up" the arrows. Be sure to put the resulting number at the top of each respective arrow.

3. Compare the numbers. The side with the bigger number is the bigger fraction. 21 > 20, so $\dfrac{3}{5}$ is greater than $\dfrac{4}{7}$.

This process generates the same numerators as before (21 and 20), and the numerators are all you need to compare. The common denominator is the same for both terms, so it doesn't matter.

If you...	Then you...	Like this:
Want to compare fractions	Do the two top calculations of the double-cross	㉘ 4 3 27 9 7

Check Your Skills

For each of the following pairs of fractions, decide which fraction is greater.

4. $\dfrac{5}{7}, \dfrac{3}{7}$

5. $\dfrac{3}{10}, \dfrac{3}{13}$

Answers can be found on page 163.

Change an Improper Fraction to a Mixed Number: Divide

What is $\frac{13}{4}$ as a mixed number? Note that $\frac{13}{4}$ is an improper fraction, because $13 > 4$.

Since the fraction bar represents division, go ahead and divide 13 by 4. Try doing this by long division:

$$
\begin{array}{r}
3 \\
4\overline{)13} \\
\underline{12} \\
1
\end{array}
$$

The number 4 goes into 13 three times, with 1 left over. Since it goes in three times, the number 3 is called the **quotient**. It represents how many whole times the denominator (4) goes into the numerator (13). The number one is called the **remainder**. It represents what is left over.

So $\frac{13}{4}$ equals 3 plus a remainder of 1. This remainder of 1 is literally "left over" the 4, so write it out this way:

$$\frac{13}{4} = 3 + \frac{1}{4}$$

As a mixed number, $\frac{13}{4}$ equals $3\frac{1}{4}$.

To convert an improper fraction to a mixed number, divide the numerator by the denominator. The quotient is the integer part of the mixed number. The remainder over the denominator equals the leftover fractional part of the mixed number.

To do the division, look for the greatest multiple of the denominator that is less than or equal to the numerator. In the case of $\frac{13}{4}$, 12 is the greatest multiple of 4 that is still less than 13, and since $12 = 4 \times 3$, the number 3 is the quotient. $13 - 12 = 1$, so 1 is the remainder.

Here's another way to understand this process. Fraction addition can be done both forward and in reverse.

$$\text{Forward: } \frac{2}{7} + \frac{4}{7} = \frac{2+4}{7} = \frac{6}{7} \qquad\qquad \text{Reverse: } \frac{6}{7} = \frac{2+4}{7} = \frac{2}{7} + \frac{4}{7}$$

In other words, you can *rewrite a numerator as a sum, then split the fraction.* Try this with $\frac{13}{4}$.

Rewrite 13 as $12 + 1$, then split the fraction:

$$\frac{13}{4} = \frac{12+1}{4} = \frac{12}{4} + \frac{1}{4}$$

Since $\frac{12}{4} = 12 \div 4 = 3$, the expression becomes $\frac{13}{4} = \frac{12}{4} + \frac{1}{4} = 3 + \frac{1}{4} = 3\frac{1}{4}$.

4

If you...	Then you...	Like this:
Want to convert an improper fraction to a mixed number	Divide the numerator by the denominator OR Rewrite the numerator as a sum, then split the fraction	$\dfrac{13}{4} = 13 \div 4$ $= 3 \text{ remainder } 1$ $= 3\dfrac{1}{4}$ $\dfrac{13}{4} = \dfrac{12+1}{4}$ $= \dfrac{12}{4} + \dfrac{1}{4}$ $= 3\dfrac{1}{4}$

Check Your Skills

Change the following improper fractions to mixed numbers.

6. $\dfrac{11}{6}$

7. $\dfrac{100}{11}$

Answers can be found on pages 163–164.

Change a Mixed Number to an Improper Fraction: Add

What is $5\dfrac{2}{3}$ as an improper fraction?

First, rewrite the mixed number as a sum: $5\dfrac{2}{3} = 5 + \dfrac{2}{3}$.

Now add these two numbers together by rewriting 5 as a fraction. You can always write any integer as a fraction by putting it over 1

$$5 = \frac{5}{1} \qquad \text{This is true because } 5 \div 1 = 5.$$

So $5\dfrac{2}{3} = 5 + \dfrac{2}{3} = \dfrac{5}{1} + \dfrac{2}{3}$. At this point, you're adding fractions with different denominators, so find a common denominator.

The least common multiple of 1 and 3 is 3, so convert $\dfrac{5}{1}$ to a fraction with a 3 in its denominator.

$$\frac{5}{1} = \frac{5 \times 3}{1 \times 3} = \frac{15}{3}$$

Finally, complete the addition. Here are the steps from start to finish:

$$5\frac{2}{3} = 5 + \frac{2}{3} = \frac{5}{1} + \frac{2}{3} = \frac{15}{3} + \frac{2}{3} = \frac{15+2}{3} = \frac{17}{3}$$

If you'd like, learn this shortcut: the new numerator is $3 \times 5 + 2 = 17$. That is: (denominator)(integer part of the mixed number) + numerator = the new numerator. The denominator, 3, stays the same, so the complete fraction is $\frac{17}{3}$.

If you understand how this shortcut is equivalent to the addition process above, you'll be better able to remember the shortcut.

If you...	Then you...	Like this:
Want to convert a mixed number to an improper fraction	Convert the integer to a fraction over 1, then add it to the fractional part OR Use the shortcut: $\dfrac{(denom)(integer)+num}{denom}$	$7\dfrac{3}{8} = \dfrac{7}{1} + \dfrac{3}{8}$ $= \dfrac{56}{8} + \dfrac{3}{8}$ $= \dfrac{59}{8}$ $\dfrac{8 \times 7 + 3}{8} = \dfrac{56+3}{8} = \dfrac{59}{8}$

Check Your Skills

Change the following mixed numbers to improper fractions.

8. $3\dfrac{3}{4}$

9. $6\dfrac{3}{4}$

Answers can be found on page 164.

Simplify a Fraction: Cancel Common Factors on the Top and Bottom

Consider this problem:

$$\frac{5}{9} + \frac{1}{9} =$$

(A) $\dfrac{4}{9}$

(B) $\dfrac{6}{18}$

(C) $\dfrac{2}{3}$

You know how to add fractions with the same denominator: $\dfrac{5}{9} + \dfrac{1}{9} = \dfrac{5+1}{9} = \dfrac{6}{9}$. This is mathematically correct so far.

But $\dfrac{6}{9}$ is not among the answer choices. Try **simplifying** or **reducing** the fraction to its lowest terms.

To simplify a fraction, cancel out common factors from the numerator and denominator.

$$\frac{6}{9} = \frac{2 \times 3}{3 \times 3}$$

Since 3 is a common factor on the top and bottom, cancel it.

$$\frac{6}{9} = \frac{2 \times \cancel{3}}{3 \times \cancel{3}} = \frac{2}{3}$$

Earlier, you learned that you can multiply the top and bottom of a fraction by the same number without changing the value of the fraction. The fraction stays the same because you are multiplying the whole fraction by the equivalent of 1. For example:

$$\frac{2}{3} = \frac{2 \times 3}{3 \times 3} = \frac{6}{9}$$

Now you're just dividing the fraction by the equivalent of 1; this also leaves the value unchanged. As you divide away the $\frac{3}{3}$ (which equals 1), the look of the fraction changes from $\frac{6}{9}$ to $\frac{2}{3}$, but the value of the fraction is the same. This process works with both numbers and variables. Try reducing the following fraction:

$$\frac{18x^2}{60x} =$$

Start canceling common factors on the top and bottom. You can do so in any order. If you want, you can even break all the way down to primes, then cancel. (The math below uses the × symbol to be very explicit about all the multiplication.)

$$\frac{18x^2}{60x} = \frac{2 \times 3 \times 3 \times x \times x}{2 \times 2 \times 3 \times 5 \times x}$$

The top and the bottom each contain a 2, a 3, and an *x*. These are the common factors to cancel. Here's one way to do so:

$$\frac{18x^2}{60x} = \frac{\cancel{2} \times 3 \times \cancel{3} \times x \times \cancel{x}}{\cancel{2} \times 2 \times \cancel{3} \times 5 \times \cancel{x}} = \frac{3x}{10}$$

Here's another way to do so:

$$\frac{18x^{\cancel{2}}}{60\cancel{x}} = \frac{18x}{60} = \frac{\cancel{2} \times 9x}{\cancel{2} \times 30} = \frac{9x}{30} = \frac{\cancel{3} \times 3x}{\cancel{3} \times 10} = \frac{3x}{10}$$

If you feel comfortable canceling all at once, feel free to do so—but if this opens you up to careless mistakes, write the math out more fully. Here's a more compressed version:

$$\frac{\overset{3}{\cancel{18}}x^{\cancel{2}}}{\underset{10}{\cancel{60}}\,\cancel{x}} = \frac{3x}{10}$$

If you...	Then you...	Like this:
Want to simplify a fraction	Cancel out common factors from the top and bottom	$\dfrac{14}{35} = \dfrac{2 \times \cancel{7}}{5 \times \cancel{7}} = \dfrac{2}{5}$

Check Your Skills

Simplify the following fractions.

10. $\dfrac{25}{40}$

11. $\dfrac{16}{24}$

Answers can be found on page 164.

Multiply Fractions: Simplify First, then Multiply

What is $\dfrac{1}{2}$ of 6?

One-half of 6 is 3. When you take $\dfrac{1}{2}$ of 6, you divide 6 into two equal parts (since the denominator of $\dfrac{1}{2}$ is 2).

Then you keep one part (since the numerator of $\dfrac{1}{2}$ is 1). If your starting point is 6, then that one part equals 3.

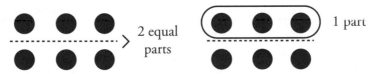

One-half *of* 6 is the same thing as one-half *times* 6. It's also the same thing as 6 divided by 2. Either way, you get 3.

$$\frac{1}{2} \times 6 = 3 \qquad\qquad \frac{6}{2} = 6 \div 2 = 3$$

Now consider this problem:

What is $\dfrac{1}{2}$ of $\dfrac{3}{4}$?

In other words, what is $\dfrac{1}{2} \times \dfrac{3}{4}$?

To multiply two fractions, multiply the tops together and multiply the bottoms together.

$$\frac{1}{2} \times \frac{3}{4} = \frac{1 \times 3}{2 \times 4} = \frac{3}{8}$$

The rule works for integers, too. Just put the integer over 1.

$$\frac{3}{4} \times \frac{5}{7} = \frac{3 \times 5}{4 \times 7} = \frac{15}{28} \qquad\qquad \frac{1}{2} \times 6 = \frac{1}{2} \times \frac{6}{1} = \frac{6}{2} = 3$$

But wait! Don't multiply immediately. Whenever possible, *cancel factors before you multiply out*, or simplify before you multiply. Take a look at these numbers; can you simplify first?

$$\frac{33}{7} \times \frac{14}{3} =$$

The terribly long way to do this multiplication is to multiply the tops, then multiply the bottoms, then reduce the numerator and denominator. You'd first have to multiply 33×14 (ugh) and then take whatever that big number is and divide it by $7 \times 3 = 21$ (double ugh).

But you *can* cancel factors before multiplying! Break the numerators into smaller factors.

$$\frac{33}{7} \times \frac{14}{3} = \frac{11 \times 3}{7} \times \frac{7 \times 2}{3} = \frac{11 \times \cancel{3}^{1}}{\cancel{7}_{1}} \times \frac{\cancel{7}^{1} \times 2}{\cancel{3}_{1}} = \frac{11 \times 2}{1 \times 1} = 22$$

You are allowed to cancel across the multiplication sign (×). In other words, a factor on top of fraction #1 can cancel with a factor on the bottom of fraction #2.

If you prefer, you can also write out the work in this way:

$$\frac{33}{7} \times \frac{14}{3} = \overset{11}{\cancel{33}} \times \frac{14}{\cancel{3}} = \frac{\overset{11}{\cancel{33}}}{\cancel{7}} \times \frac{\overset{2}{\cancel{14}}}{\cancel{3}} = 11 \times 2 = 22$$

When a factor in the denominator cancels to 1, you don't need to write it down. If *all* of the factors in the denominator cancel to 1, the answer will not be a fraction. Technically, the bottom of the calculation shown above is $1 \times 1 = 1$, but the answer $\frac{22}{1}$ simplifies to 22.

Negative signs can make fraction multiplication trickier. Again, a negative sign can appear anywhere in a fraction:

$$-\frac{2}{3} = \frac{-2}{3} = \frac{2}{-3}$$

When you multiply a fraction by -1, you put a negative sign in the fraction. Where you put it is up to you, though the most common place to put the negative sign is out in front of the fraction. For example:

$$-1 \times \frac{3}{5} = -\frac{3}{5} = \frac{-3}{5} = \frac{3}{-5}$$

In general, think of it as multiplying *either* the numerator *or* the denominator by -1.

$$-1 \times \frac{8}{7} = -\frac{8}{7} \text{ OR } \frac{-8}{7} \text{ OR } \frac{8}{-7}$$

If the fraction already contains a negative sign, then cancel out both negatives, because $-1 \times -1 = 1$.

$$-1 \times -\frac{8}{7} = -1 \times -1 \times \frac{8}{7} = \frac{8}{7}$$

$$-1 \times \frac{-8}{7} = \frac{-1 \times (-8)}{7} = \frac{8}{7}$$

If you...	Then you...	Like this:
Multiply two fractions	Multiply tops and multiply bottoms, canceling common factors first	$\frac{20}{9} \times \frac{6}{5} = \frac{\overset{4}{\cancel{20}}}{\underset{3}{\cancel{9}}} \times \frac{\overset{2}{\cancel{6}}}{\cancel{5}}$ $= \frac{4 \times 2}{3} = \frac{8}{3}$

Check Your Skills

Evaluate the following expressions. Simplify all fractions.

12. $\dfrac{3}{7} \times \dfrac{6}{10} =$

13. $\dfrac{5}{14} \times \dfrac{7}{20} =$

Answers can be found on page 164.

Square a Proper Fraction: It Gets Smaller

What is $\left(\dfrac{1}{2}\right)^2$?

Now that you can multiply fractions, you can apply exponents.

$$\left(\frac{1}{2}\right)^2 = \frac{1}{2} \times \frac{1}{2} = \frac{1}{4}$$

Notice that $\dfrac{1}{4}$ is *less* than $\dfrac{1}{2}$. When you square a number greater than 1, it gets bigger. When you square a negative number, it also gets bigger. But when you square a proper fraction (between 0 and 1), it gets *smaller*.

The same is true for greater powers (cubes, etc.). *If you square, cube, or apply any greater power to a proper fraction (between 0 and 1), the number will get smaller.*

In general, if you multiply *any* positive number by a proper fraction, the result is smaller than the original number. You are taking a *fraction* of that number. For instance, if you take $\dfrac{1}{2}$ of 3, you will get $\dfrac{1}{2} \times 3 = \dfrac{3}{2}$. The answer is smaller than the starting number, 3.

By the way, what happens if you square 0 or 1?

You get the same number! $0^2 = 0$ and $1^2 = 1$. Here are some more rules for your book:

If you...	Then you...	Like this:
Square a proper fraction (between 0 and 1)	Get a smaller number	$\left(\dfrac{1}{3}\right)^2 = \dfrac{1}{9}$ $\dfrac{1}{9} < \dfrac{1}{3}$
Square a number greater than 1 or square a negative number	Get a greater number	$2^2 = 4$ $(-3)^2 = 9$
Square 0 or 1	Get the same number	$0^2 = 0$ $1^2 = 1$

Take a Reciprocal: Flip the Fraction

The **reciprocal** of an integer is "1 over" that number. For example, the reciprocal of 5 is 1 over 5, or $\dfrac{1}{5}$.

Any number times its reciprocal equals 1:

$$5 \times \frac{1}{5} = \frac{5}{1} \times \frac{1}{5} = \frac{5}{5} = 1$$ (You could also cancel all the factors as you multiply.)

Consider this example:

What is the reciprocal of $\dfrac{2}{3}$?

To find the reciprocal of a fraction, *flip the fraction*. The reciprocal of $\dfrac{2}{3}$ is $\dfrac{3}{2}$, since the product of $\dfrac{2}{3}$ and $\dfrac{3}{2}$ is 1.

$$\frac{2}{3} \times \frac{3}{2} = \frac{6}{6} = 1$$

If you write an integer as a fraction over 1, then the flipping rule works for integers as well. The integer 9 is $\dfrac{9}{1}$, and the reciprocal of 9 is $\dfrac{1}{9}$.

Keep track of negative signs. The reciprocal of a negative fraction will also be negative.

$$\frac{-5}{6} \times \frac{6}{-5} = \frac{-30}{-30} = 1$$

The reciprocal of $\dfrac{-5}{6}$ is $\dfrac{6}{-5}$, more commonly written as $-\dfrac{6}{5}$.

If you...	Then you...	Like this:	
		Fraction	Reciprocal
Want the reciprocal of a fraction	Flip the fraction	$\dfrac{4}{7}$ $\rightarrow$	$\dfrac{7}{4}$
		$\dfrac{4}{7} \times \dfrac{7}{4} = 1$	

MANHATTAN PREP

Divide by a Fraction: Multiply by the Reciprocal

What is $6 \div 2$?

Interestingly, $6 \div 2$ gives the same result as $6 \times \dfrac{1}{2}$:

$$6 \div 2 = 6 \times \frac{1}{2} = 3$$

The numbers 2 and $\dfrac{1}{2}$ are reciprocals of each other. This pattern generalizes: *Dividing by a number is the same as multiplying by its reciprocal.* Try this example:

$$\frac{5}{6} \div \frac{4}{7} =$$

First, find the reciprocal of the second fraction (the one you're dividing *by*). Then multiply the first fraction by that reciprocal.

$$\frac{5}{6} \div \frac{4}{7} = \frac{5}{6} \times \frac{7}{4} = \frac{35}{24}$$

Sometimes you see a double-decker fraction. It's just one fraction divided by another. The longer fraction bar is the primary division.

$$\frac{\dfrac{5}{6}}{\dfrac{4}{7}} = \frac{5}{6} \div \frac{4}{7} = \frac{5}{6} \times \frac{7}{4} = \frac{35}{24}$$

This works with variables as well. Flip the bottom fraction and multiply.

$$\frac{\dfrac{3}{x}}{\dfrac{5}{x}} = \frac{3}{x} \times \frac{x}{5} = \frac{3}{\cancel{x}} \times \frac{\cancel{x}}{5} = \frac{3}{5}$$

As always, dividing by 0 is forbidden, so x cannot equal 0 in this case.

If you...	Then you...	Like this:
Divide something by a fraction	Multiply by that fraction's reciprocal	$\dfrac{3}{2} \div \dfrac{7}{11} = \dfrac{3}{2} \times \dfrac{11}{7}$

Check Your Skills

Evaluate and simplify the following expressions.

14. $\dfrac{1}{6} \div \dfrac{1}{11}$

15. $\dfrac{8}{5} \div \dfrac{4}{15}$

Answers can be found on pages 164–165.

Addition in the Numerator: Pull Out a Common Factor

If a fraction contains addition or subtraction in the numerator or denominator, tread carefully.

The fraction bar always tells you to *divide the entire numerator by the entire denominator*. To respect PEMDAS, think of the fraction bar as a grouping symbol, like parentheses. For example:

$$\frac{3x^2 + y}{2y^2 - z} = (3x^2 + y) \div (2y^2 - z)$$

Consider a cleaner example, one with simple terms and one subtraction in the numerator:

$$\frac{9x - 6}{3x}$$

The entire quantity $9x - 6$ is divided by $3x$. In other words, you have $(9x - 6) \div 3x$.

To simplify $\dfrac{9x - 6}{3x}$, you need to *find a common factor of the entire numerator and the entire denominator*. That is, you need to find a common factor that you can pull out of both the $9x$ *and* the 6, as well as the $3x$ in the denominator.

What factor does $3x$ have in common with the quantity $9x - 6$? Notice that x is not a common factor, because you can't pull it out of the *entire* numerator; the 6 does not contain an x. But you can pull a 3 out because both 9 and 6 have 3 as a factor.

In the numerator, $9x - 6 = 3 \times (3x - 2)$, or $3(3x - 2)$.

$$\frac{9x - 6}{3x} = \frac{3(3x - 2)}{3x}$$

Now cancel out the common factor on the top and bottom.

$$\frac{9x - 6}{3x} = \frac{\cancel{3}(3x - 2)}{\cancel{3}x} = \frac{3x - 2}{x}$$

The common factor could include a variable.

$$\frac{9y^2 - 6y}{12y} = \frac{\cancel{3y}(3y - 2)}{\cancel{3y}(4)} = \frac{3y - 2}{4}$$

If you feel comfortable simplifying without explicitly pulling out the common factor first, you can do so. Remember that you have to cancel from each separate term, $9y^2$, $6y$, and $12y$:

$$\frac{9y^2 - 6y}{12y} = \frac{^3\cancel{9}\,y^2 - ^2\cancel{6}\,\cancel{y}}{_4\cancel{12}\,\cancel{y}} = \frac{3y - 2}{4}$$

If you find yourself making too many careless mistakes that way, though, then pull out the common factor before you cancel.

If you...	Then you...	Like this:
Have addition or subtraction in the numerator	Pull out a factor from the entire numerator and cancel that factor with the same one in the denominator	$\dfrac{5x + 10y}{25y} = \dfrac{\cancel{5}(x + 2y)}{\cancel{5}(5y)}$ $= \dfrac{x + 2y}{5y}$

Check Your Skills

Simplify the following expression.

16. $\dfrac{4x^2 + 20xy}{12x}$

Answer can be found on page 165.

Addition in the Numerator: Split into Two Fractions (Maybe)

After you've canceled common factors, you still might not see your answer among the answer choices. In that case, you can try one more thing. Remember this?

$$\frac{13}{4} = \frac{12 + 1}{4} = \frac{12}{4} + \frac{1}{4}$$

If you have a sum in the numerator, you can rewrite the fraction as the sum of two fractions. The same is true if you have a difference (subtraction).

Consider this example again.

$$\frac{9x - 6}{3x} =$$

The first step is to cancel common factors from the numerator and denominator.

$$\frac{9x - 6}{3x} = \frac{\cancel{3}(3x - 2)}{\cancel{3}x} = \frac{3x - 2}{x}$$

It's often fine to stop there. But since you have a difference on top, you can go farther by splitting the fraction into two fractions:

$$\frac{3x-2}{x} = \frac{3x}{x} - \frac{2}{x}$$

Now you can simplify the first fraction further by canceling the common factor of x on the top and bottom. Here's the full math:

$$\frac{9x-6}{3x} = \frac{\cancel{3}(3x-2)}{\cancel{3}x} = \frac{3x-2}{x} = \frac{3\cancel{x}}{\cancel{x}} - \frac{2}{x} = 3 - \frac{2}{x}$$

That's as far as you can possibly go. Is $3 - \frac{2}{x}$ simpler than $\frac{3x-2}{x}$? In a technical sense, no. But you still might have to split the fraction, depending on the available answer choices. In fact, one of the main reasons you simplify is to make an expression or equation look like one of the answer choices.

Consider this problem involving square roots:

$$\frac{10\sqrt{2}+\sqrt{6}}{2\sqrt{2}} =$$

(A) $\frac{5+\sqrt{6}}{2}$

(B) $5 + \frac{\sqrt{6}}{2}$

(C) $5 + \frac{\sqrt{3}}{2}$

It's hard to spot a common factor in the numerator that will cancel with one in the denominator. So, if you're stuck, try splitting the fraction in two.

$$\frac{10\sqrt{2}+\sqrt{6}}{2\sqrt{2}} = \frac{10\sqrt{2}}{2\sqrt{2}} + \frac{\sqrt{6}}{2\sqrt{2}}$$

Now deal with the two fractions separately. Cancel a $\sqrt{2}$ out of the top and bottom of the first fraction.

$$\frac{10\cancel{\sqrt{2}}}{2\cancel{\sqrt{2}}} = \frac{10}{2} = 5$$

The second fraction is trickier. A rule from the Exponents & Roots chapter is that when you divide roots, you can combine the numbers under one square root sign: $\frac{\sqrt{6}}{\sqrt{2}} = \sqrt{\frac{6}{2}} = \sqrt{3}$. That's not exactly the second fraction, but it's close. Just keep the extra 2 on the bottom, separated out. Introduce a factor of 1 on top as a temporary placeholder.

$$\frac{\sqrt{6}}{2\sqrt{2}} = \frac{1\times\sqrt{6}}{2\times\sqrt{2}} = \frac{1}{2}\times\sqrt{\frac{6}{2}} = \frac{1}{2}\times\sqrt{3} = \frac{\sqrt{3}}{2}$$

Putting it all together, you have $5+\dfrac{\sqrt{3}}{2}$. The answer is (C).

If you...	Then you...	Like this:
Have addition or subtraction in the numerator	Might split the fraction into two fractions	$\dfrac{a+b}{c}=\dfrac{a}{c}+\dfrac{b}{c}$

Check Your Skills

17. $\dfrac{x+y}{xy}$ is equivalent to which of the following for all nonzero values of x and y?

(A) $\dfrac{1}{x}+\dfrac{1}{y}$

(B) $\dfrac{1+y}{y}$

(C) $\dfrac{x+1}{x}$

Answer can be found on page 165.

Addition in the Denominator: Pull Out a Common Factor, but Never Split

To simplify a fraction with addition (or subtraction) in the *denominator*, you can do one of the same things as before. You can *pull out a common factor from the denominator, and cancel with a factor in the numerator.*

Consider this example:

$$\frac{4x}{8x-12}=$$

You can factor a 4 out of $8x-12$ and cancel it with the 4 in the numerator.

$$\frac{4x}{8x-12}=\frac{4x}{4(2x-3)}=\frac{\cancel{4}x}{\cancel{4}(2x-3)}=\frac{x}{2x-3}$$

That's all legal so far. But you *cannot* go any farther. *Never split a fraction in two because of addition or subtraction in the denominator.* Consider this example:

Is $\dfrac{1}{3+4}$ equal to $\dfrac{1}{3}+\dfrac{1}{4}$?

No, because $\dfrac{1}{3+4}=\dfrac{1}{7}$, while $\dfrac{1}{3}+\dfrac{1}{4}=\dfrac{7}{12}$.

Do not be tempted to split $\dfrac{x}{2x-3}$ into anything else. That's as far as you can go.

4

If you...	Then you...	Like this:
Have addition or subtraction in the denominator	Pull out a factor from the entire denominator and cancel that factor with one in the numerator...but *never* split the fraction in two!	$\dfrac{3y}{y^2+xy}=\dfrac{3\cancel{y}}{\cancel{y}(y+x)}$ $=\dfrac{3}{y+x}$

Check Your Skills

18. $\dfrac{5a^3}{15ab^2-5a^3}$ is equivalent to which of the following?

(A) $\dfrac{a^2}{3b^2}-1$ (B) $\dfrac{a^2}{3b^2-a^2}$ (C) $\dfrac{1}{15ab^2}$

Answer can be found on page 165.

Add, Subtract, Multiply, Divide Nasty Fractions: Add Parentheses

Complicated fractions, such as $\dfrac{4x}{8x-12}$, can be a headache, but they follow the same rules of addition, subtraction, multiplication, and division as do all other fractions.

> **Addition:** Use the double-cross, or find a common denominator, then add numerators.
> **Subtraction:** Use the double-cross, or find a common denominator, then subtract numerators.
> **Multiplication:** Cancel common factors, then multiply tops and multiply bottoms.
> **Division:** Flip, then multiply.

With complicated fractions, the most important point to remember is this: *Treat the numerators and denominators as if they have parentheses around them.* This preserves the order of operations (PEMDAS).

Consider this sum:

$$\frac{1}{y+1}+\frac{2}{y}=$$

The same principle of addition holds. Do these fractions have the same denominator?

No. So use the double-cross to add. $\dfrac{1}{y+1}\overset{(1)(y)\ +\ 2(2)(y+1)}{\underset{}{\times}}\dfrac{2}{y}=\dfrac{y+(2y+2)}{y(y+1)}=\dfrac{3y+2}{y(y+1)}$

You could also write the answer as $\dfrac{3y+2}{y^2+y}$.

Consider this product:

$$\left(\frac{2w+4}{z^3+z}\right)\left(\frac{z}{2}\right)=$$

You could just multiply the tops and multiply the bottoms, but don't forget to cancel common factors as best as you can *before* you multiply. Start by pulling out factors from the ugly fraction on the left.

$$\frac{2w+4}{z^3+z} = \frac{2(w+2)}{z(z^2+1)}$$

4

Now plug that back into the product, and cancel common factors.

$$\left(\frac{2w+4}{z^3+z}\right)\left(\frac{z}{2}\right) = \left(\frac{2(w+2)}{z(z^2+1)}\right)\left(\frac{z}{2}\right) = \left(\frac{\cancel{2}(w+2)}{\cancel{z}(z^2+1)}\right)\left(\frac{\cancel{z}}{\cancel{2}}\right) = \frac{w+2}{z^2+1}$$

If you...	Then you...	Like this:
Add, subtract, multiply, or divide fractions with complicated numerators and/or denominators	Throw parentheses around those numerators and/or denominators, then proceed normally—find common denominators, cancel common factors, etc.	$\dfrac{3}{m+2} - \dfrac{2}{m} = \dfrac{(3)(m) - (2)(m+2)}{m+2 \quad m}$ $= \dfrac{3m-(2m+4)}{m(m+2)}$ $= \dfrac{m-4}{m(m+2)}$

Check Your Skills

19. $\dfrac{x+1}{x-1} - \dfrac{3}{4} =$

Answer can be found on page 165.

Fractions within Fractions: Work Your Way Out

Remember double-decker fractions in fraction division?

$$\frac{\dfrac{5}{6}}{\dfrac{4}{7}} = \frac{5}{6} \div \frac{4}{7} = \frac{5}{6} \times \frac{7}{4} = \frac{35}{24}$$

When you see a fraction within a fraction, *work your way out from the deepest level inside*. Try this example:

$$\frac{1}{1+\dfrac{1}{3}} =$$

Forget about the entire expression for a moment. Just focus on the deepest level: $1 + \dfrac{1}{3}$.

Find a common denominator.

$$1 + \frac{1}{3} = \frac{3}{3} + \frac{1}{3} = \frac{4}{3}$$

Now move up a level in the original expression.

$$\frac{1}{1 + \frac{1}{3}} = \frac{1}{\frac{4}{3}}$$

The number 1 divided by a fraction is the same as taking the reciprocal of that fraction in the denominator. Here's how that works:

$$\frac{1}{1 + \frac{1}{3}} = \frac{1}{\frac{4}{3}} = \frac{1}{1} \div \frac{4}{3} = \frac{1}{1} \times \frac{3}{4} = \frac{3}{4}$$

That's the answer. Try another one, this time a three-level problem:

$$\frac{1}{2 + \frac{1}{3 + \frac{1}{4}}} =$$

Again, start at the deepest level: $3 + \frac{1}{4}$. Turn this into a mixed fraction: $3 + \frac{1}{4} = \frac{12}{4} + \frac{1}{4} = \frac{13}{4}$. Now move up a level:

$$\frac{1}{2 + \frac{1}{3 + \frac{1}{4}}} = \frac{1}{2 + \frac{1}{\frac{13}{4}}}$$

Remember that 1 divided by a fraction is the same thing as taking the reciprocal of the fraction in the denominator:

$$\frac{1}{2 + \frac{1}{3 + \frac{1}{4}}} = \frac{1}{2 + \frac{1}{\frac{13}{4}}} = \frac{1}{2 + \frac{4}{13}}$$

Now add the two terms in the bottom part:

$$2 + \frac{4}{13} = \frac{26}{13} + \frac{4}{13} = \frac{30}{13}$$

Now replace that in the original fraction. You've almost reached the surface:

$$\cfrac{1}{2+\cfrac{1}{3+\cfrac{1}{4}}} = \cfrac{1}{2+\cfrac{1}{\cfrac{13}{4}}} = \cfrac{1}{2+\cfrac{4}{13}} = \cfrac{1}{\cfrac{30}{13}}$$

Finally, you have another 1 divided by a fraction. Take the reciprocal:

$$\cfrac{1}{2+\cfrac{1}{3+\cfrac{1}{4}}} = \cfrac{1}{2+\cfrac{1}{\cfrac{13}{4}}} = \cfrac{1}{2+\cfrac{4}{13}} = \cfrac{1}{\cfrac{30}{13}} = \frac{13}{30}$$

That was a lot of steps! If you can do that problem, then you can tackle any fraction within a fraction that you might see on the real test.

If you...	Then you...	Like this:
Encounter a fraction within a fraction	Work your way out from the deepest level inside	$\cfrac{1}{y+\cfrac{1}{\boxed{2-\cfrac{3}{y}}}}$ Focus here

Check Your Skills

20. $\dfrac{1+\dfrac{3}{4}}{2} =$

Answer can be found on page 165.

Check Your Skills Answer Key

1. $\dfrac{10x}{yz^2}$: The denominator stays the same. Add the numerators.

$$\frac{3x}{yz^2}+\frac{7x}{yz^2}=\frac{3x+7x}{yz^2}=\frac{10x}{yz^2}$$

2. $\dfrac{5}{4}$ or $1\dfrac{1}{4}$: The denominator 4 is already a multiple of the denominator 2. Because only one of the fractions needs to change, use the traditional method to solve this one.

$$\frac{1}{2}+\frac{3}{4}=\frac{1\times2}{2\times2}+\frac{3}{4}=\frac{2}{4}+\frac{3}{4}=\frac{2+3}{4}=\frac{5}{4}$$

3. $\dfrac{7}{24}$: This time, the 3 and the 8 don't share any factors, so the double-cross is the best way to proceed.

$$\frac{2}{3}-\frac{3}{8}=\frac{7}{24}$$

Here is the traditional approach:

$$\frac{2}{3}-\frac{3}{8}=\frac{2\times8}{3\times8}-\frac{3\times3}{8\times3}=\frac{16}{24}-\frac{9}{24}=\frac{16-9}{24}=\frac{7}{24}$$

4. $\dfrac{5}{7}$: The denominators of the two fractions are the same, but the numerator 5 is greater, so $\dfrac{5}{7}>\dfrac{3}{7}$.

5. $\dfrac{3}{10}$: The numerators of the two fractions are the same, but the denominator of $\dfrac{3}{10}$ is smaller, so $\dfrac{3}{10}>\dfrac{3}{13}$. Alternatively, you could double-cross.

$$\frac{3}{10}\quad\frac{3}{13}$$

39 is greater than 30, so $\dfrac{3}{10}$ is the greater fraction.

6. $1\dfrac{5}{6}$: The denominator 6 goes into 11 just once, so the quotient is 1 and the remainder is $11-6=5$. Alternatively, split the numerator into two parts.

$$\frac{11}{6}=\frac{6+5}{6}=\frac{6}{6}+\frac{5}{6}=1+\frac{5}{6}=1\frac{5}{6}$$

7. $9\dfrac{1}{11}$: Think of multiples of 11. How close can you get to 100 without going over? $11 \times 9 = 99$, with 1 left over.

$$\frac{100}{11} = \frac{99+1}{11} = \frac{99}{11} + \frac{1}{11} = 9 + \frac{1}{11} = 9\frac{1}{11}$$

8. $\dfrac{15}{4}$: The shortcut is $\dfrac{4 \times 3 + 3}{4} = \dfrac{12+3}{4} = \dfrac{15}{4}$. Here's the full path:

$$3\frac{3}{4} = 3 + \frac{3}{4} = \frac{3}{1} \times \frac{4}{4} + \frac{3}{4} = \frac{12}{4} + \frac{3}{4} = \frac{15}{4}$$

9. $\dfrac{27}{4}$: The shortcut is $\dfrac{6 \times 4 + 3}{4} = \dfrac{24+3}{4} = \dfrac{27}{4}$. The full path is:

$$6\frac{3}{4} = 6 + \frac{3}{4} = \frac{6}{1} \times \frac{4}{4} + \frac{3}{4} = \frac{24}{4} + \frac{3}{4} = \frac{27}{4}$$

10. $\dfrac{5}{8}$:

$$\frac{25}{40} = \frac{5 \times 5}{8 \times 5} = \frac{5 \times \cancel{5}}{8 \times \cancel{5}} = \frac{5}{8}$$

11. $\dfrac{2}{3}$:

$$\frac{16}{24} = \frac{2 \times 8}{3 \times 8} = \frac{2 \times \cancel{8}}{3 \times \cancel{8}} = \frac{2}{3}$$

12. $\dfrac{9}{35}$:

$$\frac{3}{7} \times \frac{6}{10} = \frac{3}{7} \times \frac{\overset{3}{\cancel{6}}}{\underset{5}{\cancel{10}}} = \frac{9}{35}$$

13. $\dfrac{1}{8}$: When a factor in the numerator cancels to 1, do still write it down; in this problem, the numerator simplifies to 1. It's safe to ignore a 1 only when a factor in the *denominator* cancels to 1.

$$\frac{5}{14} \times \frac{7}{20} = \frac{\overset{1}{\cancel{5}}}{\underset{2}{\cancel{14}}} \times \frac{\overset{1}{\cancel{7}}}{\underset{4}{\cancel{20}}} = \frac{1}{2} \times \frac{1}{4} = \frac{1}{8}$$

14. $\dfrac{11}{6}$:

$$\frac{1}{6} \div \frac{1}{11} = \frac{1}{6} \times \frac{11}{1} = \frac{11}{6}$$

MANHATTAN PREP

15. **6:**

$$\frac{8}{5} \div \frac{4}{15} = \frac{8}{5} \times \frac{15}{4} = \frac{\overset{2}{\cancel{8}}}{\cancel{5}} \times \frac{\overset{3}{\cancel{15}}}{\cancel{4}} = 6$$

16. $\dfrac{x+5y}{3}$:

$$\frac{4x^2 + 20xy}{12x} = \frac{\cancel{4x}\,(x+5y)}{\cancel{4x}\,(3)} = \frac{x+5y}{3}$$

17. **(A):** Split the fraction into two.

$$\frac{x+y}{xy} = \frac{\cancel{x}}{\cancel{x}\,y} + \frac{\cancel{y}}{x\,\cancel{y}} = \frac{1}{y} + \frac{1}{x}$$

18. **(B):** Don't split the denominator!

$$\frac{5a^3}{15ab^2 - 5a^3} = \frac{\cancel{5}\,a^{\cancel{3}\,2}}{\cancel{5}\,\cancel{a}\,(3b^2 - a^2)} = \frac{a^2}{3b^2 - a^2}$$

19. $\dfrac{x+7}{4x-4}$:

$$\frac{x+1}{x-1} - \frac{3}{4} \quad = \quad \overset{(4)(x+1)}{\underset{x-1}{x+1}} - \overset{(3)(x-1)}{\underset{4}{\frac{3}{4}}} \quad = \quad \frac{(4x+4) - (3x-3)}{4(x-1)} \quad = \quad \frac{x+7}{4x-4}$$

20. $\dfrac{7}{8}$:

$$\frac{1 + \frac{3}{4}}{2} = \frac{\frac{4}{4} + \frac{3}{4}}{2} = \frac{\frac{7}{4}}{2} = \frac{7}{4} \times \frac{1}{2} = \frac{7}{8}$$

Chapter Review: Drill Sets

Drill 1

For each of the following pairs of fractions, decide which fraction is greater.

1. $\dfrac{1}{4}, \dfrac{3}{4}$

2. $\dfrac{1}{5}, \dfrac{1}{6}$

3. $\dfrac{53}{52}, \dfrac{85}{86}$

4. $\dfrac{7}{9}, \dfrac{6}{10}$

5. $\dfrac{700}{360}, \dfrac{590}{290}$

Drill 2

Add or subtract the following fractions. Answers should be in their most simplified form. For any problems with variables in the denominator, assume that the denominator does not equal zero.

6. $\dfrac{7}{9} - \dfrac{2}{9}$

7. $\dfrac{2}{3} + \dfrac{5}{9}$

8. $\dfrac{4}{9} + \dfrac{8}{11}$

9. $\dfrac{20}{12} - \dfrac{5}{3}$

10. $\dfrac{52}{11x} + \dfrac{25}{11x}$

11. $\dfrac{a}{12} - \dfrac{b}{6} - \dfrac{b}{4}$

12. $\dfrac{u}{w} + 1$

13. $\sqrt{\dfrac{7}{5}} - \sqrt{\dfrac{5}{7}}$

   (A) $\dfrac{2}{\sqrt{35}}$

   (B) $\sqrt{35}$

   (C) $\dfrac{\sqrt{2}}{\sqrt{35}}$

14. $\dfrac{x^2 z}{yz} - \dfrac{x^2 z}{xy} + \dfrac{3xz}{y}$

   (A) $\dfrac{x^2 - 4xz}{y}$

   (B) $\dfrac{x(x + 2z)}{y}$

   (C) $\dfrac{2x^2 z + 3xz}{xyz}$

15. $\dfrac{24}{3\sqrt{2}} - \dfrac{4}{\sqrt{2}}$

   (A) $2\sqrt{2}$

   (B) 4

   (C) $8\sqrt{2}$

Drill 3

Convert the following improper fractions to mixed numbers.

16. $\dfrac{9}{4}$

17. $\dfrac{31}{7}$

18. $\dfrac{47}{15}$

19. $\dfrac{70}{20}$

20. $\dfrac{72}{12}$

Drill 4

Convert the following mixed numbers to improper fractions.

21. $3\dfrac{2}{3}$

22. $2\dfrac{1}{6}$

23. $6\dfrac{3}{7}$

24. $4\dfrac{5}{9}$

25. $12\dfrac{5}{12}$

Drill 5

Simplify the following expressions. For any problems with variables in the denominator, assume that the denominator does not equal zero.

26. $\dfrac{5}{8}-\dfrac{4}{8}$

27. $\dfrac{7}{9}-\dfrac{2}{9}$

28. $\dfrac{1}{3}+\dfrac{7}{5}$

29. $\dfrac{3}{4}-\dfrac{10}{4}$

30. $\dfrac{2\sqrt{18}}{15}$

31. $\dfrac{17^2\times 22}{11\times 34}$

32. $\dfrac{48yz^3}{12z}$

33. $\dfrac{2r\sqrt{54}}{r^2s\sqrt{12}}$

34. $\dfrac{6x^8yz^5}{46x^6y^2z^3}$

35. If $a>0$, $\dfrac{3ab^2\sqrt{50}}{\sqrt{18a^2}}$

Drill 6

Multiply or divide the following fractions. Resulting fractions should be put in their most simplified form. For any problems with variables in the denominator, assume that the denominator does not equal zero.

36. $\dfrac{14}{20}\times\dfrac{15}{21}$

37. $\dfrac{6}{25}\div\dfrac{9}{10}$

38. $\dfrac{3}{11}\div\dfrac{3}{11}$

39. $\dfrac{x^4}{wyz}\times\dfrac{w^2z}{x^2y}$

40. $\dfrac{3^2}{4^2}\times\dfrac{2^2}{5^2}\times\dfrac{10}{3}$

41. $\dfrac{\sqrt{25}}{\sqrt{10}}\times\dfrac{\sqrt{8}}{\sqrt{15}}$

42. $\dfrac{\sqrt{12}}{5}\times\dfrac{\sqrt{60}}{2^4}\times\dfrac{\sqrt{45}}{3^2}$

43. $\dfrac{\sqrt{18}}{\sqrt{4}}\div\dfrac{\sqrt{9}}{\sqrt{18}}$

44. $\dfrac{xy^3z^4}{x^3y^4z^2}\div\dfrac{x^6y^3z}{x^3y^5z^2}$

45. $\dfrac{12^2}{9^2}\div\dfrac{6^3}{3^5}$

Drill 7

Simplify the following fractions. For any problems with variables in the denominator, assume that the denominator does not equal zero.

46. $\dfrac{6x+8}{2x}$

47. $\dfrac{9a+4b}{3ab}$

   (A) $\dfrac{13}{3}$

   (B) $\dfrac{3a+4b}{ab}$

   (C) $\dfrac{3}{b}+\dfrac{4}{3a}$

48. $\dfrac{6a}{33a+21ab}$

49. $\dfrac{2y\sqrt{5}}{5y\sqrt{20}-2y\sqrt{45}}$

50. $\dfrac{8x^2+40x}{32x-24x^2}$

Drill 8

Simplify the following expressions. Final answers should be in their most simplified forms, but it is not necessary to convert improper fractions into mixed fractions. For any problems with variables in the denominator, assume that the denominator does not equal zero.

51. $\dfrac{3+4}{1+2}-\dfrac{1+2}{3+4}$

52. $\dfrac{3}{x+2}\times\dfrac{1}{5}$

53. $\dfrac{7}{n+3}\times\dfrac{n+1}{2}$

54. $\dfrac{x+2}{4}+\dfrac{x+3}{4}$

55. $\dfrac{-t+1}{t-2}\times\dfrac{-t}{2}$

56. $\dfrac{b+6}{6}-\dfrac{3+b}{6}$

57. $\dfrac{x(3+\sqrt{3})}{9}-\dfrac{x}{3}$

58. $\dfrac{3x^2+3y}{40}+\dfrac{x^2+y}{8}$

Drill 9

Match the following expressions to their simplified forms. For any problems with variables in the denominator, assume that the denominator does not equal zero.

59. $\dfrac{4t}{6}\times\dfrac{-3}{t-3}$

   (A) $\dfrac{-2t}{t-3}$

   (B) $\dfrac{4t-3}{6t-18}$

   (C) $\dfrac{2}{3}$

60. $\dfrac{x+3}{15}\times\dfrac{10}{x+3}$

   (A) $\dfrac{2}{3}$

   (B) $2x+6$

   (C) $\dfrac{2(x+3)}{3}$

61. $\dfrac{m^3}{m-2}\times\dfrac{m+3}{m^2}$

   (A) $m+1$

   (B) $\dfrac{m^2+3m}{m-2}$

   (C) $\dfrac{m^3+3m^2}{2m}$

62. $\dfrac{(n+2n)}{n^4} \times \dfrac{(2n)^2}{(15n-5n)}$

(A) $\dfrac{2n^2+4n^3}{15n^4-5n^5}$

(B) $\dfrac{6}{5n^2}$

(C) $\dfrac{n^7}{n^{16}}$

Drill 10

Simplify the following complex fractions. For any problems with variables in the denominator, assume that the denominator does not equal zero.

63. $\dfrac{3}{3+\dfrac{3}{4}}$

64. $\dfrac{8}{2-\dfrac{2}{3}}$

65. $\dfrac{\dfrac{1}{2}+\dfrac{1}{3}}{\dfrac{7}{6}-\dfrac{3}{4}}$

66. $\dfrac{1}{1-\dfrac{2}{y+1}}$

(A) $\dfrac{y+3}{y+1}$

(B) $\dfrac{y}{y-1}$

(C) $\dfrac{y+1}{y-1}$

Drill Sets Solutions

Drill 1

1. $\frac{3}{4}$: When denominators are the same, the *greater* numerator is the *greater* fraction. The numerator of $\frac{3}{4}$ is greater, so $\frac{3}{4} > \frac{1}{4}$.

2. $\frac{1}{5}$: When numerators are the same, the *smaller* denominator is the *greater* fraction. The denominator of $\frac{1}{5}$ is smaller, so $\frac{1}{5} > \frac{1}{6}$.

3. $\frac{53}{52}$: Finding a common denominator or using the double-cross would both involve ugly multiplication. Instead, consider estimating using some things you know about fractions. In the first fraction, $\frac{53}{52}$, the numerator is greater than the denominator, so the fraction is greater than 1. In the second fraction, $\frac{85}{86}$, the denominator is greater than the numerator, so the fraction is less than 1. Therefore, $\frac{53}{52} > \frac{85}{86}$.

4. $\frac{7}{9}$: Consider using what you know about fractions to compare the relative size of these. The first fraction $\frac{7}{9}$ has both a greater numerator and a smaller denominator than the second fraction. Therefore, $\frac{7}{9} > \frac{6}{10}$. Alternatively, use the double-cross: 70 > 54.

5. $\frac{590}{290}$: Comparing these using the double-cross is going to involve some very ugly math! Try simplifying and estimating. First, simplify each fraction by dropping the extra zeros! Now compare $\frac{70}{36}$ and $\frac{59}{29}$. The first fraction is greater than 1 but less than 2, because 70 is less than twice 36 ($2 \times 36 = 72$). The second fraction is greater than 2, because 59 is more than twice 29 ($2 \times 29 = 58$). So $\frac{590}{290} > \frac{700}{360}$.

Drill 2

6. $\dfrac{5}{9}$: The denominators are already the same, so subtract the numerators.

$$\frac{7}{9} - \frac{2}{9} = \frac{7-2}{9} = \frac{5}{9}$$

7. $\dfrac{11}{9}$: Only the first fraction needs to change, so the traditional method may be faster than the double-cross.

$$\frac{2}{3} + \frac{5}{9} = \frac{2}{3} \times \frac{3}{3} + \frac{5}{9} = \frac{6}{9} + \frac{5}{9} = \frac{6+5}{9} = \frac{11}{9}$$

8. $\dfrac{116}{99}$: The denominators don't share any factors, so use the double-cross.

$$\frac{4}{9} + \frac{8}{11} = \overset{44}{\underset{9}{4}} \overset{+}{\times} \overset{72}{\underset{11}{8}} = \frac{116}{99}$$

9. $\mathbf{0}$: Only the second fraction needs to change, so the traditional method may be faster than the double-cross.

$$\frac{20}{12} - \frac{5}{3} = \frac{20}{12} - \frac{5}{3} \times \frac{4}{4} = \frac{20}{12} - \frac{20}{12} = 0$$

10. $\dfrac{7}{x}$: The denominators are already the same. Add the numerators and reduce.

$$\frac{52}{11x} + \frac{25}{11x} = \frac{77}{11x} = \frac{7}{x}$$

11. $\dfrac{a-5b}{12}$: Find a common denominator and subtract. Because both 6 and 4 are factors of 12, 12 is the lowest common denominator.

$$\frac{a}{12} - \frac{b}{6} - \frac{b}{4} = \frac{a}{12} - \frac{2b}{12} - \frac{3b}{12} = \frac{a-2b-3b}{12} = \frac{a-5b}{12}$$

12. $\dfrac{u+w}{w}$: The common denominator of $\dfrac{u}{w}$ and 1 is w.

$$\frac{u}{w} + 1 = \frac{u}{w} + \frac{w}{w} = \frac{u+w}{w}$$

13. **(A):** First, break out the square root signs.

$$\sqrt{\frac{7}{5}} - \sqrt{\frac{5}{7}} = \frac{\sqrt{7}}{\sqrt{5}} - \frac{\sqrt{5}}{\sqrt{7}}$$

Then use the double-cross.

Now, you can simplify. $\sqrt{(7)(7)}$ reduces to 7 and $\sqrt{(5)(5)}$ reduces to 5.

$$\frac{7-5}{\sqrt{35}} = \frac{2}{\sqrt{35}}$$

14. **(B):** Start by simplifying the individual fractions.

$$\frac{x^2 z}{yz} - \frac{x^2 z}{xy} + \frac{3xz}{y} = \frac{x^2 \cancel{z}}{y\cancel{z}} - \frac{x^{\cancel{2}} z}{\cancel{x} y} + \frac{3xz}{y} = \frac{x^2}{y} - \frac{xz}{y} + \frac{3xz}{y}$$

Now you have common denominators, so you can add and subtract.

$$\frac{x^2}{y} - \frac{xz}{y} + \frac{3xz}{y} = \frac{x^2 - xz + 3xz}{y} = \frac{x^2 + 2xz}{y}$$

Glance at the answers. No match yet, but can you see a way to manipulate what you have to match one of the answers?

$$\frac{x^2 + 2xz}{y} = \frac{x(x+2z)}{y}$$

15. **(A):** Glance at the answers. They aren't fractions, so there must be some way to eliminate the denominators. Keep that in mind. First, find a common denominator to combine the two terms. Multiply the second term by $\frac{3}{3}$.

$$\frac{24}{3\sqrt{2}} - \frac{4}{\sqrt{2}} = \frac{24}{3\sqrt{2}} - \frac{12}{3\sqrt{2}} = \frac{24-12}{3\sqrt{2}} = \frac{12}{3\sqrt{2}} = \frac{4}{\sqrt{2}}$$

When you see a root on the bottom of a fraction, get rid of it by multiplying by that root over itself. In this case, the root is $\sqrt{2}$, so multiply the fraction by $\frac{\sqrt{2}}{\sqrt{2}}$.

$$\frac{4}{\sqrt{2}} \times \frac{\sqrt{2}}{\sqrt{2}} = \frac{4\sqrt{2}}{2} = 2\sqrt{2}$$

Drill 3

16. $2\frac{1}{4}$:

$$\frac{9}{4} = \frac{8+1}{4} = \frac{8}{4} + \frac{1}{4} = 2 + \frac{1}{4} = 2\frac{1}{4}$$

17. $4\frac{3}{7}$:

$$\frac{31}{7} = \frac{28+3}{7} = \frac{28}{7} + \frac{3}{7} = 4 + \frac{3}{7} = 4\frac{3}{7}$$

18. $3\frac{2}{15}$:

$$\frac{47}{15} = \frac{45+2}{15} = \frac{45}{15} + \frac{2}{15} = 3 + \frac{2}{15} = 3\frac{2}{15}$$

19. $3\frac{1}{2}$:

$$\frac{70}{20} = \frac{60+10}{20} = \frac{60}{20} + \frac{10}{20} = 3 + \frac{10}{20} = 3 + \frac{1}{2} = 3\frac{1}{2}$$

20. **6:** This one simplifies to an integer.

$$\frac{72}{12} = 6$$

Drill 4

21. $\frac{11}{3}$: Via the shortcut, the numerator is $(3)(3) + 2 = 11$, and the denominator remains 3. Here's the full calculation:

$$3\frac{2}{3} = 3 + \frac{2}{3} = \frac{3 \times 3}{1 \times 3} + \frac{2}{3} = \frac{9}{3} + \frac{2}{3} = \frac{11}{3}$$

22. $\frac{13}{6}$: Via the shortcut, the numerator is $(6)(2) + 1 = 13$, and the denominator remains 6. Here's the full calculation:

$$2\frac{1}{6} = 2 + \frac{1}{6} = \frac{2 \times 6}{1 \times 6} + \frac{1}{6} = \frac{12}{6} + \frac{1}{6} = \frac{13}{6}$$

MANHATTAN PREP

23. $\dfrac{45}{7}$: Via the shortcut, the numerator is $(7)(6) + 3 = 45$, and the denominator remains 7. Here's the full calculation:

$$6\dfrac{3}{7} = 6 + \dfrac{3}{7} = \dfrac{6 \times 7}{1 \times 7} + \dfrac{3}{7} = \dfrac{42}{7} + \dfrac{3}{7} = \dfrac{45}{7}$$

24. $\dfrac{41}{9}$: Via the shortcut, the numerator is $(9)(4) + 5 = 41$, and the denominator remains 9. Here's the full calculation:

$$4\dfrac{5}{9} = 4 + \dfrac{5}{9} = \dfrac{4 \times 9}{1 \times 9} + \dfrac{5}{9} = \dfrac{36}{9} + \dfrac{5}{9} = \dfrac{41}{9}$$

25. $\dfrac{149}{12}$: Via the shortcut, the numerator is $(12)(12) + 5 = 149$, and the denominator remains 12. Here's the full calculation:

$$12\dfrac{5}{12} = 12 + \dfrac{5}{12} = \dfrac{12 \times 12}{1 \times 12} + \dfrac{5}{12} = \dfrac{144}{12} + \dfrac{5}{12} = \dfrac{149}{12}$$

Drill 5

26. $\dfrac{1}{8}$:

$$\dfrac{5}{8} - \dfrac{4}{8} = \dfrac{5 - 4}{8} = \dfrac{1}{8}$$

27. $\dfrac{5}{9}$:

$$\dfrac{7}{9} - \dfrac{2}{9} = \dfrac{7 - 2}{9} = \dfrac{5}{9}$$

28. $\dfrac{26}{15}$ OR $1\dfrac{11}{15}$:

$$\dfrac{1}{3} + \dfrac{7}{5} = \dfrac{26}{15} \text{ or } 1\dfrac{11}{15}$$

29. $-\dfrac{7}{4}$ OR $-1\dfrac{3}{4}$:

$$\dfrac{3}{4} - \dfrac{10}{4} = \dfrac{3 - 10}{4} = \dfrac{-7}{4} \text{ OR } -1\dfrac{3}{4}$$

30. $\dfrac{2\sqrt{2}}{5}$: Begin by simplifying the square root in the numerator. When simplifying a square root, always look for factors that are perfect squares; in this example, $18 = 2 \times 9 = 2 \times 3^2$. The 3^2 can be removed from the square root to become 3.

$$\frac{2\sqrt{18}}{15} = \frac{2\sqrt{2\times 3\times 3}}{15} = \frac{2\times \cancel{3} \times \sqrt{2}}{\cancel{3}\times 5} = \frac{2\sqrt{2}}{5}$$

31. **17** :

$$\frac{17^2 \times 22}{11\times 34} = \frac{17 \times \cancel{17} \times \cancel{2} \times \cancel{11}}{\cancel{11} \times \cancel{2} \times \cancel{17}} = 17$$

32. $4yz^2$: Cancel a 12 from both 48 and 12. Use your exponent rules to simplify z.

$$\frac{48\,yz^3}{12z} = \frac{\overset{4}{\cancel{48}}\,yz^{3-1}}{\cancel{12}} = 4\,yz^2$$

33. $\dfrac{3\sqrt{2}}{rs}$: To begin, simplify the square roots in the numerator and denominator by looking for factors that have pairs.

$$\begin{aligned}\sqrt{54} &= \sqrt{2\times 3\times 3\times 3} = 3\sqrt{2\times 3}\\ \sqrt{12} &= \sqrt{2\times 2\times 3} = 2\sqrt{3}\end{aligned}$$

Because the numbers remaining inside the square roots have a factor of 3 in common, it's useful to leave the numerator broken into the root of 2 and 3.

$$3\sqrt{2\times 3} = 3\sqrt{2}\sqrt{3}$$

Therefore:

$$\frac{2r\sqrt{54}}{r^2s\sqrt{12}} = \frac{2r\left(3\sqrt{2}\sqrt{3}\right)}{r^2 s\left(2\sqrt{3}\right)} = \frac{\cancel{2}\,\cancel{r}\left(3\sqrt{2}\,\cancel{\sqrt{3}}\right)}{r^{\cancel{2}} s\left(\cancel{2}\,\cancel{\sqrt{3}}\right)} = \frac{3\sqrt{2}}{rs}$$

34. $\dfrac{3x^2z^2}{23y}$: There are two good ways to simplify a fraction with variables raised to powers. One approach is to use exponent rules to rewrite the expression so that the cancellations are more clear.

$$\frac{6x^8yz^5}{46x^6y^2z^3} = \frac{\overset{3}{\cancel{6}} \times \cancel{x^6} \times x^2 \times \cancel{y} \times \cancel{z^3} \times z^2}{\underset{23}{\cancel{46}} \times \cancel{x^6} \times \cancel{y} \times y \times \cancel{z^3}} = \frac{3x^2z^2}{23y}$$

Alternatively, if you are comfortable with the exponent rules, use the rules to simplify directly.

$$\frac{6}{46} \times \frac{x^8}{x^6} \times \frac{y}{y^2} \times \frac{z^5}{z^3} = \frac{3}{23} x^2 y^{-1} z^2$$

To combine these into one fraction, leave x^2 and z^2 in the numerator but place y in the denominator because $y^{-1} = \frac{1}{y}$.

$$\frac{3}{23} x^2 y^{-1} z^2 = \frac{3x^2 z^2}{23y}$$

35. $5b^2$: Begin by simplifying the square roots then pull any squares out.

$$\sqrt{50} = \sqrt{2 \times 25} = 5\sqrt{2}$$
$$\sqrt{18a^2} = \sqrt{2 \times 9 \times a^2} = 3a\sqrt{2}$$

Cancel common terms on the top and bottom.

$$\frac{3ab^2\sqrt{50}}{\sqrt{18a^2}} = \frac{\cancel{3}\,\cancel{a}b^2 \times 5\cancel{\sqrt{2}}}{\cancel{3}\,\cancel{a}\,\cancel{\sqrt{2}}} = 5b^2$$

Drill 6

36. $\dfrac{1}{2}$: Remember, you *can* cancel across the multiplication sign.

$$\frac{14}{20} \times \frac{15}{21} = \frac{^2\cancel{14}}{20} \times \frac{15}{\cancel{21}_3} = \frac{^2\cancel{14}}{_4\cancel{20}} \times \frac{\cancel{15}^3}{\cancel{21}_3} = \frac{^1\cancel{2}}{\cancel{4}_2} \times \frac{\cancel{3}^1}{\cancel{3}_1} = \frac{1}{2}$$

37. $\dfrac{4}{15}$: This is starting further left than those prior flip the second fraction to multiply.

$$\frac{6}{25} \div \frac{9}{10} = \frac{6}{25} \times \frac{10}{9} = \frac{^2\cancel{6}}{_5\cancel{25}} \times \frac{\cancel{10}^2}{\cancel{9}_3} = \frac{4}{15}$$

38. **1:**

$$\frac{3}{11} \div \frac{3}{11} = \frac{3}{11} \times \frac{11}{3} = \frac{\cancel{3} \times \cancel{11}}{\cancel{11} \times \cancel{3}} = 1$$

4

39. $\dfrac{x^2 w}{y^2}$:

$$\frac{x^4}{wyz} \times \frac{w^2 z}{x^2 y} = \frac{x^4}{wy\cancel{z}} \times \frac{w^2 \cancel{z}}{x^2 y} = \frac{x^{4-2} w^{2-1}}{y^2} = \frac{x^2 w}{y^2}$$

40. $\dfrac{3}{10}$: Simplify the bases to their prime components, then cancel. 4^2 is the same as $\left(2^2\right)^2$, which equals $(2^2)(2^2)$.

$$\frac{3^2}{4^2} \times \frac{2^2}{5^2} \times \frac{10}{3} = \frac{3^{\cancel{2}}}{\left(2^{\cancel{2}}\right)\left(2^{\cancel{2}}\right)} \times \frac{2^{\cancel{2}}}{5^{\cancel{2}}} \times \frac{\cancel{2} \times \cancel{5}}{\cancel{3}} = \frac{3}{10}$$

41. $\dfrac{2}{\sqrt{3}}$: Combine everything under one square root sign (you're allowed to do this because everything is multiplication or division), and simplify.

$$\frac{\sqrt{25}}{\sqrt{10}} \times \frac{\sqrt{8}}{\sqrt{15}} = \sqrt{\frac{25 \times 8}{10 \times 15}} = \sqrt{\frac{\overset{5}{\cancel{25}} \times \overset{4}{\cancel{8}}}{\underset{5}{\cancel{10}} \times \underset{3}{\cancel{15}}}} = \sqrt{\frac{\overset{\cancel{5}}{\cancel{25}} \times \overset{4}{\cancel{8}}}{\underset{\cancel{5}}{\cancel{10}} \times \underset{3}{\cancel{15}}}} = \sqrt{\frac{4}{3}} = \frac{2}{\sqrt{3}}$$

42. $\dfrac{1}{4}$: Begin by factoring the roots, keeping an eye on what they have in common with each other and with the terms on the bottom. Then combine everything into one big fraction.

$$\frac{\sqrt{12}}{5} \times \frac{\sqrt{60}}{2^4} \times \frac{\sqrt{45}}{3^2} = \frac{\sqrt{4}\sqrt{3} \times \sqrt{4}\sqrt{15} \times \sqrt{3}\sqrt{15}}{5 \times \left(2^2 \times 2^2\right) \times 3^2}$$

Note that you can combine each pair of roots in the numerator to get integers that will cancel with the denominator.

$$\frac{\sqrt{3}\sqrt{3}\sqrt{4}\sqrt{4}\sqrt{15}\sqrt{15}}{5 \times 4 \times 4 \times 3 \times 3} = \frac{\cancel{3} \times \cancel{4} \times \cancel{15}}{\cancel{5} \times \cancel{4} \times 4 \times \cancel{3} \times \cancel{3}} = \frac{1}{4}$$

43. **3:** To divide by a fraction, multiply by its reciprocal.

$$\frac{\sqrt{18}}{\sqrt{4}} \div \frac{\sqrt{9}}{\sqrt{18}} = \frac{\sqrt{18}}{\sqrt{4}} \times \frac{\sqrt{18}}{\sqrt{9}}$$

Feel free to simplify the perfect squares as soon as you spot them.

$$\frac{\sqrt{18}}{\sqrt{4}} \times \frac{\sqrt{18}}{\sqrt{9}} = \frac{18}{2 \times 3} = \frac{18}{6} = 3$$

44. $\dfrac{yz^3}{x^5}$: To divide, multiply by the reciprocal.

$$\frac{xy^3z^4}{x^3y^4z^2} \div \frac{x^6y^3z}{x^3y^5z^2} = \frac{xy^3z^4}{x^3y^4z^2} \times \frac{x^3y^5z^2}{x^6y^3z}$$

If you'd like, first rearrange to place the like terms together (to minimize careless mistakes). Cancel any terms that match exactly.

$$\frac{(x)\cancel{(x^3)}}{\cancel{(x^3)}(x^6)} \times \frac{\cancel{(y^3)}(y^5)}{(y^4)\cancel{(y^3)}} \times \frac{(z^4)\cancel{(z^2)}}{\cancel{(z^2)}(z)} = \frac{x}{x^6} \times \frac{y^5}{y^4} \times \frac{z^4}{z}$$

For the remaining terms, use exponent rules to simplify the like variables.

$$\frac{x}{x^6} \times \frac{y^5}{y^4} \times \frac{z^4}{z} = x^{(1-6)}y^{(5-4)}z^{(4-1)} = x^{-5}y^1z^3 = \frac{yz^3}{x^5}$$

45. **2:** Begin by multiplying by the reciprocal.

$$\frac{12^2}{9^2} \div \frac{6^3}{3^5} = \frac{12^2}{9^2} \times \frac{3^5}{6^3}$$

Break the larger numbers down into numbers with similar bases, then use exponent rules to simplify.

$$\frac{12^2}{9^2} \times \frac{3^5}{6^3} = \frac{(2\times6)^2}{(3\times3)^2} \times \frac{3^5}{6^3} = \frac{2^2\times6^2}{3^2\times3^2} \times \frac{3^5}{6^3} = \frac{2^2}{1} \times \frac{3^5}{3^4} \times \frac{6^2}{6^3} = \frac{2^23^1}{6^1} = \frac{12}{6} = 2$$

Drill 7

46. $3 + \dfrac{4}{x}$ **OR** $\dfrac{3x+4}{x}$: When the numerator of a fraction consists of two or more terms added together, but the denominator is a single term, you can split the fraction into two fractions, and then simplify further.

$$\frac{6x+8}{2x} = \frac{6x}{2x} + \frac{8}{2x}$$

Now simplify both fractions. (Don't cancel across the two fractions; that isn't allowed when adding or subtracting.)

$$\frac{6x}{2x} + \frac{8}{2x} = \frac{^3\cancel{6}\cancel{x}}{\cancel{2}\cancel{x}} + \frac{\cancel{8}^4}{\cancel{2}x} = 3 + \frac{4}{x}$$

Alternatively, you can leave this in the starting form and cancel out the common term of 2.

$$\frac{6x+8}{2x} = \frac{\cancel{2}(3x+4)}{\cancel{2}x} = \frac{3x+4}{x}$$

47. **(C):** Split this fraction into two fractions with a common denominator of $3ab$, and then simplify further.

$$\frac{9a+4b}{3ab}=\frac{9a}{3ab}+\frac{4b}{3ab}=\frac{^3\cancel{9}\cancel{a}}{\cancel{3}\cancel{a}b}+\frac{4\cancel{b}}{3a\cancel{b}}=\frac{3}{b}+\frac{4}{3a}$$

48. $\dfrac{2}{11+7b}$: Be careful when dealing with addition or subtraction in the denominator; you can't split these into two separate fractions. Instead, look for a common term that you can cancel.

$$\frac{6a}{33a+21ab}=\frac{3a\times2}{(3a\times11)+(3a\times7b)}=\frac{\cancel{3a}\times2}{\cancel{3a}(11+7b)}=\frac{2}{11+7b}$$

49. $\dfrac{1}{2}$: Begin by simplifying the square roots in the denominator.

$$\frac{2y\sqrt{5}}{5y\sqrt{20}-2y\sqrt{45}}=\frac{2y\sqrt{5}}{5y\sqrt{4}\sqrt{5}-2y\sqrt{9}\sqrt{5}}=\frac{2y\sqrt{5}}{5y\left(2\sqrt{5}\right)-2y\left(3\sqrt{5}\right)}$$

All three terms have a common factor of $2y\sqrt{5}$. Pull this factor out of each term.

$$\frac{2y\sqrt{5}}{5y\left(2\sqrt{5}\right)-2y\left(3\sqrt{5}\right)}=\frac{\cancel{2y\sqrt{5}}}{\cancel{2y\sqrt{5}}(5)-\cancel{2y\sqrt{5}}(3)}=\frac{1}{5-3}=\frac{1}{2}$$

If you feel comfortable canceling from all three terms without pulling out the common factor first, feel free to do so. Make sure to cancel a 2, a y, and a $\sqrt{5}$ from each of the three terms, the one on the top and the two on the bottom.

$$\frac{2y\sqrt{5}}{5y\left(2\sqrt{5}\right)-2y\left(3\sqrt{5}\right)}=\frac{\cancel{2}\cancel{y}\cancel{\sqrt{5}}}{5\cancel{y}\left(\cancel{2}\cancel{\sqrt{5}}\right)-\cancel{2}\cancel{y}\left(3\cancel{\sqrt{5}}\right)}=\frac{1}{5-3}=\frac{1}{2}$$

50. $\dfrac{x+5}{4-3x}$: Notice that every term has the common factor of $8x$. Pull this out and cancel.

$$\frac{8x^2+40x}{32x-24x^2}=\frac{\cancel{8x}(x+5)}{\cancel{8x}(4-3x)}=\frac{x+5}{4-3x}$$

Drill 8

51. $\dfrac{40}{21}$: Begin by simplifying each fraction.

$$\frac{3+4}{1+2}-\frac{1+2}{3+4}=\frac{7}{3}-\frac{3}{7}$$

MANHATTAN PREP

Use the double-cross method to subtract.

$$\overset{49}{7} \overset{-}{\underset{3}{\diagdown}} \overset{9}{3} = \frac{40}{21}$$

52. $\dfrac{3}{5x+10}$:

$$\frac{3}{x+2} \times \frac{1}{5} = \frac{3 \times 1}{(x+2) \times 5} = \frac{3}{5x+10}$$

53. $\dfrac{7n+7}{2n+6}$:

$$\frac{7}{n+3} \times \frac{n+1}{2} = \frac{7 \times (n+1)}{(n+3) \times 2} = \frac{7n+7}{2n+6}$$

54. $\dfrac{2x+5}{4}$:

$$\frac{x+2}{4} + \frac{x+3}{4} = \frac{(x+2)+(x+3)}{4} = \frac{2x+5}{4}$$

55. $\dfrac{t^2-t}{2t-4}$:

$$\frac{-t+1}{t-2} \times \frac{-t}{2} = \frac{(-t+1) \times (-t)}{(t-2) \times 2} = \frac{t^2-t}{2t-4}$$

56. $\dfrac{1}{2}$: When subtracting fractions with more than one term in the numerator, put the subtracted term in parentheses to remind yourself to distribute the negative sign.

$$\frac{b+6}{6} - \frac{3+b}{6} = \frac{b+6-(3+b)}{6} = \frac{b+6-3-b}{6} = \frac{3}{6} = \frac{1}{2}$$

57. $\dfrac{x\sqrt{3}}{9}$:

$$\frac{x(3+\sqrt{3})}{9} - \frac{x}{3} = \frac{3x+x\sqrt{3}}{9} - \frac{3x}{9} = \frac{(3x+x\sqrt{3})-(3x)}{9} = \frac{x\sqrt{3}}{9}$$

58. $\dfrac{x^2+y}{5}$:

$$\frac{3x^2+3y}{40}+\frac{x^2+y}{8}=\frac{3x^2+3y}{40}+\frac{5x^2+5y}{40}=\frac{\left(3x^2+3y\right)+\left(5x^2+5y\right)}{40}=\frac{8x^2+8y}{40}$$

Don't stop yet! All three terms are divisible by 8.

$$\frac{8x^2+8y}{40}=\frac{\cancel{8}x^2+\cancel{8}y}{\cancel{40}_5}=\frac{x^2+y}{5}$$

Drill 9

59. **(A):** Simplify before you multiply. Take a 2 out of the 4 and 6, then take a 3 out of the 3 and –3.

$$\frac{4t}{6}\times\frac{-3}{t-3}=\frac{^2\cancel{4}t}{\cancel{6}_{\cancel{3}}}\times\frac{\cancel{-3}^{-1}}{t-3}=\frac{2\times t\times-1}{t-3}=\frac{-2t}{t-3}$$

60. **(A):** Simplify before you multiply.

$$\frac{x+3}{15}\times\frac{10}{x+3}=\frac{\cancel{(x+3)}}{\cancel{15}_3}\times\frac{^2\cancel{10}}{\cancel{(x+3)}}=\frac{2}{3}$$

61. **(B):** Simplify before you multiply. m^3 divided by m^2 equals m^1, which is just m.

$$\frac{m^3}{m-2}\times\frac{m+3}{m^2}=\frac{m^{\cancel{3}}}{m-2}\times\frac{m+3}{\cancel{m^2}}=\frac{m(m+3)}{m-2}=\frac{m^2+3m}{m-2}$$

62. **(B):** First, combine the like terms in the numerator of the first fraction and the denominator of the second fraction.

$$\frac{(n+2n)}{n^4}\times\frac{(2n)^2}{(15n-5n)}=\frac{3n}{n^4}\times\frac{4n^2}{10n}$$

If you like, rearrange to place the numbers and variables near each other (to minimize careless mistakes), then simplify.

$$\frac{(3)(4)}{(10)}\times\frac{(n)(n^2)}{(n^4)(n)}=\frac{(3)(^2\cancel{4})}{(\cancel{10}_5)}\times\frac{(n^{1+2})}{(n^{4+1})}=\frac{6}{5}\times n^{3-5}=\frac{6}{5}\times n^{-2}=\frac{6}{5n^2}$$

If you feel comfortable with exponents, you can do the exponent simplification in one long step (but, if you do, use parentheses to make sure you keep the signs straight!).

$$\frac{(n)(n^2)}{(n^4)(n)} = n^{(1+2)-(4+1)} = n^{3-5} = n^{-2}$$

Drill 10

63. $\frac{4}{5}$: Begin by simplifying the denominator.

$$\frac{3}{3+\dfrac{3}{4}} = \frac{3}{\dfrac{12}{4}+\dfrac{3}{4}} = \frac{3}{\dfrac{15}{4}}$$

Dividing by $\dfrac{15}{4}$ is the same as multiplying by $\dfrac{4}{15}$.

$$\frac{3}{\dfrac{15}{4}} = 3 \times \frac{4}{15} = \cancel{3} \times \frac{4}{\cancel{15}_5} = \frac{4}{5}$$

64. **6:** Begin by simplifying the denominator:

$$\frac{8}{2-\dfrac{2}{3}} = \frac{8}{\dfrac{6}{3}-\dfrac{2}{3}} = \frac{8}{\dfrac{4}{3}}$$

Dividing by $\dfrac{4}{3}$ is the same as multiplying by $\dfrac{3}{4}$.

$$\frac{8}{\dfrac{4}{3}} = 8 \times \frac{3}{4} = \cancel{8}^2 \times \frac{3}{\cancel{4}} = 6$$

65. **2:** To begin, simplify the numerator and the denominator.

$$\frac{\dfrac{1}{2}+\dfrac{1}{3}}{\dfrac{7}{6}-\dfrac{3}{4}} = \frac{\dfrac{3}{6}+\dfrac{2}{6}}{\dfrac{14}{12}-\dfrac{9}{12}} = \frac{\dfrac{5}{6}}{\dfrac{5}{12}}$$

Now divide.

$$\frac{\dfrac{5}{6}}{\dfrac{5}{12}} = \frac{5}{6} \times \frac{12}{5}$$

Simplify before you multiply.

$$\frac{5}{6} \times \frac{12}{5} = \frac{\cancel{5}}{\cancel{6}} \times \frac{{}^{2}\cancel{12}}{\cancel{5}} = 2$$

66. **(C):** Work from the inside out. First, combine the terms in the denominator.

$$\frac{1}{1 - \dfrac{2}{y+1}} = \frac{1}{\dfrac{y+1}{y+1} - \dfrac{2}{y+1}} = \frac{1}{\dfrac{(y+1)-(2)}{y+1}} = \frac{1}{\dfrac{y-1}{y+1}}$$

A numerator of 1 divided by a fraction is just the reciprocal of that fraction (no matter how ugly that fraction is).

$$\frac{1}{\dfrac{y-1}{y+1}} = \frac{y+1}{y-1}$$

Fractions, Decimals, Percents, & Ratios

In this chapter...

- Four Ways to Express Parts of a Whole
- Convert 0.25 to 25%: Move the Decimal Point Two Places Right
- Convert 0.25 or 25% to $\frac{1}{4}$: Put 25 over 100 and Simplify
- Convert $\frac{1}{4}$ to 0.25 or 25%: Long-Divide 1 by 4
- Multiply a Decimal by a Power of Ten: Shift the Decimal Point
- Add or Subtract Decimals: Line Up the Decimal Points
- Multiply Two Decimals: Ignore Decimal Points at First
- Multiply a Decimal and a Big Number: Trade Decimal Places
- Divide Two Decimals: Move Points in the Same Direction to Kill Decimals
- 20% of \$55 = 0.2 × \$55
- Percent Change: Divide Change in Value by Original Value
- Percent of a Percent of: Multiply Twice
- Ratio: Part-to-Part and Part-to-Whole
- Ratios and Percents: Convert Fractions to Percents

Fractions, Decimals, Percents, & Ratios

5

In This Chapter, You Will Learn To:

- Understand relationships among fractions, decimals, percents, and ratios
- Convert from one form to another

Four Ways to Express Parts of a Whole

Say you have the shaded part of this orange. You can express how much you have in four ways.

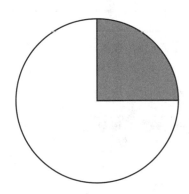

1. You have $\frac{1}{4}$ of the orange. **Fraction**

2. You have 0.25 of the orange. **Decimal**

3. You have 25% of the orange. **Percent**

4. The ratio of your piece to the whole orange is 1 part to 4 parts, or 1 : 4. **Ratio**

Any of these four forms can express a *part-to-whole relationship*. The main difference between the forms is how you think about the whole:

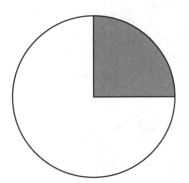

$\frac{1}{4}$ = 1 out of 4 pieces of the whole

0.25 = 0.25 of the whole

25% = 25 out of 100 pieces of the whole

1 : 4 = ("1 to 4") 1 out of 4 pieces of the whole

In other words, what is each form "out of"? What is the whole that you are dividing by?

Fractions are *out of* the denominator (4 in this case).

Decimals are *out of* 1 (the whole). You've already done the division.

Percents are *out of* 100. *Percent* literally means "per hundred," or divided by 100.

Part-to-whole ratios are *out of* the second term in the ratio (4 in this case). Ratios can also be part-to-part; you'll learn more about this later. A ratio can be written with a colon between the two numbers (3 : 7) or as a fraction ($\frac{3}{7}$).

Which form is most useful depends on the problem at hand. You might say any of the following:

The container is $\frac{1}{2}$ full.

The container is filled to 0.5 of its capacity.

The container is 50% full.

The ratio of the contents of the container to its total capacity is 1 to 2.

By the way, the part can be greater than the whole.

I ate $\frac{5}{4}$ boxes of cereal. (I ate more than one box.)

I ate 1.25 boxes of cereal.

I ate 125% of one box of cereal.

The ratio of what I ate to a whole box of cereal was 5 to 4.

Convert 0.25 to 25%: Move the Decimal Point Two Places Right

Decimals are out of 1. Percents are out of 100. So, to convert a decimal to a percent, move the decimal point to the *right two places*. Add zeros if necessary:

$$0.53 = 53\% \qquad 0.4 = 0.40 = 40\% \qquad 0.03 = 3\% \qquad 1.7 = 1.70 = 170\%$$

A percent might still contain a visible decimal point when you're done.

$$0.4057 = 40.57\% \qquad 0.002 = 0.2\% \qquad 0.0005 = 0.05\%$$

Note that, when converting from a decimal to a percent, the new number seems greater than the original. In reality, the two are equal; they represent the exact same number. But the way you write the number makes it *look* greater in percent form and smaller in decimal form. This can help you to remember to move the decimal point to the *right* when converting to the percent form.

To convert a percent to a decimal, *go in reverse*. That is, move the decimal point two places to the *left*. If the decimal point isn't visible, it's actually just before the percent sign. Add zeros if necessary as you move left.

$$39\% = 39.\% = 0.39 \qquad 60\% = 0.60 = 0.6 \qquad 8\% = 0.08 \qquad 225\% = 2.25$$

$$13.4\% = 0.134 \qquad 0.7\% = 0.007 \qquad 0.001\% = 0.00001$$

Remember: The decimal form of the number *looks* smaller than the percent form. That can help you to remember to move the decimal point to the *left* when converting to decimal form. Here are a couple more rules for your book:

If you…	Then you…	Like this:
Want to convert a decimal to a percent	Move the decimal point two places to the right to make the number seem greater (though it isn't really)	$0.036 = 3.6\%$
Want to convert a percent to a decimal	Move the decimal point two places to the left to make the number seem smaller (though it isn't really)	$41.2\% = 0.412$

Check Your Skills

1. Convert 0.035 to a percent.

Answer can be found on page 217.

Convert 0.25 or 25% to $\frac{1}{4}$: Put 25 over 100 and Simplify

The decimal 0.25 is twenty-five one-hundredths. Rewrite that as 25 over 100.

$$0.25 = \frac{25}{100}$$

Now simplify by canceling common factors from the top and bottom.

$$0.25 = \frac{25}{100} = \frac{\overset{1}{\cancel{25}}}{\underset{4}{\cancel{100}}} = \frac{1}{4}$$

When you convert a decimal to a fraction, put a power of 10 (10, 100, 1,000, etc.) in the denominator of the fraction. Which power of 10? It depends on how far the decimal goes to the right.

Put as many zeros in your power of 10 as you have digits to the right of the decimal point.

0.3	=	$\frac{3}{10}$
Zero point three	is	three-tenths, or three over ten
0.23	=	$\frac{23}{100}$
Zero point two three	is	twenty-three one-hundredths
0.007	=	$\frac{7}{1,000}$
Zero point zero zero seven	is	seven one-thousandths

As with any fractions, cancel common terms to simplify.

$$0.4 = \frac{4}{10} = \frac{\overset{2}{\cancel{4}}}{\underset{5}{\cancel{10}}} = \frac{2}{5} \qquad 0.75 = \frac{75}{100} = \frac{\overset{3}{\cancel{75}}}{\underset{4}{\cancel{100}}} = \frac{3}{4}$$

In the second case, you cancel 25 from the top and bottom, leaving 3 and 4.

In the numerator, keep any zeros in the middle of two numbers, such as the 0 between the 1 and the 2 in 0.0102 in the problem shown below. Otherwise, drop any zeros (such as the 0's to the left of the 1). However, base the number of zeros in the denominator on the total number of starting decimal places (before you dropped any zeros). In the example below, there are four decimal places in 0.0102, so there are four zeros in the power of 10 in the denominator.

$$0.0102 = \frac{102}{10,000} = \frac{\overset{51}{\cancel{102}}}{\underset{5,000}{\cancel{10,000}}} = \frac{51}{5,000}$$

To convert a percent to a fraction, write the number over 100. Remember that *percent* literally means "per hundred." For example:

$$45\% = \frac{45}{100} = \frac{\overset{9}{\cancel{45}}}{\underset{20}{\cancel{100}}} = \frac{9}{20} \qquad 8\% = \frac{8}{100} = \frac{\overset{2}{\cancel{8}}}{\underset{25}{\cancel{100}}} = \frac{2}{25}$$

Alternatively, you can first convert the percent to a decimal by moving the decimal place. Then follow the process given earlier.

$$2.5\% = 0.025 = \frac{25}{1,000} = \frac{\overset{1}{\cancel{25}}}{\underset{40}{\cancel{1,000}}} = \frac{1}{40}$$

If you don't convert to a decimal first, be sure to write the fraction over 100.

$$2.5\% = \frac{2.5}{100}$$

You'll learn how to divide decimals a little farther on.

If you...	Then you...	Like this:
Want to convert a decimal to a fraction	Put the digits to the right of the decimal point over the appropriate power of 10, then simplify	$0.036 = \frac{36}{1,000}$ $= \frac{9}{250}$
Want to convert a percent to a fraction	Write the percent over 100, then simplify *OR* Convert first to a decimal, then follow the process for converting decimals to fractions	$4\% = \frac{4}{100}$ $= \frac{1}{25}$ $3.6\% = 0.036$ $0.036 = \frac{36}{1,000}$ $= \frac{9}{250}$

Check Your Skills

2. Convert 0.375 to a fraction.
3. Convert 24% to a fraction and simplify fully.

Answers can be found on page 217.

Convert $\frac{1}{4}$ to 0.25 or 25%: Long-Divide 1 by 4

A fraction represents division. The decimal equivalent is the result of that division.

To convert a fraction to a decimal, long-divide the numerator by the denominator. As you're doing the math, keep track of the decimal point on top (in the solution), but don't worry about keeping the decimals down below.

$\frac{1}{4} = ?$ Divide 1 by 4. | $\frac{5}{8} = ?$ Divide 5 by 8.

$$\begin{array}{r} 0.25 \\ 4\overline{)1.00} \\ -8 \\ \hline 20 \\ -20 \\ \hline 0 \end{array}$$ $\frac{1}{4} = 0.25$ | $$\begin{array}{r} 0.625 \\ 8\overline{)5.000} \\ -48 \\ \hline 20 \\ -16 \\ \hline 40 \\ -40 \\ \hline 0 \end{array}$$ $\frac{5}{8} = 0.625$

On the GMAT, most cases in which you might need to do this math will involve common fractions that you can memorize. For instance, $\frac{1}{4}$ is a common fraction. Memorize the fact that $\frac{1}{4} = 0.25 = 25\%$. At the end of this section, you'll find more common fractions to memorize.

In some cases, the decimal never ends because the long division never ends. You get a repeating decimal.

$$\frac{1}{3} = 0.333... = 0.\overline{3}$$
$$\begin{array}{r} 0.33... \\ 3\overline{)1.000} \\ -9 \\ \hline 10 \\ -9 \\ \hline 10 \\ ... \end{array}$$

If the denominator contains only 2's and/or 5's as factors, the decimal will end (this is called a *terminating decimal* because it terminates, or ends). In this case, you can find the decimal equivalent using the earlier method: Multiply the numerator and denominator by the same number—whatever number turns the denominator into a power of 10. For example:

$$\frac{1}{4} = \frac{1 \times 25}{4 \times 25} = \frac{25}{100} = 0.25 \qquad\qquad \frac{1}{20} = \frac{1 \times 5}{20 \times 5} = \frac{5}{100} = 0.05$$

However, if the denominator contains factors other than 2's and 5's, you must use long division to convert to a percent (this is because powers of 10 are only multiples of 2 and 5).

To convert a fraction to a percent, first convert it to a decimal, then convert the decimal to a percent.

$$\frac{1}{2} = \frac{1 \times 5}{2 \times 5} = \frac{5}{10} = 0.5 = 50\%$$

If you...	Then you...	Like this:
Want to convert a fraction to a decimal	Do long division *OR* Multiply the top and bottom by the same number such that the denominator becomes a power of 10, but only if the denominator contains only 2's and 5's as factors	$\dfrac{7}{8} \rightarrow 8\overline{)7.000}\,^{0.875}$ $\dfrac{1}{50} = \dfrac{1 \times 2}{50 \times 2}$ $= \dfrac{2}{100}$ $= 0.02$

Memorize the following conversions. Flash cards are a great tool to help; grab some index cards and start writing.

Tenths and Fifths

Fraction	Decimal	Percent
$\dfrac{1}{10}$	0.1	10%
$\dfrac{2}{10} = \dfrac{1}{5}$	0.2	20%
$\dfrac{3}{10}$	0.3	30%
$\dfrac{4}{10} = \dfrac{2}{5}$	0.4	40%
$\dfrac{5}{10} = \dfrac{1}{2}$	0.5	50%
$\dfrac{6}{10} = \dfrac{3}{5}$	0.6	60%
$\dfrac{7}{10}$	0.7	70%

Fraction	Decimal	Percent
$\dfrac{8}{10} = \dfrac{4}{5}$	0.8	80%
$\dfrac{9}{10}$	0.9	90%
$\dfrac{10}{10} = \dfrac{5}{5} = 1$	1.0	100%
$\dfrac{11}{10}$	1.1	110%
$\dfrac{12}{10} = \dfrac{6}{5}$	1.2	120%

Eighths and Fourths

Fraction	Decimal	Percent
$\dfrac{1}{8}$	0.125	12.5%
$\dfrac{2}{8} = \dfrac{1}{4}$	0.25	25%
$\dfrac{3}{8}$	0.375	37.5%
$\dfrac{4}{8} = \dfrac{2}{4} = \dfrac{1}{2}$	0.5	50%
$\dfrac{5}{8}$	0.625	62.5%
$\dfrac{6}{8} = \dfrac{3}{4}$	0.75	75%
$\dfrac{7}{8}$	0.875	87.5%
$\dfrac{8}{8} = \dfrac{4}{4} = 1$	1	100%
$\dfrac{10}{8} = \dfrac{5}{4}$	1.25	125%
$\dfrac{12}{8} = \dfrac{6}{4} = \dfrac{3}{2}$	1.5	150%

For the set above, note that $\frac{1}{8}$ is half of $\frac{2}{8}$. You may already know that $\frac{2}{8} = \frac{1}{4} = 25\%$. Use this to help memorize the fact that $\frac{1}{8}$ is half that, or 12.5%. Every eighth fraction then increases by another 12.5%.

Thirds

Fraction	Decimal	Percent
$\frac{1}{3}$	0.3333…	33.33…%
$\frac{2}{3}$	0.6666…	66.66…%
$\frac{3}{3} = 1$	1	100%

You're almost done!

Fraction	Decimal	Percent
$\frac{1}{100}$	0.01	1%
$\frac{1}{20}$	0.05	5%

Check Your Skills

4   Change $\frac{3}{5}$ to a decimal.

5. Convert $\frac{3}{8}$ to a percent.

Answers can be found on page 217.

Multiply a Decimal by a Power of 10: Shift the Decimal Point

Decimals are tenths, hundredths, thousandths, and so on. One-tenth is a power of 10, namely 10^{-1}. One-hundredth is also a power of 10, namely 10^{-2}.

You can write any decimal as a fraction with a power of 10 in the denominator, or as a product involving a power of 10. For example, $0.03 = \frac{3}{100} = \frac{3}{10^2}$. The power of 10 determines where the decimal point is. In this example, the power of 10 is 2. In the decimal form, the decimal point is two places to the left of 3.

So if you multiply or divide a decimal by a power of 10, you move the decimal point to the right or to the left.

If you multiply by 10 itself, you shift the decimal point one place to the right.

$$0.004 \times 10 = 0.04$$

The 10 cancels with one power of 10 in the denominator.

$$\frac{4}{1,000} \times 10 = \frac{4}{1,00\cancel{0}} \times \cancel{10} = \frac{4}{100}$$

You can also see it in terms of exponents. The additional 10 increases the overall exponent from -3 to -2.

$$4 \times 10^{-3} \times 10 = 4 \times 10^{-2}$$

If you multiply by 100, or 10^2, you shift the decimal point two places to the right.

$$0.004 \times 100 = 0.4 \qquad \text{That is,} \quad \frac{4}{1,000} \times 100 = \frac{4}{10} \qquad 4 \times 10^{-3} \times 10^2 = 4 \times 10^{-1}$$

When you multiply by a power of 10, the exponent of that power is the number of places you move the decimal. If the power of 10 is positive, move the decimal to the *right* to make the number *greater*.

$$43.8723 \times 10^3 = 43,872.3 \quad \text{Move the decimal 3 places to the right.}$$

If you divide by a power of 10, move to the *left* to make the number *smaller*.

$$782.95 \div 10 = 78.295 \quad \text{Move the decimal 1 place to the left.}$$

$$57,234 \div 10^4 = 5.7234 \quad \text{Move the decimal 4 places to the left.}$$

If you're asked to multiply by a negative power of 10, flip the power to positive and divide instead. Move the decimal to the left to make the number smaller, since you're dividing.

$$4 \times 10^{-3} = 4 \div 10^3 = 0.004 \quad \text{Move 3 places to the left.}$$

Likewise, if you're asked to divide by a negative power of 10, change the power to positive and multiply instead. Move the decimal to the right to make the number greater, since you're multiplying.

$$62 \div 10^{-2} = 62 \times 10^2 = 6,200 \quad \text{Move 2 places to the right.}$$

All of these procedures work the same for repeating decimals.

$$\frac{1}{3} \times 10 = 0.333... \times 10 = 3.33... \quad \text{Move 1 place to the right.}$$

If you…	Then you…	Like this:
Multiply a decimal by a positive power of 10	Move the decimal point right a number of places, corresponding to the exponent of the 10	$0.007 \times 10^2 = 0.7$ $7 \div 10^{-2} = 7 \times 10^2 = 700$
Divide a decimal by a positive power of 10	Move the decimal point left a number of places, corresponding to the exponent of the 10	$6 \div 10^3 = 0.006$ $6 \times 10^{-2} = 6 \div 10^2 = 0.06$

Check Your Skills

Multiply. Give each answer as a single value.

6. 32.753×10^2
7. $43,681 \times 10^{-4}$

Answers can be found on pages 217–218.

Add or Subtract Decimals: Line Up the Decimal Points

When you add or subtract decimals, write the decimals vertically, with the decimal points lined up.

$$0.3 + 0.65 = \qquad\qquad 0.65 - 0.5 =$$

$$
\begin{array}{r}
0.3 \\
+\ 0.65 \\
\hline
0.95
\end{array}
\qquad\qquad
\begin{array}{r}
0.65 \\
-\ 0.50 \\
\hline
0.15
\end{array}
$$

You can add zeros on the right to help you line up. For instance, turn 0.5 into 0.50 before you subtract it from 0.65.

If you…	Then you…	Like this:
Add or subtract decimals	Line up the decimal points vertically	$\begin{array}{r} 4.035 \\ +0.120 \\ \hline 4.155 \end{array}$

Check Your Skills

Add or subtract. Give each answer as a single value.

8. $3.128 + 0.045$
9. $1.8746 - 0.313$

Answers can be found on page 218.

Multiply Two Decimals: Ignore Decimal Points at First

Consider this example:

$$0.25 \times 0.5 =$$

First, multiply the numbers together as if they were integers. In other words, ignore the decimal points.

$$25 \times 5 = 125$$

Now count all the digits to the right of the original decimal points.

0.25 has 2 digits to the right.   0.5 has 1 digit to the right.

There were a total of three digits originally to the right, so move the decimal point of the answer three places to the *left*, in order to compensate. In other words, since there were three digits to the right of the decimal originally, the result should also have three digits to the right of the decimal.

125 becomes 0.125.   Therefore, $0.25 \times 0.5 = 0.125$.

Here's why this process works:

$$0.25 = 25 \times 10^{-2} \qquad\qquad 0.5 = 5 \times 10^{-1}$$
$$0.25 \times 0.5 = (25 \times 10^{-2}) \times (5 \times 10^{-1}) = 125 \times 10^{-3} = 0.125$$

The powers of 10 tell you where to put the decimal point. Here is another example:

$3.5 \times 20 =$	There is one digit to the right of the decimal point.
$35 \times 20 = 700$	Ignore the decimals and multiply.
$3.5 \times 20 = 70.0$	Account for the one decimal place in 3.5 by moving the final decimal point one
$= 70$	place to the left.

Count the zeros to the right of the decimal point as well.

$0.01 \times 0.05 =$	There are four digits (including zeros) to the right of the decimal points.
$1 \times 5 = 5$	Ignore the decimals and multiply.
$0.01 \times 0.05 = 0.0005$	Account for the original four decimal places by moving the decimal point four places to the left.

If you...	Then you...	Like this:
Multiply two decimals	Ignore the decimal points, multiply integers, then place the decimal point by counting the original number of decimals	$0.2 \times 0.5 = ?$ $2 \times 5 = 10$ $10 \rightarrow 0.10$ $0.2 \times 0.5 = 0.1$

Check Your Skills

Multiply. Give each answer as a single value.

10. 0.6×1.1
11. 0.004×0.032

Answers can be found on page 218.

Multiply a Decimal and a Big Number: Trade Decimal Places

Now consider this example:

$$4{,}000{,}000 \times 0.0003 =$$

When one number is very big and the other one is very small, you can trade powers of 10 from the big one (4,000,000) to the small one (0.0003). In other words, move one decimal point *left* and the other one *right*. Just make sure that you move the same number of places.

This multiplication would be easier if you had no decimals at all. To make this happen, move the decimal in 0.0003 to the right four places to get 3. To compensate, move the decimal in 4,000,000 to the left four places. That makes that number more manageable, too.

$$4{,}000{,}000 \times 0.0003 = 4{,}000{,}000 \times 0.0003 = 400 \times 3 = 1{,}200$$

You can justify these maneuvers with powers of 10.

$$4{,}000{,}000 \times 0.0003 = (4 \times 10^6) \times (3 \times 10^{-4}) = 12 \times 10^{6-4} = 12 \times 10^2 = 1{,}200$$

If you...	Then you...	Like this:
Multiply a small decimal and a big number	Trade decimal places from the big number to the decimal	$50{,}000 \times 0.007 =$ $50 \times 7 = 350$

Check Your Skills

Multiply. Give the answer as a single value.

12. $520{,}000 \times 0.0004$

Answer can be found on page 218.

Divide Two Decimals: Move Points in the Same Direction To Kill Decimals

When you divide decimals, first write the division as a fraction if it isn't in that form already.

$$\frac{300}{0.05} =$$

Now move the decimals in the *same* direction on the top and bottom. This is the same as multiplying the top and bottom by the same power of 10. Do this to eliminate decimals.

In this case, turn 0.05 into 5 by moving its decimal two places to the right. Then do the same thing on top. Add zeros as necessary.

$$\frac{300}{0.05} = \frac{300_{\rightarrow\rightarrow}}{0.05_{\rightarrow}} = \frac{30,000}{5} = 6,000$$

This is equivalent to multiplying the top and bottom by 100.

$$\frac{300}{0.05} = \frac{300 \times 100}{0.05 \times 100} = \frac{30,000}{5} = 6,000$$

One decimal may need more moves than the other. Try this example:

$$\frac{12.39}{0.003} =$$

The 12.39 only needs two moves to get rid of the decimal, while 0.003 needs three moves. Go with the greater number of moves. You can always add zeros to the other number.

$$\frac{12.39}{0.003} = \frac{12.39_{\rightarrow\rightarrow}}{0.003_{\rightarrow\rightarrow}} = \frac{12,390}{3} = 4,130$$

If you…	Then you…	Like this:
Divide two decimals	Move the decimal points in the same direction to eliminate decimals as far as you can	$\frac{0.002_{\rightarrow\rightarrow\rightarrow}}{0.0004_{\rightarrow\rightarrow\rightarrow}} = \frac{20}{4} = 5$

Check Your Skills

13. Simplify $\dfrac{0.00084}{0.00007}$.

Answer can be found on page 218.

20% of \$55 = 0.2 × \$55

In everyday life, percents are the most common way of expressing part-to-whole relationships. You often see signs advertising "25% off," but you don't see as many signs advertising "$\frac{1}{4}$ off" or "0.75 of the original price." So your intuition about percents is probably pretty good, and that's useful on the GMAT.

However, percents are not necessarily the most useful form for actual *computation*. If you need to crunch numbers, think about what form would be easiest to use: *fractions, decimals, or percents*.

Consider this problem:

30% of \$60 =

The word *of* means *times* in math terms. In other words, *of* indicates multiplication.

You could start by taking 10% of 60. This is the same as $(0.1)(60) = 6$. Since 30% is three times as much as 10%, multiply: $6 \times 3 = 18$.

Alternatively, you could convert 30% to a decimal, trade decimal places, and then multiply.

$$30\% \text{ of } \$60 = 0.30 \times \$60 = 3 \times \$6 = \$18$$

You even have a third option: use the fraction form of 30%.

$$30\% \text{ of } \$60 = \frac{30}{100} \times \$60 = \frac{3\cancel{0}}{10\cancel{0}} \times \$60 = \frac{3}{1\cancel{0}} \times \$6\cancel{0} = \$18$$

Which path did you find the easiest?

A problem could also be worded as a question.

What is 20% of $55?

In the Word Problems chapter, you'll learn more about translating words into math. For now, know these translations:

What	can be translated as	x	(some variable)
is	can be translated as	$=$	(the equals sign)

Translate the full question to math as follows:

What	is	20%	of	$55?
x	$=$	0.20	$\times$	$55

Now crunch the numbers on the right. Note that when there are zeros at the end of a decimal, you don't count those zeros when counting decimals.

$0.20 \times \$55 =$ For purposes of counting the decimal point, do not include the 0 after the 2.

$0.2 \times \$55 =$ Compute $2 \times \$55 = \$110$, then move the decimal point.

$0.2 \times \$55 = \$11$

Alternatively, translate 20% to a fraction rather than to a decimal.

$$20\% = \frac{20}{100} = \frac{1}{5}$$

$$\frac{1}{5} \times \$55 = \frac{1}{\cancel{5}} \times {}^{11}\cancel{\$55} = \$11$$

Or, find 10% and then multiply by 2 to get 20%.

$$(10\%)(55) = (0.1)(55) = 5.5$$

$$5.5 \times 2 = 11$$

The translation gets a little tougher when you encounter the phrase "what percent." Consider this example:

What percent of 125 is 25?

Use a variable to represent the word *what*. Remember that the word percent by itself means "divided by 100," so it can be translated as $\dfrac{}{100}$.

As a result, "what percent" can be translated as $\dfrac{x}{100}$.

Translate the question now.

What percent	of	125	is	25?
$\dfrac{x}{100}$	$\times$	125	$=$	25

You can now find the answer by solving for x. Solving equations for x will be covered in depth in the Equations chapter later in this book. Here's how to solve this question:

$$\frac{x}{100} \times 125 = 25$$

$$\frac{x}{\overset{}{\underset{4}{100}}} \times \overset{5}{\cancel{125}} = 25$$

$$\frac{x}{4} \times 5 = 25$$

$$\frac{x}{4} = 5$$

$$x = 20$$

In practice, use something other than $\times$ (multiplication sign) to indicate multiplication when you have an x (variable) around, so that you don't mix up $\times$ and x on your paper. You can use parentheses or a big dot.

$$\left(\frac{x}{100}\right)125 = 25 \qquad\qquad \frac{x}{100} \bullet 125 = 25$$

Here's a last example:

16 is 2% of what?

Translate word by word. Change 2% either to 0.02 or to $\dfrac{2}{100} = \dfrac{1}{50}$.

16	is	2%	of	what?
16	$=$	0.02	$\times$	x

Now solve for x.

$$16 = (0.02)x$$

$$\frac{16}{0.02} = x$$

$$\frac{16}{0.02} = x$$

$$\frac{1,600}{2} = x$$

$$800 = x$$

If you…	Then you…	Like this:
See "30% of"	Convert 30% into a decimal or fraction, then multiply; alternatively, when appropriate, find 10%, then multiply by 3 to reach 30%	30% of 200 = 0.30 × 200 = 60 10% of 200 = (0.1)(200) = 20 30% = 20 × 3 = 60
See "what percent of"	Turn what percent into $\frac{x}{100}$, then multiply	What percent of 200 is 60? $\left(\dfrac{x}{100}\right)200 = 60$

Check Your Skills

Translate the following and solve.

14. 21 is 30% of what number?

Answer can be found on page 219.

Percent Change: Divide Change in Value by Original Value

Consider this example.

> You have $200 in a bank account. You deposit an additional $30 in that account. By what percent did the value of the bank account increase?

Whenever some amount changes and you care about percents, set up this equation:

> Original + Change = New

This equation holds true in two ways. First, it holds true for the actual amounts or values, which in this case are in dollars. This is unsurprising. Here is the first equation:

Original value	+	Change in value	=	New value
$200	+	$30	=	$230

MANHATTAN PREP

This equation *also* holds true for percents, as long as you mean percents *of the original value.* For example:

Original percent (% of original)	+	Change percent (% of original)	=	New percent (% of original)
100%	+	?	=	?

The original percent is always 100%, since the original value is always 100% of itself.

The change percent is better known as the **percent change**.

You had $200 in your bank account. You added $30. What percent of $200 is $30?

Turn *what percent* into $\frac{x}{100}$, translate the rest, and solve for *x*.

$$\left(\frac{x}{100}\right)200 = 30$$

$$\left(\frac{x}{\cancel{100}}\right)2\cancel{00} = 30$$

$$2x = 30$$

$$x = 15$$

The percent change is 15%.

Alternatively, if you feel pretty comfortable working with percentages, you can try a "back-of-the-envelope" approach. How can you get to the value of 30 using some combination of "easy" small percentages of the original number?

200 = 100%	The starting number is always 100% of itself.
20 = 10%	20 (or 10%) is close to 30, but not quite there…
10 = 5%	…add 10 (or 5% more) to get to 30!
	20 + 10 = 30, which represents 10% + 5% = 15%.

Therefore, 15% is the percent change.

To do this kind of back-of-the-envelope calculation in the future, break the starting 100% figure down into more manageable pieces: 50%, 10%, 5%, or 1%. Then add up (or subtract) what you need in order to find the right percent.

So the original percent is 100%, and the percent change is 15%. What is the new percent? Add them up!

Original percent (% of original)	+	Change percent (% of original)	=	New percent (% of original)
100%	+	15%	=	115%

In the future, you can use a formula to calculate the percent change more directly. The percent change equals the change in value divided by the original value.

$$\text{Percent change (as \% of original)} = \frac{\text{Change in value}}{\text{Original value}}$$

$$\frac{\text{Change in value}}{\text{Original value}} = \frac{\$30}{\$200} = \frac{\overset{15}{\cancel{\$30}}}{\underset{100}{\cancel{\$200}}} = \frac{15}{100} = 15\%$$

5

The additional \$30 corresponds to a 15% change in the value of the account. Take note of the way that the math was simplified. You're looking for a percent, so you want the denominator to be 100 (since *per cent* means *of 100*). Don't simplify to $\frac{3}{20}$, since you'd just have to do more math to figure out what percent that is.

You can also directly calculate the *new percent*. Here's the formula:

$$\text{New percent (as \% of original)} = \frac{\text{New value}}{\text{Original value}}$$

$$\frac{\text{New value}}{\text{Original value}} = \frac{\$230}{\$200} = \frac{115}{100} = 115\%$$

As last time, make the denominator 100; divide by 2 and you're there.

If the value of the account *decreases*, the equations still hold true. You just have a negative change. In other words, subtract the change this time. Consider this example:

> You have \$200 in a bank account. You make a withdrawal that reduces the value of the account by 40%. How much money remains in the account?

Solve for the new percent first. A 40% decrease from the original is a negative 40% change.

Original percent (% of original)	+	Change percent (% of original)	=	New percent (% of original)
100%	+	−40%	=	60%

If you take out 40%, what's left is 60% of the original. Now find that new value.

$$\text{New percent (as \% of original)} = \frac{\text{New value}}{\text{Original value}}$$

$$60\% = \frac{\text{New value}}{\$200}$$

$$\left(\frac{60}{100}\right)200 = x$$

$$\left(\frac{60}{\cancel{100}}\right)2\cancel{00} = x$$

$$120 = x$$

Therefore, $120 remains in the account.

Alternatively, you could use the back-of-the-envelope approach. How can you get to 60% using values for some combination of 50%, 10%, 5%, and 1%?

60% = 50% + 10%

200 = 100%	The original value is always 100% of itself.
100 = 50%	50% is half of the original value.
20 = 10%	To find 10%, move the decimal one place to the left.

Therefore, 60% = 100 + 20 = 120, so $120 remains in the account.

If you...	Then you...	Like this:
Need to find percent change of an original percent	Use the formula: $\% \text{ Change} = \dfrac{\text{Change in value}}{\text{Original value}}$	Original = $200; $30 added: $\dfrac{\$30}{\$200} = 15\%$
Need to find a new percent of an original percent	Use the formula: $\text{New } \% = \dfrac{\text{New value}}{\text{Original value}}$	Original = $200; $30 added: $\dfrac{230}{200} = 115\%$

If you learn the following shortcuts, you'll make your job easier on the GMAT.

A percent INCREASE of...	...is the same as this NEW percent...	...which is the same as multiplying the ORIGINAL VALUE by...
10%	110%	1.1
20%	120%	1.2, or $\dfrac{6}{5}$
25%	125%	1.25, or $\dfrac{5}{4}$
50%	150%	1.5, or $\dfrac{3}{2}$
100%	200%	2

A percent DECREASE of…	…is the same as this NEW percent…	…which is the same as multiplying the ORIGINAL VALUE by…
10%	90%	0.9
20%	80%	0.8, or $\dfrac{4}{5}$
25%	75%	0.75, or $\dfrac{3}{4}$
50%	50%	0.5, or $\dfrac{1}{2}$
75%	25%	0.25, or $\dfrac{1}{4}$

Percent more than is just like *percent increase*. You do exactly the same math. Consider this example:

> $230 is what percent more than $200?

Think of $230 as the new value and $200 as the original value. Again, 230 is 15% more than the starting point of $200.

Likewise, *percent less than* is just like *percent decrease*. Consider this example:

> $120 is what percent less than $200?

Think of $120 as the new value and $200 as the original value. Again, you'll get a 40% decrease or difference.

Which number you call the original value matters. The original value is always after the word *than*. It's the value you're comparing the other value *to*.

> $230 is what percent *more than* $200?

Therefore, $200 is the original value. You're comparing $230 to a starting point of $200, not the other way around.

Finally, watch out for the language *percent OF* versus *percent MORE THAN*. These two expressions don't mean the same thing. Consider these examples:

> 30 is what percent *of* 20?

> 30 is what percent *more than* 20?

For the first question (*of*), you are including the original 20 as part of the percent calculation. Since 20 is 100% of 20, you have to have at least 100% already. Then, you still have to get up to 30. What additional percentage do you need to add to get from 20 to 30?

20 = 100%

10 = 50%

20 + 10 = 30

100% + 50% = 150%

In other words, 30 is 150 percent *of* 20. Translate the equation to check the math if you're not confident.

$$30 = \frac{150}{100} \times 20$$

$$30 = \frac{15\cancel{0}}{1\cancel{0}\cancel{0}} \times 2\cancel{0}$$

$$30 = 30$$

In contrast, the second question (*more than*) is asking you to find only the *increase* from 20 to 30. The baseline 100% that 20 represents is *not* included in this calculation. This time, only count the difference: 30 − 20 = 10.

What percent of the original number does 10 represent?

20 = 100%

10 = 50%

In other words, 30 is 50 percent *more than* 20. Again, check the math if you're not sure; use the percent change formula, since *more than* is a signal to use percent change.

$$\% \text{ change } = \frac{10}{20} = \frac{50}{100} = 50\%$$

The math above works the same way for *less than* problems, except you'll be subtracting the change rather than adding it.

By the way, did you happen to notice that the answer to the first one (150%) is exactly 100% more than the second one (50%)? This isn't a coincidence! It will always be the case that the *percent of* question will be 100% more than the *percent more than* question for the exact same original and resulting numbers.

Recall how the *percent of* question includes the original number in the calculation but the *percent more than* question does not? The original number is always 100% of itself, so the *percent of* calculation will always include this 100% and the *percent more than* question will not.

Keep *percent of* and *percent more than* or *percent less than* distinct; they mean different things!

If you...	Then you...	Like this:
Need to find a *percent more than* or *percent less than*	Treat the problem like a percent increase or a percent decrease	$230 is what % more than $200? $$\frac{\$30}{\$200} = 15\%$$
Need to find a *percent of*	Translate the equation and solve *OR* Use back-of-the-envelope approach; set the starting number to 100%	50 is what % of 25? $$50 = \frac{x}{100}(25)$$ $$50 = \frac{x}{4}$$ $$200 = x$$ $$25 = 100\%$$ $$50 = 200\%$$

Check Your Skills

15. What is the percent decrease from 90 to 72?

Answer can be found on page 219.

Percent of a Percent of: Multiply Twice

Consider this example:

What is 120% of 150% of 30?

These are *percents of,* so turn the percents into decimal or fractional equivalents and multiply 30 by *both* of those equivalents. Don't forget to simplify before you multiply.

$$120\% = \frac{6}{5} \qquad 150\% = \frac{3}{2}$$

120% of 150% of 30 =

$$\frac{6}{5} \times \frac{3}{2} \times 30 = \frac{\overset{3}{\cancel{6}}}{5} \times \frac{3}{\cancel{2}} \times 30 = \frac{\overset{3}{\cancel{6}}}{\cancel{5}} \times \frac{3}{\cancel{2}} \times \overset{6}{\cancel{30}} = 9 \times 6 = 54$$

Percent changes often come one after the other. *When you have successive percent changes, multiply the original value by each new percent* (converted to a suitable fraction or decimal).

Consider another example.

> The price of a share, originally $50, goes up by 10% on Monday and then by 20% on Tuesday. What is the overall change in the price of a share, in dollars?

A percent increase of 10% is equivalent to a new percent of 110%, or multiplying the original value by 1.1 or $\frac{11}{10}$.

A percent increase of 20% is equivalent to a new percent of 120%, or multiplying the original value by 1.2 or $\frac{6}{5}$.

Compute the new value by multiplying the original value by each of these factors.

$$\$50 \times \frac{11}{10} \times \frac{6}{5} = \$50 \times \frac{11}{10} \times \frac{6}{5} = 11 \times 6 = \$66$$

The change in value is $66 − $50 = $16.

Notice that that change is *not* 30% of $50 = $15. Never *add* successive percents (e.g., 10% and 20%). If you add the percents, the answer will be approximately right ($15 is *close* to $16), but it will not be the exact number.

If you...	Then you...	Like this:
Have successive percent changes	Multiply the original value by the new percents for *each* percent change	$50 is increased by 10%, and the result is increased by 20% $$\$50\left(\frac{11}{10}\right)\left(\frac{6}{5}\right) = \$66$$

Check Your Skills

16. What is 80% of 75% of 120?

Answer can be found on page 219.

Ratio: Part-to-Part and Part-to-Whole

Ratios or proportions express a particular kind of relationship between two quantities. That relationship is division. Consider this example:

> For every 2 bananas in a certain basket of fruit there are 3 apples.

This relationship can be rewritten this way:

$$\frac{\text{Number of bananas}}{\text{Number of apples}} = \frac{2}{3}$$

In words, the number of bananas divided by the number of apples is $\frac{2}{3}$.

In the example above, the ratio is expressing a *part-to-part relationship*. There are 2 "parts" bananas to 3 "parts" apples (though you still have only whole pieces of fruit).

You could also write this same information as a *part-to-whole relationship*. There are 2 bananas for every 5 pieces of fruit (because $2 + 3 = 5$), and there are 3 apples for every 5 pieces of fruit.

$$\frac{\text{Number of bananas}}{\text{Number of apples}} = \frac{2}{3} \qquad \frac{\text{Number of apples}}{\text{Total pieces}} = \frac{3}{5}$$

The language and symbols of ratios are peculiar. Note the following equivalent expressions:

For every 2 bananas, there are 3 apples.

There are 2 bananas for every 3 apples.

The ratio of bananas to apples is 2 to 3.

The ratio of bananas to apples is 2 : 3.

The ratio of bananas to apples is $\frac{2}{3}$.

Next, the ratio, by itself, does not actually indicate how many bananas and apples there really are. In other words, *a ratio tells you the relationship between two things, but not necessarily the actual numbers of those two things.*

In this case, there are at least 2 bananas and at least 3 apples in this basket—but there may be more. There could also be 4 bananas and 6 apples, or 6 bananas and 9 apples, or 20 bananas and 30 apples, and so on.

Notice what those pairs of numbers have in common? The number of bananas divided by the number of apples must equal $\frac{2}{3}$. There are many different possible combinations of actual numbers that will make this true.

By the way, use full words for the units *bananas* and *apples*. *Never* write 2B to mean 2 bananas or 3A to mean 3 apples because you may confuse those labels with variables. Single letters (such as *B* and *A*) should always represent variables, not units. The expression 2B would mean "2 times the number of bananas."

If you know that the ratio of bananas to apples is 2 to 3 and you are given one of the real numbers, then you can figure out the other real number. For instance, if there are 15 apples, then how many bananas are there?

	Part (bananas)	Part (apples)	Whole/Total
Ratio	2	3	$2 + 3 = 5$
Actual		15	

If you know that the 15 apples represent 3 parts of the ratio, then you can calculate a new number: **the unknown multiplier**. The unknown multiplier is the number by which you multiply the *ratio* to get to the *actual* number. In this case, the unknown multiplier is 5, because $3 \times 5 = 15$.

The unknown multiplier is always the same for all parts of a ratio. Once you know what it is, apply it to everything in the ratio.

	Part (bananas)	Part (apples)	Whole/Total
Ratio	2	3	5
× Unknown Multiplier	× 5	× 5	× 5
= Actual	10	15	25

Now you also know the actual number of bananas (10) and the actual total number of pieces of fruit (25).

When you don't yet know what the unknown multiplier is, call it x, and write out an algebraic representation for the actual numbers.

	Part (bananas)	Part (apples)	Whole/Total
Ratio	2	3	5
×	x	x	x
Actual	$2x$	$3x$	$5x$

If there are 12 bananas, how many apples are there?

Set up what you know: $12 = 2x$ = the actual number of bananas, so $x = 6$. The actual number of apples, therefore, is $3x$ = $3(6) = 18$.

Take a look at the table again. The actual number of bananas is always $2x$, and the actual number of apples is always $3x$. This formulation *guarantees* the ratio of 2 to 3.

$$\frac{\text{Number of bananas}}{\text{Number of apples}} = \frac{2x}{3x} = \frac{2\cancel{x}}{3\cancel{x}} = \frac{2}{3}$$

The unknown multiplier x is a common factor that cancels out to leave $\dfrac{2}{3}$, every single time.

Since the actual values will always simplify down to the same ratio, you can always set up an algebraic representation to solve. Consider this new problem:

> The ratio of apples to bananas in a certain display is 4 to 7. If there are 63 bananas, how many apples are there?

The ratio of apples to bananas is 4 : 7. The actual number of apples is $4x$, and the actual number of bananas is $7x$, where x represents the unknown multiplier. The problem states that there are 63 actual bananas, so set up an equation to solve:

$$7x = 63$$
$$x = 9$$

Now plug in the unknown multiplier to solve for the number of apples: $4x = 4(9) = 36$. There are 36 apples.

Alternatively, you can set up the table.

	Apples	Bananas	Total
R	4	7	
×	× 9	× 9	
A	36	63	

You don't need to fill out every cell in the table. Feel free to fill in only the parts you need to answer the question. Consider this example:

> The ratio of apples to bananas in a certain display is 4 to 7. If there are 28 apples, how many total pieces of fruit are there?

Again, you can set up an equation or use the table to solve—use what you find easier.

This time, you need the ratio total, which is equal to the sum of the individual parts of the ratio: $4 + 7 = 11$. The actual number of apples is $4x$ and the actual number of pieces of fruit is $11x$. Therefore:

$4x = 28$

$x = 7$

Total pieces of fruit = $11x = 11 \times 7 = 77$

Here's the table approach.

	A	B	Total
R	4	7	11
×	× 7		× 7
A	28		77

If there are 28 apples, then there are 77 total pieces of fruit.

If you…	Then you…	Like this:			
Are told that "the ratio of sharks to dolphins is 3 to 13"	Write each quantity in terms of the unknown multiplier OR Create the table	Sharks = 3x Dolphins = 13x			
			S	D	Total
		R	3	13	
		×			
		A	3x	13x	

MANHATTAN PREP

Check Your Skills

17. The ratio of blue marbles to white marbles in a bag is 3 : 5. If there are 15 white marbles in the bag, how many blue marbles are in the bag?

Answer can be found on page 220.

Ratios and Percents: Convert Fractions to Percents

You can now write two-way ratios between any two components.

Cars : Trucks = 2 : 3
Cars : Total Vehicles = 2 : 5
Trucks : Total Vehicles = 3 : 5

You can use this information to determine percents of the whole. Because there is a 2 : 5 ratio of cars to vehicles, $\frac{2}{5}$, or 40%, of the vehicles are cars. Likewise, $\frac{3}{5}$, or 60%, of the vehicles are trucks.

Here are a few other common Part : Part ratios and the resulting percents of the whole.

Cars : Trucks	Cars : Trucks : Total	Cars : Total	Trucks : Total
1 : 1	1 : 1 : 2	1 : 2 50%	1 : 2 50%
1 : 2	1 : 2 : 3	1 : 3 33.33…%	2 : 3 66.66…%
1 : 3	1 : 3 : 4	1 : 4 25%	3 : 4 75%

Consider this problem:

A bouquet contains white roses and red roses. If the ratio of white to red roses is 5 : 3, what percent of all the roses are red?

(A) 37.5%   (B) 40%   (C) 60%   (D) 62.5%   (E) 80%

Set up a Part : Part : Whole ratio using just the top row of the standard ratio table:

	White	Red	Total
R	5	3	8

The ratio of red to total is 3 to 8, or $\frac{3}{8}$. As a percent, $\frac{3}{8}$ = 37.5%. The correct answer is (A).

If you are given the percents of the two parts of the whole, you can set up a Part : Part : Whole ratio with the percents. Use 100 for the whole. Then reduce by removing common factors and you'll have the ratio. Here's an example.

If 20% of the animals in a certain zoo are skunks, what is the ratio of non-skunk animals to skunks in the zoo?

The Part + Part = Whole equation is Skunks + Non-skunks = Animals. If 20% of the animals are skunks, then 100% − 20% = 80% are non-skunks. Reduce those numbers as far as possible to get the ratio.

	S	N-S	Total
%	20%	80%	100%
R	1	4	5

The three numbers share a common factor of 20. Take out that common factor, and you have 1 : 4 : 5 as the ratio of skunks to non-skunks to total animals at the zoo.

Thus, the ratio of non-skunk animals to skunks is 4 to 1. When answering ratio questions, double-check the order in which you were asked to present the desired categories. A ratio of 1 to 4 would be incorrect for this question.

Try this problem:

> A car lot contains only sedans and trucks. There are 4 sedans for every 5 trucks on the lot. If there are 12 sedans on the lot, how many total vehicles are there?

Set up the table and solve.

	S	T	Total
R	4	5	9
×	× 3		× 3
A	12		27

Alternatively, set up an equation.

> Number of sedans = $4x$ = 12 sedans
> $x = 3$

Now plug in this multiplier to find the total number of vehicles.

> Total number of vehicles = $(4 + 5)x = 9(3) = 27$ vehicles

Notice that when the quantities are counting real things, you have to stick to positive integers: 1, 2, 3, etc. In that case, the unknown multiplier itself is restricted to positive integers as well. In other words, the parts and the whole must be multiples of the numbers in the ratio.

Take the bananas and apples example again.

> Bananas : Apples : Pieces of fruit = 2 : 3 : 5

The number of bananas is $2x$, and x must be an integer, so the number of bananas must be even (a multiple of 2).

Likewise, the number of apples ($3x$) must be a multiple of 3, and the total number of pieces of fruit ($5x$) must be a multiple of 5. If the GMAT asks you what *could* be the total number of pieces of fruit, then the right answer will be a multiple of 5, and the four wrong answers will not be.

In real life, you encounter ratios in recipes. You usually have more than two ingredients. But you can still use the unknown multiplier.

Take this recipe:

> 3 cups of olive oil
> \+ 1 cup of vinegar
> \+ ½ cup of lemon juice
> \+ ½ cup of mustard   = 5 cups of salad dressing

What if you need 7.5 cups of salad dressing for a big party? Find the unknown multiplier.

> Cups of salad dressing: $5x = 7.5$
> Therefore: $x = 1.5$

The multiplier is 1.5. Every ingredient is multiplied by the same factor (1.5 in this case). Note that you can have a non-integer multiplier when you are working with something that can be split into fractional parts, such as the number of cups of salad dressing. You couldn't do this for a problem about people; you don't want to have half of a person!

Cups of olive oil	$= 3x$	$= 3(1.5)$	$= 4.5$ cups
Cups of vinegar	$= 1x$	$= 1(1.5)$	$= 1.5$ cups
Cups of lemon juice	$= \dfrac{1}{2}x$	$= \dfrac{1}{2}(1.5)$	$= \dfrac{3}{4}$ cup
Cups of mustard	$= \dfrac{1}{2}x$	$= \dfrac{1}{2}(1.5)$	$= \dfrac{3}{4}$ cup

If you...	Then you...	Like this:
Have two parts that make a whole and that have a ratio of 3 to 4	Write the Part : Part : Whole ratio as 3 : 4 : 7, and use the unknown multiplier as needed	Oranges = $3x$ Apples = $4x$ so Pieces of fruit = $7x$

Check Your Skills

18. A flowerbed contains only roses and tulips. If the ratio of tulips to the total number of flowers in the bed is 5 : 11, and there are 121 flowers in the bed, how many roses are there?

Answer can be found on page 220.

Check Your Skills Answer Key

1. **3.5%:** Make the number seem greater; move the decimal to the right two places: $0.035 = 3.5\%$.

2. $\dfrac{3}{8}$: If you notice that 375 and 1,000 are both divisible by 125, then you can perform the simplification in one step. If not, simplify by smaller numbers until you can't go any further. The solution below shows dividing the top and bottom by 5 first and then dividing the top and bottom by 25.

$$0.375 = \frac{\overset{75}{\cancel{375}}}{\underset{200}{\cancel{1,000}}} = \frac{\overset{3}{\cancel{75}}}{\underset{8}{\cancel{200}}} = \frac{3}{8}$$

3. $\dfrac{6}{25}$:

$$24\% = \frac{\overset{6}{\cancel{24}}}{\underset{25}{\cancel{100}}} = \frac{6}{25}$$

4. **0.6:** This one is on the list to memorize. Because the denominator is 5, you can multiply the numerator and denominator by the same number to turn the denominator into a power of 10.

$$\frac{3}{5} \times \frac{2}{2} = \frac{6}{10} = 0.6$$

Alternatively, perform long division to convert a fraction to a decimal.

$$
\begin{array}{r}
0.6 \\
5\overline{)3.0} \\
-30 \\
\hline
0
\end{array}
$$

5. **37.5%:** This one is also on the list to memorize. Alternatively, perform long division.

$$
\begin{array}{r}
0.375 \\
8\overline{)3.000} \\
24 \\
\hline
60 \\
56 \\
\hline
40 \\
40 \\
\hline
0
\end{array}
$$

6. **3,275.3:**

$$32.753 \times 10^2 = 3,275.3$$

7. **4.3681:**

$$43{,}681 \times 10^{-4} = 43{,}681 \div 10^4 = 4.3681$$

8. **3.173:** Make sure to carry over the 1 from the units digit column. Since $8 + 5 = 13$, then 3 becomes the units digit and the tens digit becomes $4 + 2 + 1 = 7$.

$$\begin{array}{r} 3.128 \\ +\ \ 0.045 \\ \hline 3.173 \end{array}$$

9. **1.5616:**

$$\begin{array}{r} 1.8746 \\ -\ \ 0.3130 \\ \hline 1.5616 \end{array}$$

10. **0.66:**

$$0.6 \times 1.1 =$$
$$6 \times 11 = 66$$
$$0.6 \times 1.1 = 0.66$$

11. **0.000128:**

$$0.004 \times 0.032$$
$$4 \times 32 = 128$$
$$0.004 \times 0.032 = 0.000128$$

12. **208:** Move the decimal in 520,000 to the left four places and move the decimal in 0.0004 to the right four places.
$$520{,}000 \times 0.0004 = 52 \times 4 = 208$$

13. **12:** Move each decimal to the right five places.

$$\frac{0.00084}{0.00007} = \frac{84}{7} = 12$$

14. **70:**

21	=	$\frac{30}{100}$	×	x
21	is	30 percent	of	what number?

$$21 = \frac{30}{100}x$$

$$\frac{10\cancel{0}}{3\cancel{0}} \times 21 = x$$

$$\frac{10 \times \overset{7}{\cancel{21}}}{{}_1\cancel{3}} = x$$

$$70 = x$$

15. **20%:** To find the percent decrease, focus on the amount by which 90 was reduced. Since $90 - 72 = 18$, then:

$$\frac{18}{90} = \frac{{}^2\cancel{18}}{{}_{10}\cancel{90}} = \frac{2}{10} = 20\%$$

Alternatively, use the back-of-the-envelope approach. How do you go from 90 to 18?

$$90 - 100\%$$
$$9 = 10\%$$

Multiply 9 by 2 to get 18, so multiply 10% by 2 to get 20%.

16. **72:** Convert 80% and 75% to fractions: $80\% = \frac{4}{5}$ and $75\% = \frac{3}{4}$. Set up the equation and solve.

$$x = \frac{\cancel{4}}{5} \times \frac{3}{\cancel{4}} \times 120$$

$$x = \frac{\cancel{4}}{\cancel{5}} \times \frac{3}{\cancel{4}} \times \overset{24}{\cancel{120}}$$

$$x = 3 \times 24 = 72$$

17. **9:** The ratio of blue to white is 3 : 5. There are 15 white marbles, so set the 15 equal to $5x$, and solve for the unknown multiplier.

$$5x = 15$$
$$x = 3$$

Therefore, the number of blue marbles is $3x$, which is $3(3) = 9$.

Alternatively, use the table to solve.

	B	W	Total
R	3	5	
×	× 3	× 3	
A	9	15	

18. **66:** If the ratio of tulips to all flowers is 5 : 11, then roses must represent $11 - 5 = 6$ in the ratio. The ratio of roses to tulips to all flowers is 6 : 5 : 11.
Use the total number of flowers, 121, to find the unknown multiplier.

$$11x = 121$$
$$x = 11$$

The total number of roses is $6x$, which is $6(11) = 66$.

Chapter Review: Drill Sets

Drill 1

1. Fill in the missing information in the chart below. See the third line for an example.

Fraction	Decimal	Percent
		1%
$\frac{1}{20}$		
$\frac{1}{10}$	0.1	10%
$\frac{1}{8}$		
	0.2	
		25%
	0.3	
		33.33…%
$\frac{3}{8}$		
		40%
$\frac{1}{2}$		
	0.6	
		66.66…%
		70%
	0.75	
$\frac{4}{5}$		
	0.875	
$\frac{9}{10}$		
		100%
	1.1	
$\frac{6}{5}$		
		125%
	1.5	

Drill 2

2. Convert 45% to a decimal.
3. Convert 0.20 to a percent.
4. Convert $\frac{4}{5}$ to a percent.
5. Convert 13.25% to a decimal.
6. Convert $\frac{6}{20}$ to a percent.
7. Convert 0.304 to a percent.
8. Convert 0.02% to a decimal.
9. Convert 0.375 to a fraction.
10. Convert $\frac{3}{2}$ to a percent.

Drill 3

Simplify the following expressions. Answers in the explanations may appear in more than one form (e.g., fraction and decimal).

11. $\frac{1}{2} \times 50\%$

12. $25\% - 0.1$

13. $\frac{2}{3} + 0.3$

14. $\frac{16}{5} \div 0.8$

15. $\frac{3}{8} \div 10\%$

16. What is 30% of $3.50?

17. What is 0.3 times 110%?

18. Simplify $\frac{2}{5} + 20\% + 0.7$.

19. Simplify $1.5 \div \left(\frac{5}{8} - 50\% \right)$.

20. Simplify $190\% - \left(1.2 \div \frac{4}{5} \right)$.

Drill 4

Simplify the following expressions.

21. 6.75×10^3
22. $1 + 0.2 + 0.03 + 0.004$
23. 0.27×2
24. 72.12×10^{-3}
25. 0.6×0.4
26. $0.48 + 0.02$
27. $\frac{4}{0.2}$
28. 20×0.35
29. $\frac{54.197}{10^2}$
30. $\frac{12.6}{0.3}$

Drill 5

Simplify the following expressions.

31. $2{,}346 \times 10^{-2}$
32. $1.21 + 0.38$
33. $\frac{6}{0.5}$
34. 2.1×0.04
35. 0.03×0.05
36. $0.370 + 0.042$
37. $\frac{3.2}{0.04}$
38. $0.6(50) + 0.25(120)$
39. $\frac{0.49}{0.07}$
40. $100 \times 0.01 \times 0.01$

Drill 6

41. 4.672×10^4 equals which of the following?
    (A) 4,672
    (B) 46,720
    (C) 467,200

42. 337×10^{-4} equals which of the following?
    (A) 3,370,000
    (B) 0.0337
    (C) 0.0000337

43. 8.25×10^5 equals which of the following?
    (A) 825×10^7
    (B) 825×10^4
    (C) 825×10^3

44. 0.003482 equals which of the following?
    (A) 34.82×10^{-4}
    (B) 34.82×10^2
    (C) 34.82×10^4

45. 12.12×10^{-3} equals which of the following?

    (A) -1.21×10^3
    (B) 0.00001212×10^3
    (C) 0.01212×10^3

Drill 7

46. What is 15% of 40?
47. 12 is 5% of what number?
48. 4 is what percent of 32?
49. 7% of 9 is what percent of 7?
50. 25% of 30 is 75% of what number?
51. What percent of 6 is 37.5% of 160?
52. If 14 is added to 56, what is the percent increase?
53. What is the percent increase from 50 to 60?
54. What number is 40% more than 30?
55. What is 60% less than 60?

Drill 8

56. If *m* is reduced by 55%, the resulting number is 90. What is the value of *m*?
57. If 75 reduced by *x* percent is 54, what is the value of *x*?
58. If *x* is 15% more than 20, what is 30% of *x*?
59. What is 50% of 12% of 50?
60. What is 120% of 30% of 400?
61. If 45% of 80 is *x* percent more than 24, what is the value of *x*?
62. 10% of 30% of what number is 200% of 6?
63. If $q \neq 0$, what percent of 25% of *q* is *q* percent of 20?
64. If $a \neq 0$, 200% of 4% of *a* is what percent of $\dfrac{a}{2}$?

65. If positive integer *m* is first increased by 20%, then decreased by 25%, and finally increased by 60%, the resulting number is what percent of *m*?

Drill 9

66. If there are 20 birds and 6 dogs in a park, which of the following is the ratio of dogs to birds?
    (A) 3 : 13
    (B) 3 : 10
    (C) 10 : 3

67. In a class of 24 students made up of only juniors and seniors, 12 are juniors. Which of the following is the ratio of juniors to seniors in the class?
    (A) 1 : 1
    (B) 1 : 2
    (C) 2 : 1

68. If there are 45 red marbles and 35 green marbles in a bag, which of the following is the ratio of green to red marbles?
    (A) 9 : 16
    (B) 7 : 9
    (C) 9 : 7

69. There are 21 trout and 24 catfish in a pond. There are no other fish in the pond. What is the ratio of catfish to the total number of fish in the pond?
    (A) 7 : 15
    (B) 8 : 15
    (C) 7 : 8

Drill 10

70. Fill in the missing information in the table below.

1 : 2	=	3 : __	=	__ : 14	=	__ : 22
1 : __	=	4 : 20	=	__ : 25	=	15 : __
3 : __	=	__ : 8	=	__ : 36	=	33 : 44
__ : 7	=	20 : __	=	40 : 56	=	60 : __
4 : 11	=	__ : 22	=	36 : __	=	__ : 132

Drill 11

71. A recipe calls for 1 cup of cheese and $\frac{1}{2}$ cup of sauce in order to make 1 pizza. If Bob used 15 cups of sauce to make pizzas, how much cheese did he use?

72. On a safari, Sofia saw only giraffes and lions. If she saw 7 giraffes for every 3 lions, and she saw 60 animals in total, how many lions did she see?

    (A) 18
    (B) 21
    (C) 42

73. The ratio of oranges to peaches to strawberries in a fruit basket is 2 : 3 : 4. If there are 8 oranges, how many pieces of fruit are in the basket?

74. A certain automotive dealer sells only cars and trucks and currently has 51 trucks for sale. If the ratio of cars for sale to trucks for sale is 1 to 3, how many cars are for sale?

75. Mustafa has invented a new dance in which he moves 3 steps forward for every 4 steps he moves back. If the dance requires 49 steps in total, how many total steps forward has Mustafa taken at the completion of the dance?

    (A) 7
    (B) 21
    (C) 28

76. A steel manufacturer combines 98 ounces of iron with 2 ounces of carbon to make 1 sheet of steel. How much iron is used in $\frac{1}{2}$ of a sheet of steel?

77. To make a 64-ounce smoothie, Malin must use 4 bananas, 2 apples, 6 cups of yogurt, and 8 teaspoons of protein powder. How many cups of yogurt will she need to make a 16-ounce smoothie?

Drill Sets Solutions

Drill 1

1.

Fraction	Decimal	Percent
$\dfrac{1}{100}$	0.01	1%
$\dfrac{1}{20}$	0.05	5%
$\dfrac{1}{10}$	0.1	10%
$\dfrac{1}{8}$	0.125	12.5%
$\dfrac{1}{5}$	0.2	20%
$\dfrac{1}{4}$	0.25	25%
$\dfrac{3}{10}$	0.3	30%
$\dfrac{1}{3}$	0.3333…	33.33…%
$\dfrac{3}{8}$	0.375	37.5%
$\dfrac{2}{5}$	0.40	40%
$\dfrac{1}{2}$	0.50	50%
$\dfrac{3}{5}$	0.6	60%
$\dfrac{2}{3}$	0.6666…	66.66…%
$\dfrac{7}{10}$	0.7	70%
$\dfrac{3}{4}$	0.75	75%

5

Fraction	Decimal	Percent
$\dfrac{4}{5}$	0.8	80%
$\dfrac{7}{8}$	0.875	87.5%
$\dfrac{9}{10}$	0.9	90%
1	1.0	100%
$\dfrac{11}{10}$	1.1	110%
$\dfrac{6}{5}$	1.2	120%
$\dfrac{5}{4}$	1.25	125%
$\dfrac{3}{2}$	1.5	150%

Drill 2

2. **0.45:** To convert from a percent to a decimal, move the decimal point two places to the left (to make it appear *smaller*), so 45% becomes 0.45.

3. **20%:** To convert from a decimal to a percent, move the decimal point two places to the right (to make it appear *greater*) and add a percent sign, so 0.20 becomes 20%.

4. **80%:** This one is on the conversion list to memorize. Alternatively, perform long division to find the decimal form, then convert to a percent.

   Step 1: $4 \div 5 = 0.8$ $5\overline{)4.0}^{\,0.8}$
   Step 2: 0.8 becomes 80%

   An additional shortcut is to convert the denominator to 100 by multiplying both the numerator and denominator by 20.

   $$\dfrac{4}{5} \times \dfrac{20}{20} = \dfrac{80}{100} = 80\%$$

5. **0.1325:** 13.25% becomes 0.1325.

MANHATTAN PREP

6. **30%:** $\dfrac{6}{20}$ simplifies to $\dfrac{3}{10}$, which is on the list to memorize. Alternatively, perform long division to find the

decimal form, then convert to a percent.

$$\begin{array}{ll} \text{Step 1: } 6 \div 20 = 0.30 & \underline{0.3} \\ \text{Step 2: } 0.30 \text{ becomes } 30\% & 20\overline{)6.0} \end{array}$$

An additional shortcut is to convert the denominator to 100 by multiplying both the numerator and denominator by 5.

$$\frac{6}{20} \times \frac{5}{5} = \frac{30}{100} = 30\%$$

7. **30.4%:** 0.304 becomes 30.4%.

8. **0.0002:** Careful! To convert from a percent to a decimal, still move the decimal point two places to the *left*, even though this creates a really small number, as 0.02% becomes 0.0002.

9. $\dfrac{3}{8}$ **:** This one is on the list to memorize. Alternatively, 0.375 becomes $\dfrac{375}{1,000}$, which reduces to $\dfrac{3}{8}$.

10. **150%:** This one is on the list to memorize. Alternatively, perform long division to find the decimal form, then convert to a percent.

$$\begin{array}{ll} \text{Step 1: } 3 \div 2 = 1.5 & \underline{1.5} \\ \text{Step 2: } 1.5 \text{ becomes } 150\% & 2\overline{)3.0} \end{array}$$

An additional shortcut is to convert the denominator to 100 by multiplying both the numerator and denominator by 50.

$$\frac{3}{2} \times \frac{50}{50} = \frac{150}{100} = 150\%$$

Drill 3

11. $\frac{1}{4}$ or 25%:

$\frac{1}{2} \times 50\% =$ Convert percent to fraction because fractions are easier to multiply than percents.

$\frac{1}{2} \times \frac{50}{100} =$ Simplify before you multiply.

$\frac{1}{2} \times \frac{1}{2} =$

$\frac{1}{4}$ or 25%

12. **15% or 0.15:**

$25\% - 0.1 =$

$25\% - 10\% =$ Convert decimal to percent because 1) it's easier to add or subtract integers, and 2) 0.1 is easy to convert to a percent (if you don't already have it memorized).

15%

13. $\frac{29}{30}$:

$\frac{2}{3} + 0.3 =$ Convert decimal to fraction because $\frac{2}{3}$ is a repeating decimal (that is, it can't be converted to an easy decimal form).

$\frac{2}{3} + \frac{3}{10} =$

$\overset{20}{\underset{3}{2}} \overset{+}{\times} \overset{3}{\underset{10}{}} \overset{9}{} = \frac{29}{30}$ Use the double-cross to add.

14. **4:**

$\frac{16}{5} \div 0.8 =$ Convert decimal to fraction because 1) this decimal is a "have this memorized" decimal, and 2) you will then be able to simplify before multiplying.

$\frac{16}{5} \div \frac{4}{5} =$

$\frac{16}{5} \times \frac{5}{4} =$

$\frac{\overset{4}{\cancel{16}}}{\cancel{5}} \times \frac{\cancel{5}}{\cancel{4}} = 4$ Simplify before you multiply.

15. **3.75 or $\dfrac{15}{4}$ or $3\dfrac{3}{4}$:**

$\dfrac{3}{8} \div 10\% =$ Convert percent to fraction because fractions are easier to divide than percents.

$\dfrac{3}{8} \div \dfrac{1}{10} =$

$\dfrac{3}{8} \times \dfrac{10}{1} =$

$\dfrac{3}{\cancel{8}_{4}} \times \dfrac{\cancel{10}^{5}}{1} =$ Simplify before you multiply.

$\dfrac{15}{4}$

16. **$1.05:**

30% of $3.50   How can you get to 30% using the "easy" percentages of 50%, 10%, 5%, or 1%?
100%: $3.50
10%: $0.35   Take 10% of $3.50.
(0.35)(3) = $1.05   Multiply by 3 to get 30%.

17. **0.33 or $\dfrac{33}{100}$ or 33%:** If you feel comfortable taking percents, you can take 10% of 0.3 and add that to 100% of 0.3 to get 110% of 0.3.

100% of 0.3 is 0.3
10% of 0.3 is 0.03 (move the decimal one place to the left)
0.3 + 0.03 = 0.33

Alternatively, convert both values to fractions (because fractions are easier to simplify and multiply), and solve from there.

$0.3 \times 110\% = \dfrac{3}{10} \times \dfrac{11\cancel{0}}{10\cancel{0}} = \dfrac{33}{100} = 33\% = 0.33$

18. **130% or $\dfrac{13}{10}$ or 1.3:** Note that all of the forms are part of your memorized lists. It's easier to add integers (in the form of percents) than decimals or fractions, so convert all three terms to percents.

$$\frac{2}{5} + 20\% + 0.7 =$$

$$40\% + 20\% + 70\% =$$

$$130\%$$

19. **12 or 1,200%:**

$$1.5 \div \left(\frac{5}{8} - 50\% \right) =$$ Convert percent to fraction because 50% is easier to convert than $\dfrac{5}{8}$.

$$1.5 \div \left(\frac{5}{8} - \frac{1}{2} \right) =$$

$$1.5 \div \left(\frac{5}{8} - \frac{4}{8} \right) =$$

$$= 1.5 \div \left(\frac{1}{8} \right) =$$

$$\frac{3}{2} \div \frac{1}{8} =$$ Convert decimal to fraction because 1) 1.5 is easier to convert than $\dfrac{1}{8}$,

$$\frac{3}{2} \times \frac{8}{1} =$$ and 2) it's easier to divide fractions as factors often cancel.

$$\frac{3}{\cancel{2}} \times \frac{\cancel{8}^{4}}{1} =$$

$$12$$

20. **40% or 0.4 or $\dfrac{2}{5}$:**

$$190\% - \left(1.2 \div \dfrac{4}{5}\right) =$$ Convert decimal to fraction because fractions are easier to divide than decimals.

$$190\% - \left(\dfrac{6}{5} \div \dfrac{4}{5}\right) =$$

$$190\% - \left(\dfrac{6}{5} \times \dfrac{5}{4}\right) =$$

$$190\% - \left(\dfrac{3}{2}\right) =$$

$$190\% - 150\% =$$ Convert fraction to percent because $\dfrac{3}{2}$ is easier to convert than 190%, and percents are easier to subtract.

$$40\%$$

Drill 4

21. **6,750:** Move the decimal to the right three places.

$$6.75 \times 10^3 = 6,750$$

22. **1.234:** Line up the decimals and add.

$$\begin{array}{r} 1.000 \\ + \ 0.200 \\ + \ 0.030 \\ + \ 0.004 \\ \hline 1.234 \end{array}$$

23. **0.54:** First, ignore the decimals and multiply the numbers. Then move the decimal two places to the left to account for the two decimals in the initial problem.

$$0.27 \times 2 =$$
$$27 \times 2 = 54$$
$$0.27 \times 2 = 0.54$$

24. **0.07212:** Move the decimal three places to the left.

$$72.12 \times 10^{-3} = 0.07212$$

25. **0.24:** First, ignore the decimals and multiply the numbers. Then move the decimal two places to the left to account for the two decimals in the initial problem.

$$0.6 \times 0.4 =$$
$$6 \times 4 = 24$$
$$0.6 \times 0.4 = 0.24$$

26. **0.50:** Line up the decimal points and add.

$$\begin{array}{r} 0.48 \\ + \ 0.02 \\ \hline 0.50 \end{array}$$

27. **20:** Multiply the top and bottom by 10 to get rid of the decimal.

$$\frac{4}{0.2} \times \frac{10}{10} = \frac{40}{2} = 20$$

28. **7:** Trade off a decimal place to make the math easier.

$$20 \times 0.35 =$$
$$2 \times 3.5 = \qquad \text{Take a decimal from 20 and give it to 0.35.}$$
$$2 \times 3.5 = 7$$

29. **0.54197:** Divide by 100, or move the decimal two places to the left.

$$\frac{54.197}{10^2} = \frac{54.197}{100} = 0.54197$$

30. **42:** Multiply the top and bottom by 10, or move each decimal one place to the right, in order to get integers.

$$\frac{12.6}{0.3} \times \frac{10}{10} = \frac{126}{3} = 42$$

Drill 5

31. **23.46:** Move the decimal two places to the left.

$$2{,}346 \times 10^{-2} = 23.46$$

32. **1.59:** Line up the decimal points and add.

$$\begin{array}{r} 1.21 \\ + \; 0.38 \\ \hline 1.59 \end{array}$$

33. **12:** Multiply the top and bottom by 10 (or move the decimal one place to the right on both the top and bottom).

$$\frac{6}{0.5} \times \frac{10}{10} = \frac{60}{5} = 12$$

34. **0.084:** Ignore the decimals and multiply the numbers. Then move the decimal three places to the left.

$$2.1 \times 0.04 = ?$$
$$21 \times 4 = 84$$
$$2.1 \times 0.04 = 0.084$$

35. **0.0015:** Ignore the decimals and multiply the numbers. Then move the decimal four places to the left.

$$0.03 \times 0.05 = ?$$
$$3 \times 5 = 15$$
$$0.03 \times 0.05 = 0.0015$$

36. **0.412:** Line up the decimals, then add.

$$\begin{array}{r} \overset{1}{0.3}70 \\ + \; 0.042 \\ \hline 0.412 \end{array}$$

37. **80:** Multiply the top and bottom by 100 (or move both decimal points to the right two places) to get rid of the decimals. Then simplify.

$$\frac{3.20}{0.04} \times \frac{100}{100} = \frac{320}{4} = 80$$

38. 60: Convert the decimals to fractions because fractions are easier to multiply. Then simplify.

$$0.6(50) + 0.25(120) =$$

$$\left(\frac{3}{5} \times 50\right) + \left(\frac{1}{4} \times 120\right) =$$

$$\left(\frac{3}{\cancel{5}} \times \cancel{50}^{10}\right) + \left(\frac{1}{\cancel{4}} \times \cancel{120}^{30}\right) =$$

$$30 + 30 =$$

$$60$$

39. 7: Multiply the top and bottom by 100 (or move the decimal point two places to the right on the top and bottom).

$$\frac{0.49}{0.07} \times \frac{100}{100} = \frac{49}{7} = 7$$

40. 0.01: Ignore the decimals and multiply the numbers first, then insert the missing decimal by moving the decimal point four places to the left.

$$100 \times 0.01 \times 0.01 = ?$$
$$100 \times 1 \times 1 = 100$$
$$100 \times 0.01 \times 0.01 = 0.01$$

Drill 6

41. (B): The answer choices don't use a power of 10, so you need to multiply that 10^4 into the starting number. Since the exponent is a positive 4, move the decimal four places to the right.

$$4.6720$$

The number becomes 46,720.

42. (B): Multiplying by 10^{-4} will make the resultant number smaller. Because the exponent is -4, move the decimal four places to the left.

$$0337.$$

The number becomes 0.0337.

43. (C): Glance at the answers. All are 825 multiplied by a power of 10. What math occurs to turn 8.25 into 825?

$$8.25$$

In other words, 8.25 increases by two decimal places to 825. In order to balance out that increase, reduce the exponent by 2; 10^5 becomes 10^3. The new form of the number is 825×10^3.

44. **(A):** Glance at the answers. All start with the form 34.82, so first figure out how may decimal places you need to move in order to get to that number.

$$0.00\underset{\smile\smile\smile\smile}{3482}$$

The number 0.003482 increased by four decimal places. In order to balance out that increase, multiply by a power of 10^{-4}, since the exponent is equivalent to the number of decimal places moved: 34.82×10^{-4}.

You can also write the original number this way: 0.003482×10^0 (note that $10^0 = 1$). Therefore, if you add four decimal points to the starting number, then subtract four from the exponent: $0.003482 \times 10^0 = 34.82 \times 10^{-4}$.

45. **(B):** Glance at the answers. Each one uses the form 10^3. If you change the exponent from −3 to 3, how do you need to change the starting number?

To go from −3 to 3, add 6. If the exponent adds 6, then the starting number needs to lose six decimal places.

$$\underset{\smile\smile\smile\smile\smile\smile}{000012}.12$$

The number becomes 0.00001212×10^3.

Drill 7

46. **6:**

What	is	15%	of	40?
x	$=$	$\dfrac{15}{100}$	$\times$	40

$$x = \frac{15}{100} \times 40$$

$$x = \frac{3}{20} \times 40$$

$$x = \frac{3}{\cancel{20}} \times {}^2\cancel{40}$$

$$x = 6$$

47. **240:**

12	is	5%	of	what number?
12	$=$	$\dfrac{5}{100}$	$\times$	x

$$12 = \frac{5}{100} \times x$$

$$12 = \frac{1}{20} \times x$$

$$20(12) = x$$

$$x = 240$$

48. **12.5%:**

4	is	what percent	of	32?
4	=	$\dfrac{x}{100}$	×	32

$$4 = \frac{x}{100} \times 32$$

$$400 = x \times 32$$

$$\frac{400}{32} = x$$

$$\frac{100}{8} = x$$

$$12.5 = x$$

49. **9%:**

7%	of	9	is	what percent	of	7
$\dfrac{7}{100}$	×	9	=	$\dfrac{x}{100}$	×	7

$$\frac{7}{100} \times 9 = \frac{x}{100} \times 7 \qquad \text{Multiply both sides by 100.}$$

$$7 \times 9 = x \times 7$$

$$9 = x$$

50. **10:** Use your memorized equivalents for 25% and 75%.

25%	of	30	is	75%	of	what?
$\dfrac{1}{4}$	×	30	=	$\dfrac{3}{4}$	×	x

$$\frac{1}{4} \times 30 = \frac{3}{4} \times x \qquad \text{Multiply both sides by 4.}$$

$$30 = 3 \times x$$

$$10 = x$$

51. **1,000%:** 37.5% is on the list of common equivalents to memorize.

What percent	of	6	is	37.5%	of	160
$\dfrac{x}{100}$	$\times$	6	=	$\dfrac{3}{8}$	$\times$	160

$$\frac{x}{100} \times 6 = \frac{3}{8} \times 160 \qquad \text{Simplify before you multiply.}$$

$$\frac{x}{100} \times 6 = \frac{3}{\cancel{8}} \times \cancel{160}^{\,20}$$

$$\frac{x}{100} \times 6 = 60$$

$$\frac{x}{100} = 10$$

$$x = 1,000$$

52. **25% increase:** In this percent change problem, the change is 14 and the original number is 56. Use the Percent Change formula.

$$\text{Percent change} = \frac{\text{Change}}{\text{Original}}$$

$$\frac{14}{56} = \frac{1}{4} = 25\%$$

53. **20% increase:** If the increase is 50 to 60, then the change is 60 − 50 = 10, and 50 is the original number. Use the Percent Change formula:

$$\text{Percent change} = \frac{\text{Change}}{\text{Original}}$$

$$\frac{10}{50} = \frac{1}{5} = 20\%$$

54. **42:** There are two ways to represent "40% more than 30." The first is a literal translation—30 plus an additional 40% of 30.

$$x = 30 + \left(\frac{40}{100} \times 30 \right)$$

Find 40% of 30, then add to 30.

100% = 30	Find 10% of 30.
10% = 3	
(10%)(4) = 40%	To find 40%, multiply 10% by 4.
(3)(4) = 12	
30 + 12 = 42	Add 30 + 40% of 30.

Alternatively, 40% more than a number is the same as 100% of that number plus an additional 40%, or 140%. In that case, "40% more than 30" can be represented this way:

$$x = \frac{140}{100} \times 30$$

$$x = \frac{14\cancel{0}}{1\cancel{0}\cancel{0}} \times 3\cancel{0}$$

$$x = 42$$

55. **24:** You can use fractions to set this up:

$$x = 60 - \left(\frac{60}{100} \times 60 \right)$$

60% of 60 is equivalent to 10% of 60 multiplied by 6. Do the math in two steps: 10% of 60 is 6, and $6 \times 6 = 36$. Therefore:

$$x = 60 - 36 = 24$$

Alternatively, "60% less than" 60 is equivalent to "40% of" 60.

$$x = \frac{40}{100} \times 60$$

40% of 60 is equivalent to 10% of 60 multiplied by 4. Do the math in two steps: 10% of 60 is 6, and $6 \times 4 = 24$.

Drill 8

56. **200:** If m is *reduced* by 55%, then 45% of *m* remains. Use the 45% figure in the translation.

$$0.45m = 90$$ Multiply both sides by 100 to get rid of the decimal.

$$45m = 9,000$$ Simplify before you divide!

$$m = \frac{^{2}\cancel{9,000}}{\cancel{45}}$$ The 90 and 45 cancel. Don't forget about the two leftover zeros!

$$m = 200$$

Glance at the answer in the context of the question stem. Does it make sense? When 200 is reduced by 55%, the answer is 90. In other words, 200 is reduced by a little more than half, so what remains (90) is a little less than half; the answer does make sense.

When you have lots of zeros or are shifting decimals, you may want to double-check the solution in this way to make sure that it makes sense. If you had gotten an answer of 2, for example, you would have asked yourself: Does it make sense that 2 reduced by 55% equals 90? No! In this way, you might catch a careless mistake.

57. **28:** Translate the problem. As always, simplify before you multiply.

$$75 - \left(\frac{x}{100} \times 75\right) = 54$$

$$75 - 54 = \frac{75x}{100}$$

$$21 = \frac{3x}{4}$$

$$^{7}\cancel{21}\left(\frac{4}{\cancel{3}}\right) = x$$

$$28 = x$$

You could also use the percent change formula. If 75 has been reduced to 54, then the change is $75 - 54 = 21$. The original number is 75. Use the formula:

$$\text{Percent change} = \frac{\text{Change}}{\text{Original}}$$

$$\frac{21}{75} = \frac{7}{25}$$

Now what? Get the denominator to be 100 so that the number is expressed as a percent.

$$\frac{7}{25} = \frac{28}{100} = 28\%$$

58. **6.9 or $\dfrac{69}{10}$** : There are two equations—"x is 15% more than 20" and "what is 30% of x?" Also, the question stem specifies a variable named x already, so translate the word *what* as a different variable. Use y. Now set up your equations:

$$x = \frac{115}{100} \times 20$$

$$y = \frac{3}{10} \times x$$

Solve the first equation for x.

$$x = \frac{115}{100} \times 20$$

$$= \frac{115}{\cancel{100}_{5}} \times \cancel{20}$$

$$= \frac{115}{5}$$

$$= 23$$

Plug $x = 23$ into the second equation to find y.

$$y = \frac{3}{10} \times 23$$

$$y = \frac{69}{10}$$

$$y = 6.9$$

59. **3:** Use a fractional representation here because fractions are easier to multiply:

$$x = \frac{1}{2} \times \frac{12}{100} \times 50$$

$$x = \frac{1}{2} \times \frac{6}{\cancel{50}} \times \cancel{50}$$

$$x = 3$$

60. **144:** Translate and simplify. Note that there are three zeros on top and three on the bottom; cancel them all.

$$x = \frac{120}{100} \times \frac{3}{10} \times 400$$

$$x = \frac{12\cancel{0}}{1\cancel{00}} \times \frac{3}{1\cancel{0}} \times 4\cancel{00}$$

$$x = 12 \times 3 \times 4$$

$$x = 144$$

61. **50:** Translate and simplify. Because the translation is decently long, it might be helpful to figure out the parts separately.

For the left-hand side of the equation, you can make 45% by adding 10% + 10% + 10% + 10% + 5%, or 10% four times and 5% once. First, find the individual percentages: 10% of 80 is 8 and 5% of 80 is half of 8, or 4. Now solve:

$$(8)(4) + 4 = 36$$

Alternatively, you can make 45% by taking 50% − 5%. Again, find the individual percentages first: 50% of 80 is 40. To get 5% from 50%, move the decimal one place to the left: 40 becomes 4. Now subtract:

$$40 − 4 = 36$$

Either way, the equation in the question stem is now "36 is x percent more than 24." This is a percent change problem! The original number is the "more than" number, 24. The change is the difference between the two numbers: 36 − 24 = 12. Use the Percent Change formula to solve:

$$Percent\ change = \frac{12}{24} = \frac{1}{2} = 50\%$$

Note that the answer is 50, not 50%. The question stem refers to x percent and asks for x by itself. If you plug 50 for x into the question stem, the equation will then say 50%.

62. **400:** Use your memorized percent equivalents. If you know that 200% = 2, you can skip the first line of math and go straight to the second.

$$\frac{1}{10} \times \frac{3}{10} \times x = \frac{200}{100} \times 6$$
$$\frac{1}{10} \times \frac{3}{10} \times x = 2 \times 6$$
$$x = \left(2 \times \cancel{6}^{\,2}\right)\left(\frac{100}{\cancel{3}}\right)$$
$$x = 400$$

63. **80%:** The question already contains a variable (q), so use another variable to represent the unknown "what" percent. Try n.

$$\frac{n}{100} \times \frac{1}{4} \times q = \frac{q}{100} \times 20$$
$$\frac{n}{\cancel{100}} \times \frac{1}{4} \times \cancel{q} = \frac{\cancel{q}}{\cancel{100}} \times 20$$
$$\frac{n}{4} = 20$$
$$n = 80$$

64. **16%:**

$$\frac{200}{100} \times \frac{4}{100} \times a = \frac{x}{100} \times \frac{a}{2}$$

$$2 \times \frac{4}{100} \times a = \frac{x}{100} \times \frac{a}{2} \qquad \text{Divide both sides by } a.$$

$$2 \times 4 = \frac{x}{2} \qquad \text{Multiply both sides by 100.}$$

$$2 \times 2 \times 4 = x$$

$$16 = x$$

65. **144%:** Assign a new variable for "what" percent. Try x. Notice that both sides of the equation below are multiplied by the variable m. Cancel it immediately (since it is not zero), and solve for x.

$$m \times \frac{120}{100} \times \frac{75}{100} \times \frac{160}{100} = \frac{x}{100} \times m$$

$$\frac{6}{5} \times \frac{3}{4} \times \frac{8}{5} = \frac{x}{100}$$

$$\frac{6}{5} \times \frac{3}{4} \times \frac{8^{2}}{5} = \frac{x}{100}$$

$$\frac{36}{25} = \frac{x}{100}$$

$$^{4}100 \times \frac{36}{25} = x$$

$$144 = x$$

Drill 9

66. **(B):** The information was given in the order birds : dogs, but the question asks about dogs : birds. Make sure to put the info in the right order. If there are 6 dogs and 20 birds in the park, the ratio of dogs to birds is 6 : 20. Divide by 2 to simplify this ratio to its base form, 3 : 10.

67. **(A):** If 12 of 24 students in the class are juniors, then the remainder, 24 − 12 = 12, are seniors. Therefore, the ratio of juniors to seniors in the class is 12 : 12. Divide by 12 to simplify the ratio to its base form, 1 : 1.

68. **(B):** The question first presents the information in the order of red marbles to green, but the question asks about the ratio of green to red. There are 35 green to 45 red, or 35 : 45. Divide each number by 5 to simplify the ratio to its base form, 7 : 9.

69. **(B):** If there are 21 trout and 24 catfish, then there are 21 + 24 = 45 total fish in the pond. The ratio of catfish to the total is therefore 24 : 45. Simplify the ratio to its base form. The number 3 is a factor of both numbers, so divide by 3 to get 8 : 15.

Drill 10

70. If the table does not give you the most basic form of the ratio, find that basic form first. Use it to find the other answers.

1 : 2	=	3 : **6**	=	**7** : 14	=	**11** : 22
1 : **5**	=	4 : 20	=	**5** : 25	=	15 : **75**
3 : **4**	=	**6** : 8	=	**27** : 36	=	33 : 44
5 : 7	=	20 : **28**	=	40 : 56	=	60 : **84**
4 : 11	=	**8** : 22	=	36 : **99**	=	**48** : 132

Drill 11

71. **30 cups:** The ratio of cheese to sauce is $1 : \dfrac{1}{2}$, and Bob uses 15 cups of sauce. Use the table to find the unknown multiplier.

	Cheese	Sauce	Total
R	1	$\dfrac{1}{2}$	
×	× 30	× 30	
A	**30**	15	

72. **(A):** The ratio of giraffes to lions is 7 : 3, and Sofia saw 60 animals total. Set up a table to figure out how many lions she saw.

	G	L	Total
R	7	3	10
×		× 6	× 6
A		18	60

73. **36 pieces of fruit:** The ratio of oranges to peaches to strawberries is 2 : 3 : 4, and there are 8 oranges total. Set up a table to solve for the number of pieces of fruit.

	O	P	S	Total
R	2	3	4	9
×	× 4			× 4
A	8			**36**

74. **17 cars:** The ratio of cars to trucks is 1 : 3, and there are 51 trucks for sale. Set up a table to solve for the number of cars.

	C	T	Total
R	1	3	
×	× 17	× 17	
A	17	51	

75. **(B):** The ratio of forward to back is 3 : 4, and the dance consists of 49 steps in total. Use a table to determine how many forward steps Mustafa takes.

	F	B	Total
R	3	4	7
×	× 7		× 7
A	21		49

76. **49 ounces:** The ratio of iron to carbon to sheets of steel is 98 : 2 : 1. You can set up a table to find how much iron to use to make just $\frac{1}{2}$ of a sheet of steel. But reflect for a moment first.

You might notice that $\frac{1}{2}$ of a sheet of steel is exactly half of 1 full sheet of steal. As a result, you would need half as much iron, or $\frac{98}{2} = 49$ ounces. No table needed!

MANHATTAN PREP

77. $1\frac{1}{2}$ **cups:** The ratio of bananas to apples to yogurt to protein powder is 4 : 2 : 6 : 8 for a 64-ounce smoothie. Set up a table to determine the number of cups of yogurt needed to make a 16-ounce smoothie. Note that, in this case, the total is the 64 ounces of smoothie, not the total number of various ingredients.

	B	A	Y	P	**Total ounces in smoothie**
R	4	2	6	8	64
×			$\times \dfrac{1}{4}$		$\times \dfrac{1}{4}$
A			$1\dfrac{1}{2}$		16

Alternatively, you might notice that a 16-ounce smoothie is exactly one-quarter of a 64-ounce smoothie. As a result, Malin will need one-quarter as much yogurt, or $6 \times \dfrac{1}{4} = 1.5$, or $1\dfrac{1}{2}$ cups.

Equations

In this chapter...

- Expressions Don't Have Equals Signs

- An Equation Says "Expression A = Expression B"

- Golden Rule of Equations: Do the Same Thing to Both Sides

- Isolate a Variable: Work Your Way In by Doing PEMDAS in Reverse

- Clean Up an Equation: Combine Like Terms and Eliminate Denominators

- Variables in the Exponent: Make the Bases Equal

- Systems of Equations

- Kill an Equation and an Unknown: (A) Isolate, Then Substitute

- Kill an Equation and an Unknown: (B) Combine Equations

- Three or More Variables: Isolate the Expression You Want

Chapter 6

Equations

In This Chapter, You Will Learn To:

- Manipulate expressions and equations to solve for variables

Manipulating expressions and equations is at the core of algebra. The first step is to understand the distinction between expressions and equations.

Expressions Don't Have Equals Signs

An **expression** such as $3y + 8z$ ultimately represents a number. It has a value, although you may not know that value. The expression $3y + 8z$ contains numbers that are known (3 and 8) and unknown (y and z) and that are linked by arithmetic operations (in this case, $+$ and $\times$).

Here are more expressions:

$$12 \qquad x - y \qquad 2w^3 \qquad 4(n + 3)(n + 2) \qquad \frac{\sqrt{x}}{3b - 2}$$

These all have one thing in common: They do *not* have an equals sign. An expression never contains an equals sign.

When you **simplify** an expression, you reduce the number of separate terms. You might also pull out and cancel common factors. In other words, you make the expression simpler. However, *you never change the expression's value as you simplify.* Examples of simplifying equations are in the table:

Unsimplified		Simplified	How
$3x + 4x$	$\longrightarrow$	$7x$	Combine like terms
$\dfrac{2y^2}{3} + \dfrac{3y^2}{5}$	$\longrightarrow$	$\dfrac{19y^2}{15}$	Find a common denominator and then combine
$x + xy$	$\longrightarrow$	$x(1 + y)$	Pull out a common factor
$\dfrac{3x^2}{6x}$	$\longrightarrow$	$\dfrac{x}{2}$	Cancel common factors

At times you might go in reverse. For instance, you might **distribute** a common factor.

$$x(1 + y) \longrightarrow x + xy$$

Or you might multiply the top and bottom of a fraction by the same number to change its look. The result may seem even *less* simplified, temporarily. But by finding a common denominator, you can add fractions and get a simpler final result. For example:

Unsimplified		Even less simple		Simplified
$\frac{w}{2} + \frac{w}{4}$	$\longrightarrow$	$\frac{w \times 2}{2 \times 2} + \frac{w}{4}$	$\longrightarrow$	$\frac{3w}{4}$

As you simplify an expression (or even complicate one), the value of the expression must never change.

When you *evaluate* an expression, you figure out its value—the actual number represented by that expression.

To evaluate an expression, *substitute numbers in for any variables, then simplify*. In other words, *swap out the variables*, replacing them with numbers. Then do the arithmetic.

Some people say "plug and chug." You *plug* in the values of the variables, then you *chug* through the simplification. Some people also call this "subbing in."

Whatever you call this process, you have to know the values of the variables to evaluate the expression. Otherwise, you're stuck.

Finally, remember PEMDAS! Follow PEMDAS when you plug and chug. Consider this example:

Evaluate the expression $3\sqrt{2x}$ given that x has the value of 8.

First, substitute in 8 for x.

$3\sqrt{2x}$ becomes $3\sqrt{2(8)}$

Now simplify the expression.

$$3\sqrt{2(8)} = 3\sqrt{16} = 3 \times 4 = 12$$

You have now evaluated the expression $3\sqrt{2x}$ when $x = 8$. For that particular value of x, the value of the expression is 12.

Pay attention to negative signs, especially if the value you're subbing in is negative. Put in parentheses to obey PEMDAS. Consider this example:

If $y = -2$, what is the value of $3y^2 - 7y + 4$?

Substitute -2 for y. Put parentheses around the -2 to clarify that you're subbing in negative 2, not subtracting 2 somehow. Therefore:

$3y^2 - 7y + 4$ becomes $3(-2)^2 - 7(-2) + 4$

Now simplify.

$$3(-2)^2 - 7(-2) + 4 = 3(4) - (-14) + 4 = 12 + 14 + 4 = 30$$

Be sure to square the negative sign and to subtract -14 (in other words, add 14). The value of the expression is 30.

You might have to plug into expressions in answer choices. Here's another one:

> If $y = 6$, then which of the following expressions has the value of 20?
>
> (A) $y + 14$ (B) $y - 14$ (C) $20y$

When you substitute 6 in for y in the answer choices, only $y + 14$ results in 20. The answer is (A).

Other expressions involving y could also equal 20 when $y = 6$, such as $2y + 8$ or $y^2 - 16$. On the GMAT, you would not be forced to pick between these expressions, because they'd all be correct answers to this question.

If you...	Then you...	Like this:
Simplify an expression	Combine like terms or perform other legal algebra moves	$3x + 4x$ becomes $7x$
Evaluate an expression	Substitute numbers in for unknowns, then simplify	When $x = 2$, $7x$ becomes $7(2)$ or 14

An Equation Says "Expression A = Expression B"

An equation is a complete sentence that has a subject, a verb, and an object. The sentence always takes this form:

Subject *equals* object.

One expression equals another expression.

$2x$	$-$	z	$=$	y	$+$	4
Two x	minus	z	equals	y	plus	four

An equation always sets one expression ($2x - z$) equal to another expression ($y + 4$).

Everything you know about simplifying or evaluating expressions applies in the world of equations, because equations are made up of expressions.

You can *simplify* an expression on just one side of an equation, because you are not changing the value of that expression. So the equation still holds true, even though you're ignoring the other side.

For instance, simplify the left side but leave the right side alone.

$3x + 5x = y$ becomes $8x = y$

You can also *evaluate* an expression on just one side. For instance, say you have $\frac{8x}{15} = y$ and you know that $x = 5$. Then you can plug and chug just on the left side:

$$\frac{8x}{15} = y \qquad \text{becomes} \qquad \frac{8(5)}{15} = y \qquad \text{and finally} \qquad \frac{8}{3} = y$$

Throughout all these changes on the left side, the right side has remained y.

If all you could do to equations was to simplify or evaluate expressions, then your toolset would be limited. However, you can do much more.

You can truly *change* both sides. You can actually alter the values of the two expressions on either side of an equation.

You just have to follow the Golden Rule.

Golden Rule of Equations: Do the Same Thing to Both Sides

You can change the value of the *left* side any way you want…

… as long as you change the *right* side in *exactly the same way*.

Take this example:

$$x + 5 = 8$$

If you subtract 5 from the left side, you must subtract 5 from the right side. You get a new equation with new expressions. If the first equation isn't lying, then the second equation is true, too.

$$\begin{array}{rr} x+5= & 8 \\ -5 & -5 \\ \hline x= & 3 \end{array}$$

Here is a table of the major Golden Rule moves you can do to both sides of an equation.

1. **Add the same thing** to both sides. <ul><li>That "thing" can be a number or a variable expression.</li><li>Show the addition underneath to be safe. (Later, if you feel comfortable with the steps, you can stop writing out the addition.)</li></ul>	$\begin{array}{r} y-6 = 15 \\ +6 \quad +6 \\ \hline y = 21 \end{array}$
2. **Subtract the same thing** from both sides.	$\begin{array}{rr} z+4 &= k \\ -4 & -4 \\ \hline z &= k-4 \end{array}$

3. **Multiply both sides by the same thing.** • Put parentheses in so that you multiply *entire* sides.	$$n + m = \frac{3w}{4}$$ $$4 \times (n+m) = \left(\frac{3w}{4}\right) \times 4$$ $$4n + 4m = 3w$$

4. **Divide both sides by the same thing**
   (except 0, of course).
    •   Extend the fraction bar all the way so that you divide *entire* sides.
	$$a + b = 5d$$ $$\frac{a+b}{5} = \frac{5d}{5}$$ $$\frac{a+b}{5} = d$$

5. **Square both sides**, cube both sides, etc. • Put parentheses in so you square or cube *entire* sides.	$$x + \sqrt{2} = \sqrt{7w}$$ $$\left(x + \sqrt{2}\right)^2 = \left(\sqrt{7w}\right)^2$$ $$\left(x + \sqrt{2}\right)^2 = 7w$$
6. **Take the square root of both sides**, the cube root of both sides, etc. • Extend the radical so you square-root or cube-root *entire* sides.	$$z^3 = 64$$ $$\sqrt[3]{z^3} = \sqrt[3]{64}$$ $$z = 4$$

One warning about square-rooting both sides of an equation: The equation usually splits into *two* separate equations. For example:

$$x^2 = 49$$
$$\sqrt{x^2} = \sqrt{49} \qquad \text{Square-root both sides}$$

$$x = 7 \quad \textbf{OR} \quad x = -7$$

There are two numbers that, when squared, equal 49. Remember that when negative numbers are squared, they become positive. So when you take a square root of a squared number, you'll need to find the negative solution as well. For example:

When you square $y = 6$ you always get $y^2 = 36$.
But if you solve $y^2 = 36$ you get $y = 6$ OR $y = -6$.

Essentially, the square hides the fact that the base could be positive or negative, leaving you with two possible solutions.

Perform the same action to an entire side of an equation. Pretend that the expression on each side of the equation is surrounded by parentheses—and actually write those parentheses in as necessary. Consider this equation:

$$x + 4 = \frac{x}{2}$$

To multiply both sides by 2, add in parentheses.

$$2(x+4) = \left(\frac{x}{2}\right)2$$

Now simplify. Distribute the 2 to both the x and the 4 and cancel the 2's on the right.

$$2x + 8 = x$$

This is why multiplying to get rid of a denominator is sometimes called *cross-multiplication*. You can imagine that the 2 that *was* in the denominator on the right side moves to the left side, where it is multiplied by the $x + 4$. Cross-multiplication is even more useful when both sides have denominators to begin with.

Let's go back to the equation at hand. You can simplify further with more Golden Rule moves: subtracting x from both sides, and then subtracting 8.

$$
\begin{array}{rcl}
2x + 8 &=& x \\
-x & & -x \\
\hline
x + 8 &=& 0 \\
-8 & & -8 \\
\hline
x &=& -8
\end{array}
$$

You now have x by itself on one side, so the equation says that the value of x is -8. What you did here was *isolate the variable* or *solve for the variable*.

To isolate x, *get x by itself on one side of the equation.* The equation should wind up reading "$x = \ldots$"

The thing on the right side is often a number, as in the case above ($x = -8$).

In a more complicated equation, the right side could be an expression that contains other variables. Either way, the important thing when you isolate x on the left is that the right side *cannot* have any terms containing x. Otherwise, you haven't truly *isolated* the x on the left side.

You can isolate the x on the *right* side if you want, of course. If you do that, make sure that the *left* side has no terms containing x.

When you get "$x = $ a number" or "a number $= x$," then you have *solved the equation.* The number you get is a *solution* to the equation.

When you plug a solution into an equation (i.e., into the *variable* in an equation), you make the equation true. For example:

"4 is a solution to the equation $2x + 7 = 15$."

This sentence means that if $x = 4$, that equation is true.

If you have more than one variable in an equation, you may still want to isolate one variable for some reason. Consider this example:

If $3x + 5y = 12$, what is x in terms of y?

"What is x in terms of y" means "get x by itself and put y and everything else on the opposite side of the equals sign."

For example, "*a* in terms of *b*" is the right side of this equation:

$$a = 3 + b^2$$

There cannot be any *a*'s on the right side. And there are only *a*'s on the left side.

To get *x* in terms of *y*, isolate *x* on one side by applying Golden Rule moves to the given equation.

$$3x + 5y = 12$$
$$\underline{-5y \qquad -5y}$$
$$3x \qquad = 12 - 5y$$

$$x = \frac{12 - 5y}{3}$$

So *x* in terms of *y* is this expression: $\dfrac{12 - 5y}{3}$. This contains no *x*'s. If you're looking for "*x* in terms of *y*," the answer will contain *y*'s, not *x*'s.

If you want *y* in terms of *x* instead, then isolate *y* on one side. You'll get this expression on the other side: $\dfrac{12 - 3x}{5}$.

If you...	Then you...	Like this:
Want to change an expression on one side of an equation	Apply the Golden Rule: Change both sides in exactly the same way	$y - 3 = 9$ $\underline{+3 \quad +3}$ $y = 12$
Want to isolate the variable *x* in an equation	Perform Golden Rule moves and simplify until the equation reads "*x* = something else"	$7x + 4 = 18$ $\underline{-4 \quad -4}$ $7x = 14$ $\dfrac{7x}{7} = \dfrac{14}{7}$ $x = 2$
Need *x* in terms of *y*	Perform Golden Rule moves and simplify until the equation reads "*x* = everything else"	$7x + 4 = y$ $\underline{-4 \quad -4}$ $7x = y - 4$ $\dfrac{7x}{7} = \dfrac{y-4}{7}$ $x = \dfrac{y-4}{7}$

Check Your Skills

1. If $\sqrt{x + 2} = 4$, what is *x*?
2. If $\dfrac{y - 3}{x} = 2$, what is *y* in terms of *x*?

Answers can be found on page 273.

Isolate a Variable: Work Your Way In by Doing PEMDAS in Reverse

If an expression is complicated, you might get confused about how to isolate the variable inside.

Consider the following equation:

$$5(x-1)^3 - 30 = 10$$

The expression on the left side is a complicated recipe that builds from the inside out.

1.	Start with x.	x
2.	Subtract 1.	$x - 1$
3.	Cube the result.	$(x-1)^3$
4.	Multiply by 5.	$5(x-1)^3$
5.	Subtract 30.	$5(x-1)^3 - 30$

The recipe follows PEMDAS, as you'd expect. The result of this recipe equals 10, because that's what the equation says:

$$5(x-1)^3 - 30 = 10$$

To isolate x on the left, you need to work your way through from the outside in. So you need to *undo* the PEMDAS steps by working in the *reverse order*.

The last step of the recipe was to subtract 30. To undo that step first, add 30 to both sides.

$$
\begin{array}{rcl}
5(x-1)^3 + 30 & = & 10 \\
+30 & & +30 \\
\hline
5(x-1)^3 & = & 40
\end{array}
$$

You have now gotten rid of 30 on the left side. You've "moved" it to the other side.

Now undo the previous step of the original recipe, which was to multiply by 5. Divide both sides by 5.

$$\frac{5(x-1)^3}{5} = \frac{40}{5}$$

$$(x-1)^3 = 8$$

Next, undo the cubing. The opposite of exponents is roots, so take the cube root of both sides.

$$\sqrt[3]{(x-1)^3} = \sqrt[3]{8}$$

$$(x-1) = 2$$

You don't need the parentheses anymore, so drop them.

$$x - 1 = 2$$

Finally, undo the subtraction by adding 1 to both sides, and you get $x = 3$.

In summary, you *added* 30, then *divided* by 5, then got rid of the *exponent*, then simplified what was inside the *parentheses*. You did PEMDAS backwards, from the outside in.

If you want to isolate a variable deep inside an expression, but you are unsure about the order of steps to perform, do PEMDAS in reverse. Try another example.

If $4\sqrt{x-6} + 7 = 19$, what is the value of *x*?

A/S

M/D

E

P

Here's the solution path. First, *subtract* 7 from both sides.

$$
\begin{array}{r}
4\sqrt{x-6} + 7 = 19 \\
-7 \quad -7 \\
\hline
4\sqrt{x-6} \quad = 12
\end{array}
$$

Next, *divide* both sides by 4.

$$
\frac{\cancel{4}\sqrt{x-6}}{\cancel{4}} = \frac{12}{4}
$$
$$
\sqrt{x-6} = 3
$$

Now, undo the square root by *squaring* both sides.

$$
\sqrt{x-6} = 3
$$
$$
\left(\sqrt{x-6}\right)^2 = (3)^2
$$
$$
x-6 = 9
$$

Finally, *add* 6 to both sides, and you end up with *x* = 15.

The original equation did not contain explicit parentheses, but the square root symbol extended over two terms: $\sqrt{x-6}$. That's just like putting parentheses around *x* − 6 and raising that whole quantity to the $\frac{1}{2}$ power: $(x-6)^{\frac{1}{2}}$.

A square root sign acts like parentheses when it extends over more than one term. Likewise, a fraction bar acts like parentheses when it's stretched over multiple terms.

If you...	Then you...	Like this:
Want to isolate a variable inside an expression	Follow PEMDAS in reverse as you undo the operations in the expression—in other words, work your way in from the outside	$2y^3 - 3 = 51$ $\underline{+ 3 \quad + 3}$ $2y^3 \quad = 54$ $\dfrac{2y^3}{2} = \dfrac{54}{2}$ $y^3 = 27$ $\sqrt[3]{y^3} = \sqrt[3]{27}$ $y = 3$

Check Your Skills

Solve for x.

3. $3(x + 4)^3 - 5 = 19$

4. $\sqrt[3]{(x+5)} - 7 = -8$

Answers can be found on page 273.

Clean Up an Equation: Combine Like Terms and Eliminate Denominators

What happens when x shows up in multiple places in an equation? Consider this question:

If $\dfrac{5x - 3(4 - x)}{2x} = 10$, what is x?

To isolate x, you have to get all the x's together on one side. How? *Combine like terms.*

If there is a denominator, get rid of that right away, especially if the denominator contains x. *Always get variables out of denominators.*

This should be the first move in the case above. Undo the division by multiplying both sides by the entire denominator, which is $2x$.

$$2x\left(\dfrac{5x - 3(4 - x)}{2x}\right) = (10)2x$$
$$5x - 3(4 - x) = 20x$$

At this point, to combine like terms, get x out of the parentheses. Distribute the -3 on the left side (be careful with the negative sign).

$$5x - 3(4 - x) = 20x$$
$$5x - 12 + 3x = 20x$$

Now combine like terms. First add $5x$ and $3x$ on the left side.

$$5x - 12 + 3x = 20x$$
$$8x - 12 = 20x$$

Next, subtract $8x$ from both sides and immediately combine like terms on the right.

$$\begin{array}{r} 8x - 12 = 20x \\ -8x \qquad -8x \\ \hline -12 = 12x \end{array}$$

The right side could be written as $20x - 8x$, but you should combine into $12x$ as you perform the subtraction.

Why subtract $8x$ rather than $20x$? If you subtract $8x$, you get all the x terms on one side and numbers on the other side. You also get a positive coefficient on the x (i.e., positive 12). These results are both nice to have.

Finally, divide by 12 to isolate x on the right.

$$\frac{-12}{12} = \frac{12x}{12}$$
$$-1 = x$$

You now have the answer to the question: $x = -1$.

If you...	Then you...	Like this:
Have a variable in multiple places in an equation	Combine like terms, which might be on different sides of the equation	$\begin{array}{r} 9y + 30 = 12y \\ -9y \qquad -9y \\ \hline 30 = 3y \end{array}$
Have a variable in a denominator	Multiply to eliminate the denominator right away	$\dfrac{2z - 3}{z} = 4$ $z\left(\dfrac{2z - 3}{z}\right) = 4(z)$ $2z - 3 = 4z$

Check Your Skills

Solve for x.

5. $\dfrac{2x + 6(9 - 2x)}{x - 4} = -3$

Answer can be found on page 273.

Variables in the Exponent: Make the Bases Equal

If a variable is in the exponent, the typical PEMDAS moves aren't going to help much. Consider this example:

If $3^x = 27^4$, what is x?

The key is to rewrite the terms so they have the *same base*. Usually, the best way to do this is to *factor bases into primes*.

On the left side, 3 is already a prime, so leave it alone. On the right side, 27 is not prime. Since $27 = 3^3$, replace 27 with 3^3. Put in parentheses to keep the exponents straight.

$$3^x = (3^3)^4$$

Simplify the right side by applying the "two exponent" rule: $(3^3)^4 = 3^{3 \times 4} = 3^{12}$. Therefore:

$$3^x = 3^{12}$$

In words, this equation says, "3 raised to the power of x is equal to 3 raised to the power of 12."

This is only true if x itself is equal to 12.

$$3^x = 3^{12} \longrightarrow x = 12$$

Once the bases are the same, the exponents must be the same.

This rule has exactly three exceptions: a base of 1, a base of 0, and a base of -1. The exceptions occur because more than one exponent of these particular bases results in the same number. For example:

$$1^2 = 1^3 = \ldots = 1 \qquad 0^2 = 0^3 = \ldots = 0 \qquad (-1)^2 = (-1)^4 = 1, \text{ while } (-1)^1 = (-1)^3 = -1$$

However, for every other base, the rule works. Try this example:

If $4^y = 8^{y+1}$, what is the value of 2^y?

(A) -8

(B) $\dfrac{1}{8}$

(C) $\dfrac{1}{4}$

(D) 1

(E) 8

Look at the answer choices. Since none of them contain a y, that's your clue that the equation can be manipulated to find the value of y. You just need to figure out how!

Look at the given equation. The variable y is in two exponents.

$$4^y = 8^{y+1}$$

To figure out what this tells you about y, make the bases the same. Rewrite both 4 and 8 as powers of 2.

$$4 = 2^2 \quad 8 = 2^3$$

$$4^y = 8^{y+1} \longrightarrow (2^2)^y = (2^3)^{y+1}$$

Next, apply the "two exponent" rule on both sides.

$$(2^2)^y = (2^3)^{y+1}$$

$$2^{2y} = 2^{3(y+1)}$$

Now that the bases are the same (and the common base is not 1, 0, or −1), you can set the exponents equal to each other. Write a brand-new equation that expresses this fact.

$$2y = 3(y + 1)$$

At this point, solve for y. To start, distribute the 3 on the right.

$$2y = 3y + 3$$

Next, subtract $2y$ from both sides to combine like terms.

$$0 = y + 3$$

Finally, subtract 3 from both sides.

$$-3 = y$$

Now that you've solved for y, find the value of 2^y, which is what the question asked. To do this, replace y with −3.

$$2^y = 2^{-3} = \frac{1}{8}$$

The correct answer is (B).

If you...	Then you...	Like this:
Have a variable in an exponent or exponents	Make the bases equal, usually by breaking the given bases down to primes	$3^x = 27^4$ $3^x = (3^3)^4$ $3^x = 3^{12}$ $x = 12$

Check Your Skills

6. If $4^6 = 64^{2x}$, what is the value of 16^x?

Answer can be found on page 274.

Systems of Equations

Many GMAT problems will force you to deal with two variables. In most of those cases, you'll also have two equations. For example:

(a) $2x - 3y = 16$ (b) $y - x = -7$

A group of more than one equation is often called a *system of equations*. Solving a system of two equations with two variables, for example, x and y, means finding values for x and y that make both equations true *at the same time*.

The systems of equations discussed in this section only have one solution. That is, only one set of values of x and y makes the system work.

To solve a system of two equations and two unknowns, you can use either of two good strategies:

1.   Isolate, then substitute   2.   Combine equations

These strategies are similar at a high level. In both, here's what you do:

1. Kill off one equation and one unknown.
2. Solve the remaining equation for the remaining unknown.
3. Plug back into one of the original equations to solve for the other variable.

However, the two strategies take very different approaches to step #1: how to kill off one equation and one unknown. Let's examine these approaches in turn.

Kill an Equation and an Unknown: (A) Isolate, Then Substitute

This strategy is also known as *substitution*. Consider this system again:

(a) $2x - 3y = 16$ (b) $y - x = -7$

To follow the substitution strategy, first isolate one variable in one of the equations. Next, substitute into the other equation.

Which variable should you isolate? The one you *don't* ultimately want. If the problem asks for x, first isolate y.

Why y? Because the variable you first isolate is the one you will then kill off. You're left with one equation containing x—the variable you want. This way, you save work.

Conversely, if the problem asks for y, first isolate x, so you can kill it off early.

Let's say that the question asks for the value of x. Then you want to isolate y in one of the given equations. In which equation should you isolate your variable? The one that's easier to deal with.

In the example above, it looks easier to isolate y in equation (b). All you have to do is add x to both sides. So go ahead and do so.

$$
\begin{array}{ll}
\text{(a)} \quad 2x - 3y = 16 & \text{(b)} \quad y - x = -7 \\
& \qquad \underline{ + x \qquad + x} \\
& \qquad y \quad\;\; = -7 + x \\
& \qquad y \quad\;\; = \;\; x - 7
\end{array}
$$

By the way, when you use this method, it's good practice to write the two equations in the system side by side. That way, you can do algebra down your page to isolate one variable without running into the other equation.

Now you have expressed y in terms of x. Since $y = x - 7$, you can replace y with $(x - 7)$ anywhere you see y. This will remove any references to y in the first equation. In essence, you are killing off y. Now go ahead and replace the y in the first equation:

(a) $2x - 3y = 16$ (b) $y - x = -7$

$$\frac{+x \qquad\qquad +x}{}$$

$$y \qquad = -7 + x$$

$$y \qquad = \ x - 7$$

$2x - 3(x - 7) = 16$

When you sub in an expression such as $x - 7$, place parentheses around the expression. This way, you avoid PEMDAS errors.

Now that you have killed off one variable (y) and one equation (the second one), you have just one variable left (x) in one equation. Solve for that variable:

$2x - 3(x - 7) = 16$	
$2x - 3x + 21 = 16$	Distribute the -3.
$-x + 21 = 16$	Combine $2x$ and $-3x$ (like terms).
$-x = -5$	Subtract 21 from both sides.
$x = 5$	Multiply both sides by -1.

At this point, you're done if the question only asks for x. If the question asks for $x + y$ or some other expression involving both x and y, then you need to solve for y. Do so by plugging your value of x into either of the original equations.

Which equation should you plug back into? The one in which you isolated y. In fact, you should plug into the revised form of that equation—the one that looks like "$y = $ something." This is the easiest way to solve for y, so this is the equation you'll want to use:

$y = x - 7$

To start, swap out x and replace it with 5, since you found that $x = 5$.

$y = (5) - 7$

$y = -2$

Now you have the complete solution: $x = 5$ and $y = -2$. These are the *solutions* of the system; in other words, these are the values that make *both* of the original equations true at the same time:

(a) $2x - 3y = 16$ (b) $y - x = -7$

$2(5) - 3(-2) = 16$ $(-2) - (5) = -7$

True   True

If you...	Then you...	Like this:
Have two equations and two unknowns	Isolate one unknown, then substitute into the other equation	$2x - 3y = 16$ and $y - x = -7$ $y = -7 + x = x - 7$ $2x - 3(x - 7) = 16$ ... $x = 5$ $y = -2$

Check Your Skills

Solve for x and y.

7. $6y + 15 = 3x$
    $x + y = 14$

Answer can be found on page 274.

Kill an Equation and an Unknown: (B) Combine Equations

Substitution will always work. But some GMAT problems can be solved more easily with another method, known as *combination* or *elimination*.

Here's how combination works. You can always *add two equations together*. Just add the left sides up and put the result on the left, then add the right sides up and put that result on the right.

$$x = 4$$
$$+\ y = 7$$
$$\overline{x + y = 4 + 7}$$

Why is this allowed? You are actually adding the same thing to both sides of an equation. Since y equals 7, you can legally add y on the left side of $x = 4$ and add 7 on the right side. You are making the same change on each side of the first equation.

In this example, the resulting equation ($x + y = 11$) is more complicated than the starting equations. However, adding equations can sometimes actually eliminate a variable—*and that's why you do it*.

Consider this system of equations:

$$a + b = 11 \qquad a - b = 5$$

What happens when you add these equations together?

$$a + b = 11$$
$$+\ \underline{a - b = 5}$$
$$2a\ \ = 16$$

The *b*'s cancel out of the resulting equation completely. It's now easy to solve for *a*.

$$2a = 16 \quad \longrightarrow \quad a = 8$$

Finally, solve for *b* by plugging back into one of the original equations.

$$a + b = 11 \quad \longrightarrow \quad (8) + b = 11 \quad \longrightarrow \quad b = 3$$

So the complete solution to the original system of equations is *a* = 8 and *b* = 3.

If you solve that system by substitution, you will need to take a few more steps. Every extra step takes time and presents an additional opportunity for error. If you learn to combine equations to eliminate, you can often kill off a variable easily and safely.

Combination isn't restricted to adding equations. You can also subtract equations. Say you are given these two equations:

$$5n + m = 17 \qquad\qquad 2n + m = 11$$

Since "+ *m*" shows up in both equations, we can kill *m* by subtracting the second equation from the first.

$$\begin{array}{r} 5n + m = 17 \\ -\ \underline{2n + m = 11} \\ 3n \ = 6 \end{array}$$

Realize that you are subtracting the whole left side, as well as the right side. If you are concerned that you might not follow PEMDAS, put in parentheses around the whole equation.

$$\begin{array}{r} 5n + m = 17 \\ -\ \underline{\left(2n + m = 11\right)} \\ 3n \ = 6 \end{array}$$

Now you can solve for *n*, then plug back in to get *m*.

$$3n = 6 \quad \longrightarrow \quad n = 2$$

$$2n + m = 11 \quad \longrightarrow \quad 2(2) + m = 11 \quad \longrightarrow \quad m = 7$$

To set up a good elimination, you can even multiply a whole equation by a number. That's the same thing as multiplying the left side and the right side by the same number. This is a Golden Rule move.

Consider this system of equations from earlier:

$$\text{(a)} \qquad 2x - 3y = 16 \qquad\qquad \text{(b)} \qquad y - x = -7$$

To take the combination approach, first rewrite the equations vertically and line up the variables. Here, you *want* to write one equation below the other (not *next to* each other as you do with substitution). Space the terms to line up *x* with *x* and *y* with *y*.

$$2x - 3y = 16$$
$$-x + y = -7$$

If you add the equations now, neither variable will die; you're left with $x - 2y = 9$. That's not helpful.

However, if you multiply the second equation by 2 on both sides, you'll be able to cancel when you add.

$$2x - 3y = 16 \qquad \longrightarrow \qquad 2x - 3y = 16$$
$$2(-x + y) = (-7)2 \qquad \longrightarrow \qquad -2x + 2y = -14$$

Now add. The $2x$ term will cancel with the $-2x$ term:

$$2x - 3y = 16$$
$$+ \quad -2x + 2y = -14$$
$$-y = 2$$
$$y = -2$$

Finally, use this value of y in one of the original equations to solve for x.

$$y - x = -7 \quad \longrightarrow \quad (-2) - x = -7 \quad \longrightarrow \quad -x = -5 \quad \longrightarrow \quad x = 5$$

This is the same solution as before. In this case, you only saved a little work by combining equations to eliminate rather than isolating and substituting. However, some problems are *much* easier to solve by combining equations. Take a look at this last example:

For this system of equations, what is the value of $x + y$?

$$\frac{1}{2}x + \frac{1}{3}y = 3$$
$$2x + y = 11$$

If you try direct substitution, you will need to make a lot of messy calculations involving fractions.

Instead, try combination. First, multiply the top equation through by 6 to eliminate all fractions.

$$6\left(\frac{1}{2}x + \frac{1}{3}y\right) = (3)6$$
$$3x + 2y = 18$$

Next line up the two given equations, which now look much better.

$$3x + 2y = 18$$
$$2x + y = 11$$

Before going further, consider: What does the question specifically ask for? It does not ask for x or y separately. Rather, it asks for $x + y$.

You can certainly solve for one of the variables, then find the other. But there's a shortcut.

If you look carefully, you might notice that you can solve for $x + y$ directly by *subtracting* the equations.

$$3x + 2y = 18$$
$$-(2x + y = 11)$$
$$\overline{ x + y = 7}$$

Ta-da! The answer to the question is 7.

Combination isn't always appropriate. Become very comfortable with substitution as a default method. But as you spot opportunities to eliminate a variable by adding or subtracting equations, seize those opportunities.

If you...	Then you...	Like this:
Have two equations and two unknowns	Add or subtract equations to eliminate a variable	$2x - 3y = 16$ and $y - x = -7$ Multiply 2nd equation by 2: $2(y - x) = (-7)2$ Add equations: $-2x + 2y = -14$ $+2x - 3y = 16$ $\overline{ -y = 2}$ $y = -2$

Check Your Skills

Solve for x and y.

8. $x + 4y = 10$
    $y - x = -5$

Answer can be found on page 274.

Three or More Variables: Isolate the Expression You Want

A few problems involve even more than two variables. Fortunately, all the procedures you've learned so far still work.

Focus on exactly what the question asks for and isolate that on one side of the equation. Try this example:

If $\sqrt{\dfrac{a}{b}} = c$ and $abc \neq 0$, what is the value of b in terms of a and c?

Since the question asks for b, you should isolate b. The answer will contain a and c, because the question asks for an expression "in terms of" a and c.

Take the given equation and do Golden Rule moves to isolate b.

$$\sqrt{\frac{a}{b}} = c$$

$$\left(\sqrt{\frac{a}{b}}\right)^2 = c^2 \qquad \text{Square both sides.}$$

$$\frac{a}{b} = c^2$$

$$b\left(\frac{a}{b}\right) = \left(c^2\right)b \qquad \text{Multiply both sides by } b.$$

$$a = c^2 b$$

$$\frac{a}{c^2} = \frac{c^2 b}{c^2} \qquad \text{Divide both sides by } c^2.$$

$$\frac{a}{c^2} = b$$

The answer to the question is $\dfrac{a}{c^2}$.

By the way, the "non-equation" $abc \neq 0$ was only there to prevent division by zero. You rarely wind up using this sort of information in any other way.

Here is another tough question:

$$\frac{w}{x-y} = 3 \qquad\qquad y - x = 4$$

In the system of equations above, what is the value of w?

(A) -12

(B) $-\dfrac{3}{4}$

(C) $\dfrac{3}{4}$

(D) $\dfrac{4}{3}$

(E) 12

You are asked for the value of w, so you want to manipulate the equations to get "$w = \ldots$"

Notice that the answer choices are all numbers. This means that the other variables x and y must disappear along the way.

MANHATTAN PREP

One approach to this problem is to isolate x or y in the second equation, then substitute into the first equation. This way, you at least get rid of one variable. It's a start—let's see where it goes.

Isolate y by adding x to both sides of the second equation.

$$
\begin{array}{rcr}
y - x = & & 4 \\
+\ x & & +x \\
\hline
y & = & x+4
\end{array}
$$

Now substitute $x + 4$ into the first equation in place of y. Be sure to put parentheses around $x + 4$.

$$\frac{w}{x-y} = 3$$

$$\longrightarrow \quad \frac{w}{x-(x+4)} = 3$$

$$\longrightarrow \quad \frac{w}{x-x-4} = 3$$

$$\longrightarrow \quad \frac{w}{-4} = 3$$

Look what happened—the variable x disappeared as well. This is a good sign. If x didn't cancel out, then you'd be in trouble. You can solve for w now.

$$\frac{w}{-4} = 3 \qquad \longrightarrow \qquad w = -12 \qquad \text{The answer is (A).}$$

Another approach to the problem is to recognize that $x - y$ is very similar to $y - x$. In fact, one is the negative version of the other.

$$x - y = -(y - x)$$

If you recognize this, then multiply the second equation by -1 so that it has $x - y$ on one side:

$$
\begin{array}{c}
y - x = 4 \\
(-1)(y - x) = (4)(-1) \\
x - y = -4
\end{array}
$$

Now you can *substitute for a whole expression*. That is, you can swap out $x - y$ in the first equation and replace that entire thing with -4.

$$\frac{w}{x-y} = 3 \qquad \overset{\displaystyle \longleftarrow}{} \quad \boxed{x - y = -4}$$

$$\frac{w}{(-4)} = 3$$

This gets you to the same point as the first method, and you end up with $w = -12$.

However many variables and equations you have, pay close attention to what the question is asking for.

- If the question asks for the variable x, isolate x, so you have "$x = ...$"
- If the question asks for x in terms of y, after you isolate x on one side of the equation, the other side should contain y.
- If the question asks for $x + y$, isolate that expression, so you have "$x + y = ...$"
- If a variable does not appear in the answer choices, help it vanish. Isolate it and substitute for it in another equation.
- If an expression such as $x - y$ shows up in two different equations, feel free to substitute for it so that the whole thing disappears.

If you...	Then you...	Like this:
Have three or more unknowns	Isolate whatever the question asks for, and use substitution to eliminate unwanted variables	If $a + b - c = 12$ and $c - b = 8$, what is the value of a? Isolate a: $a = 12 + c - b$ Substitute for $c - b$: $a = 12 + (8)$ $a = 20$

Check Your Skills

9. If $\dfrac{a}{c} + \dfrac{b}{3c} = 1$, what is c in terms of a and b?

Answer can be found on page 275.

Check Your Skills Answer Key

1. **14:** In order to find the value of x, isolate x on one side of the equation.

$$\sqrt{x+2} = 4$$
$$\left(\sqrt{x+2}\right)^2 = 4^2$$
$$x+2 = 16$$
$$x = 14$$

2. **$2x + 3$:** In order to find y in terms of x, isolate y on one side of the equation.

$$\frac{y-3}{x} = 2$$
$$\cancel{x}\left(\frac{y-3}{\cancel{x}}\right) = (2)x$$
$$y-3 = 2x$$
$$y = 2x+3$$

3. **$x = -2$:**

$$3(x+4)^3 - 5 = 19$$

$3(x+4)^3 = 24$	Add 5 to both sides.
$(x+4)^3 = 8$	Divide both sides by 3.
$(x+4) = 2$	Take the cube root of both sides.
$x = -2$	Remove the parentheses and subtract 4 from both sides.

4. **$x = -6$:**

$$\sqrt[3]{(x+5)} - 7 = -8$$

$\sqrt[3]{(x+5)} = -1$	Add 7 to both sides.
$x+5 = -1$	Cube both sides and remove parentheses.
$x = -6$	Subtract 5 from both sides.

5. **$x = 6$:**

$$\frac{2x + 6(9-2x)}{x-4} = -3$$

$2x + 6(9-2x) = -3(x-4)$	Multiply by the denominator $(x-4)$.
$2x + 54 - 12x = -3x + 12$	Simplify grouped terms by distributing (be careful of the signs!).
$-10x + 54 = -3x + 12$	Combine like terms ($2x$ and $-12x$).
$54 = 7x + 12$	Add $10x$ to both sides.
$42 = 7x$	Subtract 12 from both sides.
$6 = x$	Divide both sides by 7.

6. **16:** You could answer this question by breaking each base down to a power of 2, but you'll save some time if you notice that all three bases in the question (4, 64, and 16) are powers of 4. Solve for x by rewriting 64 as 4^3.

$$4^6 = 64^{2x}$$
$$4^6 = (4^3)^{2x}$$
$$4^6 = 4^{6x}$$
$$6 = 6x$$
$$1 = x$$

If $x = 1$, then $16^x = 16^1 = 16$.

7. **$x = 11, y = 3$:**

(a) $6y + 15 = 3x$
      $2y + 5 = x$

(b) $x + y = 14$

Divide the first equation by 3 to isolate x.

$$(2y + 5) + y = 14$$
$$3y + 5 = 14$$
$$3y = 9$$
$$y = 3$$

Substitute $(2y + 5)$ for x in the second equation and solve for y.

$$x + (3) = 14$$
$$x = 11$$

Substitute $y = 3$ in the second equation to solve for x.

8. **$x = 6, y = 1$:** Notice you have positive x in the first equation and negative x in the second equation. Rearrange the second equation and line it up under the first equation.

$$x + 4y = 10$$
$$\underline{-x + y = -5}$$
$$5y = 5$$
$$y = 1$$

Now that you know $y = 1$, plug it back into either equation to solve for x.

$$x + 4y = 10$$
$$x + 4(1) = 10$$
$$x = 6$$

9. $\dfrac{3a+b}{3}$ OR $a+\dfrac{b}{3}$: The wording "c in terms of…" means that you have to isolate c on one side of the equation. To do so, first combine the fractions on the left side of the equation to combine like terms.

$$\frac{a}{c}+\frac{b}{3c}=1$$

$$\frac{3a}{3c}+\frac{b}{3c}=1$$

$$\frac{3a+b}{3c}=1$$

$$\frac{3a+b}{3}=c$$

If you split the numerator, then you would get:

$$\frac{\cancel{3}a}{\cancel{3}}+\frac{b}{3}=c$$

$$a+\frac{b}{3}=c$$

Chapter Review: Drill Sets

Drill 1

1. If $x = 2$, what is the value of $x^2 - 4x + 3$?
2. If $x = 3$, what is the value of $x + \sqrt{48x}$?
3. If $x = -4$, what is the value of $\dfrac{5 - x}{3} - x^2$?
4. If $c = 100$ and $p = 30c^2 - c$, what is the value of p?
5. If $y - 3 = \dfrac{xy}{2}$ and $x = 3$, what is the value of y?

Drill 2

Solve for the variable in the following equations.

6. $14 - 3x = 2$
7. $3(7 - x) = 4(1.5)$
8. $7x + 13 = 2x - 7$
9. $3t^3 - 7 = 74$
10. $\dfrac{z - 4}{3} = -12$
11. $1{,}200x + 6{,}000 = 13{,}200$
12. $\sqrt{x} = 3 \times 5 - 20 \div 4$
13. $-(y)^3 = -27$
14. $2 - \dfrac{\sqrt{2x + 2}}{2} = -1$
15. $5\sqrt{x} + 6 = 51$

Drill 3

Solve for x in the following equations.

16. $3x + 2(x + 2) = 2x + 16$
17. $\dfrac{3x + 7}{x} = 10$
18. $4(-3x - 8) = 8(-x + 9)$
19. $3x + 7 - 4x + 8 = 2(-2x - 6)$
20. $2x(4 - 6) = -2x + 12$
21. $\dfrac{3(6 - x)}{2x} = -6$

22. $\dfrac{13}{x + 13} = 1$
23. $\dfrac{10(-3x + 4)}{10 - 5x} = 2$
24. $\dfrac{15 - 3(5x - 3)}{3 - 2x} = 6$
25. $\dfrac{50(10 + 3x)}{50 + 7x} = 50$

Drill 4

Solve for the values of both variables in each system of equations using substitution. The explanations will use substitution to solve.

26. $7x - 3y = 5$
    $y = 10$
27. $y = 4x + 10$
    $y = 7x - 5$
28. $2h - 4k = 0$
    $k = h - 3$
29. $5x - 3y = 17$
    $2x - y = 8$
30. $12b = 2g$
    $4g - 3b = 63$

Drill 5

Solve for the values of both variables in each system of equations using elimination. The explanations will use elimination to solve.

31. $x - y = 4$
    $2x + y = 5$
32. $x + 2y = 5$
    $x - 4y = -7$
33. $a + b = 8$
    $2a + b = 13$
34. $7m - 2n = 1$
    $3m + n = 6$

35. $y - 2x - 1 = 0$
    $x - 3y - 1 = 0$

36. $\dfrac{1}{3}r - \dfrac{1}{6}s = 0$

    $2r + \dfrac{1}{2}s - 3 = 0$

Drill 6

Solve for the values of both variables in each system of equations. Decide whether to use substitution or elimination. Explanation will use one of the two methods and explain why that is the better solution method.

37. $5x + 2y = 12$

    $y = \dfrac{1}{2}x + 3$

38. $y - 1 = x + 2$
    $2y = x + 1$

39. $8a - 2b - 5 = 0$
    $2b + 4a - 4 = 0$

40. $3x = 6 - y$
    $6x - y = 3$

41. $x = 2y - \dfrac{1}{2}$

    $y - x = -\dfrac{3}{2}$

Drill 7

Solve for the indicated value in each system of equations.

42. $4x + y + 3z = 34$
    $4x + 3z = 21$

    What is y?

43. $\dfrac{x - 3}{y - 2} = 4z$

    What is the value of x in terms of y and z?

    (A) $4yz - 8z + 3$
    (B) $4yz - 5$
    (C) $y - 8z - 3$

44. $3x + 5y + 2z = 20$
    $6x + 4z = 10$

    What is y?

45. $\dfrac{a - b}{4} = c + 1$

    $c = b + 2$

    What is b in terms of a?

Drill 8

Solve for the indicated value in each system of equations.

46. $\dfrac{a + b}{c + d} = 10$

    $3d = 15 - 3c$

    What is $a + b$?

47. $x = \dfrac{y}{5}$

    $2z - 1 = \dfrac{x + y}{2}$

    What is z in terms of x?

48. $2^{x+y} = \sqrt{z - 2}$

    $x = 2 - y$

    What is z?

49. $\dfrac{3x}{z + 4} = 4$

    $4z = 3y$

    What is $x - y$?

    (A) $4z + 3$

    (B) $\dfrac{16}{3}$

    (C) $\dfrac{4}{3}$

Drill Sets Solutions

Drill 1

1. **−1:** To evaluate the expression, replace x with 2.

$$x^2 - 4x + 3 =$$
$$(2)^2 - 4(2) + 3 =$$
$$4 - 8 + 3 = -1$$

2. **15:** To evaluate the expression, replace x with 3. Rather than multiply 48 by 3, pull a 3 out of 48 in order to create a perfect square that you can then remove from under the square-root symbol.

$$x + \sqrt{48x} =$$
$$3 + \sqrt{48(3)} =$$
$$3 + \sqrt{(16)(3)(3)} =$$
$$3 + (4)(3) =$$
$$3 + 12 = 15$$

3. **−13:** To evaluate the expression, replace x with −4 everywhere in the equation. Be extra careful with the negative signs; use parentheses to help keep track.

$$\frac{5-x}{3} - x^2 =$$
$$\frac{5-(-4)}{3} - (-4)^2 =$$
$$\frac{5+4}{3} - (16) =$$
$$\frac{9}{3} - 16 =$$
$$3 - 16 = -13$$

4. **299,900:** To find the value of p, first replace c with 100.

$$p = 30c^2 - c$$
$$p = 30(100)^2 - 100$$
$$p = 30(10,000) - 100$$
$$p = 300,000 - 100 = 299,900$$

5. **−6:** First, replace x with 3 in the equation.

$$y - 3 = \frac{xy}{2}$$

$$y - 3 = \frac{(3)\,y}{2}$$

Now, to find the value of y, isolate y on one side of the equation.

$$y - 3 = \frac{3y}{2}$$
$$2(y - 3) = 3y$$
$$2y - 6 = 3y$$
$$-6 = y$$

Drill 2

6. **4:** Apply PEMDAS in reverse.

$$
\begin{aligned}
14 - 3x &= 2 \\
-3x &= -12 &&\text{Subtract 14.} \\
x &= 4 &&\text{Divide by } -3.
\end{aligned}
$$

7. **5:** Apply PEMDAS in reverse.

$$
\begin{aligned}
3(7 - x) &= 4(1.5) \\
21 - 3x &= 6 &&\text{Distribute.} \\
-3x &= -15 &&\text{Subtract 21.} \\
x &= 5 &&\text{Divide by } -3.
\end{aligned}
$$

8. **−4:** Apply PEMDAS in reverse.

$$
\begin{aligned}
7x + 13 &= 2x - 7 \\
5x + 13 &= -7 &&\text{Subtract } 2x. \\
5x &= -20 &&\text{Subtract 13.} \\
x &= -4 &&\text{Divide by 5.}
\end{aligned}
$$

9. **3:** Apply PEMDAS in reverse.

$$
\begin{aligned}
3t^3 - 7 &= 74 \\
3t^3 &= 81 &&\text{Add 7.} \\
t^3 &= 27 &&\text{Divide by 3.} \\
t &= 3 &&\text{Take the cube root.}
\end{aligned}
$$

10. **−32:** Apply PEMDAS in reverse.

$$\frac{z-4}{3} = -12$$

$z - 4 = -36$ Multiply by 3.

$z = -32$ Add 4.

11. **6:** Apply PEMDAS in reverse.

$$1{,}200x + 6{,}000 = 13{,}200$$

$1{,}200x = 7{,}200$ Subtract 6,000.

$x = 6$ Divide by 1,200.

12. **100:** Note that the right side contains no variables. First, simplify that side using standard PEMDAS rules.

$$\sqrt{x} = 3 \times 5 - 20 \div 4$$
$$\sqrt{x} = (3 \times 5) - (20 \div 4)$$
$$\sqrt{x} = 15 - 5$$
$$\sqrt{x} = 10$$

$x = 100$ Square both sides.

13. **3:** Be careful with the negatives!

$$-(y)^3 = -27$$

$(y)^3 = 27$ Divide by −1.

$y = 3$ Take the cube root.

14. **17:**

$$2 - \frac{\sqrt{2x+2}}{2} = -1$$

$-\dfrac{\sqrt{2x+2}}{2} = -3$ Subtract 2 from both sides.

$\sqrt{2x+2} = 6$ Multiply by −2.

$2x + 2 = 36$ Square.

$2x = 34$ Subtract 2.

$x = 17$ Divide by 2.

15. **81:**

$$5\sqrt{x} + 6 = 51$$

$$5\sqrt{x} = 45 \qquad \text{Subtract 6.}$$

$$\sqrt{x} = 9 \qquad \text{Divide by 5.}$$

$$x = 81 \qquad \text{Square}$$

Drill 3

16. **4:**

$$3x + 2(x + 2) = 2x + 16$$

$$3x + 2x + 4 = 2x + 16$$

$$5x + 4 = 2x + 16$$

$$3x + 4 = 16$$

$$3x = 12$$

$$x = 4$$

17. **1:**

$$\frac{3x + 7}{x} = 10$$

$$3x + 7 = 10x$$

$$7 = 7x$$

$$1 = x$$

18. **−26:**

$$4(-3x - 8) = 8(-x + 9)$$

$$-12x - 32 = -8x + 72$$

$$-32 = 4x + 72$$

$$-104 = 4x$$

$$-26 = x$$

19. **−9:**

$$3x + 7 - 4x + 8 = 2(-2x - 6)$$

$$-x + 15 = -4x - 12$$

$$3x + 15 = -12$$

$$3x = -27$$

$$x = -9$$

20. **−6:**

$$2x(4 - 6) = -2x + 12$$

$$2x(-2) = -2x + 12$$

$$-4x = -2x + 12$$

$$-2x = 12$$

$$x = -6$$

21. **−2:**

$$\frac{3(6-x)}{2x} = -6$$
$$3(6-x) = -6(2x)$$
$$18 - 3x = -12x$$
$$18 = -9x$$
$$-2 = x$$

22. **0:**

$$\frac{13}{x+13} = 1$$
$$13 = 1(x+13)$$
$$13 = x + 13$$
$$0 = x$$

23. **1:**

$$\frac{10(-3x+4)}{10-5x} = 2$$
$$10(-3x+4) = 2(10-5x)$$
$$-30x + 40 = 20 - 10x$$
$$40 = 20 + 20x$$
$$20 = 20x$$
$$1 = x$$

24. **2:**

$$\frac{15-3(5x-3)}{3-2x} = 6$$
$$15 - 3(5x-3) = 6(3-2x)$$
$$15 - 15x + 9 = 18 - 12x$$
$$24 - 15x = 18 - 12x$$
$$24 = 18 + 3x$$
$$6 = 3x$$
$$2 = x$$

25. **−10:**

$$\frac{\cancel{50}(10+3x)}{50+7x} = {}^{1}\cancel{50}$$
$$(10 + 3x) = (50 + 7x)$$
$$10 = 50 + 4x$$
$$-40 = 4x$$
$$-10 = x$$

Drill 4

26. **$x = 5$, $y = 10$:** Equation 1 is $7x - 3y = 5$, and equation 2 is $y = 10$.

Eq. (1):　　　　　　　Eq. (2):
$7x - 3y = 5$　　　　$y = 10$
$7x - 3(10) = 5$　　　　　　　　　　Substitute 10 for y in Eq. (1) and solve for x.
$7x - 30 = 5$
$7x = 35$
$x = 5$

27. **$x = 5$, $y = 30$:**

Eq. (1):　　　　　　　Eq. (2):
$y = 4x + 10$　　　　$y = 7x - 5$
　　　　　　　　　　$(4x + 10) = 7x - 5$　　　Substitute $(4x + 10)$ for y in
　　　　　　　　　　$10 = 3x - 5$　　　　　　Eq. (2), and solve for x.
　　　　　　　　　　$15 = 3x$
　　　　　　　　　　$5 = x$

$y = 4(5) + 10$　　　　　　　　　　　Substitute 5 for x in Eq. (1),
$y = 30$　　　　　　　　　　　　　　and solve for y.

28. **$h = 6$, $k = 3$:**

Eq. (1):　　　　　　　Eq. (2):
$2h - 4k = 0$　　　　$k = h - 3$

$2h - 4(h - 3) = 0$　　　　　　　　Substitute $(h - 3)$ for k in Eq. (1),
$2h - 4h + 12 = 0$　　　　　　　　and solve for h.
$-2h = -12$
$h = 6$

　　　　　　　　　　$k = (6) - 3$　　　　　Substitute 6 for h in Eq. (2),
　　　　　　　　　　$k = 3$　　　　　　　　and solve for k.

29. **$x = 7$, $y = 6$:**

Eq. (1):　　　　　　　Eq. (2):
$5x - 3y = 17$　　　　$2x - y = 8$

　　　　　　　　　　$-y = -2x + 8$　　　　Isolate y in Eq. (2).
　　　　　　　　　　$y = 2x - 8$

$$5x - 3(2x - 8) = 17$$
$$5x - 6x + 24 = 17$$
$$-x + 24 = 17$$
$$-x = -7$$
$$x = 7$$

Substitute $(2x - 8)$ for y in Eq. (1), and solve for x.

$$y = 2(7) - 8$$
$$y = 14 - 8$$
$$y = 6$$

Substitute 7 for x in the rephrased Eq. (2) to solve for y.

30. **$b = 3$, $g = 18$:**

Eq. (1):   Eq. (2):
$$12b = 2g$$ $$4g - 3b = 63$$

$$6b = g$$

Isolate g in Eq. (1).

$$4(6b) - 3b = 63$$
$$24b - 3b = 63$$
$$21b = 63$$
$$b = 3$$

Substitute $(6b)$ for g in Eq. (2), and solve for b.

$$6(3) = g$$
$$18 = g$$

Substitute 3 for b in the rephrased Eq. (1) to solve for g.

Drill 5

31. **$x = 3$, $y = -1$:** Notice that the first equation has the term $-y$ while the second equation has the term $+y$. If you add the equations together, these two terms will cancel.

$$x - y = 4$$
$$+(2x + y = 5)$$
$$\overline{ 3x = 9}$$

Therefore, $x = 3$. Plug this value into the first equation.

$$x - y = 4$$
$$(3) - y = 4$$
$$-y = 1$$
$$y = -1$$

32. **$x = 1$, $y = 2$:** Both equations have the term $+x$, so eliminate the variable x by subtracting the second equation from the first.

$$
\begin{array}{r}
x + 2y = 5 \\
-(x - 4y = -7) \\
\hline
2y + 4y = 5 + 7
\end{array}
$$

The new equation simplifies to $6y = 12$, or $y = 2$. Then plug this value for y into the first equation and solve for x.

$$
\begin{aligned}
x + 2y &= 5 \\
x + 2(2) &= 5 \\
x + 4 &= 5 \\
x &= 1
\end{aligned}
$$

Be very careful to change the sign of each term in the second equation when subtracting (e.g, $-4y$ becomes $-(-4y) = +4y$, and -7 becomes $-(-7) = +7$). Alternatively, you could have multiplied the entire second equation by -1 to get $-x + 4y = 7$ and then added this equation to the first.

$$
\begin{array}{r}
x + 2y = 5 \\
+ (-x + 4y = 7) \\
\hline
6y = 12
\end{array}
$$

This yields the same solution: $y = 2$ and $x = 1$.

33. **$a = 5$, $b = 3$:** Both equations have the term $+b$, so eliminate the variable b by subtracting the second equation from the first.

$$
\begin{array}{r}
a + b = 8 \\
- (2a + b = 13) \\
\hline
- a = -5
\end{array}
$$

Hence, $a = 5$. Plug this value for a into the first equation, and solve for b.

$$
\begin{aligned}
a + b &= 8 \\
(5) + b &= 8 \\
b &= 3
\end{aligned}
$$

34. **$m = 1$, $n = 3$:** None of the variables have the same coefficient (the number in front of a variable), so no variables will cancel as the equations are currently written. Multiply one of the equations by a constant so that one of the variables will then cancel when you add or subtract the equations.

The second equation has an n, and the first equation has a $-2n$. Multiply the second equation by 2 to get $6m + 2n = 12$, then add the two equations.

$$7m - 2n = 1$$
$$\underline{+\left(6m + 2n = 12\right)}$$
$$13m \quad\;\; = 13$$

Therefore, $m = 1$. Plug this value into the second equation and solve for n.

$$3m + n = 6$$
$$3(1) + n = 6$$
$$n = 3$$

35. $x = -\dfrac{4}{5}$, $y = -\dfrac{3}{5}$: First, manipulate the two equations so that the variables are nicely aligned on the left-hand side and the constant terms are all on the right.

$$-2x + y = 1$$
$$x - 3y = 1$$

Multiply one of the equations by a constant that will allow you to cancel one of the variables when you add or subtract. There are multiple correct ways to do this; one way is to multiply the second equation by 2, thereby replacing it with the equation $2x - 6y = 2$, then add the original first equation to the new second equation.

$$-2x + y = 1$$
$$\underline{+\left(2x - 6y = 2\right)}$$
$$-5y = 3$$

Therefore, $y = -\dfrac{3}{5}$. Glance at the two original equations. Which one is easiest to use to solve for x? In either case, you're still going to have to deal with the fractional value for y, but the second equation is a little easier because the x variable has a coefficient of 1. In other words, you won't have to divide at the end in order to solve.

$$x - 3\left(-\dfrac{3}{5}\right) = 1$$
$$x + \dfrac{9}{5} = 1$$
$$x = \dfrac{5}{5} - \dfrac{9}{5}$$
$$x = -\dfrac{4}{5}$$

36. **$r = 1$, $s = 2$:** The coefficients in this problem are messy. Take a little time to think about the best way to proceed. It might be easiest to eliminate the fractions in both equations before proceeding.

Notice that if you multiply the first equation by 6, you will cancel out all denominators. Do the same for the second equation by multiplying everything by 2.

$$2r - s = 0$$
$$4r + s - 6 = 0$$

Notice that the coefficients on s are both 1 but with different signs. This means that when you add the equations, they will cancel. Next, rearrange the second equation so that the constant terms are on the right side.

$$2r - s = 0$$
$$\underline{+\left(4r + s = 6\right)}$$
$$6r \quad = 6$$

Then, plug $r = 1$ into the first equation to get:

$$2(1) - s = 0$$
$$2 = s$$

Drill 6

37. **$x = 1$, $y = 3.5$:** When one of the two equations is already solved for one of the variables, substitution is usually the better method. In this particular problem, the second equation is solved for y, so take the right-hand side of the second equation and substitute it for y in the first equation.

$$5x + 2\left(\frac{1}{2}x + 3\right) = 12$$
$$5x + x + 6 = 12$$
$$6x = 6$$
$$x = 1$$

Plug this value for x into either of the original equations to solve for y; in this case, it will be easiest to use the equation that was used for the substitution (since it is already solved for y).

$$y = \frac{1}{2}x + 3$$
$$y = \frac{1}{2}(1) + 3$$
$$y = 3.5 \text{ or } 3\frac{1}{2}$$

38. **$x = -5$, $y = -2$:** For this system of equations, either method would be appropriate. Both equations would require some manipulation before you could stack-and-add, and neither equation is already solved for one of its variables. When neither method seems to have an advantage, pick whichever you like best.

If you use substitution, it might be easier to solve the first equation for y: $y = x + 3$. Then substitute this into the second equation.

$$2(x + 3) = x + 1$$
$$2x + 6 = x + 1$$
$$x = -5$$

Plug this into the equation used for the substitution step.

$$y = x + 3$$
$$y = (-5) + 3$$
$$y = -2$$

If you use elimination, manipulate the first equation to combine the constant terms ($y = x + 3$). Now the two equations have the same order, and the coefficient on x is the same, so if you subtract the second from the first, the variable x will disappear.

$$\begin{array}{r} y = x + 3 \\ -(2y = x + 1) \\ \hline -y = 2 \end{array}$$

Therefore, $y = 2$; plug this value in for y in either equation to solve for x: $x = -5$.

39. **$a = \dfrac{3}{4}$, $b = \dfrac{1}{2}$:** Even though some manipulations will be required to line up the variables nicely in this system, elimination is the optimal method because the $-2b$ in the first equation will cancel the $+2b$ in the second. Start by rearranging the two equations.

$$8a - 2b = 5$$
$$4a + 2b = 4$$

Then add them together.

$$\begin{array}{r} 8a - 2b = 5 \\ +(4a + 2b = 4) \\ \hline 12a = 9 \end{array}$$

Therefore, $a = \dfrac{9}{12} = \dfrac{3}{4}$. Plug this value into one of the two original equations, and solve for b. Note that the second equation has a $4a$ term, which will cancel nicely with the fraction $\dfrac{3}{4}$.

$$2b + 4\left(\dfrac{3}{4}\right) - 4 = 0$$
$$2b + 3 - 4 = 0$$
$$2b = 1$$
$$b = \dfrac{1}{2}$$

40. **$x = 1, y = 3$:** For this system of equations, either method would be appropriate. Both equations would require some manipulation before you could stack-and-add, and neither equation is already solved for one of its variables. When neither method seems to have an advantage, pick whichever you like best.

To solve via substitution, isolate y in the first equation to get $y = 6 - 3x$, and then substitute this for y in the second equation.

$$6x - (6 - 3x) = 3$$
$$6x - 6 + 3x = 3$$
$$9x = 9$$
$$x = 1$$

Next, plug $x = 1$ into the same equation used above for the substitution step.

$$y = 6 - 3x$$
$$y = 6 - 3(1)$$
$$y = 3$$

To solve using the elimination method, rearrange the first equation to get $3x + y = 6$, and then add the equations together to eliminate y.

$$\begin{array}{r} 3x + y = 6 \\ +(6x - y = 3) \\ \hline 9x \quad\;\; = 9 \end{array}$$

Plug $x = 1$ into either of the equations to solve for y.

$$3x + y = 6$$
$$3(1) + y = 6$$
$$y = 3$$

41. **$x = 3.5$, $y = 2$:** The first equation is solved for x, which points to substitution. At the same time, the first equation has $+x$ on the left side while the second equation has $-x$. Either method will work; choose the one you like best.

To solve using the elimination method, rearrange the equations to line up all the variables. Next, add the two equations in order to eliminate the x term.

$$x - 2y = -\frac{1}{2}$$
$$+ \left(-x + y = -\frac{3}{2}\right)$$
$$\overline{\qquad -y = -2 \qquad}$$

Therefore, $y = 2$. Plug this into the first equation, since that equation already isolates x on one side.

$$x = 2y - \frac{1}{2}$$
$$x = 2(2) - \frac{1}{2}$$
$$x = 3.5$$

To solve by substitution, take the first equation, which is already solved for x, and substitute into the second equation.

$$y - \left(2y - \frac{1}{2}\right) = -\frac{3}{2}$$
$$y - 2y + \frac{1}{2} = -\frac{3}{2}$$
$$-y = -\frac{3}{2} - \frac{1}{2}$$
$$-y = -2$$

Therefore, $y = 2$. As before, plug this value into the first equation to get $x = 3.5$.

Drill 7

42. **13:** This question contains only two equations, but three variables. To isolate y, you need to get rid of both x and z. Try to eliminate both variables at the same time. The coefficients of x and z are the same in both equations, so subtract the second equation from the first to eliminate both.

$$4x + y + 3z = 34$$
$$-\left(4x \qquad + 3z = 21\right)$$
$$\overline{\qquad\qquad y = 13 \qquad}$$

43. **(A):** To find the value of x in terms of the other variables, isolate x on one side of the equation, and put everything else on the other side. Begin by getting rid of the fraction.

$$\frac{x-3}{y-2} = 4z$$
$$x-3 = 4z(y-2)$$
$$x = 4z(y-2)+3$$

The answers don't contain parentheses, so distribute to get rid of them.

$$x = 4yz - 8z + 3$$

44. **3:** In order to isolate y, you need to eliminate both x and z. Find a way to eliminate both variables at the same time.

Notice that the coefficients for x and z in the second equation (6 and 4, respectively) are exactly double their coefficients in the first equation (3 and 2, respectively). If you divide the second equation by 2, the coefficients will be the same.

$$\longrightarrow 3x+5y+2z = 20$$
$$3x+5y+2z = 20 \longrightarrow 3x+2z = 5$$
$$6x+4z = 10$$

Now, subtract the second equation from the first.

$$3x+5y+2z = 20$$
$$-(3x \qquad +2z = 5)$$
$$\overline{\qquad\qquad 5y = 15}$$
$$y = 3$$

45. $b = \dfrac{a-12}{5}$**:** To solve for b in terms of a, isolate b on one side of the equation, and put everything else on the other side. Furthermore, you will need to eliminate the variable c, because the question does not mention c.

The second equation is already solved for c, so start by substituting $b + 2$ for c in the first equation.

$$\frac{a-b}{4} = c+1$$
$$\frac{a-b}{4} = (b+2)+1$$

Now isolate b on one side of the equation.

$$\frac{a-b}{4} = b+3$$
$$a-b = 4(b+3)$$
$$a-b = 4b+12$$
$$a-12 = 5b$$
$$\frac{a-12}{5} = b$$

Drill 8

46. **$a + b = 50$:** In order to find the value of $a + b$, you need to eliminate c and d from the first equation, but there are only two equations total. Is there a way to eliminate $c + d$ at once?

Try manipulating the second equation to give you $c + d$.

$$3d = 15 - 3c$$
$$3c + 3d = 15$$
$$c + d = 15$$

Next, substitute $c + d = 5$ into the first equation and isolate $a + b$.

$$\frac{a+b}{c+d} = 10$$
$$\frac{a+b}{(5)} = 10$$
$$a+b = 50$$

47. **$z = \dfrac{3x+1}{2}$:** In order to solve for z in terms of x, you need to isolate z on one side of an equation that contains only the variable x and plain numbers on the other side of the equals sign. In other words, you have to get rid of the y somehow. Therefore, kill off y by isolating it in the first equation.

$$x = \frac{y}{5}$$
$$5x = y$$

Now substitute. In the second equation, replace y with $5x$.

$$2z - 1 = \frac{x+y}{2}$$
$$2z - 1 = \frac{x+(5x)}{2}$$

Finally, isolate z.

$$2z - 1 = \frac{6x}{2}$$
$$2z - 1 = 3x$$
$$2z = 3x + 1$$
$$z = \frac{3x + 1}{2}$$

48. **18:** In order to isolate z, you have to eliminate x and y. The combination $x + y$ is in the exponent of the first equation, so try to isolate that same combination (or combo) in the second equation.

$$x = 2 - y$$
$$x + y = 2$$

In the first equation, substitute 2 for the combo $x + y$, then solve for z.

$$2^{x+y} = \sqrt{z - 2}$$
$$2^{(2)} = \sqrt{z - 2}$$
$$4 = \sqrt{z - 2}$$
$$(4)^2 = (\sqrt{z - 2})^2$$
$$16 = z - 2$$
$$18 = z$$

49. **(B):** Both equations contain a z, but the question stem asks only for $x - y$. How can you get rid of that z?

First, get rid of the fraction in the first equation.

$$\frac{3x}{z + 4} = 4$$
$$3x = 4(z + 4)$$
$$3x = 4z + 16$$

You could solve the second equation for z and then substitute. However, did you notice that both equations now have a $4z$ term? You can directly substitute $3y$ for $4z$ into the equation to get rid of the z variable, then solve for $x - y$.

$$3x = 4z + 16$$
$$3x = (3y) + 16$$
$$3x - 3y = 16$$
$$x - y = \frac{16}{3}$$

Quadratic Equations

In this chapter...

- Mechanics of Quadratic Equations
  - Distribute $(a + b)(x + y) \rightarrow$ Use FOIL
  - Factor $x^2 + 5x + 6 \rightarrow$ Find the Original Numbers in $(x + ...)$ $(x + ...)$
  - Solve a Quadratic Equation: Set Quadratic Expression Equal to 0, Factor, Then Set Factors to 0
  - Solve a Quadratic Equation with No x Term: Take Positive and Negative Square Roots
  - Solve a Quadratic Equation with Squared Parentheses: Take Positive and Negative Square Roots
  - Higher Powers: Solve Like a Normal Quadratic
- Other Instances of Quadratics
  - See a Quadratic Expression in a Fraction: Factor and Cancel
  - See a Special Product: Convert to the Other Form

Chapter 7

Quadratic Equations

In This Chapter, You Will Learn To:

- Manipulate quadratic expressions and solve quadratic equations

Mechanics of Quadratic Equations

In high school algebra, you learned a number of skills for dealing with quadratic equations. You will need those skills again on the GMAT.

Let's define terms first. A **quadratic expression** contains a squared variable, such as x^2, and no higher power. The word *quadratic* comes from the Latin word for *square*. Here are a few quadratic expressions:

$$z^2 \qquad\qquad y^2 + y - 6 \qquad\qquad x^2 + 8x + 16 \qquad\qquad w^2 - 9$$

A quadratic expression can also be disguised. You might not see the squared exponent on the variable explicitly. Here are some disguised quadratic expressions:

$$z \times z \qquad\qquad (y+3)(y-2) \qquad\qquad (x+4)^2 \qquad\qquad (w-3)(w+3)$$

If you multiply these expressions out—that is, if you distribute them—then you will have exponents on the variables. Note that each expression in the second list equals the corresponding expression in the first list (once you multiply out).

A **quadratic equation** contains a quadratic expression and an equals sign.

Quadratic expression = something else

A quadratic equation usually has two solutions. That is, in most cases, *two* different values of the variable each make the equation true. Solving a quadratic equation means finding those values.

Before you can solve quadratic equations, you have to be able to distribute and factor quadratic expressions.

Distribute $(a + b)(x + y) \rightarrow$ Use FOIL

Recall that distributing means applying multiplication across a sum. For example:

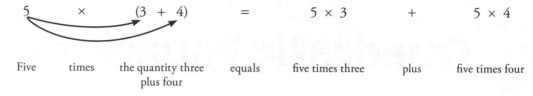

| Five | times | the quantity three plus four | equals | five times three | plus | five times four |

You can omit the multiplication sign next to parentheses. Also, the order of the product doesn't matter, and subtraction works the same way as addition. Here are more examples:

$$3(x + 2) = 3x + 6 \qquad (z - 12)y = zy - 12y \qquad w(a + b) = wa + wb$$

What if you have to distribute the product of two sums? Try this example:

$$(a + b)(x + y) =$$

Multiply every term in the first sum by every term in the second sum, then add all the products up. This is just distribution on steroids.

To make the products, use the acronym **FOIL**: **F**irst, **O**uter, **I**nner, **L**ast (or **F**irst, **O**utside, **I**nside, **L**ast). For example:

$(\boldsymbol{a} + b)(\boldsymbol{x} + y)$ F – multiply the First term in each of the parentheses: $(a)(x) = ax$
$(\boldsymbol{a} + b)(x + \boldsymbol{y})$ O – multiply the Outer term in each: $(a)(y) = ay$
$(a + \boldsymbol{b})(\boldsymbol{x} + y)$ I – multiply the Inner term in each: $(b)(x) = bx$
$(a + \boldsymbol{b})(x + \boldsymbol{y})$ L – multiply the Last terms in each: $(b)(y) = by$

Now add up the products.

$$(a + b)(x + y) = ax + ay + bx + by$$

By the way, you can even FOIL numbers. Try this example:

What is 102×301?

If you express 102 as $100 + 2$ and 301 as $300 + 1$, you can rewrite the question as a product of two sums:

What is $(100 + 2)(300 + 1)$?

Now FOIL it out.

$$(100 + 2)(300 + 1) = (100 \times 300) + (100 \times 1) + (2 \times 300) + (2 \times 1)$$
$$= 30{,}000 + 100 + 600 + 2$$
$$= 30{,}702$$

You get the same answer if you multiply these numbers in longhand. In fact, longhand multiplication is just distribution. You're essentially FOILing as you multiply the digits and add up the results.

$$102$$
$$\times\,301$$
$$\overline{102}$$
$$\underline{30{,}600}$$
$$30{,}702$$

Now try to FOIL this disguised quadratic expression: $(x + 2)(x + 3)$.

$(\boldsymbol{x} + 2)(\boldsymbol{x} + 3)$	F – multiply the First term in each of the parentheses:	$(x)(x) = x^2$
$(\boldsymbol{x} + 2)(x + \boldsymbol{3})$	O – multiply the Outer term in each:	$(x)(3) = 3x$
$(x + \boldsymbol{2})(\boldsymbol{x} + 3)$	I – multiply the Inner term in each:	$(2)(x) = 2x$
$(x + \boldsymbol{2})(x + \boldsymbol{3})$	L – multiply the Last terms in each:	$(2)(3) = 6$

Add up the products.

$$(x + 2)(x + 3) = x^2 + 3x + 2x + 6$$

Notice that you can combine the like terms in the middle ($3x$ and $2x$).

$$(x + 2)(x + 3) = x^2 + \underbrace{3x + 2x}\; + 6 = x^2 + 5x + 6$$

Now compare the expression you started with and the expression you ended up with.

$$(x + 2)(x + 3) \qquad\qquad x^2 + 5x + 6$$

Study how the numbers on the left relate to the numbers on the right.

The 2 and the 3 *multiply* to give you the 6.
The 2 and the 3 *add* to give you the 5 in $5x$.

What if you have subtraction? Attach the minus signs to the second term in each pair of parentheses. Next, multiply according to the rules of arithmetic and add the products. Try this example:

$$(y - 5)(y - 2) =$$

First, FOIL. Keep track of minus signs. Put them in the products. For example:

$(\boldsymbol{y} - 5)(\boldsymbol{y} - 2)$	F – multiply First terms:	$(y)(y) = y^2$
$(\boldsymbol{y} - 5)(y - \boldsymbol{2})$	O – multiply Outer terms:	$(y)(-2) = -2y$
$(y - \boldsymbol{5})(\boldsymbol{y} - 2)$	I – multiply Inner terms:	$(-5)(y) = -5y$
$(y - \boldsymbol{5})(y - \boldsymbol{2})$	L – multiply Last terms:	$(-5)(-2) = 10$

Finally, add the products and combine like terms.

$$(y - 5)(y - 2) = y^2 - 2y - 5y + 10 = y^2 - 7y + 10$$

Again, study how the numbers on the left relate to the numbers on the right.

The −5 and the −2 *multiply* to give you the positive 10.
The −5 and the −2 *add* to give you the −7 in −7y.

Here's one last wrinkle. In the course of doing these problems, you might encounter a sum written as $4 + z$ rather than as $z + 4$. You can FOIL it as is, or you can flip the sum around so that the variable is first. Either way works fine.

If you...	Then you...	Like this:
Want to distribute $(x + 5)(x − 4)$	FOIL it out and combine like terms	$(x + 5)(x − 4)$ $= x^2 − 4x + 5x − 20$ $= x^2 + x − 20$

Check Your Skills

FOIL the following expressions.

1. $(x + 4)(x + 9)$
2. $(y + 3)(y − 6)$

Answers can be found on page 319.

Factor $x^2 + 5x + 6$ ➡ FIND the Original Numbers in $(x + ...)(x + ...)$

FOILing is a form of distribution. So going in reverse is a form of *factoring*. To factor a quadratic expression such as $x^2 + 5x + 6$ means to *rewrite the expression as a product of two sums*. For example:

$$x^2 + 5x + 6 = (x + ...)(x + ...)$$

The form on the right is called the **factored form**. (You can call $x^2 + 5x + 6$ the **distributed form**.)

You already know the answer, because earlier you turned $(x + 2)(x + 3)$ into $x^2 + 5x + 6$.

$$(x + 2)(x + 3) = x^2 + 3x + 2x + 6 = x^2 + 5x + 6$$

Consider the relationship between the numbers one more time.

$2 + 3 = 5$, the coefficient of the x term $2 \times 3 = 6$, the constant term on the end

This is true in general. The two numbers in the factored form *add* to the x coefficient, and they *multiply* to the constant.

Now think about how to work backwards.

$$x^2 + 5x + 6 = (x + ...)(x + ...)$$

You need two numbers that multiply together to 6 and sum to 5.

Look first for factor pairs of the constant—in this case, two numbers that multiply to 6. Then check the sum.

> 2 and 3 are a factor pair of 6, because $2 \times 3 = 6$.
> 2 and 3 also sum to 5, so this is the correct pair.

> $x^2 + 5x + 6 = (x + 2)(x + 3)$

Try this slightly different example:

> $y^2 + 7y + 6 = (y + \ldots)(y + \ldots)$

The constant is the same: 6. So you need a factor pair of 6. But now the pair has to sum to 7.

Therefore, 2 and 3 no longer work. But 1 and 6 are also a factor pair of 6. So factor $y^2 + 7y + 6$ like this:

> $y^2 + 7y + 6 = (y + 1)(y + 6)$

Now try to factor this quadratic:

> $z^2 + 7z + 12 = (z + \ldots)(z + \ldots)$

Again, start with the constant. Look for a factor pair of 12 that sums to 7.

It might help to list the factor pairs of 12:

> 1×12
>
> 2×6
>
> 3×4

The only factor pair of 12 that sums to 7 is 3 and 4. Therefore:

> $3 \times 4 = 12 \qquad 3 + 4 = 7$
>
> $z^2 + 7z + 12 = (z + 3)(z + 4)$

What if you have subtraction? The same principles hold. Just think of the minus signs as part of the numbers themselves. Try this example:

> $x^2 - 9x + 18 = (x + \ldots)(x + \ldots)$

You need two numbers that multiply to 18, but now they have to add up to −9. Think about rules of negatives and positives. If the sum is negative, then at least one of the terms must be negative. And for the product to be positive, the terms must have the same sign.

> Both numbers must be negative. Neg × Neg = Pos   Neg + Neg = Neg

Again, consider listing out the factor pairs of 18, and don't forget that both terms are negative.

$$-1 \times -18$$
$$-2 \times -9$$
$$-3 \times -6$$

The answer is -3 and -6. $-3 \times -6 = 18$ $-3 + (-6) = -9$

Now, write the factored form of the quadratic expression.

$$x^2 - 9x + 18 = (x - 3)(x - 6)$$

If the constant (in the case above, 18) is positive, then the two numbers in the factored form must *both be positive* or *both be negative*, depending on the sign of the x term.

If the sign of the constant (in the case below, 12) and the x term ($7z$) are both positive, then the two numbers in factored form are positive.

$$z^2 + 7z + 12 = (z + 3)(z + 4)$$

If, on the other hand, the constant (18) is positive but the x term ($9x$) is negative, then both numbers in factored form are negative.

$$x^2 - 9x + 18 = (x - 3)(x - 6)$$

What if the constant is negative? Again, *think of the minus sign as part of the number*. Try this example:

$$w^2 + 3w - 10 = (w + \ldots)(w + \ldots)$$

You need two numbers that multiply to negative 10 and that sum to 3.

For the product to be -10, one number must be positive and the other one must be negative. That's the only way to get a negative product of two numbers.

$$\text{Pos} \times \text{Neg} = \text{Neg}$$

If the constant is negative, then in the factored form, *one number is positive and the other one is negative.*

This means that you are adding a positive and a negative to get 3:

$$\text{Pos} + \text{Neg} = 3$$

If you think about the negative as subtracting a positive, then you are looking for a difference of 3. Here's how to find the two numbers you want. First, pretend that the constant is positive. Think of the normal, positive factor pairs of 10. Which pair *differs* by 3?

$$1 \times 10$$
$$2 \times 5$$

The answer is 5 and 2.

$$5 \times 2 = 10$$

$$5 - 2 = 3$$

But now you must decide which is positive and which is negative. Because the sum is positive, it must be the case that the larger factor is the positive one.

The answer is 5 and −2. $5 \times (-2) = -10$ $5 + (-2) = 3$

Notice that −5 and 2 would give you the correct product (−10) but the incorrect sum (−5 + 2 = −3).

Now you know where to place the signs in the factored form. Place the minus sign with the 2.

$w^2 + 3w - 10 = (w + 5)(w - 2)$

When the *constant is negative*, start by testing the positive factor pairs and asking which pair *differs* by the right amount.

Once you find a good factor pair for the constant (say 5 and 2), then determine which term is negative and which is positive by asking whether the sum is negative or positive. If the sum is positive, the larger term must be positive. If the sum is negative, the larger term must be negative. If you're ever not sure, try both possibilities!

Consider this example:

$y^2 - 4y - 21 = (y + \ldots)(y + \ldots)$

You need two numbers that multiply to *negative* 21 and that sum to *negative* 4.

Again, one number must be positive, while the other is negative.

Start by looking for the positive factor pairs of 21. Which pair *differs* by 4?

Only 7 and 3 work. $7 \times 3 = 21$ $7 - 3 = 4$

Now you need to make one number negative, so that the product is now −21 and the *sum* is now −4. Which number should be negative?

The sum is negative, so make the larger term negative. Because 7 is larger than 3, 7 is the negative term.

$(-7) \times 3 = -21$ $(-7) + 3 = -4$

Write the factored form:

$y^2 - 4y - 21 = (y - 7)(y + 3)$

Finally, the GMAT can make factoring a quadratic expression harder in a couple of ways.

(1) Every term in the expression is multiplied through by a common numerical factor, including the x^2 term.

$3x^2 + 21x + 36 = \ldots$

In this case, *pull out the common factor first*. Put parentheses around what's left. Then factor the quadratic expression as usual.

$3x^2 + 21x + 36 = 3(x^2 + 7x + 12) = 3(x + 3)(x + 4)$

If the x^2 term is negative, factor out a common factor of -1 *first*. That will flip the sign on every term.

$$-x^2 + 9x - 18 = \ldots$$

Pull out the -1, which becomes a minus sign outside a set of parentheses. Don't forget to flip the sign of every term. Then factor the quadratic expression as usual.

$$-x^2 + 9x - 18 = -(x^2 - 9x + 18) = -(x - 3)(x - 6)$$

(2) Sometimes the x^2 term has a coefficient, but you can't divide it out without creating fractions for the other terms. *Avoid fractional coefficients at all costs.* If you cannot pull out a common factor from the x^2 term without turning coefficients into fractions, then keep a coefficient on one or even both x's in your factored form. At this point, *experiment with factor pairs of the constant* until you get a match. Try this example:

$$2z^2 - z - 15 = \ldots$$

Don't factor a 2 out of all the terms. Rather, set up the parentheses on the right. Put a $2z$ in one set.

$$2z^2 - z - 15 = (2z + \ldots)(z + \ldots)$$

At least you've got the F of FOIL covered.

What you already know how to do is still useful. Since the constant is negative (-15), one of the numbers must be negative, while the other must be positive.

Pretend for a minute that the constant is positive 15. You still need a factor pair of 15. There are only two factor pairs of 15:

$$1 \times 15 = 15 \qquad 3 \times 5 = 15$$

But which pair do you want? Which number becomes negative? And where does that one go—with the $2z$ or the z?

The middle term is your guide. The coefficient on the z term is only -1, so it's very unlikely that the "1 and 15" factor pair will work. The numbers must be 3 and 5, with a minus sign on exactly one of them. This covers the L of FOIL.

Finally, experiment. Try the numbers in different configurations. Examine only the OI of FOIL (Outer and Inner) to see whether you get the right middle term.

$$2z^2 - z - 15 = (2z + \ldots)(z + \ldots) = (2z + 3)(z - 5)? \quad \textbf{FOIL} \longrightarrow (2z)(-5) + 3z \text{ does not equal } -z$$

Learn after each attempt. Since $-10z$ and $3z$ are too far apart, swap the numbers.

$$2z^2 - z - 15 = (2z + \ldots)(z + \ldots) = (2z - 5)(z + 3)? \quad \textbf{FOIL} \longrightarrow (2z)(3) - 5z \text{ equals } z, \text{ not } -z$$

The coefficient, 1, is correct this time, but not the sign. Switch the signs.

$$2z^2 - z - 15 = (2z + \ldots)(z + \ldots) = (2z + 5)(z - 3)? \quad \textbf{FOIL} \longrightarrow (2z)(-3) + 5z \text{ equals } -z \quad \text{YES}$$

So $2z^2 - z - 15$ factors into $(2z + 5)(z - 3)$. You can always check your work by FOILing the result.

$$(2z + 5)(z - 3) = 2z^2 - 6z + 5z - 15 = 2z^2 - z - 15$$

If you're ever in doubt, FOIL it back out! Luckily, you won't often see a FOIL this complex on the GMAT. (You might even decide that a problem this complex isn't worth your time.)

If you…	Then you…	Like this:
Want to factor $x^2 + 11x + 18$	Find a factor pair of 18 that sums to 11	$x^2 + 11x + 18$ $= (x + 9)(x + 2)$ $9 + 2 = 11$ $9 \times 2 = 18$
Want to factor $x^2 - 8x + 12$	Find a factor pair of 12 that sums to 8, then make both numbers negative	$x^2 - 8x + 12$ $= (x - 6)(x - 2)$ $(-6) + (-2) = -8$ $(-6) \times (-2) = 12$
Want to factor $x^2 + 6x - 16$	Find a factor pair of 16 that *differs* by 6, then make the bigger number *positive* so that the sum is 6 and the product is −16	$x^2 + 6x - 16$ $= (x + 8)(x - 2)$ $8 + (-2) = 6$ $8 \times (-2) = -16$
Want to factor $x^2 - 5x - 14$	Find a factor pair of 14 that *differs* by 5, then make the bigger number *negative* so that the sum is −5 and the product is −14	$x^2 - 5x - 14$ $= (x - 7)(x + 2)$ $(-7) + 2 = -5$ $(-7) \times 2 = -14$
Want to factor $-2x^2 + 16x - 24$	Factor out −2 from all terms first, then factor the quadratic expression normally	$-2x^2 + 16x - 24$ $= -2(x^2 - 8x + 12)$ $= -2(x - 6)(x - 2)$

Check Your Skills

Factor the following expressions.

3. $x^2 + 14x + 33$
4. $x^2 - 14x + 45$
5. $x^2 + 3x - 18$
6. $x^2 - 5x - 66$

Answers can be found on page 319.

Solve a Quadratic Equation: Set Quadratic Expression Equal to 0, Factor, Then Set Factors to 0

So far, you've dealt with quadratic expressions—distributing them and factoring them.

Now how do you solve quadratic *equations*? Try this example:

> If $x^2 + x = 6$, what are the possible values of x?

Notice that you are asked for *possible* values of x. Usually, two different values of x will make a quadratic equation true. In other words, expect the equation to have two solutions.

The best way to solve most quadratic equations involves a particular property of the number 0. For example:

If $ab = 0$, then either $a = 0$ or $b = 0$ (or both, potentially).

In words, if the product of two numbers is 0, then you know that at least one of the numbers is 0. (This is known as the Zero Product rule.)

This is true no matter how complicated the factors. For example:

If $(a + 27)(b - 12) = 0$, then either $a + 27 = 0$ or $b - 12 = 0$ (or both).

In words, if the quantity $a + 27$ times the quantity $b - 12$ equals 0, then at least one of those quantities must be 0.

This gives you a pathway to solve quadratic equations.

1. Rearrange the equation to make one side equal 0. The other side will contain a quadratic expression.
2. Factor the quadratic expression. The equation will look like this:
    (Something)(Something else) $= 0$
3. Set each factor equal to 0.
    Something $= 0$ or   Something else $= 0$

These two equations will be much easier to solve. Each one will give you a possible solution for the original equation.

Try this with the problem above. First, rearrange the equation to make one side equal to 0.

$$\begin{array}{rcl} x^2 + x &=& 6 \\ -6 && -6 \\ \hline x^2 + x - 6 &=& 0 \end{array}$$

Next, factor the quadratic expression on the left side.

$$x^2 + x - 6 = 0$$
$$(x + 3)(x - 2) = 0$$

Finally, set each factor (the quantities in parentheses) equal to 0, and solve for x in each case.

$$\begin{array}{ccc} x + 3 = 0 && x - 2 = 0 \\ x = -3 & \text{or} & x = 2 \end{array}$$

Now you have the two possible values of x, which are the two solutions to the original equation.

$$\begin{array}{lll} x^2 + x = 6 & x \text{ could be } -3 & (-3)^2 + (-3) = 6 \\ & \text{or } x \text{ could be } 2 & 2^2 + 2 = 6 \end{array}$$

By the way, the two equations you get at the end can't both be true at the same time. What $x^2 + x = 6$ tells you is that x must equal either -3 or 2. The value of x is one or the other; it's not both simultaneously. The variable has multiple *possible* values.

The solutions of a quadratic equation are also called its **roots**.

If an additional condition is placed on the variable, you can often narrow down to one solution. Try this example:

If $y < 0$ and $y^2 = y + 30$, what is the value of y?

First, solve the quadratic equation. Rearrange it so that one side equals 0.

$$
\begin{array}{rl}
y^2 & = \; y + 30 \\
\underline{-y - 30 \quad -y - 30} & \\
y^2 - y - 30 & = \; 0
\end{array}
$$

Next, factor the quadratic expression.

$$y^2 - y - 30 = 0$$
$$(y - 6)(y + 5) = 0$$

Set each factor equal to 0.

$$
\begin{array}{ccc}
y - 6 = 0 & & y + 5 = 0 \\
y = 6 & \text{or} & y = -5
\end{array}
$$

At this point, you can definitively say that y is either 6 or -5. Go back to the question, which gives the additional condition that $y < 0$. Since y is negative, y cannot be 6. Thus, the answer to the question is -5. The quadratic equation gave you two possibilities, but only one of them fits the constraint that $y < 0$.

Occasionally, a quadratic equation has only one solution on its own. Try this example:

If $w^2 - 8w + 16 = 0$, what is the value of w?

The quadratic equation already has one side equal to 0, so go ahead and factor the quadratic expression:

$$w^2 - 8w + 16 = 0$$
$$(w - 4)(w - 4) = 0$$

The two factors in parentheses happen to be identical. In this special case, you don't get two separate equations and two separate roots.

$$
\begin{array}{ccc}
w - 4 = 0 & \text{so} & w = 4
\end{array}
$$

The only solution is 4.

Lastly, *never factor before you set one side equal to 0*. Try this example:

> If z is positive and $z^2 + z - 8 = 4$, what is the value of z?

You might be tempted to factor the left side right away. But the Zero Product rule only works when the product equals 0. Why? Imagine the easier example that $xy = 4$. Must it be true that $x = 4$ or $y = 4$? No! They could both equal 2, or you could have a combination of non-integer values. This means that you can really only solve these quadratics when you set them equal to 0.

Avoid the temptation to factor right away, and instead rearrange to make the right side 0 first.

$$\begin{array}{rcl} z^2 + z - 8 &=& 4 \\ -4 & & -4 \\ \hline z^2 + z - 12 &=& 0 \end{array}$$

Now factor the left side.

$$z^2 + z - 12 = 0$$
$$(z + 4)(z - 3) = 0$$

Finally, set each factor equal to 0 and solve for z.

$$z + 4 = 0 \qquad \text{or} \qquad z - 3 = 0$$

Thus, z equals either -4 or 3. Since you are told that z is positive, z must be 3.

It's legal to factor a quadratic expression whenever you want to. But if you factor the expression *before* setting one side equal to zero, your factors don't tell you anything useful. You can't set them individually to 0.

When you solve a quadratic equation, always set one side equal to 0 *before* you factor.

If you...	Then you...	Like this:
Want to solve $x^2 + 11x = -18$	Rearrange to make one side 0, factor the quadratic side, then set the factors equal to 0	$x^2 + 11x = -18$ $x^2 + 11x + 18 = 0$ $(x + 9)(x + 2) = 0$ $(x + 9) = 0$ or $(x + 2) = 0$ $x = -9$ or $x = -2$

Check Your Skills

Solve the following quadratic equations.

7. $x^2 + 2x - 35 = 0$
8. $x^2 - 15x = -26$

Answers can be found on page 320.

Solve a Quadratic Equation with No *x* Term: Take Positive and Negative Square Roots

Occasionally, you encounter a quadratic equation with an x^2 term but no x term. For example:

If x is negative and $x^2 = 9$, what is x?

Here's the fast way to solve: *Take positive and negative square roots.*

$$x^2 = 9$$
$$\sqrt{x^2} = \sqrt{9}$$
$$x = 3 \text{ OR } -3$$

Since you are told that x is negative, the answer to the question is -3.

You can also solve this problem using the method of the previous section. Although the method is longer in this case, it's worth seeing how it works.

1. Rearrange the equation to make one side 0:

    $$x^2 = 9$$
    $$x^2 - 9 = 0$$

2. Factor the quadratic expression. The strange thing is that there is no x term, but you can imagine that it has a coefficient of 0.

    $$x^2 - 9 = 0$$
    $$x^2 + 0x - 9 = 0$$

    Because the constant (-9) is negative, you need a factor pair of 9 that *differs* by 0. In other words, you need 3 and 3. Make one of these numbers negative to fit the equation as given.

    $$x^2 + 0x - 9 = 0$$
    $$(x+3)(x-3) = 0$$

    You can FOIL the result back out to see how the x terms cancel in the middle.

    $$(x + 3)(x - 3) = x^2 - 3x + 3x - 9 = x^2 - 9$$

3. Finally, set each of the factors in parentheses equal to 0, and solve for x.

    $$x + 3 = 0 \qquad \text{OR} \qquad x - 3 = 0$$

Thus, x equals either -3 or 3. Again, the question tells you that x is negative, so -3 is the answer.

Obviously, the second method is overkill in this case. It's important to understand, though, so that you know that $x^2 - 9$ factors to $(x + 3)(x - 3)$. You'll come back to that point later in this chapter.

If you...	Then you...	Like this:
Want to solve $x^2 = 25$	Take the positive and negative square roots of both sides	$x^2 = 25$ $\sqrt{x^2} = \sqrt{25}$ $(x + 5)(x - 5) = 0$ $x = -5$ or $x = 5$

Check Your Skills

9. If $x^2 - 3 = 1$, what are all the possible values of x?

Answer can be found on page 320.

Solve a Quadratic Equation with Squared Parentheses: Take Positive and Negative Square Roots

Try this example:

If $(y + 1)^2 = 16$, what are the possible values of y?

Notice that the variable y only shows up once in your expression, not as both a y and a y^2 term (the y is isolated within the parentheses).

This means you can do this problem in either of two ways.

One way is to treat $y + 1$ as if it were a new variable, z. In other words, $z = y + 1$.

Solve $z^2 = 16$ by taking positive and negative square roots.

$$(y + 1)^2 = 16 \quad \longrightarrow \quad z^2 = 16 \quad \longrightarrow \quad z = 4 \text{ or } z = -4$$

Go back to y.

$$(y + 1)^2 = 16 \quad \longrightarrow \quad z^2 = 16 \quad \longrightarrow \quad z = 4 \text{ or } z = -4 \quad \longrightarrow \quad y + 1 = 4 \text{ or } y + 1 = -4$$

In fact, you didn't need z. You could have just taken the positive and negative square roots right away:

$$(y + 1)^2 = 16$$
$$y + 1 = 4 \text{ or } y + 1 = -4$$

Finally, solve the simpler equations for y: $y = 3$ or $y = -5$.

Alternatively, expand $(y + 1)^2$ into $(y + 1)(y + 1)$. Next, you can FOIL this product out.

$$(y + 1)(y + 1) = y^2 + y + y + 1 = y^2 + 2y + 1$$

Now solve the quadratic equation normally: set one side equal to 0, and factor.

$$y^2 + 2y + 1 = 16$$
$$y^2 + 2y - 15 = 0$$
$$(y + 5)(y - 3) = 0$$
$$y = -5 \text{ or } 3$$

Which way is faster depends on the numbers involved. With big numbers, the first way is easier.

If you...	Then you...	Like this:
Want to solve $(z - 7)^2 = 225$	Take the positive and negative square roots of both sides	$(z-7)^2 = 225$ $\sqrt{(z-7)^2} = \sqrt{225}$ $z - 7 = 15$ or $z - 7 = -15$ $z = 22$ or $z = -8$

Check Your Skills

10. If $(z + 2)^2 = 144$, what are the possible values of z?

Answer can be found on page 320.

Higher Powers: Solve Like a Normal Quadratic

If you have a higher power of x in the equation, look for solutions as if the equation were a typical quadratic: Set one side equal to 0, factor as much as you can, and then set factors equal to 0:

$$x^3 = 3x^2 - 2x$$

What are all of the roots of the equation above?

(A) −3, 1, 2
(B) −2, 1, 3
(C) 0, 1, 2
(D) 0, 1
(E) 1, 2

Recall that a *root* of an equation is a solution—a value for the variable that makes the equation true.

First, set one side of the equation equal to 0:

$$x^3 = 3x^2 - 2x$$
$$\underline{-3x^2 + 2x - 3x^2 + 2x}$$
$$x^3 - 3x^2 + 2x = 0$$

You may notice that every term on the left contains an x. In other words, x is a common factor. You might be tempted to divide both sides by x to eliminate that factor.

Resist that temptation. *Never divide an equation by x unless you know for sure that x is not 0 (x ≠ 0).* You could be dividing by 0 without realizing it.

The problem doesn't tell you that $x \neq 0$. So, rather than divide away the x, pull it out to the left and keep it around.

$$x^3 - 3x^2 + 2x = 0$$
$$x\left(x^2 - 3x + 2\right) = 0$$

Now factor the quadratic expression in the parentheses normally, and rewrite the equation.

$$x\left(x^2 - 3x + 2\right) = 0$$
$$x(x - 2)(x - 1) = 0$$

There are *three* factors on the left side: x, $(x - 2)$, and $(x - 1)$. Set each one of them equal to 0 to get *three* solutions to the original equation.

$$x = 0 \qquad\qquad x - 2 = 0 \qquad\qquad x - 1 = 0$$
$$x = 2 \qquad\qquad\qquad x = 1$$

By the way, the presence of the x^3 term should alert you that there could be three solutions. The number of the largest exponent generally signals the number of solutions (unless two of the solutions turn out to be the same number, as in the example you saw earlier in this chapter).

If you had divided away the x earlier, you would have missed the $x = 0$ solution. The question asks for all of the roots, so the answer is 0, 1, and 2, or (C).

If you...	Then you...	Like this:
Want to solve $x^3 = x$	Solve like a normal quadratic: set the equation equal to 0, factor, and set factors equal to 0	$x^3 = x$ $x^3 - x = 0$ $x\left(x^2 - 1\right) = 0$ $x(x + 1)(x - 1) = 0$ $x = 0$ or $x + 1 = 0$ or $x - 1 = 0$ $x = 0, -1,$ or 1

Check Your Skills

11. What are all of the possible solutions to the equation $x^3 - 2x^2 = 3x$?

Answer can be found on page 321.

Other Instances of Quadratics

You will come across quadratic expressions in various circumstances other than the ones already given. Fortunately, the skills of FOILing and factoring are still relevant as you try to simplify the problem.

See a Quadratic Expression in a Fraction: Factor and Cancel

Take a look at this problem:

If $x \neq -1$, then $\dfrac{x^2 - 2x - 3}{x + 1}$ is equivalent to which of the following?

(A) $x + 1$
(B) $x + 3$
(C) $x - 3$

This question doesn't involve a typical quadratic expression. However, the numerator of the fraction is a quadratic. To simplify the fraction, *factor* the quadratic expression.

$$x^2 - 2x - 3 = (x - 3)(x + 1)$$

Now substitute the factored form back into the fraction.

$$\frac{x^2 - 2x - 3}{x + 1} = \frac{(x - 3)(x + 1)}{x + 1}$$

Finally, you can cancel a common factor from the top and bottom of the fraction. The common factor is the entire quantity $x + 1$. Since that is the denominator, you cancel the whole thing out, and the fraction is gone.

$$\frac{x^2 - 2x - 3}{x + 1} = \frac{(x - 3)(x + 1)}{(x + 1)} = \frac{(x - 3)\,\cancel{(x + 1)}}{\cancel{(x + 1)}} = x - 3$$

The correct answer is (C).

The constraint that $x \neq -1$ is mentioned only to prevent division by 0 in the fraction. You don't have to use this fact directly.

If you see a quadratic expression in a numerator or denominator, try factoring the expression. Then cancel common factors.

Common factors can be disguised, of course, even when you don't have quadratics. Take a look at this example:

> If $x \neq y$, then $\dfrac{y-x}{x-y}$ is equivalent to which of the following?
>
> (A) -1
> (B) $x^2 - y^2$
> (C) $y^2 - x^2$

The numerator $y - x$ may look different from the denominator $x - y$. However, these two expressions are actually identical except for a sign change throughout.

$$y - x = -(x - y) \qquad \text{because} \qquad -(x - y) = -x + y = y - x$$

In other words, these expressions only differ by a factor of -1. The GMAT loves this little disguise. Expressions that differ only by a sign change are different by a factor of -1.

Rewrite the numerator: Pull a -1 out of the $(y - x)$ term.

$$\frac{y - x}{x - y} = \frac{-(x - y)}{x - y}$$

Now you can cancel $x - y$ from both the top and bottom. You are left with -1 on top. So the whole fraction is equal to -1.

$$\frac{y - x}{x - y} = \frac{-(x - y)}{x - y} = \frac{-\cancel{(x - y)}}{\cancel{(x - y)}} = -1$$

The correct answer is (A).

Try this last example:

> If $y \neq -8$, then $\dfrac{(y + 7)^2 + y + 7}{y + 8}$ is equivalent to which of the following?
>
> (A) $y + 7$
> (B) $y + 8$
> (C) $2y + 14$

The long way to solve this is to expand $(y + 7)^2$, then add $y + 7$, then factor and cancel. This approach will work. Fortunately, there's a faster way.

Put parentheses around the last $y + 7$ on top of the fraction.

$$\frac{(y + 7)^2 + y + 7}{y + 8} = \frac{(y + 7)^2 + (y + 7)}{y + 8}$$

This subtle change can help you see that you can factor the numerator. You can *pull out a common factor*—namely, $y + 7$—from both the $(y + 7)^2$ and from the $(y + 7)$.

When you pull out $(y + 7)$ from $(y + 7)^2$, you are left with $(y + 7)$. And when you pull out $(y + 7)$ from $(y + 7)$, you are left with 1.

$$\frac{(y + 7)^2 + (y + 7)}{y + 8} = \frac{(y + 7)\left[(y + 7) + 1\right]}{y + 8}$$

Since $y + 7 + 1 = y + 8$, you can simplify the second factor on top.

$$\frac{(y + 7)^2 + (y + 7)}{y + 8} = \frac{(y + 7)\left[(y + 7) + 1\right]}{y + 8} = \frac{(y + 7)(y + 8)}{y + 8}$$

Finally, cancel the $y + 8$ quantity from the top and bottom as a common factor of both.

$$\frac{(y + 7)^2 + (y + 7)}{y + 8} = \frac{(y + 7)\left[(y + 7) + 1\right]}{y + 8} = \frac{(y + 7)(y + 8)}{y + 8} = \frac{(y + 7)\,\cancel{(y + 8)}}{\cancel{(y + 8)}} = y + 7$$

The correct answer is (A).

The recurring principle is this: Look for ways to pull out common factors from complicated fractions and cancel them.

If you...	Then you...	Like this:
See a quadratic expression in a fraction	Factor the quadratic and cancel common factors	$(z \neq -3)$ $\dfrac{z^2 + 5z + 6}{z + 3} = \dfrac{(z + 2)(z + 3)}{(z + 3)}$ $= z + 2$

Check Your Skills

Simplify the following fraction by factoring the quadratic expression.

12. If $x \neq -3$, $\dfrac{x^2 + 7x + 12}{x + 3} =$

Answer can be found on page 321.

Answer can be found on page 321.

See a Special Product: Convert to the Other Form

Three quadratic expressions are so important on the GMAT that we call them **special products**. Here they are:

$(x + y)^2 = x^2 + 2xy + y^2$	$(x - y)^2 = x^2 - 2xy + y^2$	$(x + y)(x - y) = x^2 - y^2$
Square of a sum	**Square of a difference**	**Difference of squares**

First, memorize these forms. Second, whenever you see one of these forms, *write down both forms*. Ask yourself which form is the better one to use for this particular problem; often, the better one is the one that the problem did *not* give you outright.

The GMAT often disguises these forms using different variables, numbers, roots, and so on. For example:

$$x^2 + 8x + 16 \qquad\qquad a^2 - 4ab + 4b^2 \qquad\qquad \left(1+\sqrt{2}\right)\left(1-\sqrt{2}\right)$$

Square of a sum   Square of a difference   Difference of squares

The first example can be factored normally.

$$x^2 + 8x + 16 = (x+4)(x+4) = (x+4)^2$$

The test likes "square of a sum" and "square of a difference" because the two forms can be used to create quadratic equations that have only one solution. For instance:

$$x^2 + 8x + 16 = 0$$
$$\left(x+4\right)^2 = 0$$

There is only one solution: $x + 4 = 0$, or $x = -4$. The only number that makes $x^2 + 8x + 16 = 0$ true is -4.

The second example above, $a^2 - 4ab + 4b^2$, is tougher to factor. First, recognize that the first and last term are both perfect squares:

$$a^2 = \text{the square of } a \qquad\qquad 4b^2 = \text{the square of } 2b$$

This can provide a hint as to how to factor. Set up $(a - 2b)^2$, and FOIL it to check that it matches.

$$(a - 2b)^2 = (a - 2b)(a - 2b)$$
$$= a^2 - 2ab - 2ab + 4b^2$$
$$= a^2 - 4ab + 4b^2$$

It does, so $(a - 2b)^2$ is indeed the other form.

The third example above, $\left(1+\sqrt{2}\right)\left(1-\sqrt{2}\right)$, matches the factored form of the "difference of squares," the most important of the three special products.

In distributed or expanded form, the difference of squares has no middle term. In the process of FOILing, the Outer and the Inner terms cancel.

$$\left(1+\sqrt{2}\right)\left(1-\sqrt{2}\right) = 1^2 + \left(-\sqrt{2}\right) + \sqrt{2} + \sqrt{2}\left(-\sqrt{2}\right)$$
$$= 1^2 - \left(\sqrt{2}\right)^2$$
$$= 1 - 2$$
$$= -1$$

It's not a coincidence that the middle terms cancel. If you multiply $x + y$ by $x - y$, the middle terms, or *cross-terms*, will be $-xy$ and $+xy$, which sum to 0 and drop out every time.

As a result, don't FOIL every time you multiply a sum of two things by the difference of those same two things. You'll waste time.

Rather, match up to the "difference of squares" template. Square the first thing, and subtract the square of the second thing. Try this problem:

$$\left(3 + 2\sqrt{3}\right)\left(3 - 2\sqrt{3}\right) =$$

The two terms are 3 and $2\sqrt{3}$. Always make sure that the other expression in parentheses is the *difference* of the same exact terms. Since that's true, you can square the 3, square the $2\sqrt{3}$, and subtract the second from the first.

$$\left(3 + 2\sqrt{3}\right)\left(3 - 2\sqrt{3}\right) = 3^2 - \left(2\sqrt{3}\right)^2$$
$$= 9 - (4)(3)$$
$$= 9 - 12$$
$$= -3$$

Try this same type of special product, but going in the other direction:

$16x^4 - 9y^2 =$

To treat this as a difference of squares, figure out what each term is the square of.

$16x^4 = (4x^2)^2$ $\qquad\qquad$ $9y^2 = (3y)^2$

So the first term of the difference $(16x^4)$ is the square of $4x^2$, and the second term $(9y^2)$ is the square of $3y$.

Take those square roots ($4x^2$ and $3y$) and place them in two sets of parentheses.

$16x^4 - 9y^2 = (4x^2 \quad 3y)(4x^2 \quad 3y)$

Put a + sign in one place and a − sign in the other.

$16x^4 - 9y^2 = (4x^2 + 3y)(4x^2 - 3y)$

Now you have factored a difference of squares.

A couple of sections ago, you saw $x^2 - 9 = 0$. The left side is the difference of squares.

$x^2 - 9 = (x + 3)(x - 3)$

Now, you can factor difference-of-squares equations much more quickly; you don't have to do the full reverse FOIL process.

To match a special products template, you might have to rearrange an equation. Take a look at this example:

If $x^2 + y^2 = -2xy$, what is the sum of x and y?

You need to find $x + y$. Look at the equation. It doesn't exactly match a special product, but it does have some squares. Try rearranging the equation.

$$\begin{array}{rcl} x^2 + y^2 & = & -2xy \\ + 2xy + 2xy & & \\ \hline x^2 + 2xy + y^2 & = & 0 \end{array}$$

The left side now matches the square of a sum.

$$x^2 + 2xy + y^2 = 0$$
$$(x + y)^2 = 0$$

The right side is also now equal to 0—a double benefit of the first move you made.

Since the square of $x + y$ equals 0, you know that $x + y$ itself must equal 0. That is the answer to the question.

If you...	Then you...	Like this:
See a special product	Write down both forms, then decide which is better to use	$4w^2 - 25z^4$ $(2w)^2 - (5z^2)^2$ $(2w + 5z^2)(2w - 5z^2)$
See something close to a special product	Rearrange the equation to try to fit the special product template	$m^2 + n^2 = 2mn$ $m^2 - 2mn + n^2 = 0$ $(m - n)(m - n) = 0$ $m - n = 0$ $m = n$

Check Your Skills

Factor the following quadratic expressions.

13. $25a^4b^6 - 4c^2d^2$
14. $4x^2 + 8xy + 4y^2$

Answers can be found on page 321.

Check Your Skills Answer Key

1. $x^2 + 13x + 36$:

   $(x + 4)(x + 9)$

$(\boldsymbol{x} + \boldsymbol{4})(\boldsymbol{x} + 9)$	F — multiply First terms:	$(x)(x) = x^2$
$(\boldsymbol{x} + 4)(x + \boldsymbol{9})$	O — multiply Outer terms:	$(x)(9) = 9x$
$(x + \boldsymbol{4})(\boldsymbol{x} + 9)$	I — multiply Inner terms:	$(4)(x) = 4x$
$(x + \boldsymbol{4})(x + \boldsymbol{9})$	L — multiply Last terms:	$(4)(9) = 36$

   $x^2 + 9x + 4x + 36 \longrightarrow x^2 + 13x + 36$

2. $y^2 - 3y - 18$:

   $(y + 3)(y - 6)$

$(\boldsymbol{y} + \boldsymbol{3})(\boldsymbol{y} - 6)$	F — multiply First terms:	$(y)(y) = y^2$
$(\boldsymbol{y} + 3)(y - \boldsymbol{6})$	O — multiply Outer terms:	$(y)(-6) = -6y$
$(y + \boldsymbol{3})(\boldsymbol{y} - 6)$	I — multiply Inner terms:	$(3)(y) = 3y$
$(y + \boldsymbol{3})(y - \boldsymbol{6})$	L — multiply Last terms:	$(3)(-6) = -18$

   $y^2 - 6y + 3y - 18 \longrightarrow y^2 - 3y - 18$

3. $(\boldsymbol{x + 3})(\boldsymbol{x + 11})$: Find a pair of numbers that multiplies to +33 and sums to +14. The factor pairs 1 × 33 and 3 × 11 multiply to +33, but only 3 and 11 also sum to +14.

4. $(\boldsymbol{x - 5})(\boldsymbol{x - 9})$: Ultimately, both numbers will need to be negative because the product (45) is positive, but ignore the signs for now. Find a pair that multiplies to +45 and sums to 14. The factor pairs of 45 are 1 × 45, 3 × 15, and 5 × 9. Only 5 and 9 sum to 14. Turn both negative: −5 + −9 = −14.

5. $(\boldsymbol{x + 6})(\boldsymbol{x - 3})$: The final term is negative, so you need one positive and one negative term. The middle term is positive, so the larger of the two numbers has to be the positive one. Finally, you need something that multiplies to −18 but whose *difference* is +3. The factor pairs 1 × 18, 2 × 9, and 3 × 6 multiply to 18. The difference of 3 and 6 is 3, so this is the correct pair. Make the 6 positive and the 3 negative.

6. $(\boldsymbol{x + 6})(\boldsymbol{x - 11})$: The final term is negative, so there will be one positive and one negative term. The middle term is also negative, so the larger of the two numbers has to be negative. You need something that multiplies to −66 and whose difference is −5. The pairs 1 × 66, 2 × 33, 3 × 22, and 6 × 11 multiply to 66. The difference of 6 and 11 is 5, so this is the correct pair. Make the 11 negative and the 6 positive.

7. **$x = 5$ or -7:** Find a factor pair that multiplies to 35 and has a difference of 2. The pair 5 times 7 multiplies to 35, and the difference between the factors is 2. The middle term is positive, so the larger of the two numbers (7) is positive.

$$x^2 + 2x - 35 = 0$$
$$(x - 5)(x + 7) = 0$$

$x - 5 = 0$ OR $x + 7 = 0$
$x = 5$ $x = -7$

8. **$x = 2$ or 13:** Set the equation equal to 0, then solve.

$$x^2 - 15x = -26$$
$$x^2 - 15x + 26 = 0$$

The pair 2×13 multiply to 26 and sum to 15

$$x^2 - 15x + 26 = 0$$
$$(x - 2)(x - 13) = 0$$

$x - 2 = 0$ OR $x - 13 = 0$
$x = 2$ $x = 13$

9. **$x = 2$ or -2:** Since there is no x term, you can isolate x^2 on one side of the equation. Next, take the square root of both sides.

$$x^2 - 3 = 1$$
$$x^2 = 4$$
$$\sqrt{x^2} = \sqrt{4}$$
$$x = \pm 2$$

10. **$z = 10$ or -14:** Begin by taking the square root of both sides. Remember to include the negative solution as well:

$$(z + 2)^2 = 144$$
$$\sqrt{(z + 2)^2} = \sqrt{144}$$

$z + 2 = 12$ OR $z + 2 = -12$
$z = 10$ $z = -14$

11. **$x = -1$, 0, or 3:** Begin by setting the equation equal to 0.

$$x^3 - 2x^2 = 3x$$
$$x^3 - 2x^2 - 3x = 0$$

Notice that all the terms contain x. Factor x out of the left side of the equation. Then factor the quadratic and solve for x.

$$x^3 - 2x^2 - 3x = 0$$
$$x(x^2 - 2x - 3) = 0$$
$$x(x - 3)(x + 1) = 0$$

$x = 0$ $x - 3 = 0$ $x + 1 = 0$
                $x = 3$ $x = -1$

The three values of x that will make the equation true are 0, 3, and -1.

12. **$x + 4$:** Factor the numerator, then cancel.

$$\frac{x^2 + 7x + 12x}{x + 3} = \frac{(x+3)(x+4)}{(x+3)} = x + 4$$

13. **$(5a^2b^3 + 2cd)(5a^2b^3 - 2cd)$:** Any expression that contains one term subtracted from another can be expressed as a difference of squares. Take the square root of each term. The square root of $25a^4b^6$ is $5a^2b^3$, and the square root of $4c^2d^2$ is $2cd$. In one set of parentheses, add the square roots; in the other, subtract: $(5a^2b^3 + 2cd)(5a^2b^3 - 2cd)$.

14. This is a more complicated version of the form $(x + y)^2 = x^2 + 2xy + y^2$. Take the square root of the first term to get $(2x)$ and the square root of the last term to get $(2y)$: $4x^2 + 8xy + 4y^2 = (2x + 2y)(2x + 2y)$.

Chapter Review: Drill Sets

Drill 1

Distribute the following expressions.

1. $(x + 2)(x - 3)$
2. $(2s + 1)(s + 5)$
3. $(5 + a)(3 + a)$
4. $(3 - z)(z + 4)$
5. $(3p + 2q)(p - 2q)$

Drill 2

Solve the following equations. List all possible solutions.

6. $x^2 - 2x = 0$
7. $z^2 = -5z$
8. $y^2 + 4y + 3 = 0$
9. $r^2 - 10r = 24$
10. $y^2 + 3y = 0$
11. $y^2 + 12y + 36 = 0$
12. $a^2 - a - 12 = 0$
13. $x^2 + 9x - 90 = 0$
14. $2a^2 + 6a + 4 = 0$
15. $2b^3 + 6b^2 - 36b = 0$

Drill 3

Simplify the following expressions.

16. If $a \neq b$, then $\dfrac{a^2 - b^2}{a - b}$ is equivalent to which of the following?
    - (A) $a - b$
    - (B) $a + b$
    - (C) $a^2 + b^2$

17. If $|r| \neq |s|$, then $\dfrac{r^2 + 2rs + s^2}{r^2 - s^2}$ is equivalent to which of the following?
    - (A) $\dfrac{r + s}{r - s}$
    - (B) $\dfrac{r - s}{r + s}$
    - (C) $2rs$

18. If $x \neq 1$, then $\dfrac{5x^3}{x - 1} - \dfrac{5x^2}{x - 1}$ is equivalent to which of the following?
    - (A) $\dfrac{x}{x - 1}$
    - (B) $5x^2$
    - (C) 0

19. If $y \neq -5$, then $\dfrac{y + 5 - (y + 5)^2}{y + 5}$ is equivalent to which of the following?
    - (A) $y + 5$
    - (B) $2y$
    - (C) $-y - 4$

20. If $m \neq -7$, then $\dfrac{m^2 + 2m}{m + 7} + \dfrac{49 + 12m}{m + 7}$ is equivalent to which of the following?
    - (A) 1
    - (B) $(m + 7)^2$
    - (C) $m + 7$

Drill 4

Simplify the following expressions.

21. If $z \neq -1$, then $\dfrac{4z^2 - 12z - 16}{2z + 2}$ is equivalent to which of the following?

   (A) $z - 4$

   (B) $2z - 8$

   (C) $4z - 16$

22. If $c \neq -5$, then $\dfrac{5ab + abc}{abc^2 + 10abc + 25ab}$ is equivalent to which of the following?

   (A) $\dfrac{1}{(c+5)^2}$

   (B) $c + 5$

   (C) $\dfrac{1}{c+5}$

23. If $x \neq 0$ or 1, then $\dfrac{\left(x^5 - x^3\right)}{\left(x^3 - x^2\right)} \times \dfrac{x}{5}$ is equivalent to which of the following?

   (A) $\dfrac{x^2}{5}$

   (B) $\dfrac{x^3 - x^2}{5}$

   (C) $\dfrac{x^3 + x^2}{5}$

24. If $x \neq 2$, then $\left(x^2 - 7x + 10\right) \times \dfrac{x + 5}{x - 2}$ is equivalent to which of the following?

   (A) $x^2 - 25$

   (B) $x^2 + 10x + 25$

   (C) $x + 5$

25. If $x \neq 3$, then $\dfrac{x^2 - 6x + 9}{3 - x}$ is equivalent to which of the following?

   (A) $x - 3$

   (B) $3 - x$

   (C) $(x - 3)^2$

Chapter Review: Drill Sets

Drill 1

1. $x^2 - x - 6$:

   $(x + 2)(x - 3)$

   $x^2 - 3x + 2x - 6$

   $x^2 - x - 6$

2. $2s^2 + 11s + 5$:

   $(2s + 1)(s + 5)$

   $2s^2 + 10s + s + 5$

   $2s^2 + 11s + 5$

3. $15 + 8a + a^2$:

   $(5 + a)(3 + a)$

   $15 + 5a + 3a + a^2$

   $15 + 8a + a^2$

4. $-z^2 - z + 12$:

   $(3 - z)(z + 4)$

   $3z + 12 - z^2 - 4z$

   $-z^2 - z + 12$

5. $3p^2 - 4pq - 4q^2$:

   $(3p + 2q)(p - 2q)$

   $3p^2 - 6pq + 2pq - 4q^2$

   $3p^2 - 4pq - 4q^2$

Drill 2

6. $x = 0$ or 2:

   $$x^2 - 2x = 0$$
   $$x(x - 2) = 0$$

   $x = 0$ \qquad\qquad $(x - 2) = 0$

   \qquad\qquad\qquad\qquad $x = 2$

7. $z = 0$ or -5:

   $$z^2 = -5z$$
   $$z^2 + 5z = 0$$
   $$z(z + 5) = 0$$

   $z = 0$ \qquad\qquad $(z + 5) = 0$

   \qquad\qquad\qquad\qquad $z = -5$

8. **$y = -1$ or -3:**

$$y^2 + 4y + 3 = 0$$
$$(y + 1)(y + 3) = 0$$

$$(y + 1) = 0 \qquad\qquad (y + 3) = 0$$
$$y = -1 \qquad\qquad\qquad y = -3$$

9. **$r = -2$ or 12:**

$$r^2 - 10r = 24$$
$$r^2 - 10r - 24 = 0$$
$$(r + 2)(r - 12) = 0$$

$$(r + 2) = 0 \qquad\qquad (r - 12) = 0$$
$$r = -2 \qquad\qquad\qquad r = 12$$

10. **$y = 0$ or -3:**

$$y^2 + 3y = 0$$
$$y(y + 3) = 0$$

$$y = 0 \qquad\qquad (y + 3) = 0$$
$$\qquad\qquad\qquad y = -3$$

11. **$y = -6$:** If you notice that the two factors are identical (both are $y + 6$), then you don't have to solve each one. The answer will be the same.

$$y^2 + 12y + 36 = 0$$
$$(y + 6)(y + 6) = 0$$

$$(y + 6) = 0 \qquad\qquad (y + 6) = 0$$
$$y = -6 \qquad\qquad\qquad y = -6$$

12. **$a = 4$ or -3:**

$$a^2 - a - 12 = 0$$
$$(a - 4)(a + 3) = 0$$

$$(a - 4) = 0 \qquad\qquad (a + 3) = 0$$
$$a = 4 \qquad\qquad\qquad a = -3$$

13. **$x = -15$ or 6:**

$$x^2 + 9x - 90 = 0$$
$$(x + 15)(x - 6) = 0$$

$$(x + 15) = 0 \qquad\qquad (x - 6) = 0$$
$$x = -15 \qquad\qquad\qquad x = 6$$

14. **$a = -2$ or -1:** Ignore the 2 term that you pull out front because it doesn't contain a variable.

$$2a^2 + 6a + 4 - 0$$
$$2(a^2 + 3a + 2) = 0$$
$$2(a + 2)(a + 1) = 0$$

$$(a + 2) = 0 \qquad\qquad\qquad\qquad (a + 1) = 0$$
$$a = -2 \qquad\qquad\qquad\qquad\qquad\; a = -1$$

15. **$b = 0, -6,$ or 3:** The $2b$ term that you pull out front does have to be set equal to 0, because it contains a variable.

$$2b^3 + 6b^2 - 36b = 0$$
$$2b(b^2 + 3b - 18) = 0$$
$$2b(b + 6)(b - 3) = 0$$

$$2b = 0 \qquad\qquad\qquad (b + 6) = 0 \qquad\qquad\qquad (b - 3) = 0$$
$$b = 0 \qquad\qquad\qquad\; b = -6 \qquad\qquad\qquad\quad\; b = 3$$

Drill 3

16. **(B):** The key to simplifying this expression is to recognize the special product:

$$a^2 - b^2 = (a + b)(a - b)$$

After replacing the original numerator with $(a + b)(a - b)$, cancel the $(a - b)$ in the numerator with the $(a - b)$ in the denominator.

$$\frac{a^2 - b^2}{a - b} = \frac{(a + b)\,\cancel{(a - b)}}{\cancel{(a - b)}} = a + b$$

17. **(A):** Both the numerator and the denominator contain special products. Factor each one to find common terms to cancel.

$$\frac{r^2 + 2rs + s^2}{r^2 - s^2} = \frac{\cancel{(r + s)}\,(r + s)}{\cancel{(r + s)}\,(r - s)} = \frac{r + s}{r - s}$$

18. **(B):** First perform the subtraction to combine the two terms:

$$\frac{5x^3}{x - 1} - \frac{5x^2}{x - 1} = \frac{5x^3 - 5x^2}{x - 1}$$

Next, pull out the common term ($5x^2$) in the numerator.

$$\frac{5x^3 - 5x^2}{x - 1} = \frac{5x^2\,\cancel{(x - 1)}}{\cancel{(x - 1)}} = 5x^2$$

19. **(C):** It is tempting to expand the quadratic term in the numerator, but notice all those y's and 5's? Also, none of the answer choices are fractions, so the denominator must cancel out somehow.

Group the $y + 5$ terms.

$$\frac{(y + 5) - (y + 5)^2}{(y + 5)}$$

You can cancel a $(y + 5)$ from each term (remember that the numerator contains two separate terms, separated by the subtraction sign).

$$\frac{(y + 5) - (y + 5)^2}{(y + 5)} = \frac{1 - (y + 5)}{1} = -y - 4$$

If you think you might make a mistake doing it that way, you can first pull the common $y + 5$ term out of the numerator.

$$\frac{(y + 5) - (y + 5)^2}{(y + 5)} = \frac{(y + 5)\left[1 - (y + 5) \right]}{(y + 5)} = 1 - y - 5 = -y - 4$$

20. **(C):** The denominators are the same, so add the fractions:

$$\frac{m^2 + 2m}{m + 7} + \frac{49 + 12m}{m + 7} = \frac{m^2 + 14m + 49}{m + 7}$$

None of the answer choices are fractions, so find a way to eliminate the denominator. Start by factoring the numerator.

$$\frac{m^2 + 14m + 49}{m + 7} = \frac{(m + 7)(m + 7)}{(m + 7)} = m + 7$$

Drill 4

21. **(B):** Simplify this problem by factoring a 4 out of the numerator and a 2 out of the denominator.

$$\frac{4z^2 - 12z - 16}{2z + 2} = \frac{{}^2\!\!\cancel{4}\left(z^2 - 3z - 4\right)}{\cancel{2}\,(z + 1)} = \frac{2\left(z^2 - 3z - 4\right)}{(z + 1)}$$

The answers don't contain fractions, so the denominator must cancel somehow. Factor the numerator.

$$\frac{2\left(z^2 - 3z - 4\right)}{(z + 1)} = \frac{2\,(z + 1)(z - 4)}{(z + 1)} = 2\,(z - 4) = 2z - 8$$

MANHATTAN PREP

22. **(C):** This might seem nearly impossible to factor. Glance at the answers. Notice anything?

The variables *a* and *b* have disappeared. It must mean that these variables will cancel out as you solve! Notice that every term has an *ab* piece; factor it out and cancel.

$$\frac{5ab + abc}{abc^2 + 10abc + 25ab} = \frac{\cancel{ab}\,(5+c)}{\cancel{ab}\,(c^2 + 10c + 25)} = \frac{5+c}{c^2 + 10c + 25}$$

That's more manageable. None of the answers matches yet, so factor the denominator to see whether you can cancel any further.

$$\frac{5+c}{c^2 + 10c + 25} = \frac{5+c}{(c+5)(c+5)} = \frac{\cancel{(c+5)}}{\cancel{(c+5)}\,(c+5)} = \frac{1}{c+5}$$

23. **(C):** There's no obvious way to proceed through this question. The best bet is to try to simplify before multiplying. Notice that x^3 can be factored out of the numerator and x^2 can be factored out of the denominator.

$$\frac{\left(x^5 - x^3\right)}{\left(x^3 - x^2\right)} \times \frac{x}{5} = \frac{x^3\left(x^2 - 1\right)}{x^2\left(x - 1\right)} \times \frac{x}{5}$$

Cancel x^2 from the top and bottom. Also, the numerator now contains $(x^2 - 1)$. Factor this.

$$\frac{x^3\left(x^2 - 1\right)}{x^2\left(x - 1\right)} \times \frac{x}{5} =$$

$$\frac{x^{\cancel{3}^1}\,(x+1)\,\cancel{(x-1)}}{\cancel{x^2}\,\cancel{(x-1)}} \times \frac{x}{5} =$$

$$\frac{x\,(x+1)\times x}{5}$$

Glance at the answer choices. None of the numerators in the answer choices has parenthetical expressions, so multiply the numerator out.

$$\frac{x\,(x+1)(x)}{5} = \frac{x^2\,(x+1)}{5} = \frac{x^3 + x^2}{5}$$

24. **(A):** Simplify before you multiply. Are there any common factors to cancel?

$$\left(x^2 - 7x + 10\right) \times \frac{x+5}{x-2} =$$

$$\frac{(x-5)\,(x-2)}{1} \times \frac{x+5}{x-2} =$$

$$(x-5)(x+5) =$$

$$x^2 - 25$$

25. **(B):** Glance at the answers: no fractions. Factor the numerator to try to cancel the denominator.

$$\frac{x^2 - 6x + 9}{3 - x} = \frac{(x-3)(x-3)}{3-x}$$

Neither of the expressions in the numerator matches the denominator. However, $(x-3) = -(3-x)$. Factor out a (-1) from the denominator, then cancel:

$$\frac{(x-3)(x-3)}{3-x} = \frac{(x-3)\,(x-3)}{-(x-3)} = \frac{x-3}{-1} = -x+3 \text{ or } 3-x$$

Beyond Equations: Inequalities & Absolute Value

In this chapter...

- An Inequality with a Variable: A Range on the Number Line

- Many Values "Solve" an Inequality

- Solve Inequalities: Isolate Variable by Transforming Each Side

- Multiply or Divide an Inequality by a Negative: Flip > to < or Vice Versa

- Absolute Value: The Distance from Zero

- Replace $|x|$ with x in One Equation and with $-x$ in Another

- Inequalities + Absolute Values: Set Up Two Inequalities

Chapter 8

Beyond Equations: Inequalities & Absolute Value

In This Chapter, You Will Learn To:

- Manipulate and solve inequalities
- Work with absolute values

An Inequality with a Variable: A Range on the Number Line

Inequalities use $<$, $>$, $\leq$, or $\geq$ to describe the relationship between two expressions. For example:

$$5 > 4 \qquad y \leq 7 \qquad x < 5 \qquad 2x + 3 \geq 0$$

Like equations, *inequalities are full sentences.* Always read from left to right.

$x < y$	x is less than y.	
$x > y$	x is greater than y.	
$x \leq y$	x is less than or equal to y.	x is at most y.
$x \geq y$	x is greater than or equal to y.	x is at least y.

You can also have two inequalities in one statement. Make a compound sentence.

$9 < g < 200$	9 is less than g, and g is less than 200.
$-3 < y \leq 5$	-3 is less than y, and y is less than or equal to 5.
$7 \geq x > 2$	7 is greater than or equal to x, and x is greater than 2.

To visualize an inequality that involves a variable, *draw the inequality on a number line*. Recall that "greater than" means "to the right of" on a number line. Likewise, "less than" means "to the left of."

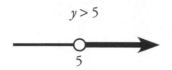

$y > 5$

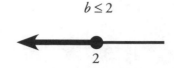

$b \leq 2$

y is to the right of 5, which is *not* included in the line (as shown by the empty circle around 5), because 5 is not a part of the solution—y is greater than 5, but not equal to 5.

b is to the left of 2 (or on top of 2). Here, 2 is included in the solution, because b can equal 2. A solid black circle indicates that you include the point itself.

Any number covered by the black arrow (or a filled-in circle) will make the inequality true and so is a possible solution to the inequality. Any number not covered by the black arrow (or covered with an empty circle) is not a solution.

If you...	Then you...	Like this:
Want to visualize an inequality	Put it all on a number line, where < means "to the left of" and > means "to the right of"	$y > 5$

Check Your Skills

Draw the following equations or inequalities on the number line provided.

1. $x > 3$

2. $b \geq -2$

3. $y = 4$

Translate the following into inequality statements.

4. z is greater than v.
5. The total amount is greater than $2,000.

Answers can be found on page 343.

Many Values "Solve" an Inequality

What does it mean to "solve an inequality"?

It means the same thing as to solve an equation: Find the value or values of x that make the inequality true. When you plug a solution back into the original equation or inequality, you get a *true statement*.

Here's what's different. Equations have only one (or just a few) value as a solution. In contrast, *inequalities give a whole range of values as solutions*—often way too many to list individually. For example:

Equation: $x + 3 = 8$	**Inequality: $x + 3 < 8$**
The solution to $x + 3 = 8$ is $x = 5$, which is the *only* number that will make the equation true.	The solution to $x + 3 < 8$ is $x < 5$. The number 5 itself is not a solution because $5 + 3 < 8$ is not a true statement.
Plug back in to check: $5 + 3 = 8$. True.	But 4 is a solution because $4 + 3 < 8$ is true. For that matter, 4.99, 3, 2, 2.87, −5, and −100 are also solutions. The list goes on.
	For all of the correct answers: (any number less than 5) $+ 3 < 8$. True.

Check Your Skills

6. If $x < 10$, what is a possible value of x?

    (A) −3
    (B) 2.5
    (C) −3/2
    (D) 9.999
    (E) All of the above

Answer can be found on page 343.

Solve Inequalities: Isolate Variable by Transforming Each Side

As with equations, your objective is to isolate a variable on one side of the inequality. When the variable is by itself, you can see what the solution (or range of solutions) really is.

For example, $2x + 6 < 12$ and $x < 3$ provide the same information. But you understand the full range of solutions more easily when you see the second inequality, which literally says that "x is less than 3."

Many manipulations are the same for inequalities as for equations. First of all, you are *always* allowed to simplify an expression on just one side of an inequality. Just don't change the expression's value.

    $2x + 3x < 45$ is the same as $5x < 45$

The inequality sign isn't involved in this simplification.

Next, some Golden Rule moves work the same way for inequalities as for equations. For instance, you can *add* anything you want to both sides of an inequality. Just make sure you do the same thing to both sides. You can also *subtract* anything you want from both sides of an inequality.

$$a - 4 > 6$$
$$\underline{+4 \quad +4}$$
$$a \qquad > 10$$

$$y + 7 < 3$$
$$\underline{-7 \quad -7}$$
$$y \quad < -4$$

You can also add or subtract variables from both sides of an inequality. It doesn't matter what the signs of the variables might be.

If you...	Then you...	Like this:
Want to add or subtract the same quantity on both sides of an inequality	Go ahead and do so	$x + y > -4$ $\underline{-y \quad -y}$ $x > -4 - y$

Check Your Skills

Isolate the variable in the following inequalities.

7. $x - 6 < 13$
8. $y + 11 \geq -13$
9. $x + 7 > 7$

Answers can be found on page 343.

Multiply or Divide an Inequality by a Negative: Flip > to < or Vice Versa

If you multiply both sides of an inequality by a positive number, leave the inequality sign alone. The same is true for division. For example:

$$\frac{x}{3} < 7$$
$$3\left(\frac{x}{3}\right) < (7)3$$
$$x < 21$$

$$4y > 12$$
$$\frac{4y}{4} > \frac{12}{4}$$
$$y > 3$$

However, *if you multiply or divide both sides of an inequality by a negative number, flip the inequality sign.* "Greater than" becomes "less than" and vice versa.

$$-2x > 10$$
$$\left(\frac{-2x}{-2}\right) < \left(\frac{10}{-2}\right)$$
$$x < -5$$

$$-b \geq 10$$
$$(-1)(-b) \leq (10)(-1)$$
$$b \leq -10$$

MANHATTAN PREP

If you didn't switch the sign, then inequalities such as $5 < 7$ would become false when you multiply them by, say, -1. You must flip the sign.

$5 < 7$	but	$-5 > -7$
5 is less than 7		-5 is greater than -7

What about multiplying or dividing an inequality by a variable? If you aren't given the sign of the variable, then avoid taking this step! If you don't know the sign of the "hidden number" that the variable represents, then you don't know whether to switch the sign.

If the problem tells you the variable is positive, or if the variable has to be positive (e.g., it counts people or measures a length), then you can go ahead and multiply or divide. If you're told the variable is negative, flip the sign when you multiply or divide by that variable. If you're not told, don't multiply or divide by that variable.

If you...	Then you...	Like this:
Multiply or divide both sides of an inequality by a *negative* number	Flip the inequality sign	$45 \quad < \quad -5w$ $\left(\dfrac{45}{-5}\right) > \left(\dfrac{-5w}{-5}\right)$ $-9 \quad > \quad w$

Check Your Skills

Isolate the variable in the following inequalities.

10. $x + 3 \geq -2$
11. $-2y < -8$
12. $a + 4 \geq 2a$

Answers can be found on pages 343–344.

Absolute Value: The Distance from Zero

The **absolute value** of a number describes how far that number is away from 0. It is the distance between that number and 0 on a number line.

The symbol for absolute value is |number|. For instance, write the absolute value of -5 as $|-5|$.

The absolute value of 5 is 5. This is how it would look on a number line:

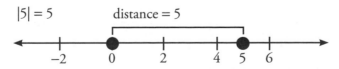

The absolute value of −5 is also 5:

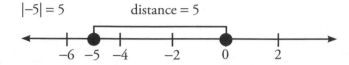

$$|-5| = 5 \qquad \text{distance} = 5$$

In either case, the number is 5 units away from 0 on the number line.

When you face an expression like $|4 - 7|$, treat the absolute value symbol like parentheses. Solve the arithmetic problem *inside* first, and then find the absolute value of the answer.

$$|4 - 7| = ?$$
$$4 - 7 = -3$$
$$|-3| = 3$$

Almost every absolute value is positive. There is one exception.

$$|0| = 0$$

Except for 0, every absolute value is positive.

Check Your Skills

Mark the following expressions as TRUE or FALSE.

13. $|3| = 3$
14. $|-3| = -3$
15. $|3| = -3$
16. $|-3| = 3$
17. $|3 - 6| = 3$
18. $|6 - 3| = -3$

Answers can be found on page 344.

Replace |x| with x in One Equation and with −x in Another

You may see a variable inside the absolute value sign.

$$|y| = 3$$

This equation has *two solutions*. There are two numbers that are 3 units away from 0, namely 3 and −3. Both of these numbers could be the value of *y*, but not simultaneously, so *y* is *either* 3 *or* −3.

When you see a variable inside an absolute value, look for the variable to have two possible values. Here is a step-by-step process for finding both solutions:

| $\lvert y \rvert = 3$ | Step 1: Isolate the absolute value expression on one side of the equation. Here, the expression is already isolated. |

| $+(y) = 3$ or $-(y) = 3$ | Step 2: Drop the absolute value signs and *set up two equations*. The first equation has the positive value of what's inside the absolute value. The second equation has the negative value. |

| $y = 3$ or $-y = 3$ | Step 3: Solve both equations. |
| $y = 3$ or $y = -3$ | There are two possible values for y. |

For equations only (*not* inequalities), you can take a shortcut and go right to "y equals plus or minus 3." This shortcut works as long as the absolute value expression is by itself on one side of the equation. As always, only use a shortcut if you know it well enough to avoid careless mistakes.

Here's a more difficult problem:

$$6 \times \lvert 2x + 4 \rvert = 30$$

To solve this problem, use the same approach.

| $6 \times \lvert 2x + 4 \rvert = 30$ | |
| $\lvert 2x + 4 \rvert = 5$ | Step 1: Isolate the absolute value expression on one side of the equation or inequality. |

| $+(2x + 4) = 5$ or $-(2x + 4) = 5$ | Step 2: Set up two equations—one positive and |
| $-2x - 4 = 5$ | one negative. |

| $2x = 1$ or $-2x = 9$ | Step 3: Solve both equations/inequalities. |

| $x = \dfrac{1}{2}$ or $x = \dfrac{-9}{2}$ | There are two possible values for x. |

If you...	Then you...	Like this:
Have a variable inside absolute value signs	Drop the absolute value and set up two equations, one positive and one negative	$\lvert z \rvert = 4$ $+(z) = 4$ or $-(z) = 4$ $z = 4$ or $z = -4$

Check Your Skills

Solve the following equations with absolute values in them.

19. $\lvert a \rvert = 6$

20. $\lvert x + 2 \rvert = 5$

21. $\lvert 3y - 4 \rvert = 17$

22. $4 \left\lvert x + \dfrac{1}{2} \right\rvert = 18$

Answers can be found on pages 344–345.

Inequalities and Absolute Values: Set Up Two Inequalities

Some tough problems include both inequalities and absolute values. To solve these problems, combine what you have learned about inequalities with what you have learned about absolute values. Try an example:

$$|x| \geq 4$$

The basic process for dealing with absolute values is the same for inequalities as it is for equations. The absolute value is already isolated on one side, so now drop the absolute value signs and *set up two inequalities*. The first inequality has the positive value of what was inside the absolute value signs, while the second inequality has the negative value.

$$+(x) \geq 4 \qquad \text{or} \qquad -(x) \geq 4$$

Next, isolate the variable in each inequality, as necessary.

$+(x) \geq 4$	or	$-(x) \geq 4$	
$x \geq 4$		$-x \geq 4$	Divide by -1 (in the negative example).
		$x \leq -4$	Remember to flip the sign when dividing by a negative.

The two solutions to the original equation are $x \geq 4$ or $x \leq -4$. Draw those two inequalities on a number line.

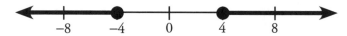

As before, any number that is covered by the black arrow will make the inequality true. Because of the absolute value, there are now two arrows instead of one, but nothing else has changed. -4 and any number to the left of -4 will make the inequality true, as will 4 and any number to the right of 4.

Looking back at the inequality $|x| \geq 4$, you can also interpret it in terms of distance. For example, $|x| \geq 4$ means "x is at least 4 units away from 0, in either direction." The black arrows indicate all numbers for which that statement is true.

Here is a harder example, with a twist:

$$|y + 3| < 5$$

Once again, the absolute value is already isolated on one side, so set up the two inequalities.

$$+(y + 3) < 5 \quad \text{or} \quad -(y + 3) < 5$$

Next, isolate the variable.

$y + 3 < 5$	or	$-y - 3 < 5$
$y < 2$		$-y < 8$
		$y > -8$

The two inequalities are $y < 2$ and $y > -8$. If you plot those results, something curious happens.

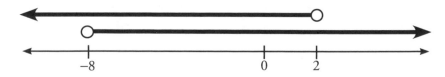

It seems as if every number should be a solution to the equation. But try plugging $y = 5$ into $|y + 3| < 5$. What happens?

It doesn't work: $|5 + 3|$ is not less than 5. In fact, the only numbers that make the inequality true are those that are true for *both* inequalities. The number line should look like this:

In other words, $-8 < y < 2$.

When the two solutions overlap, as in this example, only the numbers that fall in the range of both arrows will be solutions to the inequality, so combine the solutions into one big inequality: $-8 < y < 2$.

If your two arrows do *not* overlap, as in the first example, any number that falls in the range of *either* arrow will be a solution to the inequality, so leave the solutions as two separate inequalities: $x \geq 4$ or $x \leq -4$.

You can also interpret $|y + 3| < 5$ in terms of distance: "$(y + 3)$ is less than 5 units away from from 0, in either direction." The shaded segment indicates all numbers y for which this is true. As inequalities get more complicated, don't worry about interpreting their meaning—just solve them algebraically!

If you…	Then you…	Like this:
Have an inequality with a variable inside absolute value signs	Drop the absolute value and set up two inequalities, one positive and one negative. If the two solutions don't overlap, write *or* between them and leave them as two inequalities. If the two solutions do overlap, combine them into one big inequality.	$|z| > 4$ $+(z) > 4 \quad -(z) > 4$ no overlap $z > 4$ or $z < -4$ $|a| < 4$ $+(a) < 4 \quad -(a) > 4$ $a < 4 \quad a > -4$ overlap! $-4 < a < 4$

Check Your Skills

Solve the following inequalities with absolute values in them.

23. $|x + 1| > 2$

24. $|-x - 4| \geq 8$

25. $|x - 7| < 9$

Answers can be found on page 345.

Check Your Skills Answer Key

1.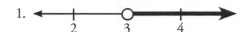

2. (number line with filled circle at -2, marks at -3, -2, -1)

3. (number line with filled circle at 4, marks at 3, 4, 5)

4. **$z > v$:** *z is greater than v is translated as $z > v$.*

5. **$a > \$2,000$:** Let a = total amount. *The total amount is greater than \$2,000* is translated as $a > 2,000$.

6. **(E):** All of the numbers in the answer choices are to the left of 10 on the number line, so all of them are possible values for x.

    (number line with open circle at 10, marks at 8, 9, 10)

7. **$x < 19$:**
$$x - 6 < 13$$
$$\underline{ +6 \quad +6}$$
$$x < 19$$

8. **$y \geq -24$:**
$$y + 11 \geq -13$$
$$\underline{-11 \qquad -11}$$
$$y \geq -24$$
$$y \geq -24$$

9. **$x > 0$:**
$$x + 7 > 7$$
$$\underline{-7 \quad -7}$$
$$x > 0$$

10. **$x \geq -5$:**
$$x + 3 \geq -2$$
$$\underline{-3 \quad -3}$$
$$x \geq -5$$

11. **$y > 4$:**

$$-2y < -8$$
$$\left(\frac{-2y}{-2}\right) > \left(\frac{-8}{-2}\right)$$
$$y > 4$$

12. **$4 \geq a$:**

$$a + 4 \geq 2a$$
$$\underline{-a \quad -a}$$
$$4 \geq a$$

13. **True:** The absolute value of 3 is 3.

14. **False:** The absolute value of -3 is *not* -3; rather, the absolute value of -3 is 3. Note that an absolute value is *never* negative.

15. **False:** The absolute value of 3 is 3. An absolute value is never negative.

16. **True:** The absolute value of -3 is 3.

17. **True:** $|3 - 6| = |-3| = 3$

18. **False:** $|6 - 3| = |3| = 3$. An absolute value is never negative.

19. **$a = 6$ or -6:**

$$|a| = 6$$

$+(a) = 6$	or	$-(a) = 6$
$a = 6$		$a = -6$

20. **$x = 3$ or -7:**

$$|x + 2| = 5$$

$+(x + 2) = 5$	or	$-(x + 2) = 5$
$x + 2 = 5$		$-x - 2 = 5$
$x = 3$		$-x = 7$
		$x = -7$

21. **$y = 7$ or $-\dfrac{13}{3}$:**

$$|3y - 4| = 17$$

$+(3y - 4) = 17$	or	$-(3y - 4) = 17$
$3y - 4 = 17$		$-3y + 4 = 17$
$3y = 21$		$-3y = 13$
$y = 7$		$y = -\dfrac{13}{3}$

22. **$x = 4$ or -5:**

$$4\left|x+\frac{1}{2}\right| = 18$$

$$\left|x+\frac{1}{2}\right| = \frac{18}{4}$$

$$\left|x+\frac{1}{2}\right| = \frac{9}{2}$$

or

$$+\left(x+\frac{1}{2}\right) = \frac{9}{2} \qquad\qquad -\left(x+\frac{1}{2}\right) = \frac{9}{2}$$

$$x+\frac{1}{2} = \frac{9}{2} \qquad\qquad -x-\frac{1}{2} = \frac{9}{2}$$

$$x = \frac{8}{2} = 4 \qquad\qquad -x = \frac{10}{2} = 5$$

$$x = -5$$

23. **$x < -3$ or $x > 1$:**

$$|x+1| > 2$$

$$+(x+1) > 2 \qquad\qquad -(x+1) > 2$$

$$x+1 > 2 \qquad\qquad -x-1 > 2$$

$$x > 1 \qquad\qquad -x > 3$$

$$x < -3$$

24. **$x \le -12$ or $x \ge 4$:**

$$|-x-4| \ge 8$$

$$+(-x-4) \ge 8 \qquad\qquad -(-x-4) \ge 8$$

$$-x-4 \ge 8 \qquad\qquad x+4 \ge 8$$

$$-x \ge 12 \qquad\qquad x \ge 4$$

$$x \le -12$$

25. **$-2 < x < 16$:**

$$|x-7| < 9$$

$$+(x-7) < 9 \qquad\qquad -(x-7) < 9$$

$$x-7 < 9 \qquad\qquad -x+7 < 9$$

$$x < 16 \qquad\qquad -x < 2$$

$$x > -2$$

Chapter Review: Drill Sets

Drill 1

Draw the following inequalities on the number line provided.

1. $x > 4$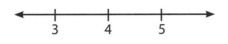

2. $a \geq 3$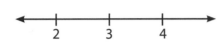

3. $y = 2$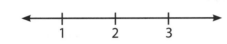

4. $x < 5$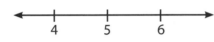

5. $6 < x$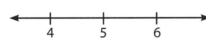

Drill 2

Translate the following into inequality statements.

6. a is less than b.
7. 5 times x is greater than 10.
8. 6 is less than or equal to $4x$.
9. The price of an apple is greater than the price of an orange.
10. The total number of members is at least 19.

Drill 3

Solve the following inequalities.

11. $x + 3 \leq -2$
12. $t - 4 \leq 13$
13. $3b \geq 12$
14. $-5x > 25$
15. $-8 < -4y$

Drill 4

Solve the following inequalities.

16. $2z + 4 \geq -18$
17. $7x + 5 \geq 10x + 14$
18. $\dfrac{b}{5} \leq 4$
19. $d + \dfrac{3}{2} < 8$
20. $\dfrac{2a}{3} > 10 - a$

Drill 5

Solve the following inequalities.

21. $3(x - 7) \geq 9$
22. $\dfrac{x}{3} + 8 < \dfrac{x}{2}$
23. $2x - 1.5 > 7$
24. $\dfrac{6(2x + 8)}{5} \leq 0$
25. $\dfrac{2(3 - x)}{5x} \leq 4$ and $x > 0$

Drill 6

Solve the following inequalities.

26. $4\sqrt{3x - 2} > 20$
27. $\dfrac{2(8 - 3x)}{7} > 4$
28. $0.25x - 3 \leq 1$
29. $2(y + 2)^3 - 5 \geq 49$
30. $\dfrac{4\sqrt[3]{5x - 8}}{3} \geq 4$

Drill 7

Solve the following absolute value equations.

31. $|x| = 5$
32. $|5a| = 15$
33. $|x + 6| = 3$
34. $|4y + 2| = 18$
35. $|1 - x| = 6$

Drill 8

Solve the following absolute value equations.

36. $3|x - 4| = 18$
37. $2|x + 0.3| = 7$
38. $|3x - 4| = 2x + 6$
39. $|6z - 3| = 4z + 11$
40. $\left|\dfrac{x}{4} + 3\right| = 0.5$

Drill 9

Solve each of the following inequalities. Then draw the solution on a number line.

41. $|x + 3| < 1$
42. $|3x| \geq 6$
43. $5 \geq |2y + 3|$
44. $6 \leq |5b - 9|$
45. $|-12a| < 15$

Drill 10

Solve each of the following inequalities. Then draw the solution on a number line.

46. $|-x| \geq 6$
47. $\dfrac{|x + 4|}{2} > 5$
48. $|z^3| \leq 27$
49. $|0.1x - 3| \geq 1$
50. $\left|\dfrac{3x}{2} + 7\right| \leq 11$

Drill 11

Solve each of the following inequalities. Then draw the solution on a number line.

51. $\left|\dfrac{-x}{5} + \dfrac{2}{3}\right| \leq \dfrac{7}{15}$
52. $|3x - 7| \geq 2x + 12$
53. $|3 + 3x| < -2x$
54. $|-9 - 5x| \leq -4x$
55. $2\left|\dfrac{7y}{4} - 7\right| < \dfrac{3y}{2} + 10$

Drill Sets Solutions

Drill 1

1. $x > 4$

2. $a \geq 3$

3. $y = 2$

4. $x < 5$

5. $6 < x$: You can flip inequalities around, moving the left side to the right and vice versa, as long as you flip the sign, too. In this case, $6 < x$ becomes $x > 6$:

Drill 2

6. $\textbf{\textit{a}} < \textbf{\textit{b}}$: *a is less than b translates as a < b.*

7. $\textbf{5\textit{x}} > \textbf{10}$: *5 times x is greater than 10* is translated as $5x > 10$.

8. $\textbf{6} \leq \textbf{4\textit{x}}$: *6 is less than or equal to 4x* is translated as $6 \leq 4x$.

9. $\textbf{\textit{a}} > \textbf{\textit{o}}$: Let a price of an apple and o equal to the price of an orange. *The price of an apple is greater than the price of an orange* is translated as $a > o$.

   Note: In this problem, the variables refer to prices—not the number of apples and oranges.

10. $\textbf{\textit{m}} \geq \textbf{19}$: Let m equal the number of members. *The total number of members is at least 19* is translated as $m \geq 19$.

Drill 3

11. **$x \leq -5$:**

$$x + 3 \leq -2$$
$$x \leq -5$$

12. **$t \leq 17$:**

$$t - 4 \leq 13$$
$$t \leq 17$$

13. **$b \geq 4$:**

$$3b \geq 12$$
$$b \geq 4$$

14. **$x < -5$:**

$$-5x > 25$$
$$x < -5$$

15. **$2 > y$:**

$$-8 < -4y$$
$$2 > y$$

Drill 4

16. **$z \geq -11$:**

$$2z + 4 \geq -18$$
$$2z \geq -22$$
$$z \geq -11$$

17. **$x \leq -3$:** The answer can also be written as $-3 \geq x$. It's more common to write the variable first.

$$7x + 5 \geq 10x + 14$$
$$5 \geq 3x + 14$$
$$-9 \geq 3x$$
$$-3 \geq x$$

18. **$b \leq 20$:**

$$\frac{b}{5} \leq 4$$
$$b \leq 20$$

19. $d < 6.5$ or $\dfrac{13}{2}$: You can choose to convert to decimals or fractions, as you prefer.

$$d + \frac{3}{2} < 8$$
$$d < 8 - \frac{3}{2}$$
$$d < 8 - 1.5$$
$$d < 6.5$$

20. $a > 6$:

$$\frac{2a}{3} > 10 - a$$
$$2a > 30 - 3a$$
$$5a > 30$$
$$a > 6$$

Drill 5

21. $x \geq 10$:

$$3(x - 7) \geq 9$$
$$x - 7 \geq 3$$
$$x \geq 10$$

22. $x > 48$: The answer can also be written $48 < x$. It is more common to put the variable first.

$$\frac{x}{3} + 8 < \frac{x}{2}$$
$$6\left(\frac{x}{3} + 8\right) < 6\left(\frac{x}{2}\right)$$
$$2x + 48 < 3x$$
$$48 < x$$

Multiply by 6 to get rid of fractions.

23. $x > 4.25$:
$$2x - 1.5 > 7$$
$$2x > 8.5$$
$$x > 4.25$$

24. **$x \leq -4$:** You are allowed to multiply or divide by a constant (a number) even when one side of the equation is 0. That side of the equation just remains 0.

$$\frac{6(2x + 8)}{5} \leq 0$$
$$6(2x+8) \leq 0$$
$$2x+8 \leq 0$$
$$2x \leq -8$$
$$x \leq -4$$

8

25. **$x \geq \dfrac{3}{11}$:** The answer can also be written $\dfrac{3}{11} \leq x$.

$$\frac{2(3-x)}{5x} \leq 4$$
$$2(3-x) \leq 20x$$
$$3-x \leq 10x$$
$$3 \leq 11x$$
$$\frac{3}{11} \leq x$$

Since $x > 0$, you can multiply both sides by $5x$ and keep the inequality sign as it is.

Drill 6

26. **$x > 9$:** Both sides of an inequality can be squared as long as both sides are positive. In this case, the square-root side of the equation must be positive because it is greater than the positive number 5.

$$4\sqrt{3x-2} > 20$$
$$\sqrt{3x-2} > 5$$
$$3x-2 > 25$$
$$3x > 27$$
$$x > 9$$

27. **$x < -2$:**

$$\frac{2(8-3x)}{7} > 4$$
$$2(8-3x) > 28$$
$$8-3x > 14$$
$$-3x > 6$$
$$x < -2$$

28. **$x \leq 16$:** If you are more comfortable working with fractions, you can convert 0.25 to $\frac{1}{4}$, before you solve:

$$0.25x - 3 \leq 1$$
$$0.25x \leq 4$$
$$x \leq 16$$

29. **$y \geq 1$:** When you take a cube root, there is only one solution: the cube has the same sign as the cube root. In this case, the cube root of positive 27 is positive 3:

$$2(y + 2)^3 - 5 \geq 49$$
$$2(y + 2)^3 \geq 54$$
$$(y + 2)^3 \geq 27$$
$$y + 2 \geq 3$$
$$y \geq 1$$

30. **$x \geq 7$:**

$$\frac{4\sqrt[3]{5x - 8}}{3} \geq 4$$
$$4\sqrt[3]{5x - 8} \geq 12$$
$$\sqrt[3]{5x - 8} \geq 3$$
$$\left(\sqrt[3]{5x - 8}\right)^3 \geq (3)^3$$
$$5x - 8 \geq 27$$
$$5x \geq 35$$
$$x \geq 7$$

Drill 7

31. **$x = 5$ or -5:**

$$|x| = 5$$

$$+(x) = 5 \qquad \text{or} \qquad -x = 5$$
$$x = 5 \qquad\qquad\qquad x = -5$$

32. **$a = 3$ or -3:**

$$|5a| = 15$$

$$+(5a) = 15 \qquad \text{or} \qquad -(5a) = 15$$
$$5a = 15 \qquad\qquad\qquad -5a = 15$$
$$a = 3 \qquad\qquad\qquad a = -3$$

33. $x = -3$ **or** -9:

$$|x + 6| = 3$$

$+(x + 6) = 3$ $-(x + 6) = 3$
$x + 6 = 3$ or $-x - 6 = 3$
$x = -3$ $-x = 9$
                        $x = -9$

34. $y = 4$ **or** -5:

$$|4y + 2| = 18$$

$+(4y + 2) = 18$ $-(4y + 2) = 18$
$4y + 2 = 18$ $-4y - 2 = 18$
$4y = 16$ or $-4y = 20$
$y = 4$ $y = -5$

35. $x = -5$ **or** 7:

$$|1 - x| = 6$$

$+(1 - x) = 6$ $-(1 - x) = 6$
$1 - x = 6$ $-1 + x = 6$
$-x = 5$ or $x = 7$
$x = -5$

Drill 8

36. $x = 10$ **or** -2: Isolate the absolute value first. Next, split into two equations and solve:

$$3|x - 4| = 18$$
$$|x - 4| = 6$$

$+(x - 4) = 6$ $-(x - 4) = 6$
$x - 4 = 6$ $-x + 4 = 6$
$x = 10$ or $-x = 2$
                      $x = -2$

37. $x = 3.2$ **or** -3.8: Isolate the absolute value first. Next, split into two equations and solve:

$$2|x + 0.3| = 7$$
$$|x + 0.3| = 3.5$$

$+(x + 0.3) = 3.5$ $-(x + 0.3) = 3.5$
$x + 0.3 = 3.5$ $-x - 0.3 = 3.5$
$x = 3.2$ or $-x = 3.8$
                         $x = -3.8$

38. $x = 10$ or $-\dfrac{2}{5}$:

$$|3x - 4| = 2x + 6$$

$$+(3x - 4) = 2x + 6 \qquad \text{or} \qquad -(3x - 4) = 2x + 6$$

$$3x - 4 = 2x + 6 \qquad\qquad\qquad -3x + 4 = 2x + 6$$

$$x - 4 = 6 \qquad\qquad\qquad\qquad 4 = 5x + 6$$

$$x = 10 \qquad\qquad\qquad\qquad -2 = 5x$$

$$-\dfrac{2}{5} = x$$

39. $z = 7$ or $-\dfrac{4}{5}$:

$$|6z - 3| = 4z + 11$$

$$+(6z - 3) = 4z + 11 \qquad \text{or} \qquad -(6z - 3) = 4z + 11$$

$$6z - 3 = 4z + 11 \qquad\qquad\qquad -6z + 3 = 4z + 11$$

$$2z - 3 = 11 \qquad\qquad\qquad\qquad 3 = 10z + 11$$

$$2z = 14 \qquad\qquad\qquad\qquad -8 = 10z$$

$$z = 7 \qquad\qquad\qquad\qquad -\dfrac{8}{10} = z$$

$$-\dfrac{4}{5} = z$$

40. $x = -10$ or -14:

$$\left|\dfrac{x}{4} + 3\right| = 0.5$$

$$+\left(\dfrac{x}{4} + 3\right) = 0.5 \qquad \text{or} \qquad -\left(\dfrac{x}{4} + 3\right) = 0.5$$

$$\dfrac{x}{4} + 3 = 0.5 \qquad\qquad\qquad -\dfrac{x}{4} - 3 = 0.5$$

$$\dfrac{x}{4} = -2.5 \qquad\qquad\qquad -\dfrac{x}{4} = 3.5$$

$$x = -10 \qquad\qquad\qquad\qquad x = -14$$

Drill 9

41. **−4 < *x* < −2:** Because the two solutions overlap, combine them into one inequality: *x* is greater than −4 *and* less than −2.

$$|x+3| < 1$$

$+(x+3) < 1$	$-(x+3) < 1$
$x+3 < 1$	$-x-3 < 1$
$x < -2$	$-x < 4$
	$x > -4$

$$-4 < x < -2$$

42. ***x* ≤ −2 or *x* ≥ 2:** The two solutions do not overlap, so leave them as two separate inequalities: *x* is less than or equal to −2 *or* greater than or equal to 2.

$$|3x| \geq 6$$

$+(3x) \geq 6$	$-(3x) \geq 6$
$3x \geq 6$	$-3x \geq 6$
$x \geq 2$	$x \leq -2$

$$x \leq -2 \text{ or } x \geq 2$$

43. **−4 ≤ *y* ≤ 1:** If you prefer to have the variable on the left-hand side, you can rewrite, as shown in the last line below. If, when rewriting, you flip the two sides of the inequality, make sure to flip the inequality sign, too. (In this problem, it isn't necessary to flip the inequalities.)

$$5 \geq |2y+3|$$

$5 \geq +(2y+3)$	$5 \geq -(2y+3)$
$5 \geq 2y+3$	$5 \geq -2y-3$
$2 \geq 2y$	$8 \geq -2y$
$1 \geq y$	$-4 \leq y$
$y \leq 1$	

$$-4 \leq y \leq 1$$

MANHATTAN PREP

44. $b \geq 3$ or $b \leq \dfrac{3}{5}$:

$$6 \leq |5b - 9|$$

$$6 \leq +(5b - 9) \qquad\qquad 6 \leq -(5b - 9)$$
$$6 \leq 5b - 9 \qquad\qquad 6 \leq -5b + 9$$
$$15 \leq 5b \qquad\qquad -3 \leq -5b$$
$$3 \leq b \qquad\qquad \dfrac{3}{5} \geq b$$

$$b \geq 3 \ \text{or} \ b \leq \dfrac{3}{5}$$

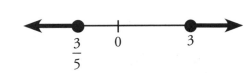

45. $-\dfrac{5}{4} < a < \dfrac{5}{4}$:

$$|-12a| < 15$$

$$+(-12a) < 15 \qquad\qquad -(-12a) < 15$$
$$-12a < 15 \qquad\qquad 12a < 15$$
$$a > -\dfrac{15}{12} \qquad\qquad a < \dfrac{15}{12}$$
$$a > -\dfrac{5}{4} \qquad\qquad a < \dfrac{5}{4}$$

$$-\dfrac{5}{4} < a < \dfrac{5}{4}$$

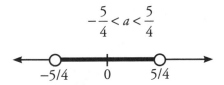

Drill 10

46. $x \leq -6$ or $x \geq 6$:

$$|-x| \geq 6$$

$$+(-x) \geq 6 \qquad\qquad -(-x) \geq 6$$
$$-x \geq 6 \qquad\qquad x \geq 6$$
$$x \leq -6$$

$$x \leq -6 \ \text{or} \ x \geq 6$$

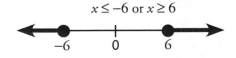

47. **$x < -14$ or $x > 6$:**

$$\frac{|x+4|}{2} > 5$$

$$|x+4| > 10$$

$+(x + 4) > 10$	$-(x + 4) > 10$
$x + 4 > 10$	$-x - 4 > 10$
$x > 6$	$-x > 14$
	$x < -14$

$$x < -14 \text{ or } x > 6$$

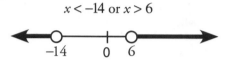

48. **$-3 \leq z \leq 3$:**

$$|z^3| \leq 27$$

$+(z^3) \leq 27$	$-(z^3) \leq 27$
$z^3 \leq 27$	$z^3 \geq -27$
$z \leq 3$	$z \geq -3$

$$-3 \leq z \leq 3$$

49. **$x \leq 20$ or $x \geq 40$:**

$$|0.1x - 3| \geq 1$$

$+(0.1x - 3) \geq 1$	$-(0.1x - 3) \geq 1$
$0.1x - 3 \geq 1$	$-0.1x + 3 \geq 1$
$0.1x \geq 4$	$-0.1x \geq -2$
$x \geq 40$	$x \leq 20$

$$x \leq 20 \text{ or } x \geq 40$$

50. $-12 \leq x \leq \dfrac{8}{3}$:

$$\left|\dfrac{3x}{2}+7\right| \leq 11$$

$+\left(\dfrac{3x}{2}+7\right) \leq 11$ $\qquad\qquad$ $-\left(\dfrac{3x}{2}+7\right) \leq 11$

$\quad\dfrac{3x}{2}+7 \leq 11$ $\qquad\qquad\quad$ $-\dfrac{3x}{2}-7 \leq 11$

$\qquad\dfrac{3x}{2} \leq 4$ $\qquad\qquad\qquad$ $-\dfrac{3x}{2} \leq 18$

$\qquad 3x \leq 8$ $\qquad\qquad\qquad\quad$ $-3x \leq 36$

$\qquad\quad x \leq \dfrac{8}{3}$ $\qquad\qquad\qquad\quad$ $x \geq -12$

$$-12 \leq x \leq \dfrac{8}{3}$$

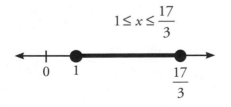

Drill 11

51. $1 \leq x \leq \dfrac{17}{3}$: The second number can also be written as a mixed fraction, $5\dfrac{2}{3}$.

$$\left|\dfrac{-x}{5}+\dfrac{2}{3}\right| \leq \dfrac{7}{15}$$

$+\left(\dfrac{-x}{5}+\dfrac{2}{3}\right) \leq \dfrac{7}{15}$ $\qquad\qquad$ $-\left(\dfrac{-x}{5}+\dfrac{2}{3}\right) \leq \dfrac{7}{15}$

$\quad -\dfrac{x}{5}+\dfrac{2}{3} \leq \dfrac{7}{15}$ $\qquad\qquad\qquad$ $\dfrac{x}{5}-\dfrac{2}{3} \leq \dfrac{7}{15}$

$15\left(-\dfrac{x}{5}+\dfrac{2}{3}\right) \leq \left(\dfrac{7}{15}\right)15$ $\qquad$ $15\left(\dfrac{x}{5}-\dfrac{2}{3}\right) \leq \left(\dfrac{7}{15}\right)15$

$\quad -3x+10 \leq 7$ $\qquad\qquad\qquad\quad$ $3x-10 \leq 7$

$\qquad -3x \leq -3$ $\qquad\qquad\qquad\qquad$ $3x \leq 17$

$\qquad\quad x \geq 1$ $\qquad\qquad\qquad\qquad\quad$ $x \leq \dfrac{17}{3}$

$$1 \leq x \leq \dfrac{17}{3}$$

52. $x \leq -1$ or $x \geq 19$:

$$|3x - 7| \geq 2x + 12$$

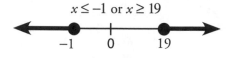

$+(3x - 7) \geq 2x + 12$	$-(3x - 7) \geq 2x + 12$
$3x - 7 \geq 2x + 12$	$-3x + 7 \geq 2x + 12$
$x - 7 \geq 12$	$7 \geq 5x + 12$
$x \geq 19$	$-5 \geq 5x$
	$-1 \geq x$

$$x \leq -1 \text{ or } x \geq 19$$

8

53. $-3 < x < -\dfrac{3}{5}$:

$$|3 + 3x| < -2x$$

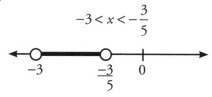

$+(3 + 3x) < -2x$	$-(3 + 3x) < -2x$
$3 + 3x < -2x$	$-3 - 3x < -2x$
$3 + 5x < 0$	$-3 < x$
$5x < -3$	
$x < -\dfrac{3}{5}$	

$$-3 < x < -\dfrac{3}{5}$$

54. $-9 \leq x \leq -1$:

$$|-9 - 5x| \leq -4x$$

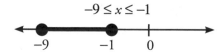

$+(-9 - 5x) \leq -4x$	$-(-9 - 5x) \leq -4x$
$-9 - 5x \leq -4x$	$9 + 5x \leq -4x$
$-9 \leq x$	$9 + 9x \leq 0$
	$9x \leq -9$
	$x \leq -1$

$$-9 \leq x \leq -1$$

55. $\frac{4}{5} < y < 12$: Isolate the absolute value, and then split into two equations.

$$2\left|\frac{7x}{4} - 7\right| < \frac{3y}{2} + 10$$

$$\left|\frac{7y}{4} - 7\right| < \frac{3y}{4} + 5$$

$$+\left(\frac{7y}{4} - 7\right) < \frac{3y}{4} + 5 \qquad\qquad -\left(\frac{7y}{4} - 7\right) < \frac{3y}{4} + 5$$

$$\frac{7y}{4} - 7 < \frac{3y}{4} + 5 \qquad\qquad -\frac{7y}{4} + 7 < \frac{3y}{4} + 5$$

$$7y - 28 < 3y + 20 \qquad\qquad -7y + 28 < 3y + 20$$

$$4y < 48 \qquad\qquad\qquad 8 < 10y$$

$$y < 12 \qquad\qquad\qquad \frac{8}{10} < y$$

$$\qquad\qquad\qquad\qquad\qquad \frac{4}{5} < y$$

$$\frac{4}{5} < y < 12$$

Word Problems

In this chapter...

- Solve Word Problems: Follow Four Steps to Turn Words into Math

- Common Word Problem Phrases

- Express Revenue as Price × Quantity

- Add Units: Add Apples to Apples

- Multiply and Divide Units: Treat Them Just Like Numbers or Variables

- Rate × Time: Distance, Follow the Units

- Rate × Time: Work, Define the Work Unit and Add Rates

- Fractions and Percents in Word Problems: *Of* Means *Times*

Chapter 9

Word Problems

In This Chapter, You Will Learn To:

- Translate and solve word problems

Solve Word Problems: Follow Four Steps to Turn Words into Math

Word problems are everywhere on the GMAT. They come in all sorts of shapes and sizes. The descriptions can be confusing and unfamiliar.

Fortunately, the process for tackling almost all word problems is fundamentally the same. You can solve word problems by asking yourself the following four questions:

1. **What do they want?**

   Identify what the problem is specifically asking for. Name that thing and write it down. This is the unknown that you care about the most.

2. **What do they give me?**

   The problem typically gives you some numbers. It also gives you relationships between things. Clearly identify all of this given information. You may have to name additional unknowns.

3. **How do I turn this information into equations?**

   An equation is a sentence: *The left side equals the right side*. You can express most relationships using the equals sign (=) or the inequalities signs. A few common relationships show up over and over again; you can learn to recognize them.

4. **How do I solve those equations for the desired value?**

   Use methods from the Equations chapter, the Quadratic Equations chapter, and so on, to manipulate the equations you've created. You'll eliminate any secondary unknowns until you find the value you want.

It is crucial to write things down. Do not wait for lightning to strike. Often, the entire process will not be completely clear from the beginning. That's fine—just start writing, and be methodical and patient.

The four questions above correspond to the four steps of a general process of solving word problems.

Consider this example:

> The annual profit for a mattress company is defined by the equation $p = 200m - 3{,}000$, where p is the profit, in dollars, and m is the number of mattresses sold. How much profit does the company make, in dollars, from the sale of 40 mattresses in a particular year?

Start with step #1: **What do they want?**

The question is asking for the *profit* in a particular year. This unknown has already been named for you. Profit is represented by p.

If you were not given a letter for the variable, you would make up your own.

Write "$p = \text{profit} = ?$" on your paper. By writing an actual question mark, you flag the most important unknown.

You may even want to draw a circle or box around this text to help you remember that it is the question. This will help you to forestall one of the most common careless mistakes on word problems: solving for the wrong thing.

Next is step #2: **What do they give me?**

In this problem, you are given two specific pieces of information:

1. The relationship between number of mattresses and profit
2. A specific number of mattresses

Step #3: **How do I turn this information into equations?**

The first bit of information is already in equation form. Write "$p = 200m - 3{,}000$."

The same relationship could have been given in words: "The profit, in dollars, is \$200 times the number of mattresses, minus a \$3,000 fixed cost." You would translate those words to the same equation.

The second bit of given information is this: There are 40 mattresses. Write "$m = 40$" on your scrap paper. This is actually a second equation.

Don't just write "40." Put information down in the form of equations.

Finally, step #4: **How do I solve the equations for the desired value?**

$$p = 200m - 3{,}000 \qquad m = 40 \qquad p = \text{profit} = ?$$

To get p, you'll need to eliminate the variable m. Plug in 40 for m in the first equation and simplify.

$p - 200(40) - 3,000$
$p = 8,000 - 3,000$
$p = 5,000$

Therefore, the answer to the problem is $5,000.

Even as the problems become more complicated, follow these same four steps. Let's try another problem:

A steel rod 50 meters long is cut into two pieces. If one piece is 14 meters longer than the other, what is the length, in meters, of the shorter piece?

Again, start with step #1: **What do they want?**

The question asks specifically for the "length ... of the shorter piece." This length is the number you want.

Since the problem did not give you a letter to represent this length, pick one. Don't just pick x. Choose a letter that will easily remind you of the quantity you are trying to find. For instance, you might choose S for "shorter." Write this down:

S = length short = ?

Note: "Length short" is shorthand for "the length of the shorter piece."

Step #2: **What do they give me?**

Reread the first sentence: "A steel rod 50 meters long is cut into two pieces."

It might not be obvious at first, but this sentence provides a relationship between a few lengths:

- The length of the whole rod, which is 50 meters
- The length of the shorter piece, which you've already called S
- The length of the longer piece (which must be longer, because the other piece is shorter)

Before trying to represent the relationship, name the length of the longer piece. Write this down:

L = length long

Now you can express the relationship between all the lengths. This relationship is very common:

Part + Part = Whole

If you break something into two parts, you can add the parts back up to get the original thing. That's true of lengths, weights, and so on.

Go ahead and do step #3 right now: **How do I turn this information into an equation?** Write this relationship down using the numbers and letters for each quantity.

$$S + L = 50$$

As you identify each relationship, you will often want to go ahead and express it on paper in the form of an equation right away. You can go back and forth between steps #2 and #3.

The equation $S + L = 50$ is a good start, but it's not enough on its own to solve for S. Go back to step #2 and ask: **What ELSE do they give me?**

Keep reading: "If one piece is 14 meters longer than the other …" Stop there. In a math problem, anything after an "if" is true. You are told that one piece is 14 meters longer than the other.

This relationship is also very common: *Different values are made equal.* You have two different values that are definitely not equal, but you are told exactly how the values differ, so you can set up an equivalence.

If the shorter piece were 14 meters longer, it would have the *same* length as the longer piece. *Same* always means *equal.* Therefore:

> Shorter piece, if made 14 meters longer = Longer piece

Now do step #3 again: **How do I turn THIS information into an equation?**

To make something 14 meters longer, add 14 meters to its length. Write the equation using letters and numbers:

$$S + 14 = L$$

Be careful not to write this equation down backward. If you need to check, mentally test a number for S and verify that the longer piece comes out longer. Alternatively, remind yourself that S is the *shorter* piece, so logically it makes sense that you have to add something to it to match the longer piece.

At last you have two equations and two variables (S and L), and you have no more information to process from the problem. Move on to step #4: **How do I solve the equations for the desired value?**

$$S + L = 50 \qquad\qquad S + 14 = L \qquad\qquad S = ?$$

Since you ultimately want S, eliminate L by replacing it in the first equation with $S + 14$.

$$S + L = 50$$
$$S + (S + 14) = 50$$
$$2S + 14 = 50$$
$$2S = 36$$
$$S = 18$$

The answer to the question is 18.

Try a harder problem. Despite new challenges, the process remains the same. As needed, move back and forth among the first three steps: Identify what the question asks for, identify given quantities and relationships, and represent those quantities as variables and those relationships as equations.

MANHATTAN PREP

Over a period of 5 days at a donut shop, the average (arithmetic mean) number of donuts sold per day was 80. In the 4 days after that period, the shop sold a total of 500 donuts. What was the average number of donuts sold per day over the entire 9-day period?

Start by identifying what they want: the average (arithmetic mean) number of donuts sold per day over 9 days. Use the letter *a* to represent this value. (Note: *arithmetic mean* is a synonym for *average*. The test will often use both terms; all you need to find is the regular average.)

$$a = \text{average \# donuts sold a day} = ?$$

The problem also mentions the concept of an average. This is one of the formulas that you need to memorize for the GMAT: The average of a group of numbers is the sum of those numbers divided by the number of terms, which is the number of numbers you have.

$$\text{Average} = \frac{\text{Sum}}{\text{\# of terms}}$$

When you see that a problem mentions some concept for which you have memorized a formula, immediately write down the "generic" form of that formula, as shown above.

Include units as well. The average is in *donuts a day*, or donuts *per* day. *Per* means *divided by*, so this unit is donuts/day or $\frac{\text{donuts}}{\text{day}}$. The sum is the total number of donuts, and you divide by the number of days. Here is the average formula customized for this problem:

$$\text{Average donuts per day} = \frac{\text{Total donuts}}{\text{Total days}}$$

To find the average, you need both the total number of donuts and the total number of days.

Do you know either of these values? Yes. You are asked for the average *over the entire 9-day period*. So the total number of days is 9.

However, the total number of donuts is unknown. Make up a variable—say, *d* for donuts.

Now rewrite the average formula.

$$a = \frac{d}{9}$$

You may not think that you've accomplished much yet, but now you know that to get *a*, you need *d*.

That's important. Now you should focus on *d*. What else can you find out about the total number of donuts sold over the 9 days?

Reread the problem. The first sentence indicates something about the donuts sold during the first 5 days. The next sentence indicates that a total of 500 donuts were sold in the last 4 days. And you are looking for *d*, the total donuts sold over all 9 days.

What is the relationship between the donuts sold during these periods?

- Donuts sold over the first 5 days
- Donuts sold over the last 4 days
- Donuts sold over all 9 days

This is Part + Part = Whole again.

$$\begin{array}{ccc} \text{Donuts sold in} & & \text{Donuts sold in} & & \text{Total donuts sold} \\ \text{the first 5 days} & + & \text{the last 4 days} & = & \text{over all 9 days} \end{array}$$

As word problems get harder, they make relationships harder to see. You also have to perform more steps.

Now you have two more unknowns to worry about on the left side of the equation above. Do you know either unknown?

Yes. You do know how many donuts were sold in the last 4 days: 500 donuts. However, the number of donuts sold in the first 5 days is still unknown. Use an n to represent that quantity and rewrite the Part + Part = Whole equation.

$n + 500 = d$

You're almost there. If you can find n, you can find d. Then you can find a, and that's the answer.

What do you know about n, the number of donuts sold over the first 5 days? You know something about that period from the first sentence: on average, 80 donuts per day were sold. Once again, you can use the average formula to create an equation. Notice that you're focusing on a different period now—just the first 5 days.

$$\text{Average donuts per day} = \frac{\text{Total donuts}}{\text{Total days}} \qquad 80 = \frac{n}{5}$$

At last, you can solve the problem. First, solve for n.

$$80 = \frac{n}{5} \quad \longrightarrow \quad 400 = n$$

Next, find d.

$$n + 500 = d \quad \longrightarrow \quad 400 + 500 = d \quad \longrightarrow \quad 900 = d$$

Finally, solve for a.

$$a = \frac{d}{9} \quad \longrightarrow \quad a = \frac{900}{9} \quad \longrightarrow \quad a = 100$$

The average number of donuts sold per day over the entire 9-day period is 100. That is, on average, 100 donuts were sold each day for 9 days.

As you solve word problems, sometimes you'll notice relationships first. At other times, you'll notice unknowns first. The order is not important. Just keep extracting information from the problem and representing that information on paper.

Turn unknowns into letters, and turn relationships into equations. Observe how the equations hook together. In the previous problem, you ultimately wanted *a*, but you needed *d* first, and before that *n*.

The last value you solve for is the one you really want (*a*). When you identify other unknowns, realize that you will likely need to solve for them first.

If you...	Then you...	Like this:
Want to solve a word problem: Kelly is three times as old as Bill. In 5 years, Kelly will be twice as old as Bill will be. How old is Bill?	Follow the four steps: 1. Identify what they want 2. Identify what they give you 3. Represent relationships as equations 4. Solve the algebra	$B = ?$ $K = 3B$ $K+5 = 2(B+5)$ $(3B)+5 = 2(B+5)$ $3B+5 = 2B+10$ $B = 5$ Bill is 5 years old.

To help you translate, here are several phrases commonly found in word problems to describe mathematical relationships. Study this list.

Common Word Problem Phrases

Addition

Add, Sum, Total (of parts), More Than: +

The sum of *x* and *y*: $x + y$

The sum of the three funds combined: $a + b + c$

If Anuj were 50 years older: $a + 50$

Six pounds heavier than Dave: $d + 6$

A group of men and women: $m + w$

The cost is marked up: $c + m$

Subtraction

Minus, Difference, Less Than: −

x minus five: $x - 5$

The positive difference between Quentin's and Rachel's heights (if Quentin is taller): $q - r$

Four pounds less than expected: $e - 4$

The profit is the revenue minus the cost: $P = R - C$

Multiplication

The product of h and k: $h \times k$

The number of reds times the number of blues: $r \times b$

One-fifth of y: $\left(\dfrac{1}{5}\right) \times y$

n persons have x beads each: total number of beads $= nx$

Ratios and Division

Quotient, Per, Ratio, Proportion: ÷ or /

Five dollars every two weeks: $\left(\dfrac{5 \text{ dollars}}{2 \text{ weeks}}\right)$ ➔ 2.5 dollars a week

The ratio of x to y: $\dfrac{x}{y}$

The proportion of girls to boys: $\dfrac{g}{b}$

Average or Mean (sum of terms divided by the total number of terms)

$$\text{Average} = \dfrac{\text{Sum}}{\text{\# of terms}}$$

The average of a and b: $\dfrac{a+b}{2}$

The average salary of the three doctors: $\dfrac{x+y+z}{3}$

A student's average score on 5 tests was 87: $\dfrac{\text{sum}}{5} = 87$ or $\dfrac{a+b+c+d+e}{5} = 87$

Check Your Skills

1. The total weight of two jugs of milk is 2.2 kilograms. The lighter jug weighs 0.4 kilogram less than the heavier jug. What is the weight of the lighter jug?

2. Jan makes a salary of $10,000 per month for 3 months. Then her salary drops to $6,000 per month. After 9 months at $6,000 per month, what will Jan's average (arithmetic mean) monthly pay be for the whole period?

Answers can be found on page 387.

Express Revenue as Price × Quantity

The GMAT expects you to know certain basic money relationships. Try this example:

> At a certain store, 7 shirts cost $63. If each shirt costs the same amount, what is the cost of 3 shirts, in dollars?

Solve the problem methodically. First, what is the question specifically asking for? It's asking for the total cost to buy 3 shirts, in dollars (represented by $). This cost for the consumer can also be thought of as revenue for the company selling the shirts.

What are you given? You are given the cost of 7 shirts ($63); again, this cost to the buyer represents revenue for the seller. You are also told that every shirt has the same price, and you are given another quantity of shirts to care about (3).

When every unit of something has the same price, you can use this equation:

Total revenue = Price × Quantity

This can also be written: **Total cost to consumer = Price × Quantity**

Name the variables R for revenue (in this case, you can also use C for cost, since that's what the problem says), P for price, and Q for quantity.

$$C = P \times Q$$

What is the question asking for again? It asks for the total cost of 3 shirts. In other words, the question asks for the value of C when $Q = 3$:

$$C = P \times 3 = ?$$

To find C, then, you need P—the price of each shirt. Price is always in dollars *per unit*. It is the cost of one unit of whatever is being sold or bought—in this case, shirts.

How can you find the price of each shirt? You know something else related to the price: "…7 shirts costs $63."

This is another instance of Total cost to consumer = Price × Quantity. You have a different quantity (7) and a different total cost ($63), but the problem says that the price per shirt is always the same. So P is the same in both equations.

Set up a second equation:

$$\$63 = P \times 7$$

Next, solve for P, the price per shirt.

$$63 = P \times 7$$
$$\frac{63}{7} = P$$
$$9 = P$$

Therefore, $P = 9$, so each shirt costs $9.

Finally, solve the other equation for the total cost of 3 shirts by substituting 9 for P.

$$C = P \times 3$$
$$C = 9 \times 3$$
$$C = 27$$

The total cost of 3 shirts is $27.

Here's how the problem would look from the store's point of view.

> A certain store sold 7 shirts for $63. If every shirt has the same price, how much revenue, in dollars, would the store receive from selling 3 shirts?

The answer is the same: $27. Instead of Total cost, write Total revenue.

> Total revenue = Price × Quantity

Or, you can focus on the units. The total on the left is in dollars, while the price is in dollars per shirt.

$$\text{Total money (\$)} = \text{Price}\left(\frac{\$}{\text{shirt}}\right) \times \text{Quantity (shirts)}$$

Try a more complicated example.

> Five apples and four bananas cost $2.10, while three apples and two bananas cost $1.20. If the cost of each apple is the same, and if the cost of each banana is the same, what is the cost of two apples and one banana?

Take this one step at a time.

The cost of five apples and four bananas is $2.10. This $2.10 is a whole made up of two parts: the cost of five apples and the cost of four bananas. Each of *those* costs is a price times a quantity. Set up an equation:

Total Cost	=	**Price × Quantity**	+	**Price × Quantity**
		for apples		for bananas

What are you given? You are given the cost of five apples and four bananas ($2.10). You are also given the cost of three apples and two bananas ($1.20).

Furthermore, you are told that the cost (or price) of each apple is the same, and likewise for bananas. These last facts allow you to use the Total cost = Price × Quantity relationship.

What are you asked for? The total cost of two apples and a banana.

The simplest unknowns to name are the price (or cost) of one apple and the price of one banana. Call these A for apple and B for banana. You're going to write everything in terms of these unknowns.

For each total cost you are given, write a separate equation.

Total Cost		Price × Quantity		Price × Quantity		
$2.10	=	$A \times 5$	+	$B \times 4$	=	$5A + 4B$
$1.20	=	$A \times 3$	+	$B \times 2$	=	$3A + 2B$

You are looking for the cost of two apples and a banana: $A \times 2 + B \times 1 = 2A + B = ?$

Solve for A and B. Try combining the equations. First, multiply the second equation by 2.

Equation 1:

$2.10 = 5A + 4B$

Equation 2:

$2(1.20) = (3A + 2B)2$

$2.40 = 6A + 4B$

Now subtract the first equation from the second.

$$
\begin{array}{rcl}
2.40 & = & 6A + 4B \\
-(2.10 & = & 5A + 4B) \\
\hline
0.30 & = & A
\end{array}
$$

Plug back into one of the original equations to solve for B.

$1.20 = 3A + 2B$ ⟶

$$
\begin{array}{rcl}
1.20 & - & 3(0.30) + 2B \\
1.20 & = & 0.90 + 2B \\
0.30 & = & 2B \\
0.15 & = & B
\end{array}
$$

Finally, answer the question.

$2A + B = 2(0.30) + (0.15) = 0.60 + 0.15 = 0.75$

The cost of two apples and one banana is $0.75.

Sometimes the price is known and the quantity is not. The cost in dollars of x books priced at $12 each is $12x$. Notice that $12x$ is also the cost of 12 pens, if each pen costs $$x$. When you write the total cost as a product of price and quantity, keep track of which is which.

Occasionally, you encounter an up-front **fixed cost**. Cell phone minutes used to be priced this way: You had a fixed cost per call (including the first 2 or 3 minutes), and then you paid for additional minutes at a certain price per minute. The equation looks like this:

Total cost = **Fixed cost** + **Price × *Additional* quantity**

Consider this example:

> The charge to reserve a box seat at Colossus Stadium is $1,000, which includes attendance at two games, plus $300 for each additional game attended. If Sam wants to spend no more than $4,000 on his box seat at Colossus Stadium, what is the maximum number of games he can attend?

What is the question looking for? The maximum number of games that Sam can attend. Call that n.

What information are you given? You are told that the cost to reserve a box seat is $1,000 (which includes two games), plus $300 each additional game. You are also told that Sam wants to spend no more than $4,000 on his seat.

Sam attends n games in all, but he had passes for two of them (included in the $1,000 up front).

So he attends $n - 2$ games at the $300 ticket price.

Finally, this is an inequality: Sam wants to spend less than or equal to $4,000. Set up an equation:

Fixed cost	+	Price × *Additional* quantity	≤	Total cost
$1,000	+	$300 × $(n - 2)$	≤	$4,000

Next, solve for n.

$$1,000 + 300(n - 2) \leq 4,000$$
$$300(n - 2) \leq 3,000$$
$$n - 2 \leq 10$$
$$n \leq 12$$

At most, Sam can attend 12 total games.

Last but not least, don't forget this classic relationship:

Profit = Revenues − Costs

This one shows up in business school quite a bit, of course! You also need it on the GMAT, sometimes in combination with the other relationships above.

If you...	Then you...	Like this:
Encounter a money relationship: "The cost of 8 watches is $1,200..."	Write the equation: Total Cost = Price × Quantity, including more items or a fixed cost as necessary	P = Price of one watch $1,200 = P \times 8$ $1,200 = 8P$ $150 = P$ One watch costs $150.

Check Your Skills

3. A candy shop sold 50 candy bars in January for $3 each. In February, the shop increased the price by $1, but its revenue from candy bar sales only increased by $10. By how many units did the number of candy bars sold decrease from January to February?

4. At a particular store, seven staplers and five coffee mugs cost $36, while two staplers and one coffee mug cost $10. If each stapler costs the same, and if each coffee mug costs the same, how much more does a stapler cost than a coffee mug?

Answers can be found on pages 388.

Add Units: Add Apples to Apples

When you solve pure algebra problems, the numbers don't represent anything in particular. In contrast, word problems have a context. Every number has a meaning. That is, every number has a natural **unit** attached.

Up to this point, the units have worked out naturally. For instance, in the steel rod question (on page 367), all the lengths were already in meters, so you could ignore the units.

$$
\begin{array}{cccccc}
S & + & L & = & 50 & \quad\quad S & + & 14 & = & L \\
\text{meters} & & \text{meters} & & \text{meters} & \text{meters} & & \text{meters} & & \text{meters}
\end{array}
$$

If some units were meters and others were feet, you couldn't add or subtract them. *When you add or subtract quantities, they must have exactly the same units.*

What is $2 plus 45 cents, if $1 = 100 cents? Choose a common unit. It doesn't matter which one you pick, but you must express both quantities in that same unit before you add.

$$
\begin{array}{cccccc}
2 & + & 0.45 & = & 2.45 & \quad\quad 200 & + & 45 & = & 245 \\
\text{dollars} & & \text{dollars} & & \text{dollars} & \text{cents} & & \text{cents} & & \text{cents}
\end{array}
$$

The result has the same unit as the original quantities. When you add or subtract units, the units do not change. For example:

$$\text{meters} + \text{meters} = \text{meters} \quad \text{dollars} - \text{dollars} = \text{dollars} \quad \text{puppies} + \text{puppies} = \text{puppies}$$

Multiply and Divide Units: Treat Them Just Like Numbers or Variables

In contrast, when you multiply units, the result has a different unit. A good example is area.

> If a room is 6 feet long and 9 feet wide, what is the area of the room?

Area is length times width, so multiply:

> Area = 6 feet × 9 feet = 54…

What happens to the feet? "Feet" times "feet" equals "feet *squared.*" Therefore:

$$\text{Area} = 6 \text{ feet} \times 9 \text{ feet} = 54 \text{ feet squared} = 54 \text{ feet}^2 = 54 \text{ square feet}$$

If you multiply two quantities that each have units, multiply the units, too.

Not every multiplication in a word problem changes the units. If Alex is twice as old as Brenda, in years, then you can represent that relationship like so:

$$\begin{array}{ccccc} A & = & 2 & \times & B \\ \text{years} & & & & \text{years} \end{array}$$

The word *twice* has no units (it just means *two times*, or 2 ×).

Some units are naturally ratios of other units. Look for the words *per*, *a*, *for every*, and so on.

$$3 \text{ books a week} = 3\frac{\text{books}}{\text{week}} \qquad\qquad 17 \text{ miles per gallon} = 17\frac{\text{miles}}{\text{gallon}}$$

Prices and averages often have units that are ratios of other units.

$$9 \text{ dollars a shirt} = 9\frac{\text{dollars}}{\text{shirt}} \qquad\qquad 100 \text{ donuts per day} = 100\frac{\text{donuts}}{\text{day}}$$

The average formula actually shows the division of units.

$$\text{Average donuts per day} = \frac{\text{Total donuts}}{\text{Total days}}$$

Likewise, the Total cost relationship demonstrates that *units cancel in the same way as numbers and variables do.*

$$\text{Total cost} = \text{Price} \times \text{Quantity}$$

$$\text{dollars} = \frac{\text{dollars}}{\text{shirt}} \times \text{shirts}$$

The units match on both sides of the equation, because you can cancel the "shirt" unit just as you would with anything else in its place.

$$\text{dollars} = \frac{\text{dollars}}{\cancel{\text{shirt}}} \times \cancel{\text{shirts}}$$

This cancellation property allows you to convert from a larger to a smaller unit, or vice versa. Try another example:

How many minutes are in two days?

First, convert 2 days into hours: 1 day = 24 hours. You could convert 2 days to 48 hours in your head, but do it on paper with unit cancellation:

$$2 \text{ days} \times \frac{24 \text{ hours}}{1 \text{ day}} = 48 \text{ hours} \qquad\qquad \cancel{\text{days}} \times \frac{\text{hours}}{\cancel{\text{day}}} = \text{hours}$$

Notice that the "day" unit cancels, leaving you with "hours" on top. The fraction you use to multiply is called a *conversion factor*. It's a fancy form of the number 1, because the top (24 hours) equals the bottom (1 day). When you write conversion factors, put the units in place first so that they cancel correctly. Then place the corresponding numbers so that the top equals the bottom.

Keep going to minutes. Set up the conversion factor using 60 minutes = 1 hour.

$$48 \text{ hours} \times \frac{60 \text{ minutes}}{1 \text{ hour}} = 2{,}880 \text{ minutes} \qquad\qquad \cancel{\text{hrs}} \times \frac{\text{min}}{\cancel{\text{hr}}} = \text{min}$$

By the way, always write out at least a few letters for every unit. "Hours" can be "hr," and "minutes" can be "min," but never write "h" or "m." You might confuse a single letter for a variable.

You can do two or more conversions in one step:

$$2 \text{ days} \times \frac{24 \text{ hours}}{1 \text{ day}} \times \frac{60 \text{ minutes}}{1 \text{ hour}} = 2{,}880 \text{ minutes} \qquad\qquad \cancel{\text{days}} \times \frac{\cancel{\text{hrs}}}{\cancel{\text{day}}} \times \frac{\text{min}}{\cancel{\text{hr}}} = \text{min}$$

A common conversion is between miles and kilometers. You don't have to know that 1 mile is approximately 1.6 kilometers; the GMAT will give you this information. However, you will have to be able to use this information to convert between these units. For example:

A distance is 30 miles. What is the approximate distance in kilometers? (1 mile = 1.6 kilometers)

Multiply the given distance by the conversion factor, which you should set up to cancel units.

$$30 \text{ miles} \times \frac{1.6 \text{ kilometers}}{1 \text{ mile}} = 48 \text{ kilometers} \qquad\qquad \cancel{\text{miles}} \times \frac{\text{km}}{\cancel{\text{miles}}} = \text{km}$$

If you…	Then you…	Like this:
Add or subtract quantities with units	Ensure that the units are the same, converting first if necessary	30 minutes + 2 hours = 30 min + 120 min = 150 min *or* $= \frac{1}{2} \text{ hr} + 2 \text{ hr} = 2\frac{1}{2} \text{ hr}$
Multiply quantities with units	Multiply the units, canceling as appropriate	$10 \frac{\text{bagels}}{\text{hr}} \times 3 \text{ hrs} = 30 \text{ bagels}$
Want to convert from one unit to another	Multiply by a conversion factor and cancel	$20 \text{ min} \times \frac{60 \text{ sec}}{1 \text{ min}} = 1{,}200 \text{ sec}$

Check Your Skills

5. How many hours are there in two weeks? Do this problem with conversion factors.
6. How long after midnight is 1:04am, in seconds?

Answers can be found on pages 388–389.

Rate × Time: Distance, Follow the Units

A **rate**, or speed, can be expressed in "miles per hour" $\left(\dfrac{\text{miles}}{\text{hour}}\right)$ or in "feet per second" $\left(\dfrac{\text{feet}}{\text{sec}}\right)$. In other words, the

unit of this kind of rate is a *distance* unit (*miles, feet*) divided by a *time* unit (*hour, second*).

$$\text{Rate} = \frac{\text{Distance}}{\text{Time}} \qquad\qquad 60 \text{ miles per hour} = \frac{60 \text{ miles}}{1 \text{ hour}}$$

You also can rearrange this relationship to isolate distance on one side.

$$\text{Rate} \times \text{Time} = \text{Distance} \qquad\qquad 60 \,\frac{\text{miles}}{\text{hour}} \times 1 \text{ hour} = 60 \text{ miles}$$

This version is very similar to the Total cost equation:

$$\text{Price} \times \text{Quantity} = \text{Total cost/Revenue} \qquad\qquad 9 \,\frac{\text{dollars}}{\text{shirt}} \times 4 \text{ shirts} = 36 \text{ dollars}$$

A price is a kind of rate, too, because it's *per* something. In distance problems, most rates are *per* time, but occasionally, you see a rate *per* something else, such as miles per gallon.

Avoid expressing rates as time divided by distance. Instead, *always put time in the denominator*. It doesn't matter how the words are expressed. "It took Joe 4 hours to go 60 miles" means that Joe's rate was 60 miles ÷ 4 hours, or 15 miles per hour.

You can combine the Rate × Time = Distance relationship with other relationships already covered. For instance, you have worked with the average formula, as in the "donuts per day" problem:

$$\text{Average donuts per day} = \frac{\text{Total donuts}}{\text{Total days}}$$

The same formula works for rates as well.

$$\text{Average miles per hour} = \frac{\text{Total miles}}{\text{Total hours}}$$

To get the totals on the top and bottom, you often need another relationship you're familiar with:

Part + Part = Whole

Miles for first part of a trip + Miles for second part = Total miles

Hours for first part of a trip + Hours for second part = Total hours

Try this problem:

Nancy takes 2 hours to bike 12 kilometers from home to school. If she bikes back home by the same route at a rate of 4 kilometers per hour, what is her average speed, in kilometers per hour, for the entire trip?

Be careful. The average rate for a journey is the *total* distance divided by the *total* time. Do not simply take an average of the rates given.

You are asked for the average rate for the whole trip. Call this a and write an equation.

$$\text{Average kilometers per hour} = a \qquad\qquad a = \frac{\text{Total kilometers}}{\text{Total hours}}$$

Do you know either of the missing numbers on the right? Yes. You can figure out the total kilometers. The route from home to school is 12 kilometers, and Nancy comes home by the *same* route, so the total kilometers is equal to $12 + 12 = 24$. This is Part + Part = Whole.

$$a = \frac{24}{\text{Total hours}}$$

Now, to find the total time in hours, use Part + Part = Whole again.

Total hours = Hours spent on the first part of the trip + Hours spent on the second part

Do you know either of *these* numbers? Yes—you have the first number directly from the problem.

Total hours = 2 hours + Hours spent on the second part

What do you know about the second part of the trip? You know that Nancy's rate was 4 kilometers per hour. You also know that this route was the *same* as for the first leg—so the distances are equal. It's easy to miss this information. Whenever the GMAT says "the same," pay attention! It always represents an equation.

Write Rate × Time = Distance again, this time just for the second leg of the journey.

$$\text{Rate} \times \text{Time} = \text{Distance} \qquad\qquad 4\,\frac{\text{kilometers}}{\text{hour}} \times \text{Time (hours)} = 12 \text{ kilometers}$$

You now have enough to solve. Call this time t.

$$4t = 12$$
$$t = 3$$

Plug into the previous equation to find the total time spent on the trip.

Total hours = 2 hours + Hours spent on the second part

Total hours = 2 hours + 3 hours

Total hours = 5 hours

Finally, plug into the first equation you wrote.

$$a = \frac{24}{\text{Total hours}} = \frac{24}{5} = 4.8$$

Nancy's average rate for the whole trip is 4.8 kilometers per hour.

Rate problems can become tricky when you have to use the same relationship repeatedly (Rate × Time = Distance). To keep the various rates, times, and distances straight, you might use subscripts or even whole words.

$t_1 = 2$ hours $t_2 = 3$ hours   Time #1 = 2 hrs   Time #2 = 3 hrs

If you have more than one time in the problem, then using t everywhere for every time is likely to lead to mistakes. Tables or grids can help keep quantities straight.

If you...	Then you...	Like this:
See a rate problem	Use Rate × Time = Distance, putting in units to keep the math correct	$7 \dfrac{\text{miles}}{\text{hr}} \times 3 \text{ hrs} = 21 \text{ miles}$

Check Your Skills

7. Amanda ran 24 miles at a rate of 3 miles per hour, then took 4 hours to run an additional 6 miles. What was her average speed for the entire run?

Answer can be found on page 389.

Rate × Time: Work, Define the Work Unit and Add Rates

Work problems are very similar to Rate-Time-Distance problems. The main difference is that work takes the place of distance.

Rate × Time = Distance   Rate × Time = Work

$20 \dfrac{\text{miles}}{\text{hour}} \times 3 \text{ hours} = 60 \text{ miles}$ $20 \dfrac{\text{chairs}}{\text{hour}} \times 3 \text{ hours} = 60 \text{ chairs}$

Define work by the task done. It could be building chairs, painting houses, manufacturing soda cans, etc. One unit of output (chairs, houses, cans) is one unit of work.

MANHATTAN PREP

If the "job" is to paint a house or fill a warehouse, you can still call that one: filling the warehouse once is one unit of output. Occasionally, it can be helpful to invent small units of work ("widgets") so that you avoid dealing with fractions. If the problem references "half a warehouse per day," say that a warehouse contains 10 boxes. The rate then becomes 5 boxes per day.

Again, always put time in the denominator. "It takes Sally 3 minutes to build a chair" should be translated as 1 chair per 3 minutes. As a rate, this translates to $\frac{1}{3}$ of a chair per minute.

$$\text{Rate} = 1 \text{ chair per } 3 \text{ minutes} \qquad\qquad \text{Rate} = \frac{1 \text{ chair}}{3 \text{ minutes}} = \frac{1}{3} \text{ chair per minute}$$

If two people or machines work at the same time side by side, you can *add* their rates. Try this example:

> Jay can build a chair in 3 hours. Kay can build a chair in 5 hours. How long will it take both of them, working together, to build 8 chairs?

First, focus on Jay. What is his rate of work? Put time in the denominator.

$$\text{Jay's rate} = \frac{1 \text{ chair}}{3 \text{ hours}} = \frac{1}{3} \text{ chair per hour}$$

In 1 hour, Jay can build $\frac{1}{3}$ of a chair.

Now, figure out Kay's rate of work.

$$\text{Kay's rate} = \frac{1 \text{ chair}}{5 \text{ hours}} = \frac{1}{5} \text{ chair per hour}$$

In 1 hour, Kay can build $\frac{1}{5}$ of a chair.

Together, then, Jay and Kay can build $\frac{1}{3} + \frac{1}{5}$ of a chair in an hour. This is the "adding rates" principle in action.

Simplify the sum of fractions.

$$\overset{5}{\underset{3}{\frac{1}{}}} \times \overset{3}{\underset{5}{\frac{1}{}}} = \frac{8}{15} \text{ chair per hour}$$

Together, Jay and Kay build $\frac{8}{15}$ of a chair in 1 hour.

Now use the full Rate × Time = Work equation. The Work is 8 chairs. The Time is unknown. Therefore:

$$\text{Rate} \times \text{Time} = \text{Work}$$

$$\frac{8}{15} \times T = 8 \text{ chairs}$$

$$T = 8\left(\frac{15}{8}\right)$$

$$T = 15$$

It takes Jay and Kay, working together, 15 hours to build 8 chairs.

As with Rate-Time-Distance problems, keep the various quantities separate. If you need to use the same equation more than once, distinguish the different cases clearly. For instance, there could be three cases in this problem: Jay working alone, Kay working alone, or the two of them working together.

If you...	Then you...	Like this:
See a work problem	Use Rate × Time = Work, choosing work units and often adding rates	$7 \dfrac{\text{goblets}}{\text{hr}} \times 3 \text{ hrs} = 21 \text{ goblets}$

Check Your Skills

8. It takes Albert 6 hours to build a shelf. Betty can do the same work twice as fast. How many shelves can Albert and Betty, working together, build in a 24-hour period?

Answer can be found on pages 389–390.

Fractions and Percents in Word Problems: *Of* Means *Times*

Many word problems involve fractional amounts or percents. Remember that word problems always have a real context. This means that fractional amounts are fractional amounts *of* something. Percents are percents *of* something. Neither fractions nor percents live in a vacuum.

As you already know, *of* means *times* in the context of fractions and percents. Try an example:

> At a birthday party, children can choose one of the following 3 flavors of ice cream: chocolate, vanilla, or strawberry. If $\dfrac{1}{2}$ of the children choose chocolate, 20% of the children choose vanilla, and the remaining 15 children choose strawberry, how many children are at the party?

First, identify what the question wants. It asks for the total number of kids at the party. Label that number *n*.

The problem contains a Part + Part = Whole relationship—or rather, Part + Part + Part = Whole.

> Kids who choose chocolate + Kids who choose vanilla + Kids who choose strawberry = Total kids

Replace all of these with variables for the moment.

$c + v + s = n$

The question gives you *s* directly. It tells you 15 kids choose strawberry, so this can be put in your equation:

$c + v + 15 = n$

MANHATTAN PREP

How many kids choose chocolate? You don't have an absolute number, but you know that $\frac{1}{2}$ of the kids choose this flavor. To emphasize the point, you can say that $\frac{1}{2}$ of *all* kids choose chocolate. Express this as an equation.

$\frac{1}{2}$ of all kids choose chocolate $\frac{1}{2}n = c$

Note that the verb—in this case, *choose*—represents the equals sign.

Likewise, 20% of the kids (all kids) choose vanilla.

20% of all kids choose vanilla $0.2n = v$

Rewrite $\frac{1}{2}n$ as $0.5n$. Replace c and v in the main Part + Part + Part equation.

$c + v + 15 = n$

$0.5n + 0.2n + 15 = n$

Now solve for n.

$0.7n + 15 = n$

$15 = 0.3n$

$150 = 3n$

$50 = n$

There are 50 kids at the party.

If you...	Then you...	Like this:
See a fraction or a percent in a word problem	Figure out what the fraction or percent is *of*, and write *of* as *times*. The verb in the sentence represents the equals sign.	$\frac{1}{2}$ of kids choose chocolate $\frac{1}{2}n = c$ 20% of kids choose vanilla $0.2n = v$

Check Your Skills

9. Every junior at Central High School studies exactly one language: 75 percent of the juniors study Gaelic, one-sixth of the juniors study Spanish, and the other 7 juniors study Tagalog. How many juniors are there at Central High School?

Answer can be found on page 390.

Check Your Skills Answer Key

1. **0.9 kg:** First, translate the information in the question stem. Then, use algebra rules to solve for the weight of the lighter jug.

$$H = \text{weight heavy}$$
$$L = \text{weight light} = ?$$

$H + L = 2.2$	"The total weight...is 2.2 kilograms."
$L = H - 0.4$	"The lighter jug weighs 0.4 kilogram less than the heavier jug."
$L + 0.4 = H$	Rearrange.
$H + L = 2.2$	Substitute.
$(L + 0.4) + L = 2.2$	
$2L + 0.4 = 2.2$	Simplify.
$2L = 1.8$	
$L = 0.9$	

2. **$7,000 per month:** First, translate. When the problem mentions something for which you know a standard formula (in this case average), write down that standard formula. Also, when the problem has multiple time periods, organize the information carefully.

First 3 months:

$$\text{Average monthly pay} = \frac{\text{Total pay for 3 months}}{\text{Months}}$$

$$\$10,000 = \frac{\text{Total pay for 3 months}}{3}$$

The total pay for the first 3 months is $10,000 × 3 = $30,000.

Last 9 months:

$$\text{Average monthly pay} = \frac{\text{Total pay for 9 months}}{\text{Months}}$$

$$\$6,000 = \frac{\text{Total pay for 9 months}}{9 \text{ months}}$$

The total pay for the last 9 months is $6,000 × 9 = $54,000.

Next, set up the formula to find the average for the overall 12-month period and solve.

$$\text{Average monthly pay} = \frac{\text{Total pay for all months}}{\text{All months}}$$

$$\text{Average monthly pay} = \frac{30,000 + 54,000}{3 + 9}$$

$$\text{Average} = \frac{\overset{7}{84},000}{\cancel{12}} = 7,000$$

9

3. **10:** The candy shop sold 50 candy bars in January, but only 40 in February, for a decrease of 10 candy bars. Here's how to do the math:

> January: Total revenue = Price × Quantity = $3 per bar × 50 bars = $150

> February: New price = Old price + $1 = $3 + $1 = $4 per bar

> New total revenue = Old revenue + $10 = $150 + $10 = $160

Total revenue	=	Price × Quantity
$160	=	$4 per bar × Q bars
40 candy bars	=	Q

> January Qty − February Qty = 50 bars − 40 bars = 10 bars

4. **$4:** If the price of one stapler is S and the price of one coffee mug is C, then $S - C$ represents the difference in price between the two items. In other words, the question is, "What is $S - C$?"

Translate the rest of the math in the question stem.

$$7S + 5C = \$36 \qquad 2S + C = \$10 \qquad S - C = ?$$

When you're asked for a combo, or combination of variables, examine the equations to see whether you can solve directly for the entire combo (in this case, $S - C$). That's faster than finding S and C individually.

Take a look at what happens when you multiply the second equation by 4.

$$2S + C = 10$$

$$8S + 4C = 40$$

Subtract the first equation from the new second equation.

$$
\begin{array}{rcl}
8S + 4C & = & 40 \\
-(7S + 5C & = & 36) \\
\hline
S - C & = & 4
\end{array}
$$

A stapler costs $4 more than a coffee mug. You might be thinking that you would never think to do this yourself. Now that you know it's possible, though, you can think about it. In the future, take a moment to examine the equations to see whether this shortcut exists. It often does! If not, you can solve for the variables individually, with substitution or elimination.

5. **336 hours:**

> 1 week = 7 days

$$2 \text{ weeks} \times \frac{7 \text{ days}}{1 \text{ week}} = 14 \text{ days} \qquad\qquad \text{weeks} \times \frac{\text{days}}{\text{week}} = \text{days}$$

MANHATTAN PREP

$$1 \text{ day} = 24 \text{ hours}$$

$$14 \text{ days} \times \frac{24 \text{ hours}}{1 \text{ day}} = 336 \text{ hours} \qquad \cancel{\text{days}} \times \frac{\text{hours}}{\cancel{\text{day}}} = \text{hours}$$

Or, in one line:

$$2 \text{ weeks} \times \frac{7 \text{ days}}{1 \text{ week}} \times \frac{24 \text{ hours}}{1 \text{ day}} = 336 \text{ hours}$$

6. **3,840 seconds:** Convert 1 hour to seconds and 4 minutes to seconds.

$$1 \text{ hours} \times \frac{60 \text{ minutes}}{1 \text{ hour}} \times \frac{60 \text{ seconds}}{1 \text{ minute}} = 3,600 \text{ seconds}$$

$$4 \text{ minutes} \times \frac{60 \text{ seconds}}{1 \text{ minute}} = 240 \text{ seconds}$$

$$3,600 \text{ seconds} + 240 \text{ seconds} = 3,840 \text{ seconds}$$

7. **2.5 miles per hour:** To find Amanda's average speed, find the total distance and the total time.

Total distance = 24 miles + 6 miles = 30 miles
Total time = time for first part of trip + 4 hours

Now find the time Amanda took for the first part of the trip.

Rate × Time = Distance
3 miles per hour × t = 24 miles
t = 8 hours

The total time is 8 + 4 = 12 hours. Finally, calculate her average speed.

$$\text{Average} = \frac{\text{Total distance}}{\text{Total time}}$$

$$a = \frac{30 \text{ miles}}{12 \text{ hours}} = 2.5 \text{ miles per hour}$$

8. **12:** First, find Albert's rate, using the formula Rate × Time = Work.

$$r \times 6 \text{ hours} = 1 \text{ shelf}$$
$$r = \frac{1 \text{ shelf}}{6 \text{ hours}}$$

Albert's rate is $\frac{1}{6}$ shelf per hour.

Betty can work twice as fast, so her rate is $2 \times \dfrac{1}{6} = \dfrac{1}{3}$ shelf per hour.

Add the rates to find their combined rate:

$$\frac{1}{6} + \frac{1}{3} = \frac{1}{6} + \frac{2}{6} = \frac{3}{6} = \frac{1}{2}$$

Together, they can build $\dfrac{1}{2}$ of a shelf per hour. Finally, calculate how much work is completed in 24 hours at their combined rate:

$$\frac{1}{2} \text{ shelf per hour} \times 24 \text{ hours} = 12 \text{ shelves}$$

9. **84:** Define variables and translate the information.

> G = the number of juniors studying Gaelic
> S = the number of juniors studying Spanish
> T = the number of juniors studying Tagalog
> J = the total number of juniors

J = total number of juniors = $G + S + T = ?$

75% of juniors study Gaelic: $\dfrac{3}{4} J = G$

One-sixth of juniors study Spanish: $\dfrac{1}{6} J = S$

The other 7 study Tagalog: $7 = T$

Now substitute these values into the equation $G + S + T = J$, and solve for J.

$$\frac{3}{4} J + \frac{1}{6} J + 7 = J$$
$$\frac{9}{12} J + \frac{2}{12} J + 7 = J$$
$$\frac{11}{12} J + 7 = J$$
$$7 = J - \frac{11}{12} J$$
$$7 = \frac{1}{12} J$$
$$(7)(12) = J$$
$$84 = J$$

Chapter Review: Drill Sets

Drill 1

Translate and solve the following problems.

1. In an office, there are 5 more computers than there are employees. If there are 10 employees in the office, how many computers are there?

2. If −5 is 7 more than z, what is $\dfrac{z}{4}$?

3. Two conference rooms have a combined capacity of 75 people. Conference Room A can accommodate 15 fewer people than Conference Room B. How many people can Conference Room B accommodate?

4. Norman is 12 years older than Michael. In 6 years, he will be twice as old as Michael. How old is Norman now?

5. Three lawyers each earn an average (arithmetic mean) of $300 per hour. How much money have they earned in total after each has worked 4 hours?

6. A clothing store bought a container of 100 shirts for $20. If the store sold all of the shirts at $0.50 per shirt, what is the store's gross profit on the box?

7. There are 2 trees in the front yard of a school. The trees have a combined height of 60 feet, and the taller tree is three times the height of the shorter tree. What is the height, in feet, of the shorter tree?

8. Louise is three times as old as Mary. In 5 years, Louise will be twice as old as Mary. How old is Mary now?

9. The average of 2, 13, and x is 10. What is x?

10. Four children collect 33 candies that fall out of a piñata. If 3 of the children pick up the same number of candies and the fourth child picks up three fewer candies than each of the other children, how many candies does the fourth child collect?

Drill 2

Translate and solve the following problems.

11. To put on a concert, a band pays $10,000 to rent a venue and another $15,000 for security; the band has no other costs. Attendees at the concert pay an average price of $40 for a ticket to the concert. If everyone who attends the concert must purchase a ticket, how many tickets must the band sell to make a gross profit of $7,000 on the concert?

12. Toshi is 7 years older than his brother Kosuke, who is twice as old as their younger sister Junko. If Junko is 8 years old, how old is Toshi?

13. A plane leaves Chicago in the morning and makes 3 flights before returning. The plane traveled twice as far on the first flight as on the second flight, and the plane traveled three times as far on the second flight as on the third flight. If the third flight was 45 miles, how many miles was the first flight?

14. It costs a certain bicycle factory $10,000 to operate for one month, plus $300 for each bicycle produced during the month. Each of the bicycles sells for a retail price of $700. The gross profit of the factory is measured by total income from sales minus the production costs of the bicycles and the factory operation cost. If 50 bicycles are produced and sold during the month, what is the factory's gross profit?

15. Arnaldo earns $11 for each ticket that he sells, plus a bonus of $2 per ticket for each ticket he sells over the first 100 tickets. If Arnaldo was paid $2,400, how many tickets did he sell?

16. If the average (arithmetic mean) of the five numbers $x - 3$, x, $x + 3$, $x + 4$, and $x + 11$ is 45, what is the value of x?

17. Ten years ago, Sana was half as old as Byron. If Byron is now 15 years older than Sana, how old will Sana be in 7 years?

18. John buys 5 books with an average (arithmetic mean) price of $9. If John then buys another book with a price of $15, what is the average price of the 6 books?

19. Alicia is producing a magazine that costs $3 per magazine to print. In addition, she has to pay $10,500 to her staff to design the issue. If Alicia sells each magazine for $10, how many magazines must she sell to break even?

20. Every week, Renee is paid $40 per hour for the first 40 hours she works and $80 per hour for each hour she works after the first 40 hours. If she earned $2,000 last week, how many hours did she work?

Drill 3

Translate and solve the following unit conversion problems.

21. An American football field is 100 yards long. What is this length in feet? (1 yard = 3 feet)

22. How many gallons of water would it take to fill a tank with a capacity of 200 pints? (1 gallon = 8 pints)

23. A 40 kilogram suitcase weighs how many pounds? (1 kilogram = 2.2 pounds)

24. Boston received 2.5 feet of snow yesterday. How many inches of snow did Boston receive? (1 foot = 12 inches)

25. What is the temperature in Fahrenheit when it is 30 degrees Celsius? $\left(C = \dfrac{5}{9}(F - 32) \right)$

26. How many minutes are there in 10 days?

27. On her bicycle, Miriam travels 50 yards in 10 seconds. How many feet does she travel in 2 minutes? (1 yard = 3 feet)

    (A) 500
    (B) 900
    (C) 1,800

28. A recipe calls for 1.6 cups of sugar and 2 quarts of flour. How many gallons is the resulting mixture of sugar and flour? (1 gallon = 4 quarts; 1 quart = 4 cups) Leave your answer in decimal form. (For you chefs: ignore the difference between dry measures and liquid measures.)

29. How many 1-inch-square tiles would it take to cover the floor of a closet that has dimensions 5 feet by 4 feet? (1 foot = 12 inches)

30. A pool has sprung a leak and is losing water at a rate of 5 milliliters per second. How many liters of water is this pool losing per hour? (1 liter = 1,000 milliliters)

Drill 4

Translate and solve the following rate problems.

31. Jiang drove away from Marksville at a constant speed of 64 miles per hour. How far was she from Marksville after 2 hours and 15 minutes of driving?

32. Tyrone began the drive from Billington to Camville at 7:30. He drove at a constant speed of 40 miles per hour for the first hour and 50 miles per hour after that. If the distance from Billington to Camville is 160 miles, at what time did Tyrone arrive in Camville?

    (A) 10:30
    (B) 10:54
    (C) 11:00

33. If Roger took 2 hours to walk to a store that is 3 miles away, and then ran home along the same path in 1 hour, what was Roger's average speed, in miles per hour, for the round trip?

34. Sue and Rob began running a 10-mile path around a lake at the same time. Sue ran at a constant rate of 8 miles per hour. Rob ran at a constant rate of $6\frac{2}{3}$ miles per hour. Sue finished running the 10-mile path how much sooner than Rob did?

35. Svetlana ran the first 5 kilometers of a 10-kilometer race at a speed of 12 kilometers per hour. At what speed will she have to run the last 5 kilometers of the race if she wants to complete the 10-kilometer race in 55 minutes?

Drill 5

Translate and solve the following work problems.

36. A factory must complete production of 1,400 plastic bottles in 4 hours. How many bottles must be produced per hour (at a constant rate) to meet this deadline?

37. A standard machine can fill 15 gallons of paint per hour. A deluxe machine fills gallons of paint at twice the rate of a standard machine. How long will it take a deluxe machine to fill 150 gallons of paint?

38. Machine A produces 15 widgets per minute. Machine B produces 18 widgets per minute. How many widgets will the machines produce together in 20 minutes?

39. At 2:00pm, a hose was placed into an empty pool and turned on. The pool, which holds 680 gallons of water, reached its capacity at 5:24pm. How many gallons of water per hour did the hose add to the pool?

40. Machine X, working alone at a constant rate, can produce a certain number of chocolates in 5 hours. Machine Y, working alone at a constant rate, can produce the same number of chocolates in 2 hours. If Machine X produces 180 chocolates per hour, how many chocolates does Machine Y produce per hour?
    (A) 72
    (B) 450
    (C) 900

Drill 6

Translate and solve the following word problems.

41. If Ken's salary were 20% higher, it would be 20% less than Lorena's. If Lorena's salary is $60,000, what is Ken's salary?

42. A $10 shirt is marked up by 30%, then by an additional 50%. What is the new price of the shirt?

43. A share of Stock Q increased in value by 20%, then decreased in value by 10%. The new value of a share of Stock Q is what percent of its initial value?

44. In a class of 200 students, 40 students earned A's on their test, while 64 of the students received B's, 18 received D's, and 6 received F's. If students can receive only A, B, C, D, or F as grades, what percent of the students received C's?

45. Akira currently weighs 160 pounds. If he must lose 8 pounds in order to qualify for a certain sporting event, what percent of his body weight must he lose in order to qualify?
    (A) 0.05%
    (B) 0.5%
    (C) 5%

Drill 7

Translate and solve the following word problems.

46. Lily stayed up all last night to watch a meteor shower from her roof. Ten percent of the meteors visible from her roof were exceptionally bright, and of these, 80 percent inspired Lily to write a haiku. If Lily was inspired to write a haiku by 20 exceptionally bright meteors, how many meteors were visible from her roof last night?

47. Bingwa the African elephant can lift 6% of his body weight using his trunk alone. If Bingwa weighs 1,000 times as much as a white-handed gibbon, how many gibbons can Bingwa lift at once with his trunk?

48. Last year, Country X received $\frac{7}{4}$ as much precipitation as Country Y, which received $\frac{2}{3}$ as much precipitation as Country Z. If Country X received 280 centimeters of precipitation, how much precipitation, in centimeters, did Country Z receive?

    (A) 160
    (B) 240
    (C) 420

49. In Farrah's workday playlist, $\frac{1}{3}$ of the songs are jazz, $\frac{1}{4}$ are R & B, $\frac{1}{6}$ are rock, $\frac{1}{12}$ are country, and the remainder are world music. What fraction of the songs in Farrah's playlist are world music?

50. At a music convention, $\frac{2}{5}$ of the attendees play no musical instrument, $\frac{1}{4}$ play exactly one musical instrument, $\frac{3}{10}$ play exactly two musical instruments, and the remaining 8 attendees play three or more musical instruments. How many people are attending the convention?

Drill 8

Translate and solve the following word problems.

51. Yemi wants to buy a blue umbrella for no more than $25. At a certain store, $\frac{3}{5}$ of the umbrellas cost more than $25, and of the remaining umbrellas, $\frac{7}{8}$ are not blue. If the store has 400 umbrellas, how many of the umbrellas meet Yemi's requirements?

    (A) 20
    (B) 140
    (C) 210

52. To make one serving of her signature punch, Mariko mixes $\frac{1}{2}$ cup of grape juice, $\frac{3}{4}$ cup of passion fruit juice, and $\frac{1}{8}$ cup of sparkling water. If Mariko makes 22 cups of punch, how many servings of punch will there be?

    (A) 16
    (B) 20
    (C) 30

53. Of the movies in Santosh's collection, $\frac{1}{3}$ are animated features, $\frac{1}{4}$ are live-action features, and the remainder are documentaries. If $\frac{2}{5}$ of the documentaries are depressing, what fraction of the films in Santosh's collection are depressing documentaries?

54. Of all the homes on Gotham Street, $\frac{1}{3}$ are termite-ridden, and $\frac{3}{5}$ of these are collapsing. What fraction of the homes are termite-ridden, but NOT collapsing?

55. A bag contains only red and green marbles. Of these, $\frac{3}{4}$ of the marbles in the bag are green. Of the green marbles, $\frac{1}{3}$ are cracked. If there are 6,000 red marbles in the bag, how many cracked green marbles are there?

Drill Sets Solutions

Drill 1

1. **15 computers:** Let c = the number of computers and e = the number of employees.

   The "more…than" translation is tricky. Which are there more of, computers or employees? There are more computers, so add 5 to the smaller group, employees: $c = e + 5$. The bigger number equals the smaller number plus 5.

   $$c = e + 5$$
   $$e = 10$$
   $$c = (10) + 5 = 15$$

2. **−3:**

   $$-5 = z + 7$$
   $$-12 = z$$

   $$\frac{z}{4} = \frac{-12}{4} = -3$$

3. **45 people:** Let a = the capacity of Conference Room A, and let b = the capacity of Conference Room B.

   $$\text{Eq 1: } a + b = 75$$
   $$\text{Eq 2: } a = b - 15$$

   The second translation is tricky. Which room can hold more people, A or B? Room B is bigger, so subtract 15 from room B to get the capacity in room A.

   The second equation already isolates a. Substitute into the first equation, and solve for b.

   $$(b - 15) + b = 75$$
   $$2b - 15 = 75$$
   $$2b = 90$$
   $$b = 45$$

4. **18 years old:** Make a table to keep track of the two people and the two points in time.

	Now	In 6 years
Norman	N	$N + 6$
Michael	M	$M + 6$

$N = M + 12$ — Translate the first sentence into an equation.

$(N + 6) = 2 (M + 6)$ — Translate the second sentence into an equation. Use the ages in 6 years, not the ages now.

$N - 12 = M$ — You want to solve for N, so rewrite the first equation to isolate the variable you *don't* want: M.

$N + 6 = 2(N - 12 + 6)$ — Insert $N - 12$ for M in the second equation and simplify.
$N + 6 = 2(N - 6)$
$N + 6 = 2N - 12$
$18 = N$

5. **$3,600:** The lawyers each earn the same amount, so calculate what one lawyer earns, then multiply by 3:

One lawyer earns:	$4 \times \$300 = \$1,200$
The three lawyers together earn:	$\$1,200 \times 3 = \$3,600$

6. **$30 profit:** Let p = profit, r = revenue, and c = cost.

While the question specifies the cost of the 100 shirts, it doesn't give you the revenue directly; use Revenue = Price (per shirt) × Quantity (of shirts). Therefore:

$$\text{Profit} = \text{Revenue} - \text{Cost}$$
$$p = (\$0.50 \times 100) - (\$20)$$
$$p = \$50 - \$20$$
$$p = \$30$$

7. **15 feet:** Let s = the height of the shorter tree and t = the height of the taller tree. Translate the equations.

$$s + t = 60$$
$$3s = t$$

The second equation is already isolated for t; substitute into the first equation and solve.

$$s + (3s) = 60$$
$$4s = 60$$
$$s = 15$$

8. **5 years old:**

	Now	In 5 years
Louise	L	$L + 5$
Mary	M	$M + 5$

$L = 3M$ — Translate the first sentence into an equation.
$(L + 5) = 2(M + 5)$ — Translate the second sentence into an equation.
$(3M + 5) = 2(M + 5)$ — Insert $3M$ for L in the second equation and solve.
$3M + 5 = 2M + 10$
$M = 5$

9. **15:**

$$\text{Average} = \frac{\text{Sum}}{\text{\# of terms}}$$
$$10 = \frac{2+13+x}{3}$$
$$30 = 2+13+x$$
$$30 = 15 + x$$
$$15 = x$$

10. **6 candies:** Let c stand for each of the three children who pick up the same number of candies. Let f stand for the fourth child. Therefore:

      Eq 1: $c + c + c + f = 33$ or $3c + f = 33$
      Eq 2: $f = c - 3$

If you substitute the second equation into the first, note that you will be solving for c, not f. Make sure to solve for f at the end.

$$3c + f = 33$$
$$3c + (c - 3) = 33$$
$$4c = 36$$
$$c = 9$$

Therefore, $f = c - 3 = 9 - 3 = 6$.

Alternatively, you can rearrange the second equation to isolate c. The second equation becomes $f + 3 = c$. When you plug into the first equation, you will be able to solve directly for f.

$$3c + f = 33$$
$$3(f + 3) + f = 33$$
$$3f + 9 + f = 33$$
$$4f = 24$$
$$f = 6$$

Drill 2

11. **800 tickets:** Let n = the number of tickets sold. Recall that Profit = Revenue − Cost. The problem indicates that the band wants a profit of $7,000. What are the revenues and the costs? Set up what you know:

      Revenue: $40n$
      Costs: $10,000 + 15,000 = 25,000$
      Profit = 7,000

$$\text{Profit} = \text{Revenue} - \text{Cost}$$
$$7{,}000 = 40n - 25{,}000$$

$$32{,}000 = 40n$$
$$\frac{32{,}000}{40} = n$$

$$\frac{3{,}200}{4} = n \qquad \text{Divide top and bottom of fraction by 10.}$$

$$800 = n \qquad \text{Divide top and bottom of fraction by 4.}$$

12. **23 years old:** Let T = Toshi's age, K = Kosuke's age, and J = Junko's age.

$$T = K + 7$$
$$K = 2J$$
$$J = 8$$

Substitute and solve.

$$K = 2 \times J = 2 \times (8) = 16$$
$$T = K + 7 = (16) + 7 = 23$$

13. **270 miles:** Let F = the distance of the first flight, S = the distance of the second flight, and T = the distance of the third flight. What is F?

$$F = 2S \qquad \text{The first flight traveled twice as far as the second flight.}$$
$$S = 3T \qquad \text{The second flight traveled three times as far as the third flight.}$$
$$T = 45$$

Substitute and solve.

$$S = 3 \times (45) = 135$$
$$F = 2 \times (135) = 270$$

14. **$10,000 profit:** Recall that Profit = Revenue − Cost. Set up equations to find the revenues and costs?

$$\text{Revenue} = 50 \times 700 = 35{,}000$$
$$\text{Cost} = 10{,}000 + (50 \times 300) = 10{,}000 + 15{,}000 = 25{,}000$$
$$\text{Profit} = \text{Revenue} - \text{Cost} = 35{,}000 - 25{,}000 = 10{,}000$$

15. **200 tickets:** Let x equal the total number of tickets sold. Therefore, $(x - 100)$ is equal to the number of tickets Arnoldo sold beyond the first 100.

$$11x + 2(x - 100) = 2{,}400$$
$$11x + 2x - 200 = 2{,}400$$
$$13x = 2{,}600$$
$$x = 200$$

16. **42:** Multiplying 45 by 5 is a little annoying (because the number is large), so don't immediately multiply. Hold off to see whether you can simplify any part of the math first.

$$\frac{(x-3)+(x)+(x+3)+(x+4)+(x+11)}{5} = 45$$

$$\frac{5x+15}{5} = 45$$

$$x + 3 = 45$$

$$x = 42$$

17. **32 years old:** Let S = Sana's age and B = Byron's age. What is $S + 7$? Set up a table:

	10 years ago	Now	7 years from now
Sana	$S - 10$	S	$S + 7$
Byron	$B - 10$	B	$B + 7$

$$S - 10 = \frac{B - 10}{2}$$

$$B = S + 15$$

Substitute the second equation into the first, and solve for S.

$$S - 10 = \frac{(S + 15) - 10}{2}$$
$$2S - 20 = S + 5$$
$$S = 25$$

You're not quite done! The question asks for $S + 7$: $(25) + 7 = 32$.

18. **$10:** To find the average, you need to know the sum John spent on all 6 books. First, find the cost of the original 5 books.

$$\frac{\text{Sum}}{\text{\# of Terms}} = \text{Average}$$

$$\text{Sum} = (\text{Average})(\text{\# of terms}) = (\$9)(5) = \$45$$

Next, find the sum of the cost for all 6 books, and use that to find the new average.

Sum of the cost of all 6 books = $45 + $15 = $60
Number of books = 6

$$\text{New Average} = \frac{\$60}{6} = \$10$$

19. **1,500 magazines:** Let m = the number of magazines sold.

$$\text{Total cost} = 3m + 10,500$$
$$\text{Total revenue} = 10m$$

Breaking even occurs when total revenue equals total cost. In other words, profit is $0. Therefore:

$$3m + 10,500 = 10m$$
$$10,500 = 7m$$
$$1,500 = m$$

20. **45 hours:** Let h equal the number of hours Renee worked. She must have worked more than 40 hours, because she earned more than ($40/hour)(40 hours) = $1,600. Therefore, let $h - 40$ represent the number of hours she worked after the first 40 hours.

$$40(40) + (h - 40)(80) = 2,000$$
$$1,600 + 80h - 3,200 = 2,000$$
$$80h - 1,600 = 2,000$$
$$80h = 3,600$$
$$h = 45$$

Drill 3

21. **300 feet:**

$$100 \ \cancel{\text{yards}} \times \frac{3 \text{ feet}}{1 \ \cancel{\text{yard}}} = 300 \text{ feet}$$

22. **25 gallons:**

$$200 \ \cancel{\text{pints}} \times \frac{1 \text{ gallon}}{8 \ \cancel{\text{pints}}} = \frac{200}{8} \text{ gallons} = 25 \text{ gallons}$$

23. **88 pounds:**

$$40 \ \cancel{\text{kilograms}} \times \frac{2.2 \text{ pounds}}{1 \ \cancel{\text{kilogram}}} = 40 \times 2.2 \text{ pounds}$$

Swap a decimal place between the 40 and the 2.2: 40 loses one decimal place to become 4, and 2.2 gains one decimal place to become 22. Now multiply:

$$4 \times 22 = 88$$

24. **30 inches:**

$$2.5 \ \cancel{\text{feet}} \times \frac{12 \text{ inches}}{1 \ \cancel{\text{foot}}} = 30 \text{ inches}$$

25. **86° Fahrenheit:** Use the conversion formula, replacing the variable C with the temperature in Celsius.

$$C = \frac{5}{9}(F-32)$$

$$30 = \frac{5}{9}(F-32)$$

$$\overset{6}{\cancel{30}} \times \frac{9}{\cancel{5}} = F - 32$$

$$54 = F - 32$$

$$86 = F$$

26. **14,400 minutes:** One day has 24 hours. Each of those hours has 60 minutes. Set up conversion ratios to solve.

$$10 \ \cancel{\text{days}} \times \frac{24 \ \cancel{\text{hours}}}{1 \ \cancel{\text{day}}} \times \frac{60 \ \text{minutes}}{1 \ \cancel{\text{hour}}} = 14,400 \ \text{minutes}$$

To make the math a little easier, multiply 24 by 6, then add two zeros.

27. **(C):** Set up conversion ratios to solve.

$$\frac{50 \ \cancel{\text{yards}}}{1\cancel{0} \ \cancel{\text{seconds}}} \times \frac{3 \ \text{feet}}{1 \ \cancel{\text{yard}}} \times \frac{6\cancel{0} \ \cancel{\text{seconds}}}{1 \ \text{minute}} = 50 \times 3 \times 6 = 900 \ \frac{\text{feet}}{\text{min}}$$

Don't stop yet! The question asks how far Miriam can travel in 2 minutes, not just 1 minute. If she can travel 900 feet in 1 minute, then she can travel 900 × 2 = 1,800 feet in 2 minutes.

Alternatively, the answers are far enough apart to allow you to estimate. If Miriam can travel 50 yards in 10 seconds, then she can travel 50 × 6 = 300 yards in 60 seconds, or 1 minute. She can travel 600 yards, then, in 2 minutes. Since there are 3 feet for every yard, the answer has to be greater than 900. (Specifically, it is 600 × 3 = 1,800, but you can stop your calculations at any point that you realize only one answer would work.)

28. **0.6 gallons:** Convert both 1.6 cups and 2 quarts into gallons using conversion ratios.

$$1.6 \ \cancel{\text{cups}} \times \frac{1 \ \cancel{\text{quart}}}{4 \ \cancel{\text{cups}}} \times \frac{1 \ \text{gallon}}{4 \ \cancel{\text{quarts}}} = \frac{1.6}{16} \ \text{gallons} = 0.1 \ \text{gallons}$$

$$2 \ \cancel{\text{quarts}} \times \frac{1 \ \text{gallon}}{4 \ \cancel{\text{quarts}}} = \frac{2}{4} \ \text{gallons} = 0.5 \ \text{gallons}$$

0.1 gallons + 0.5 gallons = 0.6 gallons

29. **2,880 tiles:** There is a hidden trap in this question. The dimensions of this room are in square feet, not feet (because 5 feet × 4 feet = 20 square feet). To avoid this trap, convert the dimensions to inches first, then multiply.

$$5 \text{ feet} \times \frac{12 \text{ inches}}{1 \text{ foot}} = 60 \text{ inches}$$

$$4 \text{ feet} \times \frac{12 \text{ inches}}{1 \text{ foot}} = 48 \text{ inches}$$

The dimensions of the closet in inches are 60 inches by 48 inches, or 60 × 48 = 2,880 square inches. Each tile is 1 square inch, so it will take 2,880 tiles to cover the floor.

30. **18 liters per hour:** There is no mandatory order for processing the conversions. Start with 5 milliliters per second, and make the appropriate conversions.

$$\frac{5 \text{ milliliters}}{\text{second}} \times \frac{60 \text{ seconds}}{1 \text{ minute}} \times \frac{60 \text{ minutes}}{1 \text{ hour}} = \frac{5 \times 60 \times 60 \text{ milliliters}}{\text{hour}}$$

Don't multiply yet. Continue with the conversion to see whether you can simplify before you multiply.

$$\frac{5 \times 60 \times 60 \text{ milliliters}}{\text{hour}} \times \frac{1 \text{ liter}}{1,000 \text{ milliliters}} = \frac{5 \times 6 \times 6 \text{ liters}}{10 \text{ hours}} = \frac{18 \text{ liters}}{\text{hour}}$$

Drill 4

31. **144 miles:** Use the $D = RT$ formula to solve for Jiang's distance. Note that the time must be converted so that it is expressed only in hours rather than hours and minutes.

$$15 \text{ min} \times \left(\frac{1 \text{ hr}}{60 \text{ min}}\right) = \frac{1}{4} \text{ hr} = 0.25 \text{ hr}$$

Therefore, 2 hours and 15 minutes is equivalent to 2.25 hours. Now set up a table and solve:

D (mi)	=	R (mi/hr)	×	T (hr)
d	=	64	×	2.25

$$\frac{64 \text{ miles}}{\text{hour}} \times 2.25 \text{ hours} = 64 \times \frac{9}{4} = 16 \times 9 = 144 \text{ miles}$$

32. **(B):** Process the math in steps. For the first hour only, Tyrone drove 40 miles per hour (mph), so he drove a total of 40 miles in that first hour. After that, he still had another 160 − 40 = 120 miles to go at a speed of 50 mph. Use the $D = RT$ formula to determine how long this took.

$$50t = 120$$
$$t = \frac{120}{50} = \frac{12}{5} = 2\frac{2}{5} = 2.4 \text{ hours}$$

Tyrone started at 7:30. As of 8:30, he had driven 40 miles. Then he took 2.4 hours to drive the remaining 120 miles. This took more than 2 hours, so the time is later than 10:30, but not as long as 2.5 hours, so the time is not yet 11:00. The only answer that works is answer (B).

If you want to calculate exactly, the math is shown below, but remember: On the GMAT, it's only necessary to find the right answer. It's not always necessary to do all of the official math!

$$\frac{2}{5} \text{ hours} \times \frac{\cancel{60}^{12} \text{ minutes}}{1 \text{ hour}} = 2 \times 12 = 24 \text{ minutes}$$

The additional time after 8:30 is 2 hours and 24 minutes, so Tyrone arrived in Camville at 10:54.

33. **2 miles per hour:** Find the average rate by dividing the total distance traveled by the total time spent traveling. In this case, Roger traveled 3 miles to the store and 3 miles back, covering a total of 6 miles in 3 hours.

$$R = \frac{(3+3) \text{ miles}}{(2+1) \text{ hours}} = \frac{6 \text{ miles}}{3 \text{ hours}} = 2 \frac{\text{miles}}{\text{hour}}$$

34. **15 minutes:** Use the $D = RT$ equation to calculate how long it took each individual to run the path. Sue ran the 10-mile path at a rate of 8 miles per hour. To get her time, set up a table and solve:

D (mi)	=	R (mi/hr)	×	T (hr)
10	=	8	×	t

$$10 = 8t$$
$$\frac{5}{4} = t$$

Therefore, Sue completed the path in 1 hour and 15 minutes.

Rob ran the 10-mile path at a rate of $6\frac{2}{3}$ mi/hr $= \frac{20}{3}$ mi/hr. To get his time, set up a table and solve:

D (mi)	=	R (mi/hr)	×	T (hr)
10	=	$\frac{20}{3}$	×	t

$$10 = \frac{20}{3}t$$

$$\frac{3}{20} \times 10 = t$$

$$\frac{3}{2} = t$$

Therefore, Rob ran the path in 1 hour and 30 minutes.

Finally, subtract Sue's time from Rob's time to calculate how much sooner Sue finished.

$$1 \text{ hour } 30 \text{ min} - 1 \text{ hour } 15 \text{ min} = 15 \text{ min}$$

35. **10 kilometers per hour:** In order to calculate Svetlana's speed during the second half of the race, first calculate how long it took her to run the first half of the race. The first half of the race is 5 kilometers in length, and Svetlana ran at a speed of 12 kilometers per hour. Set up a table and solve:

D (km)	=	R (km/hr)	×	T (hr)
5	=	12	×	t

$$5 = 12t$$

$$t = \frac{5}{12} \text{ hr}$$

To calculate the time Svetlana has available to run the second half of the race, subtract her time for the first half of the race from her goal time for the entire race. To do this calculation, first convert her goal time from minutes to hours.

$$55 \text{ min} \times \frac{1 \text{ hr}}{60 \text{ min}} = \frac{55}{60} \text{ hr} = \frac{11}{12} \text{ hr}$$

Then subtract Svetlana's time for the first half of the race from this value.

$$\frac{11}{12} \text{ hr} - \frac{5}{12} \text{ hr} = \frac{6}{12} \text{ hr} = \frac{1}{2} \text{ hr} = 0.5 \text{ hr}$$

Svetlana must complete the second 5 kilometers in 0.5 hours. Use the $D = RT$ equation to solve for Svetlana's required speed.

D (km)	=	R (km/hr)	×	T (hr)
5	=	r	×	0.5

$$5 = 0.5r$$
$$10 = r$$

Svetlana must run the second half of the race at a speed of 10 kilometers per hour in order to finish the entire race in 55 minutes.

Drill 5

36. **350 bottles per hour:** Use the $W = RT$ formula to solve for the number of bottles produced per hour.

W (bot)	=	R (bot/hr)	×	T (hr)
1,400	=	r	×	4

$$1,400 = 4r$$
$$350 = r$$

37. **5 hours:** First, calculate the rate of the deluxe machine by multiplying the rate of the standard machine by 2. If the standard machine can fill 15 gallons per hour, then the deluxe machine can fill 30 gallons per hour.

   Use the $W = RT$ formula to solve for the amount of time the machine takes to fill 150 gallons of paint.

W (gal)	=	R (gal/hr)	×	T (hr)
150	=	30	×	t

$$150 = 30t$$
$$t = \frac{15\cancel{0}}{3\cancel{0}} = \frac{15}{3} = 5$$

38. **660 widgets:** Use two separate $W = RT$ equations, one for Machine A and one for Machine B, to calculate how many widgets each machine produces in 20 minutes.

	W (wid)	=	R (wid/min)	×	T (min)
Machine A	a	=	15	×	20
Machine A	b	=	18	×	20

Machine A: $a = 15 \times 20 = 300$ widgets
Machine B: $b = 18 \times 20 = 360$ widgets

To calculate the total number of widgets produced, add the values for the individual machines:

300 widgets + 360 widgets = 660 widgets

39. **200 gallons per hour:** First, find the time it took to fill the pool.

$$5:24\text{pm} - 2:00\text{pm} = 3 \text{ hours } 24 \text{ minutes}$$

Next, convert the minutes portion of this time to hours.

$$24 \text{ min} \times \left(\frac{1 \text{ hr}}{60 \text{ min}}\right) = \frac{24}{60} \text{ hr} = \frac{2}{5} \text{ hr} = 0.4 \text{ hr}$$

It took 3.4 hours to fill the pool and the capacity of the pool is 680 gallons. Use the $W = RT$ equation to solve for the rate.

W (gal)	=	R (gal/hr)	×	T (hr)
680	=	r	×	3.4

$$680 = 3.4r$$

$$r = \frac{680}{3.4} = \frac{6800}{34} = \frac{\overset{2}{\cancel{68}}00}{\cancel{34}} = 200 \frac{\text{gallons}}{\text{hour}}$$

40. **(B):** Machine X produces 180 chocolates per hour; use the $W = RT$ formula to determine how many chocolates it produces in 5 hours.

W (choc)	=	R (choc/hr)	×	T (hr)
W	=	180	×	5

$$W = 180 \times 5$$
$$W = 900$$

Machine Y is capable of producing the same number, 900 chocolates, but in just 2 hours. Use the $W = RT$ formula again to find the rate for Machine Y.

W (choc)	=	R (choc/hr)	×	T (hr)
900	=	r	×	2

$$900 = r \times 2$$
$$450 = r$$

Drill 6

41. **$40,000:** Use decimal equivalents here, using 1 (or 100%) as a starting point and adding to 1 for an increase or subtracting from 1 for a decrease. For example, "If Ken's salary were 20% higher" can be translated as $1 + (20\%)(1) = 1 + 0.2 = 1.2$. Similarly, "20% less than" can be translated as $1 - (20\%)(1) = 1 - 0.2 = 0.8$. Therefore, 120% of Ken's salary is equal to 80% of Lorena's salary. Translate this into math and solve.

$$1.2K = 0.8(60,000)$$
$$K = \frac{0.8(60,000)}{1.2} \times \frac{10}{10}$$
$$K = \frac{8\left(\overset{5}{\cancel{60}},000\right)}{\cancel{12}}$$
$$K = 8(5,000)$$
$$K = 40,000$$

42. **$19.50:** When you are asked to multiply percents, it is usually best to use a fractional representation because you can then simplify before you multiply.

$$\$10 \times \frac{13\cancel{0}}{10\cancel{0}} \times \frac{15\cancel{0}}{10\cancel{0}}$$
$$= \$\cancel{10} \times \frac{13}{\cancel{10}} \times \frac{15}{10}$$
$$= \$13 \times \frac{3}{2}$$
$$= \$19.50$$

Multiplying by $\frac{3}{2}$, or 1.5, is the same as adding 50% of the starting number to the starting number:

$13 + \$6.50 = \$19.50$.

43. **108%:** If the stock increased 20%, then the resulting value is 120% of the original. If the stock then goes down 10%, the final value is 90% of that intermediate value.

$\frac{120}{100}$	×	$\frac{90}{100}$	×	Q	=	$\frac{x}{100}$	×	Q
120 percent	of	90 percent	of	Q	is	what percent	of	Q?

$$\frac{120}{100} \times \frac{90}{100} \times Q = \frac{x}{100} \times Q \qquad \text{Divide both sides by Q and simplify.}$$

$$\frac{6}{5} \times \frac{9}{10} = \frac{x}{100}$$

$$\frac{54}{50} = \frac{x}{100}$$

$$^2\cancel{100} \times \frac{54}{\cancel{50}_1} = x$$

$$108 = x$$

Alternatively, pretend that the initial price was \$100. If it increased in value by 20%, then the new value is \$100 + \$20 = \$120. If that new value decreases by 10%, then the final value is \$120 − \$12 = \$108. This final value is $\frac{108}{100} = 108\%$ of the starting value.

44. **36%:** Because all of the students sum to 200, write the following equation:

$$A + B + C + D + F = \text{Total}$$
$$40 + 64 + C + 18 + 6 = 200$$
$$128 + C = 200$$
$$C = 200 - 128$$
$$C = 72$$

Therefore, $\frac{72}{200}$ of the grades are C's. Percents are defined in terms of 100. Divide the top and bottom by 2 to find the percent directly.

$$\frac{72}{200} = \frac{36}{100}$$

Therefore, 36% of the students got a C.

45.   **(C):** You can use the percent change formula or you can calculate directly.

Direct calculation:
160 = 100%   This is the starting fact.
16 = 10%   Move the decimal one to the left to get 10%.
8 = 5%   Divide by 2 to get 5%.

Percent change: % change = $\dfrac{\text{change}}{\text{original}}$

$$\text{\% change} = \frac{^1\cancel{8}}{_2\cancel{160}} = \frac{1}{20}$$

This value is on the to-memorize list from the Fractions chapter: $\frac{1}{20} = 5\%$. If you forget the conversion, you can also find the percentage by making the fraction "of 100" or "per cent": $\frac{1}{20} = \frac{5}{100} = 5\%$.

Drill 7

46. **250 meteors:** Let m equal the number of meteors visible from Lily's roof. The 20 meteors that inspire Lily represent 10% of 80% of the visible meteors.

$$20 = \frac{10}{100}\left(\frac{80}{100}\right)m$$

$$20 = \frac{1}{10}\left(\frac{4}{5}\right)m$$

$$\left(\frac{50}{\cancel{4}}\right)\left(^5\cancel{20}\right) = m$$

$$250 = m$$

47. **60 gibbons:** Bingwa weighs the same as 1,000 gibbons. Therefore, he can lift 6% of this weight with his trunk.

$$\frac{6}{1\cancel{00}} \times 1,0\cancel{00} \text{ gibbons} = 6 \times 10 \text{ gibbons} = 60 \text{ gibbons}$$

48. **(B):** Let x equal the precipitation in Country X, y equal the precipitation in Country Y, and z equal the precipitation in Country Z. Translate the equations.

$$x = \frac{7}{4}y$$

$$y = \frac{2}{3}z$$

Since the question tells you the value of x and you are solving for the value of z, substitute the second equation into the first to simplify to a single equation with x and z.

$$x = \frac{7}{4}\left(\frac{2}{3}z\right)$$

$$x = \frac{7}{6}z$$

Now plug in for x and solve for z:

$$280 = \frac{7}{6}z$$

$$\left(\frac{6}{7}\right)(280) = z$$

$$(6)(40) = z$$

$$240 = z$$

49. $\dfrac{1}{6}$: In order to determine the fraction of the songs that are world music, first figure out what fraction of the songs are not world music. Add the fractions for the other types of music.

$$\text{Not world} = \frac{1}{3} + \frac{1}{4} + \frac{1}{6} + \frac{1}{12}$$
$$= \frac{4}{12} + \frac{3}{12} + \frac{2}{12} + \frac{1}{12}$$
$$= \frac{10}{12}$$
$$= \frac{5}{6}$$

Of the songs in Farrah's playlist, $\dfrac{5}{6}$ are *not* world music, so the remaining $\dfrac{1}{6}$ of the songs are world music.

50. **160 people:** Let p = the total number of people attending the convention. In order to find the total number, determine what fraction of the total the 8 people (who play three or more instruments) represent, and then use that to find the total.

You could add up the three fractions and subtract from 1—but wait! Adding fractions is annoying because you have to find a common denominator. Take a look at those fractions again: they are all on the to-memorize conversion list. Convert them to percentages.

$$\frac{2}{5} = 40\%$$

$$\frac{1}{4} = 25\%$$

$$\frac{3}{10} = 30\%$$

The sum is 40% + 25% + 30% = 95%. The 8 people who play three or more instruments must represent the remaining 5%. Use this fact to find 100%, or the total number of attendees.

5% = 8	This is the starting fact.
10% = 16	Double the number to get 10%.
100% = 160	Add a 0 to get 100%.

Drill 8

51. **(A):** First, determine how many umbrellas fit Yemi's price range. There are 400 umbrellas total, but $\frac{3}{5}$ cost more than the $25 that Yemi is willing to pay.

$$400\left(1-\frac{3}{5}\right) = \text{umbrellas under } \$25$$

$$^{8}\cancel{400}\left(\frac{2}{\cancel{5}}\right) = \text{umbrellas under } \$25$$

$$160 = \text{umbrellas under } \$25$$

There are 160 *remaining* umbrellas. According to the problem, $\frac{7}{8}$ of these are not blue, so $\frac{1}{8}$ are under $25 and blue. Therefore:

$$^{2}\cancel{160}\left(\frac{1}{\cancel{8}}\right) = \text{blue umbrellas under } \$25$$

$$20 = \text{blue umbrellas under } \$25$$

52. **(A):** First, figure out how many cups of liquid are in one serving of Mariko's punch.

$$\frac{1}{2}+\frac{3}{4}+\frac{1}{8}=\frac{4}{8}+\frac{6}{8}+\frac{1}{8}=\frac{11}{8}$$

Each serving of punch consists of $\frac{11}{8}$ cups of liquid. (This is a weird number. Don't try to turn it into a mixed fraction yet. Glance at the answers: something must cancel out later to make a "nicer" number, so just keep going.)

Next, you know that $\frac{11}{8}$ times the number of servings equals 22 cups. Let s equal the number of servings and solve:

$$\frac{11}{8}s = 22$$

$$s = 22\left(\frac{8}{11}\right)$$

$$s = 2(8) = 16$$

53. $\dfrac{1}{6}$: Begin by finding the fraction of the movies that are documentaries. Let M equal the total number of movies and d equal the number of documentaries. Notice that you can simplify the math by multiplying both sides by the common denominator, 12.

$$M = \frac{1}{3}M + \frac{1}{4}M + d$$

$$(12)(M) = \left(\frac{1}{3}M + \frac{1}{4}M + d\right)(12)$$

$$12M = 4M + 3M + 12d$$

$$5M = 12d$$

$$\frac{5}{12}M = d$$

Of the movies, $\dfrac{5}{12}$ are documentaries. Of these, $\dfrac{2}{5}$ are depressing. Therefore:

$$\frac{\cancel{5}}{12}M \times \frac{2}{\cancel{5}} = \frac{2}{12}M = \frac{1}{6}M$$

Of the movies in Santosh's collection, $\dfrac{1}{6}$ are depressing documentaries.

Alternatively, because the problem discusses only fractions (never any real numbers), you can work through the problem using a real number. Choose a number that is a multiple of all of the denominators of the fractions in the problem. In this case, choose $3 \times 4 \times 5 = 60$.

Assuming that there are 60 total movies, then $\dfrac{1}{3}$, or 20 movies, are animated, and $\dfrac{1}{4}$, or 15 movies, are live-action. The remainder, or $60 - 20 - 15 = 25$, are documentaries.

Of the documentaries, $\dfrac{2}{5}$, or $25\left(\dfrac{2}{5}\right) = 10$, documentaries are depressing. These 10 depressing documentaries represent $\dfrac{10,}{60}$ or $\dfrac{1}{6}$, of all of the movies.

54. $\dfrac{2}{15}$: Let h = the total number of homes. You know that $\dfrac{1}{3}$ of the homes are termite-ridden. If $\dfrac{3}{5}$ of the termite-ridden homes are collapsing, then $1 - \dfrac{3}{5} = \dfrac{2}{5}$ of the termite-ridden homes are NOT collapsing. Therefore:

$$\left(h \times \dfrac{1}{3}\right) \times \dfrac{2}{5} = \dfrac{2}{15}h$$

Alternatively, because the problem only mentions fractions (no real numbers), you can choose your own real number to solve. Choose a number that is a multiple of all of the denominators in the problem. In this case, choose $3 \times 5 = 15$.

Assuming that there are 15 homes total, then $\dfrac{1}{3}$, or 5 homes, are termite-ridden. Of these 5 homes, $\dfrac{3}{5}$, or 3 homes, are collapsing. That leaves 2 homes that are both termite-ridden and NOT collapsing; this represents $\dfrac{2}{15}$ of the total homes.

55. **6,000 cracked green marbles:** If $\dfrac{3}{4}$ of the marbles are green, then $\dfrac{1}{4}$ are red. If 6,000 represents $\dfrac{1}{4}$ (or 25%) of the total, then $\dfrac{3}{4}$ (or 75%) of the total is three times as much. There are $6,000 \times 3 = 18,000$ green marbles. Determine how many of these are cracked.

$$^{6}\cancel{18},000 \times \dfrac{1}{\cancel{3}} = 6,000$$

It may seem odd that you're back at 6,000. It is sometimes the case that the answer is the same as another number in the problem!

Geometry

In this chapter...

- Circles
  - Know One Thing about a Circle: Know Everything Else
  - Sector: Slice of Pizza
- Triangles
  - Sum of Any Two Sides > Third Side
  - Sum of the Three Angles = 180°
  - Same Sides = Same Angles, and Vice Versa
  - Perimeter: Sum of Sides
  - Apply Area Formula: Any Side Can Be the Base
  - Know Two Sides of a Right Triangle: Find the Third Side
- Quadrilaterals
  - Parallelogram: Cut into Triangles OR Drop Height
  - Rectangles = Parallelogram + Four Right Angles
  - Squares = Rectangle + Four Equal Sides
- Geometry: "Word" Problems with Pictures
- Coordinate Plane—Position Is a Pair of Numbers
  - Know Just One Coordinate = Find a Line
  - Know a Range = Shade a Region
  - Read a Graph = Drop a Line to the Axes
  - Plot a Relationship: Given an x, Find a y
  - Lines in the Plane: Use Slope and y-Intercept to Plot

Chapter 10

Geometry

In This Chapter, You Will Learn To:

- Work with the basic shapes that the GMAT tests, including key facts, rules, and formulas
- Apply these rules and equations to solve GMAT geometry problems
- Solve coordinate plane problems

For many students, geometry brings to mind complicated shapes and the need to memorize lots of formulas. It's true that you will need to memorize some rules and formulas, but you can generally get away with limiting your studies to triangles, squares, rectangles, circles, and the coordinate plane.

On occasion, someone will be given a more complicated shape, such as a cylinder or a rhombus, but these shapes don't often appear on the GMAT. If you like, you can choose not to study the "weird" shapes and to make a guess if one happens to pop up on your test.

In this chapter, you'll learn the properties of the basic shapes most commonly tested on the GMAT. You'll also learn how the GMAT tests your knowledge of these shapes and how to work your way through Geometry questions.

Circles

A circle is a set of points that are all the same distance from a central point. By definition, every circle has a center, usually labeled O, which is not itself a point on the circle. The **radius** of a circle is the distance between the center of the circle and a point on the circle. *Any* line segment connecting the center and *any* point on the circle is a radius (usually labeled r). All radii in the same circle have the same length. For example:

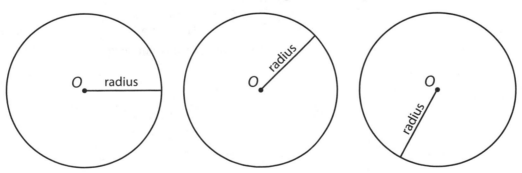

Know One Thing about a Circle: Know Everything Else

Now imagine a circle of radius 7. What else can you figure out about that circle?

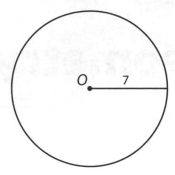

The next easiest thing to figure out is the **diameter** (usually labeled *d*), which passes through the center of a circle and connects two opposite points on the circle:

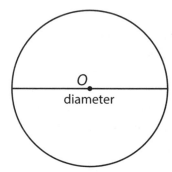

A diameter is two radii laid end to end, so it will always be exactly twice the length of the radius. This relationship can be expressed as $d = 2r$. A circle with radius 7 has a diameter of 14.

The **circumference** (usually referred to as *C*) is a measure of the distance around a circle. The circumference is essentially the perimeter of a circle:

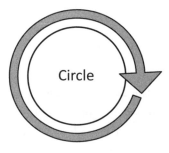

For any circle, the circumference and the diameter have a consistent relationship. If you divide the circumference by the diameter, you always get the same number: 3.14… This number has decimals that continue forever and it is indicated by the Greek letter π (pi). To recap:

$$\frac{\text{Circumference}}{\text{Diameter}} = \pi \quad \text{or} \quad \pi d = C$$

In a circle with a diameter of 14, the circumference is $\pi(14)$, or 14π. Most of the time, you will not approximate this as 43.96 (which is 14×3.14). Instead, keep it as 14π.

You can relate the circumference directly to the radius, since the diameter is twice the radius. This relationship is commonly expressed as $C = 2\pi r$. Be comfortable with using either equation.

Finally, the **area** (usually labeled A) is the space inside the circle.

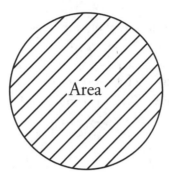

The area of a circle and its radius always have the same relationship. If you know the radius of the circle, then you can find the area using the formula $A = \pi r^2$. For a circle of radius 7, the area is $\pi(7)^2$, or 49π. *Once you know the radius, you can find the diameter, the circumference, and the area.*

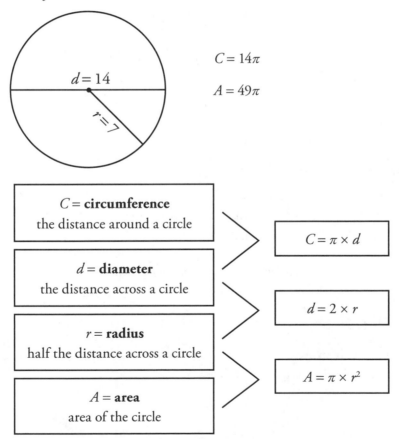

These relationships are true of any circle. What's more, *if you know any one of these values, you can determine the rest,* since they're all connected.

Say that the area of a circle is 36π. How do you find the other measures? Start with the formula for the area, which involves the radius.

$$36\pi = \pi r^2$$

Solve for the radius by isolating r.

$36\pi = \pi r^2$	Divide by π.
$36 = r^2$	Take the square root of both sides.
$6 = r$	

Now that you know the radius, multiply it by 2 to get the diameter, which is 12. Finally, to find the circumference, multiply the diameter by π. The circumference is 12π. You can fill in the measurements on your circle:

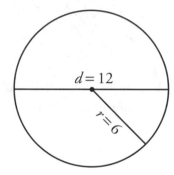

If you...	Then you...	Like this:
Know one thing about a circle	Can find out everything else about the circle by using the standard formulas	If $r = 4$, then $d = 8$, $C = 8\pi$, and $A = 16\pi$

Check Your Skills

1. The radius of a circle is 9. What is the area?
2. The circumference of a circle is 17π. What is the diameter?
3. The area of a circle is 25π. What is the circumference?

Answers can be found on page 467.

Sector: Slice of Pizza

Imagine that you have a circle with an area of 36π. Now cut it in half and make it a semicircle. Any fractional portion of a circle is known as a **sector**. Think of a sector as a slice of pizza.

MANHATTAN PREP

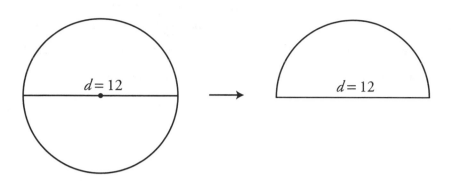

What effect does cutting the circle in half have on the basic elements of the circle? The diameter stays the same, as does the radius. But the area and the circumference are cut in half. The area of the semicircle is 18π, and the curved part of the semicircle's perimeter is 6π. When you deal with sectors, you call the remaining portion of the circumference the **arc length**. For this sector, the arc length is 6π.

If, instead of cutting the circle in half, you cut it into quarters, each piece of the circle would have $\frac{1}{4}$ the area of the entire circle and $\frac{1}{4}$ the circumference.

10

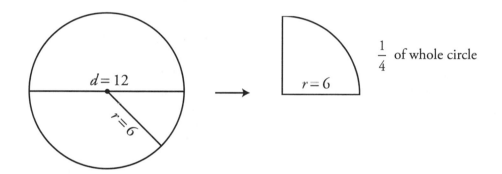

$\frac{1}{4}$ of whole circle

Now, on the GMAT, you're unlikely to be told that you have one-quarter of a circle. Rather, you would be told something about the **central angle**, which is the degree measure between two given radii. Take a look at the quarter circle. Normally, there are 360° in a full circle. What is the degree measure of the angle between the two radii? The same thing that happens to area and circumference happens to the central angle. It is now $\frac{1}{4}$ of 360°, which is 90° (you illustrate a 90° angle with a box at the angle).

$$\frac{1}{4} = \frac{90°}{360°}$$

Let's see how you can use the central angle to determine sector area and arc length. Imagine that the original circle still has area 36π, but now the sector, or slice of pie, has a central angle of 60°.

60°

What fractional amount of the circle remains if the central angle is 60°? The whole is 360°, and the part is 60°, so $\frac{60}{360}$ is the relevant fraction, which reduces to $\frac{1}{6}$. In other words, a sector with a central angle of 60° is $\frac{1}{6}$ of the entire circle. The sector area is $\frac{1}{6}$ × (Area of circle), and the arc length is $\frac{1}{6}$ × (Circumference of circle).

$$\text{Sector area} = \frac{1}{6} \times (36\pi) = 6\pi$$

$$\text{Arc length} = \frac{1}{6} \times (12\pi) = 2\pi$$

$$\frac{1}{6} = \frac{60°}{360°} = \frac{\text{Sector area}}{\text{Circle area}} = \frac{\text{Arc length}}{\text{Circumference}}$$

In the last example, the central angle indicated the fractional amount that the sector represented. But any of the three properties of a sector, namely central angle, arc length, and area, could be used to convey that same information, since all three measures are related.

Consider this example:

A sector has a radius of 9 and an area of 27π. What is the central angle of the sector?

You still need to determine the fraction of the circle that the sector represents. This time, however, use the radius to figure out the area of the whole circle. From that, you can figure out what fractional amount the sector is.

$$\text{Area} = \pi r^2 = \pi(9)^2 = 81\pi$$

$$\frac{27\pi}{81\pi} = \frac{1}{3}$$

The sector is $\frac{1}{3}$ of the entire circle. The full circle has an angle of 360°, so multiply that by $\frac{1}{3}$ to find the angle of the sector.

$$\frac{1}{3} \times 360 = 120$$

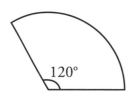

$$\frac{1}{3} = \frac{120°}{360°} = \frac{27\pi \;\text{(Sector area)}}{81\pi \;\text{(Circle area)}}$$

Every question about sectors will provide you with enough information to calculate one of the following fractions, which represent the sector as a fraction of the circle.

$$\frac{\text{Central area}}{360} \qquad \frac{\text{Sector area}}{\text{Circle area}} \qquad \frac{\text{Arc length}}{\text{Circumference}}$$

All of these fractions have the same value for the same sector of a circle (in other words, each fraction is equal). Once you know this value, you can find any measure of the sector of the original circle.

If you...	**Then you...**	**Like this:**
Encounter a sector	Figure out the fraction of the circle that the sector represents	If central angle = 45° and radius = 5, then $\text{fraction} = \frac{45}{360} = \frac{1}{8}$, and area = $\frac{1}{8}\pi r^2 = \frac{1}{8}\pi(5)^2 = \frac{25}{8}\pi$

Check Your Skills

4. A sector has a central angle of 270° and a radius of 2. What is the area of the sector?
5. A sector has an arc length of 4π and a radius of 3. What is the central angle of the sector?
6. A sector has an area of 40π and a radius of 10. What is the arc length of the sector?

Answers can be found on pages 467–468.

Triangles

Triangles are relatively common in GMAT geometry problems. You'll often find them hiding in problems that seem to be about rectangles or other shapes. Many properties of triangles are tested.

Sum of Any Two Sides > Third Side

The sum of any two side lengths of a triangle will always be greater than the third side length.

Grab your pen and draw two dots (the endpoints), then connect them with a straight line. Now use that straight line as one side of a triangle, and draw two more lines to create the full triangle. The other two lines added together have to be longer than the straight line that you started from, since the straight line is the shortest possible distance between the two endpoints.

A related idea is that any side is greater than the *difference* of the other two side lengths. Otherwise, you can't even connect the dots and draw a complete triangle. The pictures below illustrate these points:

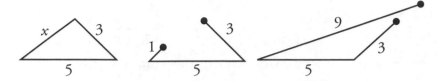

In the first triangle, what is the largest number x could be? What's the smallest? Could it be 9? 1?

x must be less than $3 + 5 = 8$

x must be greater than $5 - 3 = 2$

$2 < x < 8$

If you…	Then you…	Like this:
Want to know how long the third side of a triangle could be	Find the sum and the difference of the other two sides; the length of the third side must be less than the sum, but more than the difference	First side = 6 Second side = 4 Third side must be less than $6 + 4 = 10$ and greater than $6 - 4 = 2$

Check Your Skills

7. Two sides of a triangle have lengths 5 and 19. Can the third side have a length of 13?

8. Two sides of a triangle have lengths 8 and 17. What is the range of possible values of the length of the third side?

Answers can be found on page 468.

Sum of the Three Angles = 180°

The internal angles of a triangle must sum to 180°. As a result, if you know two angles in the triangle, you can find the third angle. Take a look at this triangle:

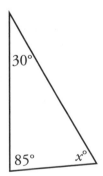

The three internal angles must sum to 180°, so $30 + 85 + x = 180$, so $x = 65$. The third angle is 65°.

MANHATTAN PREP

The GMAT can also test you in more complicated ways. Consider this triangle:

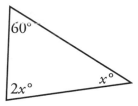

You only know one of the angles, but the other two are both given in terms of x. Again, the three angles must sum to 180°.

$$60 + x + 2x = 180$$
$$3x = 120$$
$$x = 40$$

The angle labeled x has a measure of 40°, and the angle labeled $2x$ has a measure of 80°.

By the way, a straight line also has a measure of 180°.

The GMAT does not always draw triangles to scale. On Problem Solving questions (one of the two types of GMAT Quant questions), figures will be drawn to scale unless there is a note saying that it is not drawn to scale. On Data Sufficiency questions (the other type of GMAT Quant question), the figures will not say whether they are drawn to scale, so assume they are not.

If you...	Then you...	Like this:
Know two angles of a triangle or can represent all three in terms of a single variable	Can find all angles using the "sum to 180" principle	First angle = $3x$ Second angle = $4x$ Third angle = 40° $3x + 4x + 40 = 180$ $7x = 140$ or $x = 20$

Check Your Skills

Find the missing angle(s).

9.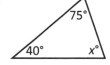

10.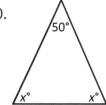

11.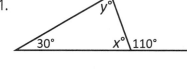

Answers can be found on pages 468–469.

Same Sides = Same Angles, and Vice Versa

Internal angles of a triangle are important on the GMAT for another reason: *sides correspond to their opposite angles.* That is, the longest side is opposite the largest angle, and the smallest side is opposite the smallest angle. Think about an alligator opening its mouth. As the angle between its upper and lower jaws increases, the distance between its top and bottom teeth gets bigger.

For example:

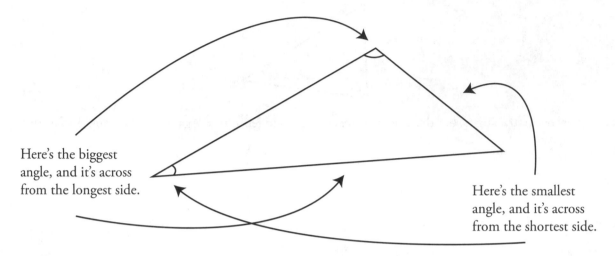

Here's the biggest angle, and it's across from the longest side.

Here's the smallest angle, and it's across from the shortest side.

10

This relationship works both ways. If you know the sides of the triangle, you can make inferences about the angles. If you know the angles, you can make inferences about the sides. (Note: In the diagram below, a two-letter designation, such as *AC*, refers to the line that lies between the points *A* and *C*. The three-letter designation. ∠*ABC*, refers to the angle traced by starting from the letter *A*, going through *B*, and ending on *C*.)

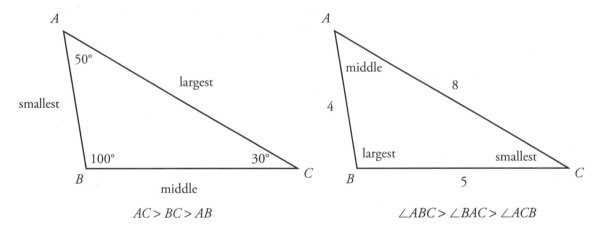

$$AC > BC > AB$$

$$\angle ABC > \angle BAC > \angle ACB$$

Lots of triangles have two or even three equal sides. These triangles also have two or three equal angles, respectively. You can classify triangles by the number of equal sides or angles that they have.

- A triangle that has two equal angles and two equal sides is an **isosceles** triangle.

- A triangle that has three equal angles (all 60°) and three equal sides is an **equilateral** triangle.

The relationship between equal angles and equal sides works in both directions. Take a look at these isosceles triangles, and think about what additional information you can infer from them:

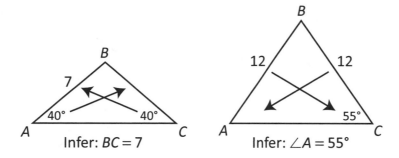

The GMAT loves isosceles triangles. Examine this challenging example:

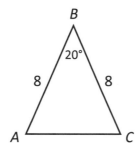

Take a look at the triangle to see what other information you can fill in. Specifically, do you know the degree measure of either angle *BAC* or angle *BCA*?

Because side *AB* is the same length as side *BC*, angle *BAC* must have the same degree measure as angle *BCA*. Label each of those angles *x*°:

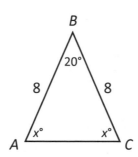

The three internal angles will sum to 180. So $20 + x + x = 180$, so $x = 80$. Therefore, the two angles, *BAC* and *BCA*, each equal 80°. You can't find the side length *AC* without more advanced math; the GMAT doesn't test that more advanced math.

If you...	Then you...	Like this:
See two equal sides in a triangle	Set the angles opposite each side equal	Two sides both equal 8, so the angles opposite those sides are equal
See two equal angles in a triangle	Set the sides opposite each angle equal	Two angles equal 30°, so the sides opposite those angles are equal

Check Your Skills

Find the value of *x*.

12.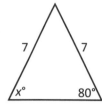

13.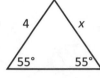

14.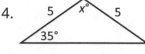

Answers can be found on pages 469–470.

Perimeter: Sum of Sides

The **perimeter** of a triangle is the sum of the lengths of all three sides. Look at the triangle below:

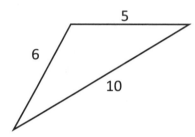

In this triangle, the perimeter is 5 + 6 + 10 = 21. This is a relatively simple property of a triangle, so often it will be used in combination with another property. Try this next problem. What is the perimeter of triangle *PQR*?

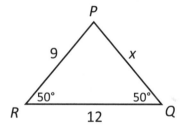

To solve for the perimeter, you need to determine the value of *x*. Because angles *PQR* and *PRQ* are both 50°, their opposite sides (*PR* and *PQ*) will have equal lengths. Therefore, side *PQ* also has a length of 9. The perimeter of triangle *PQR* is therefore 9 + 9 + 12 = 30.

Check Your Skills

Find the perimeter of each triangle.

15.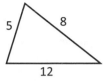

Note: Figure not drawn to scale.

16.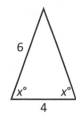

Answer can be found on page 470.

Apply Area Formula: Any Side Can Be the Base

The area of a triangle equals $\frac{1}{2} \times$ (base) × (height). In area formulas for any shape, be clear about the relationship between the base and the height. *The base and the height must be perpendicular to each other.*

In a triangle, one side of the triangle is the base. Any of the sides can be the base, but it is most common to make the bottom side the base.

The height is formed by dropping a line from the third point of the triangle straight down toward the base so that it forms a 90° angle with the base. The small square located where the height and base meet is used to denote a right angle (see the figure below). You can also say that the height is **perpendicular** to the base, or vice versa.

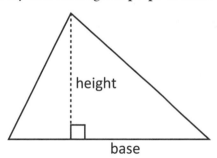

The GMAT often asks you about familiar shapes while presenting them in unfamiliar orientations. In particular, the triangle may be oriented in a way that makes it difficult to call the bottom side the base. The three triangles below are all the same triangle, but in each one a different side is the base. The diagrams also show the corresponding height.

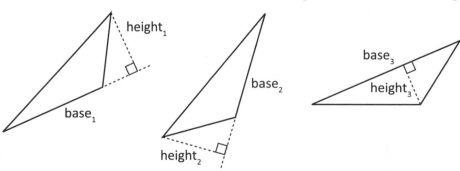

As in the first two examples, the height can be *outside* the triangle! You can extend the base farther in order to create the 90° angle. As long as there is a right angle between the base and the height, any orientation is permitted.

If you…	Then you…	Like this:
Need the area of a triangle	Apply the area formula, using *any* convenient side as the base	$A = \dfrac{1}{2}$ (base) (height) Use any side as the base; draw the right-angle height from the corner opposite the base

Check Your Skills

Find the area of each triangle.

17.

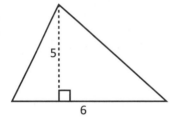

18.

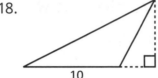

Answers can be found on page 470.

Know Two Sides of a Right Triangle: Find the Third Side

Right triangles are very common on the GMAT. A right triangle is any triangle in which one of the angles is a right angle (90°). Consider this example:

What is the perimeter of triangle *ABC*?

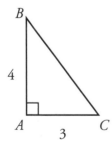

With only two sides of the triangle, how do you get the perimeter? Because this is a right triangle, you can use the Pythagorean theorem, which applies only to right triangles. According to the theorem, the lengths of the three sides of a right triangle are related by the equation $a^2 + b^2 = c^2$, where a and b are the lengths of the sides touching the right angle, also known as **legs**, and c is the length of the side opposite the right angle, also known as the **hypotenuse**.

In the given triangle, sides AB and AC are a and b (it doesn't matter which is which), and side BC is c. Therefore:

$$a^2 + b^2 = c^2$$
$$(3)^2 + (4)^2 = (BC)^2$$
$$9 + 16 = (BC)^2$$
$$25 = (BC)^2$$
$$5 = BC$$

The triangle looks like this:

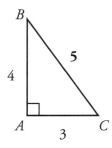

The perimeter is equal to $3 + 4 + 5 = 12$.

Often, you can take a shortcut around using the Pythagorean theorem. The GMAT favors a subset of right triangles, called *Pythagorean triples*. The triangle above is an example. The side lengths are 3, 4, and 5—all integers—and this triple is called a 3-4-5 triangle.

While there are quite a few of these triples, only a couple are useful to commit to memory for the GMAT; if you memorize them, you can save yourself from having to calculate them on the test. For each triple, the first two numbers are the lengths of the sides that touch the right angle, and the third (and greatest) number is the length of the hypotenuse.

3-4-5, or its "double" 6-8-10
5-12-13

Note that you can double, triple, or otherwise apply a common multiplier to these lengths; 3-4-5 is really a ratio of $3 : 4 : 5$.

Consider this example:

What is the area of triangle *DEF*?

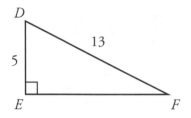

What do you need in order to find the area of triangle *DEF*? The area formula is $\frac{1}{2} \times$ (base) $\times$ (height). This is a right triangle, so sides *DE* and *EF* are already perpendicular to each other. Treat one of them as the base and the other as the height.

How do you find the length of side *EF*? First, you can always use the Pythagorean theorem to find the length of the third side of a right triangle if you know the lengths of the other two sides. In this case, the formula would look like this: $(DE)^2 + (EF)^2 = (DF)^2$.

But don't follow through on that calculation! If you have memorized the Pythagorean triples, then when you see a right triangle in which one of the legs has a length of 5 and the hypotenuse has a length of 13, you will know that the length of the other leg must be 12.

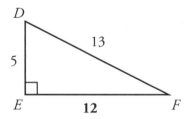

Now you have what you need to find the area of triangle *DEF*.

Area $= \frac{1}{2} \times (12) \times (5) = (6)(5) = 30$

If you...	Then you...	Like this:
Know two sides of a right triangle	Can find the third side, either by recognizing a triple or by using the full Pythagorean theorem	A leg of a right triangle has length 18, while the hypotenuse has length 30. How long is the third side? $18^2 + x^2 = 30^2$ and solve for x, or recognize that this is a multiple of the $3 : 4 : 5$ triple (each side is multiplied by 6), $x = 24$

Check Your Skills

Solve the following problems.

19.

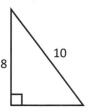

What is the length of the third side of the triangle in the figure above?

20.

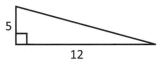

What is the length of the third side of the triangle in the figure above?

21.

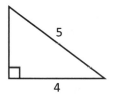

What is the area of the triangle in the figure above?

Answers can be found on page 471.

Quadrilaterals

A quadrilateral is any figure with *four* sides. Quadrilaterals can always be cut up into two triangles by slicing across the middle to connect opposite corners. Therefore, what you know about triangles could apply in a problem involving quadrilaterals. In many cases, you won't want to cut up the quadrilateral that way, but it's good to know you could.

Parallelogram: Cut into Triangles OR Drop Height

The GMAT frequently deals with **parallelograms**. A parallelogram is any four-sided figure in which the opposite sides are parallel and equal. Opposite angles are also equal, and adjacent angles (angles that are next to each other without another angle in between) add up to 180°.

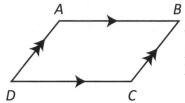

In the parallelogram above, sides *AB* and *CD* are parallel and have equal lengths. Sides *AD* and *BC* are parallel and have equal length. Angles *ADC* and *ABC* are equal. Angles *DAB* and *DCB* are equal. This is shown below:

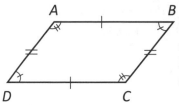

Use hash marks to indicate equal lengths or equal angles.

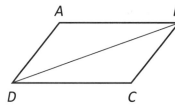

Use arrows to indicate parallel lines.

10

In any parallelogram, the diagonal will divide the parallelogram into two equal triangles.

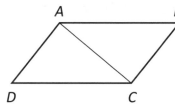

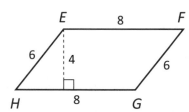

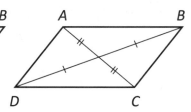

Triangle *ABD* = Triangle *BCD*　　　　Triangle *ADC* = Triangle *ABC*　　　　The diagonals also cut each other in half (bisect each other).

For any parallelogram, the perimeter is the sum of the lengths of all the sides and the area is equal to (base) × (height). With parallelograms, as with triangles, remember that the base and the height *must* be perpendicular to one another:

In the above parallelogram, what is the perimeter and what is the area? The perimeter is the sum of the sides: 6 + 8 + 6 + 8 = 28.

Alternatively, you can use one of the properties of parallelograms to calculate the perimeter in a different way. Parallelograms always have two sets of equal sides. In this parallelogram, two of the sides have a length of 6 and two of the sides have a length of 8. Therefore, the perimeter equals (2)(6) + (2)(8). You can factor out a 2 and say that the perimeter equals 2(6 + 8) = 28.

To calculate the area, you need a base and a height. It might be tempting to say that the area is 6 × 8 = 48. But the two sides of this parallelogram are not perpendicular to each other. The dotted line drawn into the figure, however, is perpendicular to side *HG*. You need to "drop a height," or draw a perpendicular line, to the base. The area of parallelogram *EFGH* is $8 \times 4 = 32$.

If you...	Then you...	Like this:
Want the perimeter or area of a parallelogram	Find all sides (for the perimeter) or drop a height (for the area)	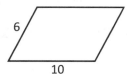 Perimeter = 2(6 + 8) = 28 Area = 8 × 4 = 32

Check Your Skills

22. What is the perimeter of the parallelogram?

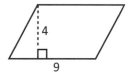

23. What is the area of the parallelogram?

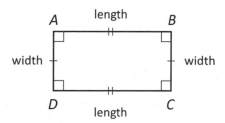

Answers can be found on pages 471–472.

Rectangles = Parallelogram + Four Right Angles

Rectangles are a specific type of parallelogram. Rectangles have all the properties of parallelograms, plus one more: *all four internal angles of a rectangle are right angles.* With rectangles, you refer to one pair of sides as the length and one pair of sides as the width. It doesn't matter which is which, though traditionally the shorter side is the width and the longer side is the length.

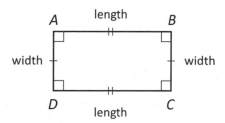

The formula for the perimeter of a rectangle is the same as for the perimeter of a parallelogram. You can sum the lengths of the four sides, or you can sum the length and the width and multiply by 2: $2(l + w)$.

The formula for the area of a rectangle is also the same as for the area of a parallelogram. But for any rectangle, the length and width are by definition perpendicular to each other, so you don't need to find a separate height. For this reason, the area of a rectangle is commonly expressed as (length) × (width), or $A = lw$.

For the following rectangle, find the perimeter and the area.

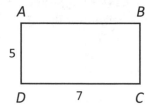

Start with the perimeter. The perimeter is $2(5 + 7) = 24$. Alternatively, $5 + 5 + 7 + 7 = 24$.

Now find the area. The formula for area is (length) × (width), or $(7)(5) = 35$.

Finally, the diagonal of a rectangle cuts the rectangle into two equal *right* triangles, with all the properties you expect of right triangles.

Check Your Skills

Find the area and perimeter of each rectangle.

24.

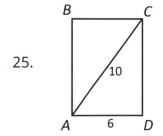

25.

Answers can be found on page 472.

Squares = Rectangle + Four Equal Sides

The most special type of rectangle is a square. *A square is a rectangle in which all four sides are equal.* Knowing only one side of a square is enough to determine the perimeter and area of a square.

For instance, if the length of the side of a square is 3, then all four sides have a length of 3:

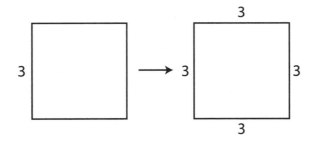

The perimeter of the square is 3 + 3 + 3 + 3, which equals 12. Alternatively, once you know the length of one side of a square, multiply that length by 4 to find the perimeter: $4s = (4)(3) = 12$.

To find the area, use the same formula as for a rectangle: Area = length × width.

But, because the shape is a square, the length and the width are equal. Therefore, the area of a square is Area = (side)², which is the side length squared.

In this case, the area is equal to s^2, or $(3)^2 = 9$.

Squares are like circles: if you know one measure, you can find everything. This is because they are both "regular" figures. All circles look like each other, and all squares look like each other. For circles, the most fundamental measure is the radius, and then you can calculate everything else. For squares, the most fundamental measure is the side length.

Geometry: "Word" Problems with Pictures

Now that you know various properties of shapes, such as perimeter and area, how do you use these properties to answer GMAT geometry questions, especially ones with more than one figure? Consider this problem:

> Rectangles *ABCD* and *EFGH*, shown below, have equal areas. The length of side *AB* is 5. What is the length of diagonal *AC*?

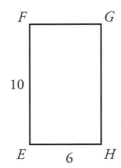 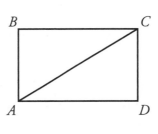

First, *draw your own copies of the shapes, and fill in everything you know.* For this problem, redraw both rectangles. Label side *AB* with a length of 5. Also, make note of what you're looking for—in this case, you want the length of diagonal *AC*. Label that diagonal with a question mark.

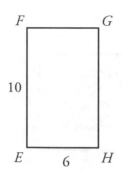

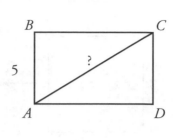

Now turn to the question. Many geometry questions are similar to the word problems discussed in Chapter 9. Both types of problems provide you with information that may be disguised. The information is related through common mathematical relationships, which also may be disguised or implied. In word problems, the information is given in words. In geometry, the information can be presented in words or visually.

So has the question above provided you with any information that can be expressed mathematically? Can you create equations?

Yes. The two rectangles have equal areas: $\text{Area}_{ABCD} = \text{Area}_{EFGH}$. You can do even better than that. The formula for area of a rectangle is Area = (length) × (width). The equation can be rewritten as $(\text{length}_{ABCD}) \times (\text{width}_{ABCD}) = (\text{length}_{EFGH}) \times (\text{width}_{EFGH})$.

The length and width of rectangle *EFGH* are 6 and 10, and the length of *AB* is 5.

$$(5) \times (\text{width}_{ABCD}) = (6) \times (10)$$
$$(5) \times (\text{width}_{ABCD}) = 60$$
$$\text{width}_{ABCD} = 12$$

Any time you learn a new piece of information, add that information to your picture.

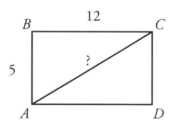

To recap, you've redrawn the shapes and filled in all the given information (such as side lengths, angles, etc.). You've made note of what the question wants. Just as you start a word problem by identifying unknowns, creating variables, and writing down givens, the first steps for geometry problems are to draw or redraw figures, add all of the given information, and confirm what you're being asked to find.

Next, you made use of additional information provided. The question stated that the two rectangles had equal areas. You created an equation to express this relationship, and then you plugged in the values you knew to solve for the width of rectangle *ABCD*. This process is identical to the process used to solve word problems—you identify relationships and create equations. After that, you solve the equations for the missing value (in this case, the width of *ABCD*).

In some ways, all you have done so far is set up the problem. In fact, aside from noting that you need to find the length of diagonal *AC*, nothing you have done so far seems to have directly helped you actually solve for that value. So far, you have found that the width of rectangle *ABCD* is 12.

So why bother solving for the width of rectangle *ABCD* when you're not even sure why you'd need it? You are *likely* to need that missing value. On the vast majority of GMAT problems, two general principles hold:

1. Intermediate steps are required to solve for the value you want.
2. The GMAT almost never provides extraneous information.

As a result, something that you *can* solve for is likely to be a stepping stone on the way to the answer.

This doesn't mean that you should run hog-wild and calculate quantities at random. Rather, as you practice these problems, you'll gain a sense of the kinds of stepping stones that the GMAT prefers.

Now that you know the width of *ABCD*, what can you figure out that you couldn't before? Take another look at the value you're looking for: the length of *AC*.

You've already identified a relationship mentioned in the question—that both rectangles have equal areas. But for many geometry problems, there are additional relationships that aren't as obvious.

The key to this problem is to recognize that *AC* is not only the diagonal of rectangle *ABCD*, but also the hypotenuse of a right triangle, because all four interior angles of a rectangle are right angles.

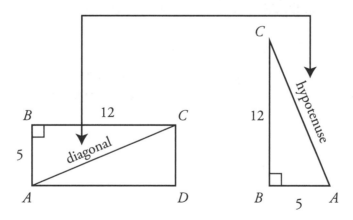

Now that you know *AC* is the hypotenuse of a right triangle, you can use two sides to find the third. One way to get the number is through the Pythagorean theorem.

This is a Pythagorean triple, though! The hypotenuse is *AC* = 13.

If you do want to use the Pythagorean theorem, sides *BC* and *AB* are the legs of the triangle, and *AC* is the hypotenuse. Therefore:

$$(BC)^2 + (AB)^2 = (AC)^2$$
$$(12)^2 + (5)^2 = (AC)^2$$
$$144 + 25 = (AC)^2$$
$$169 = (AC)^2$$
$$13 = AC$$

Let's recap what happened in the last portion of this question. You needed an insight that wasn't obvious: that the diagonal of rectangle *ABCD* is also the hypotenuse of right triangle *ABC*. Once you had that insight, you could apply "right triangle" thinking to get that unknown side. The last part of this problem required you to make inferences from the figures.

Sometimes you need to make a jump from one shape to another through a common element. For instance, you needed to see *AC* as both a diagonal of a rectangle and as a hypotenuse of a right triangle. Here, *AC* was common to both a rectangle and a right triangle, playing a different role in each.

These inferences can also make you think about what information you need to find another value.

Putting this all together, we recommend a 4-step process that you can apply to any Geometry problem.

Step 1: *Draw or redraw figures, fill in all given information, and identify the target.*
         Fill in all known angles and lengths, and make note of any equal sides or angles.

Step 2: *Identify relationships and create equations.*
         Start with relationships that are explicitly stated somewhere.

Step 3: *Solve the equations for the missing value.*
         If you can solve for a value, you will almost always need that value to answer the question.

Step 4: *Make inferences from the figures.*
         You often need to use relationships that are not explicitly stated.

Try this problem:

Rectangle *PQRS* is inscribed in circle *O* pictured below. The center of circle *O* is also the center of rectangle *PQRS*. If the circumference of circle *O* is 5π, what is the area of rectangle *PQRS*?

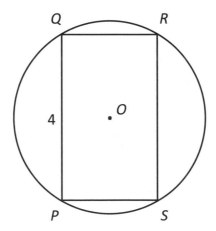

Inscribed means that the inside shape is just large enough to exactly touch the edges of the outside shape. The four corners of the rectangle just touch the circle.

First, redraw the figure on your paper and fill in all of the given information. The question didn't explicitly give you the value of any side lengths or angles, but it did say that *PQRS* is a rectangle. That means all four internal angles are right angles. This is how the GMAT tests what you know about the key properties of different shapes. Also identify what you're looking for: the rectangle's area. Here's what your picture should look like:

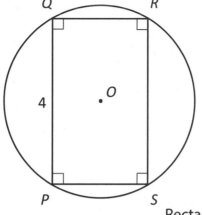

Rectangle Area = ?

Now identify relationships and create equations. The question stated that the circumference of circle O is 5π. Find the radius of the circle.

$$C = 2\pi r$$
$$5\pi = 2\pi r$$
$$5 = 2r$$
$$2.5 = r$$

If the radius is 2.5, then the diameter of circle O is 5.

Why do you find the radius and diameter? *This is how you will make a connection between the circle and the rectangle.* Now is the time to make inferences from the figures.

Ultimately, this question is asking for the area of rectangle *PQRS*. What information do you need to find that value? You have the length of *QP*. If you can find the length of either *QR* or *PS*, you can find the area of the rectangle.

What is the connection between the rectangle and the radius or diameter? Put in a diameter.

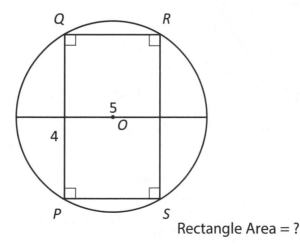

Rectangle Area = ?

That didn't help much. What if you drew the diameter so that it passed through the center but touched the circle at points *P* and *R*? The center of the circle is also the center of the rectangle, so the diameter of the circle is also the diagonal of the rectangle.

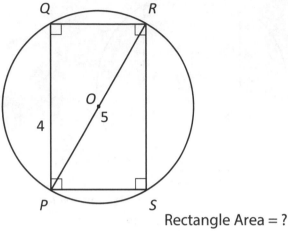

Rectangle Area = ?

Connection made! *PR* is the "bridge" between the two figures. (You could also draw the diagonal *QS*.)

Where do you go from here? You still need the length of either *QR* or *PS* (which are the same, because this is a rectangle). Can you get either one of those values? Yes. *PQR* is a right triangle. Maybe it's not oriented the way you are used to, but all the elements are there: it's a triangle and one of its internal angles is a right angle. You also know the lengths of two of the sides: *QP* and *PR*.

Triangle *PQR* is a 3-4-5 Pythagorean triple, so the length of *QR* is 3.

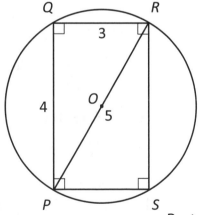

Rectangle Area = ?

At last, you have what you need to find the area of rectangle *PQRS*. Since the area is equal to (length) × (width), the area is (4) × (3) = 12.

The key insight in this problem was to realize that you could draw a diameter that would also act as the diagonal of the rectangle, linking the two figures together. You also had to recognize that *PQR* was a right triangle, even though it may have been hard to see. These kinds of insights will be crucial to success on the GMAT.

If you...	Then you...	Like this:
Face a geometry problem with more than one figure	Follow the basic 4-step process to solve, finding intermediate unknowns and looking for bridges or links between the shapes	1. Redraw, fill in, label target 2. Spot relationships & write equations 3. Solve for what you can 4. Make inferences

Check Your Skills

26. In rectangle *ABCD*, the distance from *A* to *C* is 10. What is the area of the circle tangent to sides *AD* and *BC* of the rectangle?

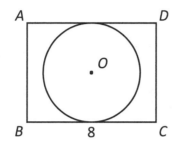

Answer can be found on pages 472-473.

Coordinate Plane—Position Is a Pair of Numbers

A **coordinate plane** is a more advanced version of a number line.

Position	Number	Number Line
"Two units right of 0"	2	*(number line with point at 2; marks −3 −2 −1 0 1 2 3)*
"One and a half units left of 0"	−1.5	*(number line with point at −1.5; marks −3 −2 −1 0 1 2 3)*

A **number line** is a ruler or measuring stick that goes as far as you want in both directions. With the number line, you can say where something is with a single number. In other words, you can link a position with a number.

You use either positive or negative numbers to indicate the position of a **point** either left or right of 0. When you are dealing with the number line, a point and a number mean the same thing.

If you're shown where the point is on the number line, you can tell the number.	*(number line with point at −2; marks −2 −1 0 1 2)* →	*The point is at −2.*
If you're told the number, you can show where the point is on the number line.	*The point is at 0.* → *(number line with point at 0; marks −2 −1 0 1 2)*	

This works even if you have only partial information about the point. If you are told something about where the point is, you can tell *something* about the number, and vice versa.

For instance, if the number is positive, then the point lies somewhere to the right of 0 on the number line. Even though you don't know the exact location of the point, you do know a range of potential values.

The number is positive.
In other words, the number
is greater than (>) 0.

→

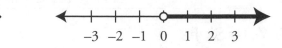

This also works in reverse. If you are given a range of potential positions on a number line, you can tell what that range is for the number:

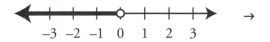

→

The number is less than (<) 0.

How does this get more complicated? What if you want to be able to locate a point that's not on a straight line, but on a page?

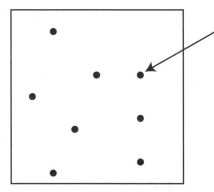

The point you want.

Now one number
line won't be enough
to tell you where the
point is.

Begin by inserting the number line into the picture. This will help you determine how far to the right or left of 0 the point is:

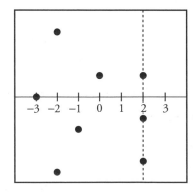

The point is two units to the right of 0.

But all three points that touch the dotted line are two units to the right of 0. You don't have enough information to determine the unique location of the point.

To locate the point, you also need to know how far up or down the dotted line the point is. For that, you'll need another number line. This number line, however, is going to be vertical. Using this vertical number line, you can measure how far above or below 0 a point is.

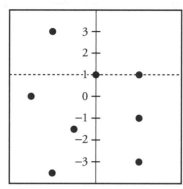

The point is one unit above 0.

Notice that this number line by itself also does not provide enough information to determine the unique location of the point.

If you combine the information from the two number lines, you can determine both how far left or right *and* how far up or down the point is.

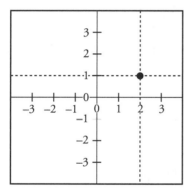

The point is 2 units to the right of 0.

AND

The point is 1 unit above 0.

Now you have a unique description of the point's position. Only one point on the page is *both* 2 units to the right of 0 *and* 1 unit above 0. On a page, you need two numbers to indicate position.

As with the number line, information can travel in either direction. If you're told the two numbers that indicate a point's location, you can place that point on the page.

The point is 3 units to the left of 0.

AND

The point is 2 units below 0.

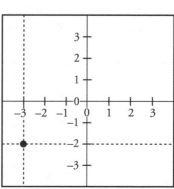

If, on the other hand, you see a point on the page, you can identify its location and extract the two numbers:

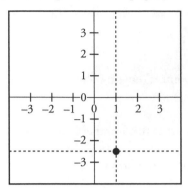

The point is 1 unit to the right of 0.

AND

The point is 2.5 units below 0.

Now that you have two pieces of information for each point, you need to keep straight which number is which. In other words, you need to know which number gives the left-right position and which number gives the up-down position:

The **x-coordinate** is the left-right number.

> Numbers to the right of 0 are positive.
> Numbers to the left of 0 are negative.

This number line is the **x-axis**.

The **y-coordinate** is the up-down number.

> Numbers above 0 are positive.
> Numbers below 0 are negative.

This number line is the **y-axis**.

The point where the x-axis and the y-axis cross is called the **origin**. This is always 0 on both axes.

Now when describing the location of a point, you can use the technical terms: x-coordinate and y-coordinate.

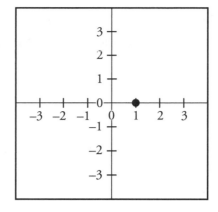

The *x*-coordinate of the point is 1 and the *y*-coordinate of the point is 0.

In short, you can say that, for this point, $x = 1$ and $y = 0$. In fact, you can go even farther. You can say that the point is at (1, 0). This shorthand always has the same basic layout. The first number in the parentheses is the *x*-coordinate and the second number is the *y*-coordinate: (*x*, *y*). One easy way to remember this is that *x* comes before *y* in the alphabet. The origin has coordinates (0, 0). For example:

The point is at (−3, −1).

OR

The point has an *x*-coordinate of −3 and a *y*-coordinate of −1.

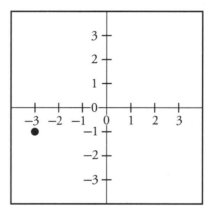

Now you have a fully functioning **coordinate plane**: an *x*-axis and a *y*-axis drawn on a page. The coordinate plane allows you to determine the unique position of any point on a **plane** (essentially, a big, flat sheet of paper).

And in case you were ever curious about what **one-dimensional** and **two-dimensional** mean, now you know. A line is one-dimensional, because you only need one number to identify a point's location. A plane is two-dimensional, because you need two numbers to identify a point's location.

If you…	Then you…	Like this:
Want to plot a point on the coordinate plane	Use the *x*-coordinate for right-left of (0, 0), and use the *y*-coordinate for up-down from (0, 0)	(3, 2) is three units right of and two units up from the origin

Check Your Skills

27. Draw a coordinate plane and plot the given points.
    1. (3, 1)
    2. (–2, 3.5)
    3. (0, –4.5)
    4. (1, 0)

28. Match each coordinate with the appropriate point on the coordinate plane.
    1. (2, –1)
    2. (–1.5, –3)
    3. (–1, 2)
    4. (3, 2)

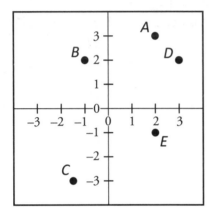

Answers can be found on page 474.

Know Just One Coordinate = Find a Line

You need to know both the *x*-coordinate and the *y*-coordinate to plot a point exactly on the coordinate plane. If you only know one coordinate, you can't tell precisely where the point is, but you can narrow down the possibilities.

Let's say that all you know is that the point is 4 units to the right of 0.

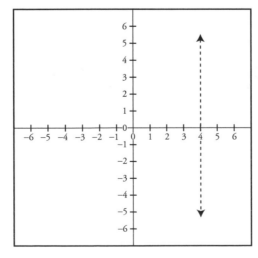

The *x*-coordinate still indicates left-right position. If you fix the left-right position but not the up-down position, then the point can only move up and down—forming a vertical line.

In this case, any point along the vertical dotted line is 4 units to the right of 0. In other words, every point on the dotted line has an *x*-coordinate of 4. You could shorten that and say $x = 4$. You don't know anything about the *y*-coordinate, which could be any number. All the points along the dotted line have different *y*-coordinates but the same *x*-coordinate, which equals 4.

So if you know that $x = 4$, then the point can be anywhere along a vertical line that crosses the *x*-axis at (4, 0). Let's try another example.

If you know that $x = -3$…

Then you know…

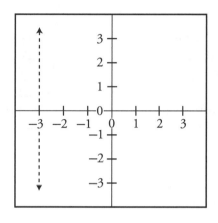

Every point on the dotted line has an *x*-coordinate of −3.

Points on the dotted line include (−3, 1), (−3, −7), (−3, 100), and so on. In general, if you know the *x*-coordinate of a point and not the *y*-coordinate, then all you can say about the point is that it lies on a vertical line.

Now imagine that all you know is the *y*-coordinate of a number. Say you know that $y = -2$. How could you represent this on the coordinate plane? In other words, what are all the points for which $y = -2$?

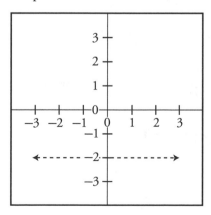

Every point 2 units below 0 fits this condition. These points form a horizontal line. You don't know anything about the *x*-coordinate, which could be any number. All the points along the horizontal dotted line have different *x*-coordinates but the same *y*-coordinate, which equals −2. For instance, (−3, −2), (−2, −2), and (50, −2) are all on the line.

Let's try another example. If you know that $y = 1$...

Then you know...

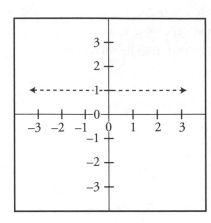

Every point on the dotted line has a y-coordinate of 1.

If you know the y-coordinate but not the x-coordinate, then you know the point lies somewhere on a horizontal line.

If you…	Then you…	Like this:
Know just one coordinate	Have either a horizontal or a vertical line	If $x = 3$, then a vertical line runs through the number 3 on the x-axis. The y-coordinate could be anything.

Check Your Skills

Draw a coordinate plane and plot the following lines.

29. $x = 6$
30. $y = -3$
31. $x = 0$

Answers can be found on pages 474–475.

Know a Range = Shade a Region

What do you do if all you know is that $x > 0$? To answer that, return to the number line for a moment. As you saw earlier, if $x > 0$, then the target is anywhere to the right of 0.

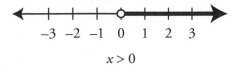

$x > 0$

Now look at the coordinate plane. All you know is that *x* is greater than 0. And you don't know *anything* about *y*, which could be any number.

How do you show all the possible points? You can shade in part of the coordinate plane: the part to the right of 0.

If you know that *x* > 0…

Then you know…

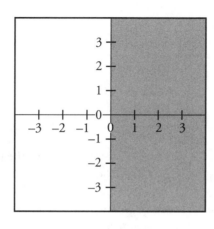

Every point in the shaded region has an *x*-coordinate greater than 0.

What if you know that *y* < 0? Then you can shade in the bottom half of the coordinate plane—where the *y*-coordinate is less than 0. The *x*-coordinate can be anything.

If you know that *y* < 0…

Then you know…

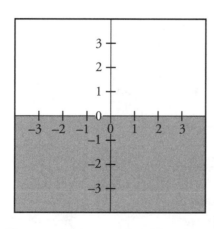

Every point in the shaded region has a *y*-coordinate less than 0.

Finally, if you know information about both *x* and *y*, then you can narrow down the shaded region.

If you know that $x > 0$ AND $y < 0$...

Then you know...

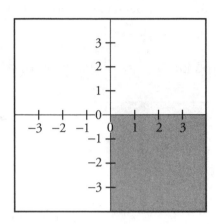

The only place where x is greater than 0 AND y is less than 0 is the bottom right quarter of the plane. So you know that the point lies somewhere in the bottom right quarter of the coordinate plane.

The four quarters of the coordinate plane are called **quadrants**. Each quadrant corresponds to a different combination of signs of x and y. The quadrants are numbered I, II, III, or IV, as shown below, starting with the top right quadrant and moving counter-clockwise:

In quadrant:	The x-coordinate is:	The y-coordinate is:
I	positive	positive
II	negative	positive
III	negative	negative
IV	positive	negative

If you...	Then you...	Like this:
Only know ranges for one or both coordinates	Can plot a shaded region corresponding to the proper range	If $x < 0$, then shade all of the points to the left of the y-axis

Check Your Skills

32. In which quadrant do the following points lie?
    1. (1, –2)
    2. (–4.6, 7)
    3. (–1, –2.5)
    4. (3, 3)

33. Which quadrant or quadrants are indicated by the following?
    1. $x < 0, y > 0$
    2. $x < 0, y < 0$
    3. $y > 0$
    4. $x < 0$

Answers can be found on pages 475–476.

Read a Graph = Drop a Line to the Axes

If you see a point on a coordinate plane, how do you determine its coordinates? To find an *x*-coordinate, drop an imaginary line down to the *x*-axis (or up to it) and find the corresponding number.

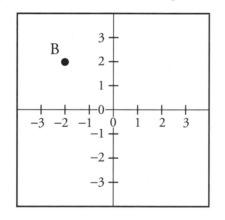   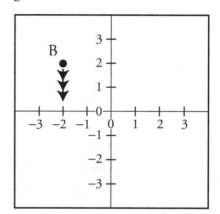

The line hits the *x*-axis at –2, so the *x*-coordinate of the point is –2. Now to find the *y*-coordinate, employ a similar technique. This time, draw a horizontal line instead of a vertical line.

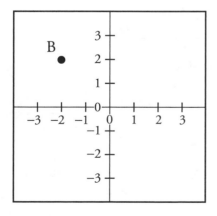   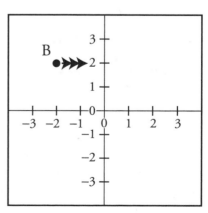

The line touches the *y*-axis at 2, which means the *y*-coordinate of the point is 2. Thus, the coordinates of point *B* are (−2, 2).

Now suppose that you know that the point is on a slanted line in the plane. Try this problem.

On the line shown, what is the *y*-coordinate of the point that has an *x*-coordinate of −4?

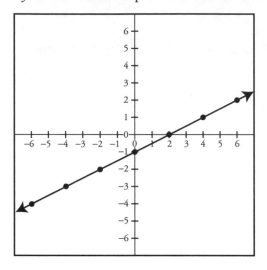

Go from the axis that you know (here, the *x*-axis) to the line that contains the point, and then to the *y*-axis (the axis you don't know).

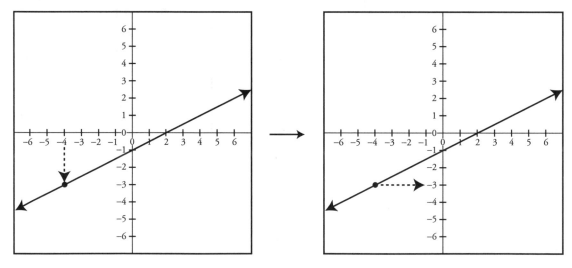

So the point on the line that has an *x*-coordinate of −4 has a *y*-coordinate of −3.

This method of locating points applies equally well to any shape or curve you may encounter on a coordinate plane. Try this next problem.

On the curve shown, what is the value of *y* when *x* = 2?

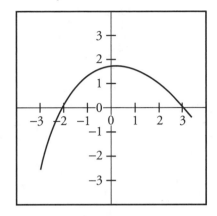

Once again, you know the *x*-coordinate, so draw a line from the *x*-axis (where you know the coordinate) to the curve, and then draw a line to the *y*-axis.

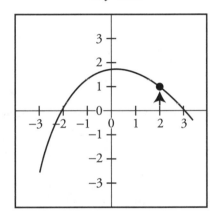 ⟶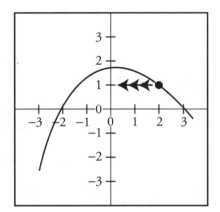

On the curve shown, the point that has an *x*-coordinate of 2 has a *y*-coordinate of 1.

Note that the GMAT will mathematically define each line or curve, so you will never be forced to guess visually where a point falls. This discussion is meant to convey how to use any graphical representation.

Check Your Skills

34. On the following graph, what is the *y*-coordinate of the point on the line that has an *x*-coordinate of –3?

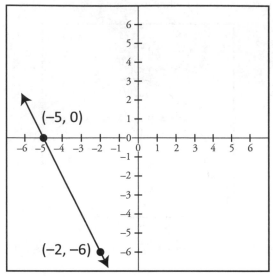

Answer can be found on page 476.

Plot a Relationship: Given an *X*, Find a *Y*

The most frequent use of the coordinate plane is to display a relationship between *x* and *y*. Often, this relationship is expressed this way: If you tell me *x*, I can tell you *y*.

As an equation, this sort of relationship looks like this:

y = some expression involving *x*

Another way of saying this is that you have *y* "in terms of" *x*.

Examples:

$$y = 2x + 1$$
$$y = x^2 - 3x + 2$$
$$y = \frac{x}{x+2}$$

If you plug a number in for *x* in any of these equations, you can calculate a value for *y*.

Take *y* = 2*x* + 1. You can generate a set of *y*'s by plugging in various values of *x*. Start by making a table.

x	*y* = 2*x* + 1
−1	*y* = 2(−1) + 1 = −1
0	*y* = 2(0) + 1 = 1
1	*y* = 2(1) + 1 = 3
2	*y* = 2(2) + 1 = 5

Now that you have some values, see what you can do with them. You can say that when *x* equals 0, *y* equals 1. These two values form a pair. You express this connection by plotting the point (0, 1) on the coordinate plane. Similarly, you can plot all the other points that represent an *x-y* pair from the table.

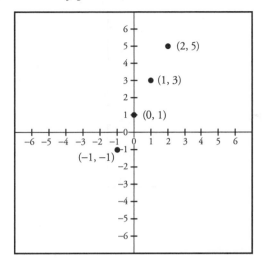

You might notice that these points seem to lie on a straight line. You're right—they do. In fact, any point that you can generate using the relationship $y = 2x + 1$ will also lie on the line.

This line is the graphical representation of $y = 2x + 1$:

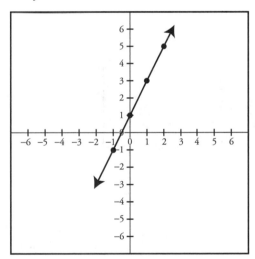

So now you can talk about equations in visual terms. In fact, that's what lines and curves on the coordinate plane are—they represent all the *x-y* pairs that make an equation true. Take a look at the following example:

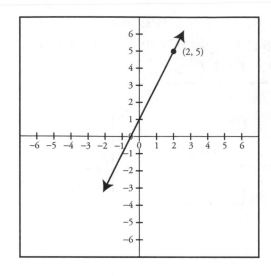

The point (2, 5) lies on the line $y = 2x + 1$. $\longleftrightarrow$ If you plug in 2 for x in $y = 2x + 1$, you get 5 for y.

You can even speak more generally, using variables.

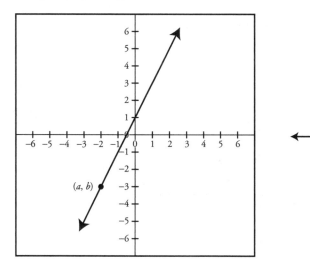

The point (a, b) lies on the line $y = 2x + 1$. $\longleftrightarrow$ If you plug in a for x in $y = 2x + 1$, you get b for y.

If you...	Then you...	Like this:
Want to plot a relationship in the x-y plane	Input values of x into the relationship, get values of y back, then plot the (x, y) pairs	Plot $y = 4 - x$ If $x = 0$, then $y = 4$, etc. Then plot $(0, 4)$, etc.

Check Your Skills

35. True or False? The point (9, 21) is on the line $y = 2x + 1$.

36. True or False? The point (4, 14) is on the curve $y = x^2 - 2$.

Answers can be found on page 476.

Lines in the Plane: Use Slope and *y*-Intercept to Plot

The relationship $y - 2x + 1$ formed a line in the coordinate plane. You can generalize this relationship. Any relationship of the following form represents a line:

$y = mx + b$ *m* and *b* represent numbers (positive or negative).

For instance, in the equation $y = 2x + 1$, $m = 2$ and $b = 1$.

A **linear equation** is one that forms a straight line when it is plotted on a coordinate plane. A linear equation does not contain any exponents and, if you put *x* and *y* on the same side of the equation, the two variables are not multiplied together.

Lines		Not Lines
$y = 3x - 2$	$m = 3, b = -2$	$y = x^2$
$y = -x + 4$	$m = -1, b = 4$	$y = \dfrac{1}{x}$
$y = \dfrac{1}{2}x$	$m = \dfrac{1}{2}, b = 0$	
These are called linear equations.		These equations are not linear.

The variables *m* and *b* have special meanings when you are dealing with linear equations. The variable *m* represents the **slope** of the line. The slope tells you how steep the line is and whether the line is rising or falling.

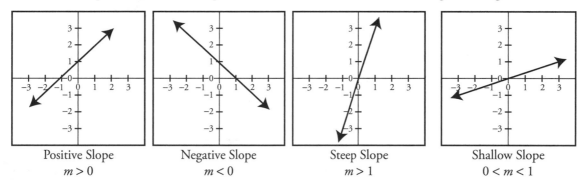

Positive Slope	Negative Slope	Steep Slope	Shallow Slope
$m > 0$	$m < 0$	$m > 1$	$0 < m < 1$

Imagine someone walking along the line from left to right. When the person is walking uphill, the slope is positive. If the person is walking downhill, the slope is negative. If the slope is very gradual, it is called a shallow slope. If it would be very hard to walk uphill, the slope is considered steep. (And if you'd be in danger of tumbling down while walking downhill, that's also very steep!)

The variable *b* represents the **y-intercept**. The *y*-intercept indicates where the line crosses the *y*-axis. Any line or curve always crosses the *y*-axis when $x = 0$. To find the *y*-intercept, plug in 0 for *x* in the equation and find *y*.

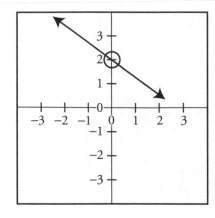
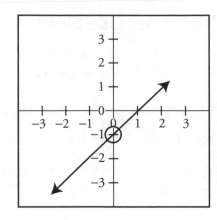

In the first image above, the *y*-intercept is 2, because the line crosses the *y*-axis at *y* = 2. In the second image, the *y*-intercept is −1.

As you saw earlier, you can graph an equation by solving the equation for various values of *x* to obtain a value of *y*, and then plot and connect those points. However, you can use *m* and *b* in a linear equation to plot a line more quickly than by plotting several points on the line. Here's how to plot the line $y = \frac{1}{2}x - 2$.

Begin with the *y*-intercept: *b* = −2, so the line crosses the *y*-axis at *y* = −2. Plot that point on the coordinate plane.

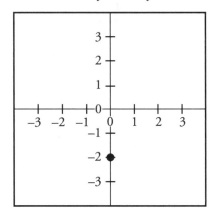

Now you're going to use the slope in order to finish drawing the line. Every slope, whether an integer or a fraction, can be thought of as a fraction. In this equation, $m = \frac{1}{2}$.

$$\frac{1}{2} \rightarrow \frac{\text{Numerator}}{\text{Denominator}} \rightarrow \frac{\text{Rise}}{\text{Run}} \rightarrow \frac{\text{Change in } y}{\text{Change in } x}$$

The numerator of the fraction indicates how many units you want to move in the *y* direction—in other words, how far up or down you want to move. The denominator indicates how many units you want to move in the *x* direction—in other words, how far left or right you want to move. For this particular equation, the slope is $\frac{1}{2}$, which means you want to move up 1 unit and right 2 units from the *y*-intercept.

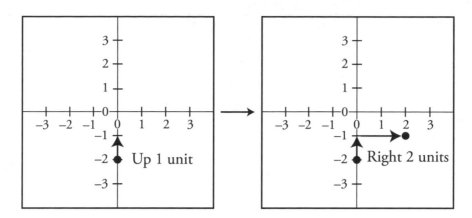

If you start from the point (0, –2) and go 1 unit up and 2 units to the right, you'll end up at the point (2, –1). The point (2, –1) is also a point on the line and a solution to the equation $y = \frac{1}{2}x - 2$. In fact, you can plug in the x value and solve for y to check that you did this correctly.

$$y = \frac{1}{2}x - 2$$
$$y = \frac{1}{2}(2) - 2$$
$$y = -1$$

If you go up another 1 unit and right another 2 units, you will end up with another point that appears on the line. Although you could keep doing this indefinitely, in reality, you need only two points to draw a line. Connect the dots and you're done! Here's what the equation will look like graphically:

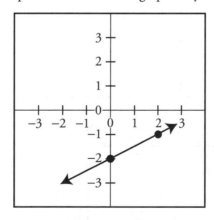

$$y = \frac{1}{2}x - 2$$

Try another one. Graph the equation $y = -\frac{3}{2}x + 4$.

Start by plotting the y-intercept. In this equation, $b = 4$, so the line crosses the y-axis at the point (0, 4).

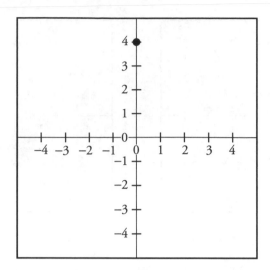

Now use the slope to find a second point. This time, the slope is $-\dfrac{3}{2}$, which is a negative slope. Associate the negative sign with the numerator: -3. To find the next point, go *down* 3 units and right 2 units.

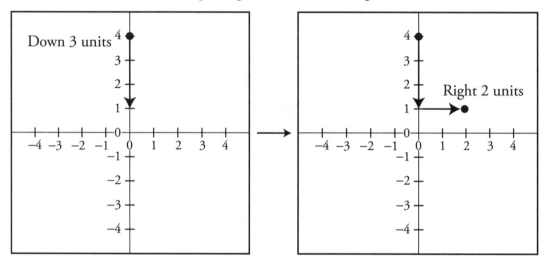

Therefore, (2, 1) is another point on the line. Now that you have 2 points, you can draw the line.

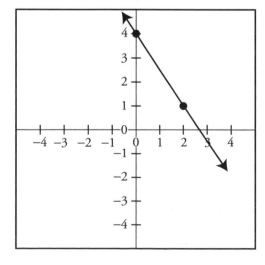

$$y = -\dfrac{3}{2}x + 4$$

If you…	Then you…	Like this:
Want to plot a linear equation in the x-y plane	Put the equation in the form of $y = mx + b$, then use m and b to draw the line	Plot $y = 4 - x$ Rearrange the equation: $y = -1x + 4$ Slope is -1, y-intercept is $(0, 4)$

Check Your Skills

For questions 37 and 38, what are the slope and y-intercept of the given lines?

37. $y = 3x + 4$
38. $2y = 5x - 12$
39. Draw a coordinate plane and graph the line $y = 2x - 4$. Identify the slope and the y-intercept.

Answers can be found on pages 476–477.

10

Check Your Skills Answer Key

1. **81π:** The formula for area is $A = \pi r^2$. The radius is 9, so the area is equal to $\pi(9)^2 = 81\pi$.

2. **17:** Circumference of a circle is either $C = 2\pi r$ or $C = \pi d$. The question asks for the diameter, so use the latter formula.

$$17\pi = \pi d$$
$$17 = d$$

3. **10π:** Both the area and circumference of a circle are defined in terms of the radius. Use the given area of 25π to find the radius.

$$A = \pi r^2$$
$$25\pi = \pi r^2$$
$$25 = r^2$$
$$5 = r$$

Now use the radius of 5 to find the circumference.

$$C = 2\pi r$$
$$C = 2\pi(5)$$
$$C = 10\pi$$

4. **3π:** If the central angle of the sector is 270°, then it is $\frac{3}{4}$ of the full circle, because $\frac{270°}{360°} = \frac{3}{4}$.

Since the radius is 2, the area of the full circle is $\pi(2)^2 = 4\pi$. The area of the sector is $\frac{3}{4} \times 4\pi = 3\pi$.

5. **240°:** Because you are given the arc length, find the circumference of the full circle and use that to determine what fraction the sector represents.

$$C = 2\pi r = 2\pi(3) = 6\pi$$

$$\text{Fraction of total} = \frac{4\pi}{6\pi} = \frac{2}{3}$$

The central angle is $\frac{2}{3} \times 360° = 240°$.

10

6. **8π:** Begin by finding the area of the whole circle; use that information to determine what fraction the sector represents.

$$\text{Area} = \pi(10)^2 = 100\pi$$
$$\text{Fraction of sector} = \frac{40\pi}{100\pi} = \frac{4}{10} = \frac{2}{5}$$

The circumference of the whole circle is $2\pi r = 20\pi$. Use this, coupled with the fraction of the sector, to determine the arc length.

$$\text{Arc length} = \frac{2}{5} \times 20\pi = 8\pi$$

7. **No:** The two known sides of the triangle are 5 and 19. The third side of the triangle must be greater than $19 - 5$ but less than $19 + 5$. In other words, the third side must be between 14 and 24. The number 13 is less than 14, so 13 cannot be the length of the third side.

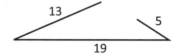

No possible triangle with these lengths.

8. **$9 <$ third side < 25:** If the two known sides of the triangle are 8 and 17, then find the range for the third side by taking the sum and the difference of the known sides.

Sum $= 8 + 17 = 25$
Difference $= 17 - 8 = 9$
The third side must be greater than 9 but less than 25.

9. **$x = 65°$:** The internal angles of a triangle sum to $180°$.

$40 + 75 + x = 180$
$115 + x = 180$
$x = 65$

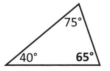

MANHATTAN PREP

10. **$x = 65°$:** The three angles of the triangle sum to 180°, so $50 + x + x = 180$.

$$50 + x + x = 180$$
$$2x = 130$$
$$x = 65$$

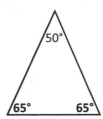

11. **$x = 70°$ and $y = 80°$:** In order to determine the missing angles of the triangle, you'll need to do a little work with the picture. Start with x. Straight lines have a degree measure of 180°, so $110 + x = 180$, and $x = 70$. Now find y.

$$30 + 70 + y = 180$$
$$y = 80$$

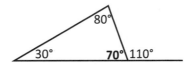

12. **$x° = 80°$:** In this triangle, two sides have the same length (so this triangle is isosceles). Therefore, the two angles opposite the two equal sides will also be equal: x must be 80°.

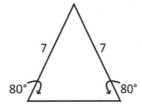

13. **$x = 4$:** In this triangle, two angles are equal (so this triangle is isosceles). The two sides opposite the equal angles must also be equal, so x must equal 4.

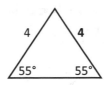

14. **$x° = 110°$:** Two sides have the same length, so the angles opposite the equal sides must also be equal. (This is an isosceles triangle.)

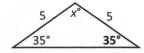

Now solve for x.

$$35 + 35 + x = 180$$
$$x = 110$$

15. **25:**

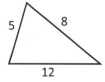

The perimeter of a triangle equals the sum of the three sides, or $5 + 8 + 12 = 25$.

16. **16:** The two angles labeled x are equal, so the sides opposite the equal angles must also be equal.

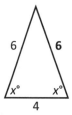

The perimeter is $6 + 6 + 4 = 16$.

17. **15:** In the triangle shown, the base is 6 and the height is 5. Therefore, you can find the area:

$$A = \frac{1}{2}bh$$
$$A = \frac{1}{2}(6)(5)$$
$$A = 15$$

18. **35:** In this triangle, the base is 10 and the height is 7. Remember that the height must be perpendicular to the base, but the height doesn't need to lie within the triangle. Now find the area:

$$A = \frac{1}{2}bh$$
$$A = \frac{1}{2}(10)(7)$$
$$A = 35$$

When you see a problem like this one on the GMAT, you will probably not be given the dotted lines; you'll likely have to realize yourself that the height can be drawn outside of the triangle.

19. **6:** This is a right triangle, so you can use the Pythagorean theorem to solve for the length of the third side. First, though, check to see whether this is one of the Pythagorean triples. It is a multiple of the 3-4-5 triangle; the sides here are 6-8-10. The third side must equal 6.

If you don't recognize the triple, you need to use the Pythagorean theorem to solve.

$$a^2 + 8^2 = 10^2$$
$$a^2 + 64 = 100$$
$$a^2 = 36$$
$$a = 6$$

20. **13:** This triangle is one of the Pythagorean triples, a 5-12-13 triangle. The hypotenuse equals 13.

Alternatively, use the Pythagorean theorem to solve.

$$5^2 + 12^2 = c^2$$
$$25 + 144 = c^2$$
$$169 = c^2$$
$$13 = c$$

21. **6:** This is a 3-4-5 triple, so the length of the third side is 3.

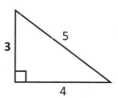

The base of the triangle is 4 and the height is 3. Plug this into the area formula.

$$A = \frac{1}{2}bh$$
$$A = \frac{1}{2}(4)(3)$$
$$A = 6$$

22. **32:** In parallelograms, opposite sides have equal lengths, so two of the sides of the parallelogram have a length of 6 and two sides have a length of 10.

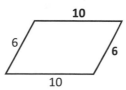

The perimeter is 2(6 + 10) = 32.

23. **36:** The area of a parallelogram is $b \times h$. In this parallelogram, the base is 9 and the height is 4, so the area is $(9) \times (4) = 36$.

24. **$A = 21$ and $P = 20$:** In rectangles, opposite sides have equal lengths, so the rectangle looks like this:

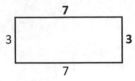

The perimeter is $2(l + w) = 2(3 + 7) = 20$. The area is $l \times w = (7)(3) = 21$.

25. **$A = 48$ and $P = 28$:** The diagonal of the rectangle creates a right triangle, so you can use the Pythagorean theorem to find the length of side CD. Alternatively, triangle ACD is a 6-8-10 triangle, so the length of side CD is 8.

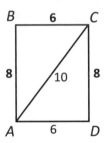

The perimeter of the rectangle is $2(l + w) = 2(8 + 6) = 28$. The area is $l \times w = (8)(6) = 48$.

26. **9π:** Redraw the diagram *without* the circle, so that you can focus on the rectangle. Add in the diagonal AC, as well as its length.

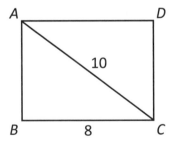

Look at right triangle *ABC*. *AC* functions not only as the diagonal of rectangle *ABCD* but also as the hypotenuse of right triangle *ABC*. Find the third side of triangle *ABC*, either using the Pythagorean theorem or by recognizing a Pythagorean triple (6-8-10).

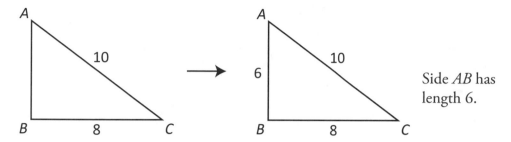

Side *AB* has length 6.

Now redraw the diagram *with* the circle but without the diagonal, since you've gotten what you need from that: the other side of the rectangle.

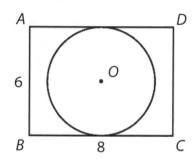

Since the circle touches both *AD* and *BC*, its diameter must be 6.

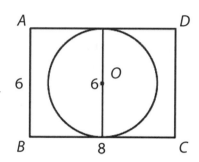

Finally, find the radius and compute the area:

$$d = 6 = 2r$$
$$3 = r$$

$$\text{Area} = \pi r^2$$
$$= \pi (3)^2$$
$$\text{Area} = 9\pi$$

27.

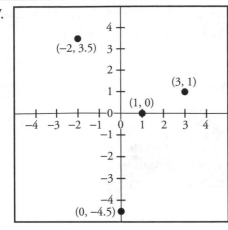

28. 1. $(2, -1)$: **E**
2. $(-1.5, -3)$: **C**
3. $(-1, 2)$: **B**
4. $(3, 2)$: **D**

29.

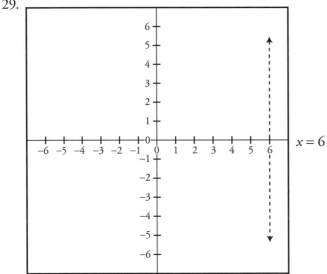

$x = 6$

30.

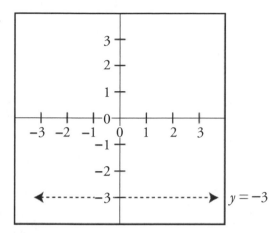

31.

$x = 0$ is the y-axis.

32. 1. (1, −2) is in **Quadrant IV**
     2. (−4.6, 7) is in **Quadrant II**
     3. (−1, −2.5) is in **Quadrant III**
     4. (3, 3) is in **Quadrant I**

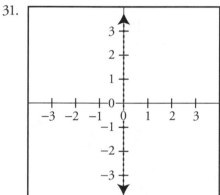

33. 1. $x < 0, y > 0$ indicates **Quadrant II**
    2. $x < 0, y < 0$ indicates **Quadrant III**
    3. $y > 0$ indicates **Quadrants I and II**
    4. $x < 0$ indicates **Quadrants II and III**

34. **$y = -4$**: The point on the line with $x = -3$ has a y-coordinate of -4.

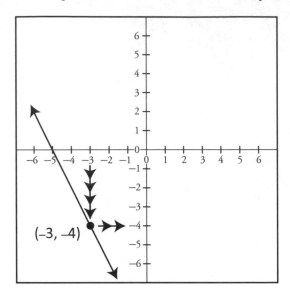

(–3, –4)

35. **False:** Test the point $(9, 21)$ in the equation $y = 2x + 1$. Plug in 9 for x to see whether you get 21 for y.

$$y = 2(9) + 1 = 19$$

Because 19 does not equal 21, the point $(9, 21)$ does not lie on the line.

36. **True:** Test the point $(4, 14)$ in the equation $y = x^2 - 2$. Plug in 4 for x to see whether you get 14 for y.

$$y = (4)^2 - 2 = 14$$

Because 14 is the desired number, the point $(4, 14)$ does lie on the curve defined by the equation $y = x^2 - 2$.

37. **slope = 3, y-intercept = 4:** The equation $y = 3x + 4$ is already in $y = mx + b$ form, so you can directly find the slope and y-intercept. The slope, m, is 3, and the y-intercept, b, is 4.

38. **slope = 2.5 (or $\frac{5}{2}$), y-intercept = –6:** To find the slope and y-intercept of a line, put the equation in $y = mx + b$ form. Next, divide the original equation by 2 to make that happen. Therefore, $2y = 5x - 12$ becomes $y = 2.5x - 6$. The slope, m, is 2.5 (or $\frac{5}{2}$) and the y-intercept, b, is -6.

39.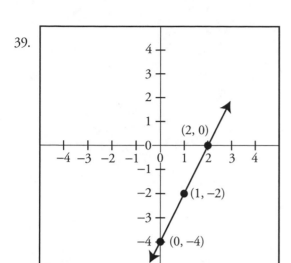

$y = 2x - 4$

slope $= 2$

y-intercept $= -4$

Think of the slope, 2, as a fraction: $\dfrac{2}{1}$. Go up 2 and to the right 1.

Chapter Review: Drill Sets

Drill 1

1. The radius of a circle is 4. What is its area?
2. The diameter of a circle is 7. What is its circumference?
3. The radius of a circle is 3. What is its circumference?
4. The area of a circle is 25π. What is its diameter?
5. The circumference of a circle is 18π. What is its area?

Drill 2

6. The area of a circle is 100π. What is its circumference?
7. The diameter of a circle is 16. Calculate its radius, circumference, and area.
8. Circle A has a circumference of 6π and circle B has an area of 8π. Which circle has the greater area?
9. Circle C has a diameter of 10 and circle D has a circumference of 12π. Which circle has the greater area?
10. Circle A has an area of 64π and circle B has an area of 16π. The radius of circle A is how many times the radius of circle B?

Drill 3

11. A sector has a central angle of 90°. If the sector has a radius of 8, what is the area of the sector?
12. A sector has a central angle of 45° and a radius of 12. What is the arc length of the sector?
13. A sector has an arc length of 7π and a diameter of 14. What is the central angle of the sector?
14. A sector has a central angle of 270°. If the sector has a radius of 4, what is the area of the sector?
15. A sector has an area of 24π and a radius of 12. What is the central angle of the sector?

Drill 4

16. The area of a sector is $\frac{1}{10}$ of the area of the full circle. What is the central angle of the sector?
17. What is the perimeter of a sector with a central angle of 60° and a radius of 18?
18. A sector has a radius of 8 and an area of 8π. What is the arc length of the sector?
19. A sector has an arc length of $\frac{\pi}{2}$ and a central angle of 45°. What is the radius of the sector?
20. Sector A has a radius of 4 and a central angle of 90°. Sector B has a radius of 6 and a central angle of 45°. Which sector has the greater area?

Drill 5

Note: Figures are not necessarily drawn to scale.

21. A triangle has two sides with lengths of 5 and 11, respectively. What is the range of values for the length of the third side?
22. The length of the hypotenuse of a right triangle is 10, and the length of one of the legs is 6. What is the length of the other leg?
23. What is the area of triangle DEF?

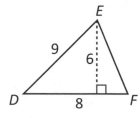

24. Which side of triangle GHI has the longest length?

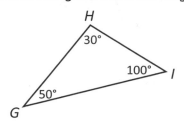

25. What is the value of x?

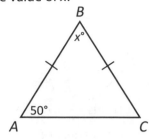

Drill 6

Note: Figures are not necessarily drawn to scale.

26. Two sides of a triangle have lengths 4 and 8. Which of the following are possible side lengths of the third side? (More than one answer may apply.)

(A) 2
(B) 4
(C) 6
(D) 8

27. What is the value of x?

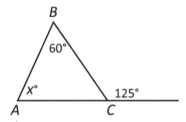

28. Isosceles triangle ABC has two sides with lengths 3 and 9. What is the length of the third side?

29. Which of the following could be the length of side AB, if x < y < z?

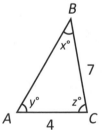

(A) 6
(B) 10
(C) 14

30. What is the area of right triangle ABC?

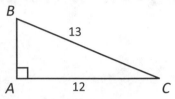

Drill 7

Note: Figures are not necessarily drawn to scale.

31. What is the perimeter of triangle ABC?

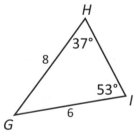

32. The area of right triangle XYZ is 12. What is the length of its hypotenuse?

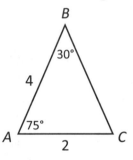

33. What is the length of side HI?

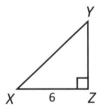

34. Which triangle has the greater perimeter?

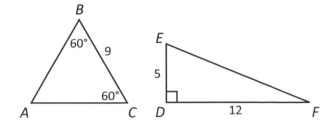

MANHATTAN PREP

35. *ZW* has a length of 3 and *XZ* has a length of 6. What is the area of triangle *XYZ*?

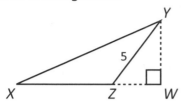

40. Rectangle *WXYZ* and rectangle *OPQR* have equal areas. What is the length of side *PQ*?

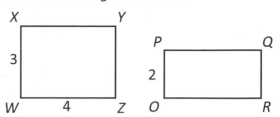

Drill 8

Note: Figures are not necessarily drawn to scale.

36. What is the perimeter of parallelogram *ABCD*?

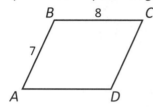

37. What is the area of parallelogram *EFGH*?

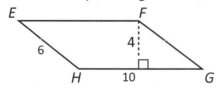

38. The rectangle and the parallelogram pictured below have the same perimeters. What is the length of side *EF*?

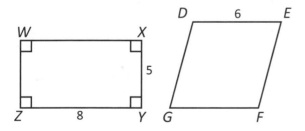

39. In parallelogram *ABCD*, triangle *ABC* has an area of 12. What is the area of triangle *ACD*?

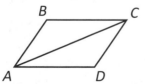

Drill 9

Note: Figures are not necessarily drawn to scale.

41. What is the area of rectangle *ABCD*?

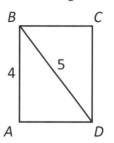

42. In rectangle *ABCD*, the area of triangle *ABC* is 30. What is the length of diagonal *AC*?

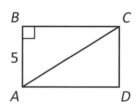

43. Rectangle *EFGH* has an area three times that of rectangle *ABCD*. What is the length of side *FG*?

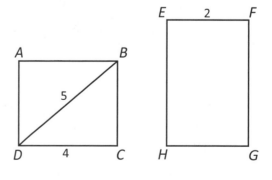

10

44. A rectangle has an area of 22 and a perimeter of 26. What are the length and width of the rectangle?

45. Right triangle *ABC* and rectangle *JKLM* have equal areas. What is the perimeter of rectangle *JKLM*?

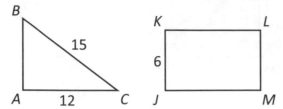

50. Right triangle *ABC* and rectangle *EFGH* have the same perimeter. What is the value of *x*?

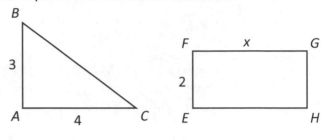

Drill 10

Note: Figures are not necessarily drawn to scale.

46. What is the perimeter of a square with an area of 25?

47. A rectangle and a square have the same area. The square has a perimeter of 32, and the rectangle has a width of 4. What is the length of the rectangle?

48. A circle is inscribed in a square, as shown in the diagram. If the area of the circle is 16π, what is the perimeter of the square?

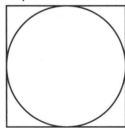

49. Square *WXYZ* has an area of 36. What is the length of diagonal *XZ*?

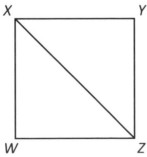

Drill 11

51. Draw a coordinate plane and plot the following points.
    1. (2, 3)
    2. (−2, −1)
    3. (−5, −6)
    4. (4, −2.5)

52. What are the *x*- and *y*-coordinates of the following points?

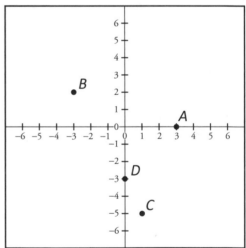

53. What is the *y*-coordinate of the point on the line that has an *x*-coordinate of 3?

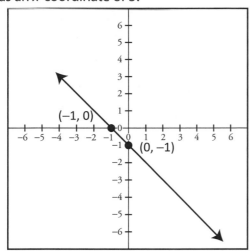

Drill 12

56. Does the point $(-3, 0)$ lie on the curve
$y = x^2 - 3$?

57. For the line $y = 3x - 4$, what is the *y*-coordinate when $x = 2$?

58. What is the *y*-intercept of the line $y = -2x - 7$?

59. Graph the line $y = \dfrac{1}{2}x + 3$.

60. Graph the line $\dfrac{1}{2}y = -\dfrac{1}{2}x + 1$.

54. What is the *x*-coordinate of the point on the line that has a *y*-coordinate of -4?

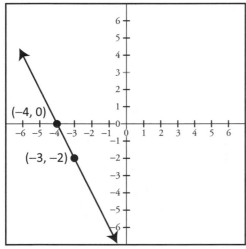

55. Does the point $(-3, 5)$ lie on the line
$y = -2x - 1$?

Drill Sets Solutions

Drill 1

1. **16π:**

$$A = \pi r^2$$
$$A = \pi(4)^2$$
$$A = 16\pi$$

2. **7π:**

$$C = \pi d$$
$$C = \pi(7) = 7\pi$$

3. **6π:**

$$C = 2\pi r$$
$$C = 2\pi(3)$$
$$C = 6\pi$$

4. **10:**

$$A = \pi r^2$$
$$25\pi = \pi r^2$$
$$25 = r^2$$
$$5 = r$$
$$d = 2r = 2(5) = 10$$

5. **81π:** The connection between circumference and area is radius. Use the circumference to solve for the radius.

$$C = 2\pi r$$
$$18\pi = 2\pi r$$
$$18 = 2r$$
$$9 = r$$

Use the radius to find the area.

$$A = \pi r^2$$
$$A = \pi(9)^2$$
$$A = 81\pi$$

Drill 2

6. **20π:**

$$A = \pi r^2$$
$$100\pi = \pi r^2$$
$$100 = r^2$$
$$10 = r$$

Use the radius to find the circumference.

$$C = 2\pi r$$
$$C = 2\pi(10)$$
$$C = 20\pi$$

7. **$r = 8$, $C = 16\pi$, and $A = 64\pi$:**

$$d = 2r$$
$$16 = 2r$$
$$8 = r$$

$$C = 2\pi r$$
$$C = 2\pi(8)$$
$$C = 16\pi$$

$$A = \pi r^2$$
$$A = \pi(8)^2$$
$$A = 64\pi$$

8. **Circle A:** Find the radius of circle A, and then calculate its area.

$$C_A = 2\pi r_A$$
$$6\pi = 2\pi r_A$$
$$3 = r_A$$

$$A_A = \pi r_A^{\,2}$$
$$A_A = \pi(3)^2$$
$$A_A = 9\pi$$

Because 9π is greater than 8π, circle A has the greater area.

9. **Circle D:** You could find the area of each circle and compare. Note, though, that it is sufficient to find the radii of both circles. The one with the greater radius will also have the greater area. Don't do more work than you're asked to do! You only need to tell which circle has the greater area; you don't need to be able to say what that area is.

$$d_C = 10$$
$$r_C = 5$$
$$C_D = 2\pi r_D$$
$$12\pi = 2\pi r_D$$
$$6 = r_D$$

Since circle D has the greater radius, it will have the greater area.

10. **Two times:** The radius of circle A is two times the radius of circle B.

Careful: Don't use the areas to determine the ratio of the two circles' radii. Find the radii.

$$A_A = \pi r_A^2 \qquad\qquad A_B = \pi r_B^2$$
$$64\pi = \pi r_A^2 \qquad\qquad 16\pi = \pi r_B^2$$
$$64 = r_A^2 \qquad\qquad 16 = r_B^2$$
$$8 = r_A \qquad\qquad 4 = r_B$$

Thus, 8 is 2 times 4.

Drill 3

11. **16π:** If the sector has a central angle of 90°, then the sector is $\dfrac{90}{360} = \dfrac{1}{4}$ of the circle. Next, find the area of the entire circle

$$A = \pi r^2$$
$$A = \pi (8)^2$$
$$A = 64\pi$$

The area of the sector is $\dfrac{1}{4}$ of the total area: $64\pi \times \dfrac{1}{4} = 16\pi$.

12. **3π:** A central angle of 45° corresponds to $\dfrac{45}{360} = \dfrac{1}{8}$ of the circle. Next, find the circumference of the entire circle.

$$C = 2\pi r$$
$$C = 2\pi (12)$$
$$C = 24\pi$$

The arc length of the sector is $\dfrac{1}{8}$ of the total circumference: $24\pi \times \dfrac{1}{8} = 3\pi$.

13. **180°:** To find the central angle of the sector, you need to determine what fraction of the full circle the sector represents. Because you were given the arc length, find the circumference of the circle, and use those two numbers to determine the fraction.

$$C = \pi d$$
$$C = \pi (14) = 14\pi$$

$$\dfrac{7\pi}{14\pi} = \dfrac{1}{2}$$

The arc length represents $\frac{1}{2}$ of the circle. The central angle, therefore, also represents $\frac{1}{2}$ of the total 360°:

$360° \times \frac{1}{2} = 180°$.

14. **12π:** The sector represents $\frac{270°}{360°} = \frac{3}{4}$ of the circle. Next, find the area of the whole circle:

$A = \pi r^2$

$A = \pi(4)^2$

$A = 16\pi$

The area of the sector is $\frac{3}{4}$ of the total area: $16\pi \times \frac{3}{4} = 12\pi$.

15. **60°:** First, find the area of the whole circle.

$A = \pi r^2$

$A = \pi(12)^2$

$A = 144\pi$

The sector represents $\frac{24\pi}{144\pi} = \frac{1}{6}$ of the circle. The central angle is also $\frac{1}{6}$ of the circle: $360° \times \frac{1}{6} = 60°$.

Drill 4

16. **36°:** If the area of the sector is $\frac{1}{10}$ of the area of the full circle, then the central angle is also $\frac{1}{10}$ of the degree measure of the full circle.

$360° \times \frac{1}{10} = 36°$

17. **6π + 36:** The perimeter of a sector equals the arc length plus two radii.

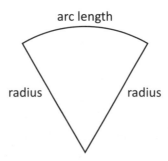

arc length

radius   radius

Begin by finding the circumference and the fraction of the total circle that the central angle represents.

$$C = 2\pi r$$
$$C = 2\pi(18) = 36\pi$$
$$\frac{\text{Central angle}}{\text{Total angle}} = \frac{60}{360} = \frac{1}{6}$$

The arc length is $\frac{1}{6}$ of the circumference: $36\pi \times \frac{1}{6} = 6\pi$.

The perimeter is $6\pi + 18 + 18 = 6\pi + 36$.

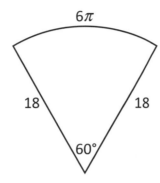

18. **2π:** First, determine what fraction of the circle the sector represents. Since you were given the area of the sector, find the area of the whole circle.

$$A = \pi r^2$$
$$A = \pi(8)^2$$
$$A = 64\pi$$
$$\frac{\text{Area of sector}}{\text{Area of circle}} = \frac{8\pi}{64\pi} = \frac{1}{8}$$

The sector represents $\frac{1}{8}$ of the circle. To find the arc length, find the circumference of the whole circle.

$$C = 2\pi r$$
$$C = 2\pi(8) = 16\pi$$
$$\text{Arc length} = 16\pi \times \frac{1}{8} = 2\pi$$

19. **2:** Begin by determining what portion of the circle the sector represents.

$$\frac{\text{Central angle}}{\text{Total angle}} = \frac{45}{360} = \frac{1}{8}$$

The sector represents $\frac{1}{8}$ of the circle. If the arc length of the sector is $\frac{\pi}{2}$, then the circumference of the whole circle is

$$\frac{\pi}{2} \times 8 = 4\pi.$$

$$C = 2\pi r$$
$$4\pi = 2\pi r$$
$$2 = r$$

20. **Sector B:** First, calculate what you can for sector A. Determine the fraction that the sector represents, the area of the entire circle, and finally the area of sector A.

$$\frac{\text{Central angle}}{\text{Total angle}} = \frac{90}{360} = \frac{1}{4}$$

$$A_A = \pi r_A^{\ 2}$$
$$A_A = \pi(4)^2$$
$$A_A = 16\pi$$

Area of sector $A = \dfrac{1}{4} \times 16\pi = 4\pi$

Calculate the equivalent information for sector B.

$$\frac{\text{Central angle}}{\text{Total angle}} = \frac{45}{360} = \frac{1}{8}$$

$$A_B = \pi r_B^{\ 2}$$
$$A_B = \pi(6)^2$$
$$A_B = 36\pi$$

Area of sector $B = \dfrac{1}{8} \times 36\pi = \dfrac{9}{2}\pi = 4.5\pi$

Because $4.5\pi > 4\pi$, the area of sector B is greater than the area of sector A.

Drill 5

21. **6 < third side < 16:** The sum of the lengths of any two sides of a triangle must be greater than the length of the third side. Therefore, the third side must be less than $5 + 11 = 16$. The third side must also be greater than the difference of the lengths of the other two sides: $11 - 5 = 6$. Therefore, the third side must be between 6 and 16.

22. **8:** This is a Pythagorean triple, a 6-8-10 triangle. When you think you may have a triple, do make sure that the longest measure corresponds to the hypotenuse. If you were told that the two *legs* were 6 and 10, then the hypotenuse could not be 8, since the hypotenuse is the longest side of the triangle.

Alternatively, use the Pythagorean theorem to solve.

$$a^2 + b^2 = c^2$$
$$6^2 + b^2 = 10^2$$
$$b^2 = 100 - 36$$
$$b^2 = 64$$
$$b = 8$$

23. **24:**

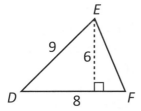

Side *DF* can act as the base, and the line dropping straight down from point *E* to touch side *DF* at a right angle can act as the height. The base is 8 and the height is 6, so you can find the area:

$$A = \frac{1}{2}bh$$

$$A = \frac{1}{2}(8)(6)$$

$$A = 24$$

24. **GH:**

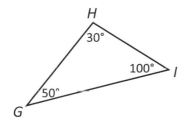

Although *GI* looks like the longest side, don't trust how the picture looks when the question states that the picture is not drawn to scale. In any triangle, the longest side is opposite the largest angle. Angle *GIH* is the largest angle in the triangle, so side *GH* is the longest side.

25. **80°:** In triangle *ABC*, sides *AB* and *BC* are equal, so their opposite angles are also equal. Therefore, angle *ACB* is also 50°.

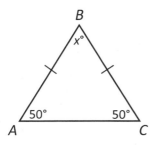

Now find angle *x*.

$$50 + 50 + x = 180$$

$$100 + x = 180$$

$$x = 80$$

Drill 6

26. **(C) and (D):** The sum of the lengths of any two sides of a triangle must be greater than the length of the third side. Therefore, the third side must be less than $4 + 8 = 12$. In addition, the third side must be greater than the difference of the other two sides: $8 - 4 = 4$. Only values between 4 and 12 are possible values for the third side of the triangle. (Note that 4 itself is not a possible value. The third side must be greater than 4.)

27. $x = 65°$: First, solve for angle BCA. A straight line equals 180°, so angle BCA equals $180 - 125 = 55$.

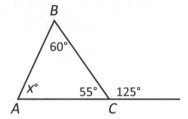

Now solve for x.

$$60 + 55 + x = 180$$
$$x = 65$$

28. **9:** This is a tricky one. If the triangle is isosceles, then two sides have equal length, but is the unknown third side 3 or 9? If the third side were 3, then the lengths of two of the sides would not sum to greater than the length of the third side, because $3 + 3$ is not greater than 9.

    Use the rule about the third side of any triangle: The third side must be greater than the difference of the other two sides but smaller than the sum of the other two sides. The third side, then, has to be between $9 - 3 = 6$ and $9 + 3 = 12$.

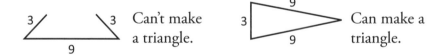

    Because 3 is not a valid possibility, the length of the third side must be 9.

29. **(B):** Start with the rule about the third side of any triangle. The third side must be between $7 - 4 = 3$ and $7 + 4 = 11$. That knocks out answer (C), 14.

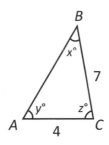

$$3 < \text{third side} < 11$$

Both 6 and 10 are still possibilities according to the rule about the third side of any triangle, though. Did the problem provide any other information that you haven't used yet?

Yes: angle x < angle y < angle z. If this is the case, then side AC < side BC < side AB, or $4 < 7 <$ side AB. Side AB cannot be 6, but it could be 10.

30. **30:** Find the base and the height. Because this is a right triangle, the base can be 12 and the height can be the leg AB. The triangle is a Pythagorean triple, so side $AB = 5$.

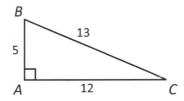

Now calculate the area.

$$A = \frac{1}{2}bh$$
$$A = \frac{1}{2}(12)(5)$$
$$A = 30$$

Drill 7

31. **10:** The perimeter is the sum of the three sides of the triangle. This triangle is not a Pythagorean triple, nor is it a right triangle, so there must be some other way to figure out the unknown third side.

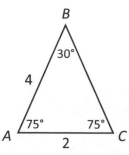

Let x equal the unknown third angle:

$30 + 75 + x = 180$

$x = 75$

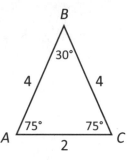

Angle *BAC* and angle *BCA* are both 75, so the triangle sides opposite those angles are also equal. Side *AB* has a length of 4, so side *BC* also has a length of 4.

The perimeter is $4 + 4 + 2 = 10$.

32. **$\sqrt{52}$ *or* $2\sqrt{13}$** : The area of a right triangle can be calculated using the two legs as the base and height, so use the given area to find the length of the unknown leg.

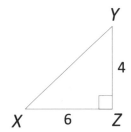

$$A = \frac{1}{2}bh$$

$$12 = \frac{1}{2}(6)h$$

$$12 = 3h$$

$$4 = h$$

Now use the Pythagorean theorem to find the length of the hypotenuse.

$a^2 + b^2 = c^2$

$4^2 + 6^2 = c^2$

$16 + 36 = c^2$

$52 = c^2$

$\sqrt{52} = c$

You can also write $\sqrt{52}$ as $\sqrt{52} = \sqrt{4 \times 13} = 2\sqrt{13}$.

33. **10:** First, calculate the value of the unknown third angle.

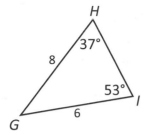

Let x = the third angle.
$37 + 53 + x = 180$
$90 + x = 180$
$x = 90$

It turns out that the third angle is a right angle! Remember that the chapter directions indicated that figures are not necessarily drawn to scale (as is always the case on Data Sufficiency problems on the GMAT). It may help to redraw the triangle in a way that more closely approximates the real dimensions.

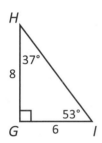

Now, you have a chance to recognize that this is a Pythagorean triple in disguise. It's a 6-8-10 triangle, so the hypotenuse equals 10:

34. **Triangle DEF:** Start with triangle *ABC*. Two of the angles equal 60°. The third angle must also be 60°, since $60 + 60 + 60 = 180$. Because the triangle is equilateral (all of the angles are the same), all of the sides are the same length, 9. The perimeter is $3(9) = 27$.

Triangle *DEF* is a right triangle and a Pythagorean triple. The hypotenuse equals 13, and the perimeter is $5 + 12 + 13 = 30$.

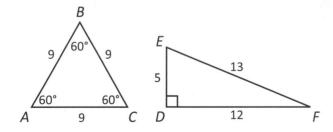

Because $30 > 27$, triangle *DEF* has the greater perimeter.

35. **12:** Redraw the diagram, and fill in everything you know about triangle *XYZ*.

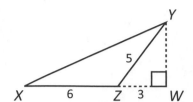

If *XZ* is the base, then *YW* can act as the height. Triangle *ZYW* is a right triangle and Pythagorean triple, a 3-4-5 triangle. Side *YW* = 4.

Now calculate the area of the triangle.

$$A = \frac{1}{2}bh$$

$$A = \frac{1}{2}(6)(4)$$

$$A = 12$$

Drill 8

36. **30:** Opposite sides of a parallelogram are equal, so side *CD* has a length of 7 and side *AD* has a length of 8. The perimeter is 2(7 + 8) = 2(15) = 30.

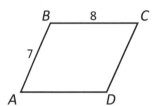

37. **40:** The area of a parallelogram is base × height. In this parallelogram, the base is 10 and the height is 4 (the base and height need to be perpendicular). The area is 10 × 4 = 40.

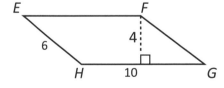

38. **7:** Start with the rectangle, since it provides enough information to calculate the perimeter.

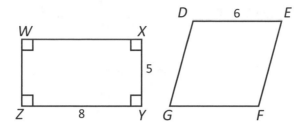

The opposite sides of a rectangle are the same length, so the perimeter of the rectangle is $2(5 + 8) = 2(13) = 26$.

The problem indicates that the perimeters of the two shapes are the same, so use this information to find the length of the unknown side of the parallelogram, *EF*.

$$26 = 2(6 + EF)$$
$$26 = 12 + 2EF$$
$$14 = 2EF$$
$$7 = EF$$

39. **12:** When you split any parallelogram by its diagonal, you create two identical triangles. In this case, since triangle *ABC* has an area of 12, triangle *ACD* must also have an area of 12.

40. **6:** Start by finding the area of rectangle *WXYZ*. The area of a rectangle = $lw = (3)(4) = 12$.

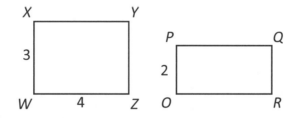

Since the two rectangles have equal areas, rectangle *OPQR* also has an area of 12. Use this information to find the length of side *PQ*. You know the length of side *OP*, so that is the width of rectangle *OPQR*. Side *PQ* is the length of rectangle *OPQR*. Therefore:

$$A = lw$$
$$12 = l(2)$$
$$6 = l$$

Drill 9

41. **12:** The area of a rectangle equals the length times the width. The length, 4, is already given. Find the width, *AD* (or *BC*).

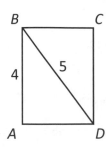

The triangle *ABD* is a Pythagorean triple—a 3-4-5 triangle. The length of side *AD* is therefore 3.

$$A = lw$$
$$A = (4)(3)$$
$$A = 12$$

42. **13:** First, use the area of the triangle to find the length of side *BC*.

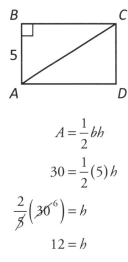

$$A = \frac{1}{2}bh$$

$$30 = \frac{1}{2}(5)h$$

$$\frac{2}{\cancel{5}}\left(\cancel{30}^{6}\right) = h$$

$$12 = h$$

The triangle is a 5-12-13 Pythagorean triple, so the length of the hypotenuse is 13. The hypotenuse, *AC*, is also the diagonal of the rectangle.

43. **18:** Use the information given for rectangle *ABCD* to find the area.

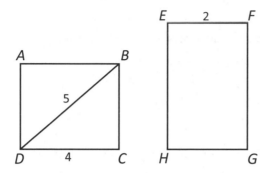

Triangle *BCD* is a 3-4-5 Pythagorean triple, so the side of length *BC* equals 3. The area of rectangle *ABCD* = lw = (3)(4) = 12.

According to the question stem, the area of rectangle *EFGH* is three times the area of rectangle *ABCD*, so the area of rectangle *EFGH* equals (3)(12) = 36. Use this information to find the length of side *FG*. Let *l* equal the length of *FG*.

$A = lw$
$36 = l(2)$
$18 = l$

44. **11 and 2:** The question stem allows you to write two equations.

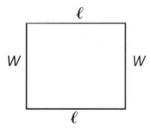

The area of the rectangle is 22, and the perimeter of the rectangle is 26.

A = lw = 22
P = $2(l + w)$ = 26

The second equation can be simplified to $l + w = 13$.

Substitute to solve for the values of the variables. In the second equation, isolate *w* (or *l*, your choice).

$l = 13 - w$

Substitute $(13 - w)$ for l in the first equation.

$(13 - w)w = 22$

$13w - w^2 = 22$ This is a quadratic, so move everything to one side to set it equal to 0.

$0 = w^2 - 13w + 22$

$0 = (w - 11)(w - 2)$ Factor the equation and solve.

$w = 11$ or $w = 2$

Which is it, 11 or 2? Plug the values into one of the original equations. What happens? It turns out that when $w = 11$, $l = 2$, and when $w = 2$, $l = 11$. Traditionally, the length is considered longer than the width, so the width is 2 and the length is 11.

45. **30:** Start with triangle *ABC*, since more information is provided for that shape.

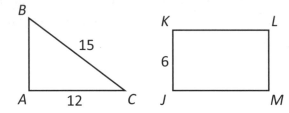

You can use the Pythagorean theorem to find side *AB*…but examine that triangle for a second. Does anything look familiar?

A 9-12-15 triangle is a 3-4-5 triangle in disguise; all of the measurements are tripled. Therefore, side $AB = 9$. Use that information to find the area of the triangle.

$A = \dfrac{1}{2}bh$

$A = \dfrac{1}{2}(12)(9)$

$A = 54$

Since the areas of the two shapes are the same, rectangle *JKLM* also has an area of 54. Use this information to find the length of the rectangle.

$A = lw$

$54 = l(6)$

$9 = l$

Now calculate the perimeter: $2(l + w) = 2(9 + 6) = 2(15) = 30$.

Drill 10

46. **20:** A square has four equal sides, so the area of a square is the length of one side squared.

$$A = s^2$$
$$25 = s^2$$
$$5 = s$$

The perimeter of a square is equal to four times the length of one side.

$$P = 4s$$
$$P = 4(5) = 20$$

47. **16:** Begin by drawing the shapes described in the problem.

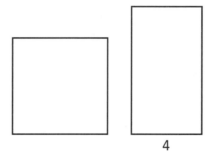

4

A square has four equal sides, so the perimeter is four times the length of one side. Let s = length of a side of the square. Solve for s, then find the area of the square.

$$4s = 32$$
$$s = 8$$
$$A = s^2 = (8)^2 = 64$$

Since the two shapes have the same area, the area of the rectangle is also 64. The width of the rectangle is 4, so solve for the length.

$$A = lw$$
$$64 = l(4)$$
$$16 = l$$

48. **32:** Whenever you're given a diagram that combines shapes, find a common link between the two shapes. When a circle is inscribed in a square, the diameter of the circle is the same as the length of one side of the square.

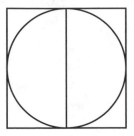

You can use the area of the circle to find the radius and then the diameter.

$$A = \pi r^2$$
$$16\pi = \pi r^2$$
$$16 = r^2$$
$$4 = r$$

If the radius is 4, then the diameter is 8. The diameter also equals one side of the square, so you can find the perimeter:

$$P = 4s$$
$$P = 4(8) = 32$$

49. $\sqrt{72}$ *or* $6\sqrt{2}$: Use the area of the square to find the length of one side.

$$A = s^2$$
$$36 = s^2$$
$$6 = s$$

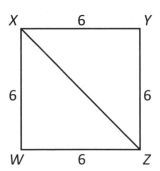

Now use the Pythagorean theorem to find the length of the diagonal *XZ*.

$$a^2 + b^2 = c^2$$
$$6^2 + 6^2 = c^2$$
$$36 + 36 = c^2$$
$$72 = c^2$$
$$\sqrt{72} = c$$

$\sqrt{72}$ can also be written as $\sqrt{72} = \sqrt{36 \times 2} = 6\sqrt{2}$.

50. **$x = 4$:** Start with the triangle. It's a 3-4-5 Pythagorean triple, so the hypotenuse is 5.

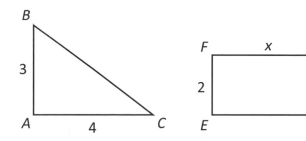

The perimeter of triangle *ABC* is $3 + 4 + 5 = 12$.

Since the two shapes have the same perimeter, the perimeter of rectangle *EFGH* is also 12. Use this information to find the value of *x*.

$$P = 2(l + w)$$
$$12 = 2(2 + x)$$
$$12 = 4 + 2x$$
$$8 = 2x$$
$$4 = x$$

Drill 11

51.

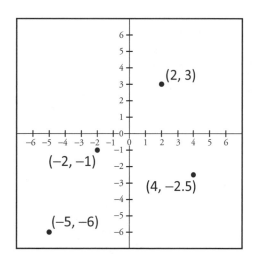

52. A. (3, 0)
     B. (−3, 2)
     C. (1, −5)
     D. (0, −3)

53. **−4:** Find $x = 3$ on the x-axis, then go straight down to the line and draw a point. Next, move straight left to the y-axis to find the corresponding y-value. The point is $(3, -4)$.

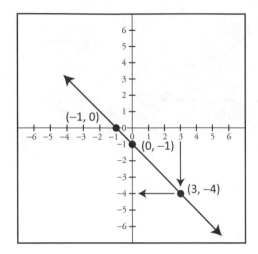

54. **−2:** Find $y = -4$ on the y-axis, then go straight left to the line and draw a point. Next, move straight up to the x-axis to find the corresponding x-value. The point is $(-2, -4)$.

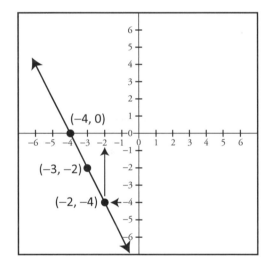

55. **Yes:** Plug the point $(-3, 5)$ into the equation $y = -2x - 1$. If the math works, then this point does lie on this line. If the math does not work, then this point does not lie on this line.

$$y = -2x - 1$$
$$(5) = -2(-3) - 1$$
$$5 = 6 - 1$$
$$5 = 5 \text{ True!}$$

The math is true, so this point does lie on this line.

Drill 12

56. **No:** Plug the point $(-3, 0)$ into the equation $y = x^2 - 3$. If the math works, then this point does lie on this curve. If the math does not work, then this point does not lie on this curve.

$$y = x^2 - 3$$
$$0 = (-3)^2 - 3$$
$$0 = 9 - 3$$
$$0 = 6 \text{ False!}$$

The math is false, so this point does not lie on this curve.

57. **2:** To find the y-coordinate, plug in 2 for x and solve for y.

$$y = 3(2) - 4$$
$$y = 6 - 4 = 2$$

The y-coordinate is 2. The point is $(2, 2)$.

58. **–7:** The equation of the line $y = -2x - 7$ is already in $y = mx + b$ form. In this form, b stands for the y-intercept, so look at the equation to find the y-intercept. The y-intercept is $b = -7$. The point is $(0, -7)$. (For the y-intercept, the x value is always 0.)

59. The equation is in $y = mx + b$ form. The y-intercept, b, is 3, so place a point at $(0, 3)$. The slope, m, is $\dfrac{1}{2}$. Count up 1 and to the right 2 to get to the point $(2, 4)$. Draw a line to connect the two points.

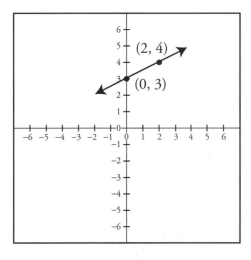

60. First, put the equation into $y = mx + b$ form. Multiply both sides by 2.

$y = -x + 2$

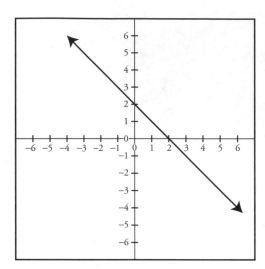

The y-intercept is 2, so place a point at (0, 2).

The slope (m) is −1, so the line drops to the right. Count down 1, right 1 and place another dot.

Draw a line to connect the two dots.

Glossary

absolute value: The distance from 0 on the number line for a particular term. E.g., the absolute value of −7 is 7, or |−7| = 7.

arc length: A section of a circle's circumference.

area: The space enclosed by a given closed shape on a plane; the formula depends on the specific shape. E.g., the area of a rectangle equals *length* × *width*.

axis: One of the two number lines (*x*-axis or *y*-axis) used to indicate position on a coordinate plane.

base: 1) In the expression b^n, the variable *b* represents the base. The base is multiplied by itself *n* times. E.g., $3^4 = 3 \times 3 \times 3 \times 3$. 2) Can refer to a side of a triangle when calculating the area of the triangle.

center (circle): The point from which any point on a circle's circumference is equidistant. The distance from the center to any point on the circumference is called the *radius*.

central angle (circle): The angle created by any two radii (lines drawn from the center of the circle to any point on the circumference).

circle: A set of points in a plane that are equidistant from a fixed center point.

circumference: The measure of the perimeter of a circle. The circumference of a circle can be found with the formula $C = 2\pi r$, where *C* is the circumference, *r* is the radius, and π is a constant (which you can approximate as 3.14).

coefficient: A number that is multiplied by a variable. In the equation $y = 2x + 5$, the coefficient of the *x* term is 2.

common denominator: When adding or subtracting fractions, first find a common denominator, generally the smallest common multiple of both numbers. (Note: You can also use the double-cross technique to add fractions.)

Example:

Given $\dfrac{3}{5} + \dfrac{1}{10}$, the two denominators are 5 and 10. The smallest multiple that works for both numbers is 10. The common denominator, therefore, is 10.

constant: In an equation or expression, a number that doesn't change. E.g., in the equation $y = 3x + 2$, the numbers 3 and 2 are constants. In the equation $y = mx + b$, *m* and *b* are also constants: once you know the value of *m* or *b* for a particular equation, it never changes. The *x* and *y*, on the other hand, are *variables*; they can have many possible values.

coordinate plane: Consists of a horizontal axis (typically labeled "*x*") and a vertical axis (typically labeled "*y*"), crossing at the number 0 on both axes.

decimal: Most commonly refers to numbers that fall in between integers, such as 1.5. An integer can be expressed in decimal form, though, such as 2.00 or 3.4×10^2. A decimal can express a part-to-whole relationship, just as a percent or fraction can.

Example:

1.2 is a decimal. The integers 1 and 2 are not decimals. An integer written as 1.0, however, is considered a decimal. The decimal 0.2 is equivalent to 20% or to $\dfrac{2}{10} = \dfrac{1}{5}$.

denominator: The bottom of a fraction. In the fraction $\dfrac{7}{2}$, 2 is the denominator.

diameter: A line segment that passes through the center of a circle and whose endpoints lie on the circle's circumference.

difference: When one number is subtracted from another, the difference is what is left over. The difference of 7 and 5 is 2, because $7 - 5 = 2$.

digit: The ten numbers 0, 1, 2, 3, 4, 5, 6, 7, 8, and 9. Used in combination to represent other numbers (e.g., 12 or 0.38).

distribute: To multiply a term across other terms. For example, given the expression $3(x + 2)$, to distribute the 3, multiply each term in the parentheses by 3: $3(x + 2) = 3x + 6$. For the reverse math, see: *factor (verb)*.

distributed form: Presenting an expression as a sum or difference. In distributed form, terms are added or subtracted. $x^2 - 1$ is in distributed form, as is $x^2 + 2x + 1$. In contrast, $(x + 1)(x - 1)$ is not in distributed form; it is in factored form.

divisible: If an integer x divided by another number y yields an integer, then x is said to be divisible by y.

Example:

Because 12 divided by 3 yields the integer 4, 12 is divisible by 3. On the other hand, 12 divided by 5 does not yield an integer. Therefore, 12 is not divisible by 5.

divisor: The part of a division operation that comes after the division sign. In the operation $22 \div 4$ (or $\dfrac{22}{4}$), 4 is the divisor. *Divisor* is also a synonym for *factor (noun)*.

equation: A combination of mathematical expressions and symbols that contains an equals sign. For example, $3 + 7 = 10$ is an equation, as is $x + y = 3$. An equation makes a statement: left side equals right side.

equilateral triangle: A triangle in which all three angles are equal (and all three are 60°); in addition, all three sides are of equal length.

even: An integer is even if it is divisible by 2. The integer 14 is even because $\dfrac{14}{2} = 7$, which is an integer.

exponent: In the expression b^n, the variable n represents the exponent. The exponent indicates how many times to multiply the base, b, by itself. For example, $4^3 = 4 \times 4 \times 4$, or 4 multiplied by itself three times.

MANHATTAN PREP

expression: A combination of numbers and mathematical symbols that does not contain an equals sign. For example, xy is an expression, as is $x + 3$. An expression represents a quantity.

factor (noun): Integers that divide evenly into an integer. For instance, 6 is a factor of 12 because $12 \div 6 = 2$, an integer. On the GMAT, problems about factors are typically limited to positive integers; in this case, factors are equal to or smaller than the integer in question. The factors of 12 are 1, 2, 3, 4, 6, and 12. Note: For any given number, 1 and the number itself are always factors of that number.

factor (verb): To pull a common factor out of multiple terms. For example, given the expression $3x + 6$, factor out the common term of 3: $3x + 6 = 3(x + 2)$. For the reverse math, see: *distribute*.

factored form: Presenting an expression as a product. In factored form, expressions are multiplied together. The expression $(x + 1)(x - 1)$ is in factored form: $(x + 1)$ and $(x - 1)$ are the factors. In contrast, $x^2 - 1$ is not in factored form; it is in *distributed form*.

factor foundation rule: If a is a factor of b, and b is a factor of c, then a is also a factor of c. For example, 2 is a factor of 10, and 10 is a factor of 60. Therefore, 2 is also a factor of 60.

factor tree: Use the "factor tree" to break any number down into its prime factors (see: *prime number*). For example:

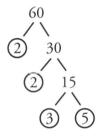

FOIL: **F**irst, **O**utside, **I**nside, **L**ast; an acronym to remember the method for converting from factored to distributed form in a quadratic equation or expression. For example, $(x + 2)(x - 3)$ is a quadratic expression in factored form. Multiply the First, Outside, Inside, and Last terms to get the distributed form.

Example:

Factored form: $(y + 2)(y - 3)$

First: $y \times y = y^2$
Outside: $y \times (-3) = -3y$
Inside: $y \times 2 = 2y$
Last: $2 \times (-3) = -6$

Distributed form: $y^2 - 3y + 2y - 6 = y^2 - y - 6$

fraction: A way to express numbers that fall in between integers (though integers can also be expressed in fractional form). A fraction expresses a part-to-whole relationship in terms of a numerator (the part) and a denominator (the whole). For example, $\frac{3}{4}$ is a fraction, as is $\frac{6}{5}$. (The latter fraction has a special name. See: *improper fraction*.)

hypotenuse: The longest side of a right triangle. The hypotenuse is opposite the right angle.

improper fraction: Fractions that are greater than 1, such as $\frac{7}{2}$. Improper fractions can also be written as mixed numbers, such as, $\frac{7}{2} = 3\frac{1}{2}$.

inequality: A comparison of quantities that have different values. There are four ways to express inequalities: less than ($<$), less than or equal to ($\leq$), greater than ($>$), or greater than or equal to ($\geq$). Inequalities can be manipulated in the same way as equations with one exception: when multiplying or dividing by a negative number, the inequality sign must be flipped to the other direction.

integers: Numbers, such as -1, 0, 1, 2, and 3, that have no fractional part. Integers include the counting numbers (1, 2, 3, ...), their negative counterparts (-1, -2, -3, ...), and 0.

interior angles: The angles that appear in the interior of a closed shape. For example, a triangle has three interior angles.

isosceles triangle: A triangle in which two of the three angles are equal; in addition, the sides opposite the two equal angles are equal in length.

line: A set of points that extend infinitely in both directions without curving. On the GMAT, lines are by definition perfectly straight. They equal 180°.

line segment: A continuous, finite section of a line. The sides of a triangle or of a rectangle are line segments.

linear equation: An equation that does not contain exponents or multiple variables multiplied together. For example, $x + y = 3$ is a linear equation, but $xy = 3$ and $y = x^2$ are not. When plotted on a coordinate plane, linear equations create lines.

mixed number: An integer combined with a proper fraction. For example, $3\frac{1}{2}$ is a mixed number. Mixed numbers can also be written as improper fractions: $3\frac{1}{2} = \frac{7}{2}$.

multiple: Multiples are integers formed by multiplying some integer by any other integer. For example, 12 is a multiple of 12 (12×1), as are 24 ($= 12 \times 2$), 36 ($= 12 \times 3$), 48 ($= 12 \times 4$), and 60 ($= 12 \times 5$). (Negative multiples are possible in mathematics, but you typically don't have to use them to get GMAT questions right. You can usually just stick with positive multiples.)

negative: Any number to the left of 0 on a number line; can be integer or non-integer.

negative exponent: Any exponent less than 0. To find a value for a term with a negative exponent, put the term containing the exponent in the denominator of a fraction and make the exponent positive, such as, $4^{-2} = \frac{1}{4^2}$. Alternatively, if the term with the negative exponent is already in the denominator of a fraction, flip the fraction and make the exponent positive: $\frac{1}{3^{-2}} = 3^2 = 9$.

number line: A straight line that represents all of the numbers from negative infinity to infinity.

numerator: The top of a fraction. In the fraction $\frac{7}{2}$, the numerator is 7.

odd: An odd integer is not divisible by 2 (i.e., division by 2 results in a non-integer value). The number 15 is odd because $\frac{15}{2} = 7.5$, which is not an integer.

order of operations: The order in which mathematical operations must be carried out in order to simplify an expression. See: *PEMDAS*.

origin: The coordinate pair (0, 0) represents the origin of a coordinate plane.

parallelogram: A four-sided closed shape composed of straight lines in which the opposite sides are equal and the opposite angles are equal.

PEMDAS: An acronym that stands for Parentheses, Exponents, Multiplication, Division, Addition, Subtraction; used to remember the order of operations.

percent: Literally, "per 100"; expresses a special part-to-whole relationship between a number (the part) and 100 (the whole). A special type of fraction or decimal that involves the number 100 (e.g., 50% = 50 out of 100).

perimeter: In a polygon, the sum of the lengths of the sides.

perpendicular: Lines that intersect at a 90° angle.

plane: A flat, two-dimensional surface that extends infinitely in every direction.

point: An object that exists in a single location on the coordinate plane. Each point has a unique *x*-coordinate and *y*-coordinate that together describe its location. For example, (1, −2) is a point.

polygon: A two-dimensional, closed shape made of line segments. For example, a triangle is a polygon, as is a rectangle. A circle is a closed shape, but it is not a polygon because it does not contain line segments.

positive: Any number to the right of 0 on a number line; can be an integer or a non-integer.

prime factorization: A number expressed as a product of its *prime numbers*. For example, the prime factorization of 60 is $2 \times 2 \times 3 \times 5$. Every number has a unique prime factorization; that is, no two numbers have the same prime factorization.

prime number: A positive integer with *exactly* two different factors: 1 and itself. The number 1 does not qualify as prime because it has only one factor, not two. The number 2 is the smallest prime number; it is also the only even prime number. The numbers 2, 3, 5, 7, 11, 13, and so on are prime.

product: The end result when two numbers are multiplied together. For example, the product of 4 and 5 is 20.

Pythagorean theorem: A formula used to calculate the sides of a right triangle: $a^2 + b^2 = c^2$, where a and b are the two sides (legs) that create the 90° angle, and c is the length of the side (hypotenuse) across from the 90° angle.

Pythagorean triple: A set of three numbers that describes the lengths of the three sides of a right triangle in which all three sides have integer lengths. Common Pythagorean triples are 3-4-5, 6-8-10, and 5-12-13.

quadrant: One-quarter of the coordinate plane. Bounded on two sides by the x- and y-axes.

quadratic expression: An expression including a variable raised to the second power (and no higher powers). Commonly of the form $ax^2 + bx + c$, where a, b, and c are constants. (A **quadratic equation** contains both a quadratic expression and an equals sign.)

quotient: The result of dividing one number by another. The quotient of $10 \div 5$ is 2.

radius: A line segment that connects the center of a circle with any point on that circle's circumference. Plural: *radii*.

reciprocal: The product of a number and its reciprocal is always 1. To get the reciprocal of an integer, put that integer in the denominator of a fraction with numerator 1. The reciprocal of 3 is $\frac{1}{3}$. To get the reciprocal of a fraction, switch the numerator and the denominator. The reciprocal of $\frac{2}{3}$ is $\frac{3}{2}$.

rectangle: A four-sided closed shape in which all of the angles equal 90° and in which the opposite sides are equal. Rectangles are also parallelograms.

right triangle: A triangle that includes a 90°, or right, angle.

root: The opposite of an exponent (in a sense). The square root of 16 (written $\sqrt{16}$) is the number (or numbers) that, when multiplied by itself, will yield 16. In this case, both 4 and −4 equal 16 when squared. However, when the GMAT provides the root sign for an even root, such as a square root, the only accepted answer is the positive root. That is, $\sqrt{16} = 4$, *not* +4 or −4. In contrast, the equation $x^2 = 16$ has *two* solutions, +4 and −4.

sector: A "wedge" or "slice of pie" of a circle, bounded by two radii and the arc connecting those two radii.

simplify (in general): Change the form of given math to a simpler form. For example, add two numbers in parentheses, combine like terms, or divide every term in an equation by the same number.

simplify (fractions): Reducing numerators and denominators to their smallest form by taking out common factors. Dividing the numerator and denominator by the same number does not change the value of the fraction.

Example:

Simplify $\frac{21}{6}$. Divide both the numerator and the denominator by a common factor, in this case, 3: $\frac{21}{6} = \frac{7}{2}$.

slope: In a coordinate plane, "rise over run," or the distance the line runs vertically over the distance the line runs horizontally. The slope of any given line is constant over the length of that line.

special products: The set of three commonly used quadratic forms found on the GMAT:

    square of a sum: $(x + y)^2 = x^2 + 2xy + y^2$

square of a difference: $(x - y)^2 = x^2 - 2xy + y^2$

difference of squares: $(x + y)(x - y) = x^2 - y^2$

square: A four-sided closed shape in which all of the angles equal 90° and all of the sides are equal. Squares are also rectangles and parallelograms.

sum: The result when two numbers are added together. The sum of 4 and 7 is 11.

term: Parts within an expression or equation that are separated by either a plus sign or a minus sign. For example, in the expression $x + 3$, "x" and "3" are each separate terms.

triangle: A three-sided closed shape composed of straight lines; the interior angles sum to 180°.

two-dimensional: A shape containing a length and a width.

variable: Letter used as a substitute for an unknown value, or number. Common letters for variables are x, y, z, and t. In contrast to a constant, a variable is a value that can change (hence the term *variable*). In the equation $y = 3x + 2$, both y and x are variables.

x-axis: A horizontal number line that indicates left-right position on a coordinate plane.

x-coordinate: The number that indicates where a point lies along the x-axis. The x-coordinate is always written first in the parentheses. The x-coordinate of (2, −1) is 2.

x-intercept: The point where a line crosses the x-axis (that is, when $y = 0$).

y-axis: A vertical number line that indicates up-down position on a coordinate plane.

y-coordinate: The number that indicates where a point lies along the y-axis. The y-coordinate is always written second in the parentheses. The y-coordinate of (2, −1) is −1.

y-intercept: The point where a line crosses the y-axis (that is, when $x = 0$). In the equation of a line $y = mx + b$, the y-intercept equals b. The coordinates of the y-intercept are (0, b).

Go beyond books.
Try us for free.

In Person

Find a GMAT course near you
and attend the first session
free, no strings attached.

**Find your city at
manhattanprep.com/gmat/classes**

Online

Enjoy the flexibility of prepping
from home or the office with
our online course.

**See the full schedule at
manhattanprep.com/gmat/classes**

On Demand

Prep where you are, when you
want with GMAT Interact™—
our on-demand course.

**Try 5 full lessons for free at
manhattanprep.com/gmat/interact**

Not sure which is right for you? Try all three!
Or, give us a call, and we'll help you figure out
which program fits you best.

Toll-Free U.S. Number 800.576.4628 | International 001 212.721.7400 | Email gmat@manhattanprep.com